DOSTOEVSKY
Reminiscences

Anna Dostoevsky

DOSTOEVSKY

Reminiscences

by ANNA DOSTOEVSKY

Translated and edited by Beatrice Stillman
Introduction by Helen Muchnic

WILDWOOD HOUSE LONDON

Text of the Russian edition on which this translation is based:
Vospominaniya by A. G. Dostoevskaya, first published by Mezhkniga,
Moscow, U.S.S.R., 1971.

All illustrations in this book courtesy of Sovfoto, New York.

First published in Great Britain 1976
Wildwood House Limited, 29 King Street, London WC2
ISBN: 07045 0202 X

This book was designed by Paula Wiener.
Typefaces used are Gael and Bulmer.
Manufacturing was done by Haddon Craftsmen.

Printed in the United States of America

for Mischa Stillman

Contents

Illustrations follow page 254.

Translator's Preface

When Anna Dostoevsky's *Reminiscences* of her life with her husband first appeared in Russia, seven years after her death in 1918, they were recognized at once as a literary event of the first magnitude. That first Russian edition of 1925 was prepared by the distinguished Dostoevsky scholar Leonid Grossman, who selected that part of Anna Dostoevsky's 798-page manuscript which described her fourteen years with Dostoevsky, from her first meeting with him in 1866 to his death in 1881. To this material Grossman appended a brief section which Anna Grigoryevna had called "Memoirists" and also her refutation of the charge made by Nikolai Strakhov many years earlier that Dostoevsky had confessed—indeed, boasted—of raping a ten-year-old girl.

The final copy of Anna Grigoryevna's manuscript (based on over thirty notebooks of rough drafts) was handwritten by her on large sheets of paper stitched into a notebook consisting of ninety-two "chapters" of greatly varying length, not always chronologically arranged, some titled and others merely numbered. It was evident that she had not succeeded in working out to her own satisfaction the definitive edition of her text. Her uncertainties are reflected in the fact that she left a number of minor stylistic variants of the same episodes without indicating her own preference. Where she left such choices open, Grossman selected the version he considered stylistically the simplest and most natural.

The present translation of the *Reminiscences* is based on the second Russian edition, published in Moscow in 1971 and edited by the Dostoevsky scholars S. V. Belov and V. A. Tunimanov. They have carried Grossman's work further by rearranging the manuscript into twelve broad chapters in chronological sequence, corresponding to the most important periods in the life of Fyodor Dostoevsky's family. This necessitated some transposition of material to where it chronologically belonged, as well as the elimination of certain redundant episodes left in the Grossman edition. Belov and Tunimanov also added, as a first chapter, Anna Grigoryevna's description of her childhood and youth and the milieu in which her extraordinary character was formed. In the book's last chapter, "After Dostoevsky's Death," they retained Anna Grigoryevna's "Answer to Strakhov" and added to it her description of her only meeting with Leo Tolstoy, not included in the Grossman edition. To this chapter the translator of the present edition has also restored the brief section "Memoirists," omitted from the second Russian edition.

The present translation continues the work of the Russian editors by deleting some further duplications discovered in the Russian text, and by making some minor rearrangements in sequence (at several points in Chapters Two, Five, Six, Seven, Eight and Ten) to make it conform with chronology. At the same time, Anna Grigoryevna's tentative titles, which she had appended to some of her brief "chapters" or, more accurately, episodes (leaving others untitled, merely numbered or with an indication of the year in which they occurred) were removed so as not to impede the flow of her narrative.

The editors of the new Russian edition of the *Reminiscences* provided a detailed and able commentary. Unfortunately, its length, its specialization, and its implicit assumptions make it unsuitable as is for general English-language readers. An educated Russian reader, for instance, can be presumed to be thoroughly familiar with Belinsky and Nekrasov, with *The Contemporary* and possibly even with the Pochvenniki—but requires commentary on aspects of English and European life which would be superfluous in an English translation.

For this reason, the translator has redone the notes to the Russian edition (while gratefully acknowledging her debt to the scholarship of the Russian editors). She has also supplied a chronology, a list of periodicals and a glossary identifying persons, literary and political groups and issues of Dostoevsky's day, with whom or with which he was intensely involved. The bibliography has been greatly reduced. Books existing in Russian only were eliminated from the bibliography, on the theory that readers of Russian can go to the Russian edition, while non-readers of Russian would find such references useless.

Anna Grigoryevna, who took utmost pains to achieve the greatest possible accuracy in her narrative, supplied a substantial number of footnotes to her own manuscript. These have been treated in several ways by the translator. Those which are anecdotal in nature have been incorporated into the text itself. Where appropriate, the remainder have been included among the general footnotes (identified by the initials A.G.D.). In a very few instances they remain where they were originally placed by their author, at the bottom of the page. In no case have they been deleted. All notations concerning gaps in Anna Grigoryevna's text were made by the Soviet editors, who had access to the original hand-written manuscript; wherever possible they have filled in these gaps by referring to letters and other sources.

The reader is reminded that the Russian language is rich in diminutives and name variants. Thus, Fyodor Mikhailovich and Fedya are one and the same person—Dostoevsky. His wife refers to him as "Fedya" only in the part of the book based on the diary she kept during the first year of their marriage. In the later sections of the book, "Fedya" refers to their son—who was also Fyodor Fyodorovich. Madame Dostoevsky herself is Anna Grigoryevna, Anya, Anechka, Nyuta, and Netochka. Their daughter Lyubov is also called Lyuba, Lyubochka, and sometimes Lilya. In the English translation of the book she wrote about her father, her name is given as Aimée.

When Dostoevsky died, Anna Grigoryevna says, her "personal life was finished" and she was "orphaned in her heart forever." And indeed, for all the public attention accorded her after her husband's death, it might be assumed that she had died with him. The astounding fact is that at the time of Dostoevsky's death in 1881, Anna Grigoryevna was only thirty-five years old. She devoted the next thirty-seven years to the preservation of his work; and despite her modest disclaimer of any scholarly or intellectual ability, her service to Russian literature has proved incalculable. With Strakhov and Orest Miller, she worked on the preparation of the *Materials for a Biography of Dostoevsky,* of which the first volume was published in her lifetime; she compiled a bibliographic index of works by Dostoevsky and critical literature on him in European and Asiatic languages, consisting of over five thousand items—a unique achievement in Russian bibliography up to that time; she published seven editions of Dostoevsky's collected works, founded a school in his name in Staraya Russa, and created a special section in the Moscow Historical Museum where his manuscripts, letters, and notebooks were preserved: a priceless collection of primary sources for the brilliant wave of Dostoevsky scholarship of recent years. All during that period, she continued to work on transcribing the shorthand notebooks containing her diaries and records of conversations with her husband, on a separate edition of his letters to her, on her *Diary of 1867,* and, for over five years, on her *Reminiscences.* During the terrible Petrograd winter of 1916–17, when the nation was shattered by war and on the eve of revolution, Anna Grigoryevna maintained her schedule of visits to the public library to verify her work on her memoirs with (as Leonid Grossman remarks) "all the stamina and verve of a young student."

The last year of her life was lived in tragic isolation from her family. In May of 1917 she left Petrograd for her summer home in the Caucasus, where she caught a particularly severe form of malaria. She tried to get back to Petrograd but did not succeed. The German march south in the spring of 1918 cut communications with Moscow, where her son Fedya (who had been sending her small sums of money from time to time) was living. She had recovered from the malaria, but was weakened and had suffered a series of small strokes. She was then living in Yalta, reduced to a state of destitution and actual hunger. After a period of semi-starvation she bought two pounds of fresh-baked bread, still hot, and in her hunger she ate all of it. Nine days later, utterly alone, she died in agony of acute intestinal inflammation. She was buried in Yalta far from her nearest and dearest.

Her "Testamentary Notebook" had asked that she be laid to rest side by side with Fyodor Mikhailovich at the Alexander Nevsky monastery in Petersburg—and that her grave be marked not by a separate monument, but only by a few lines inscribed on his monument. Fifty years later, in 1968, thanks to the tireless effort of Fedya's son Andrey—a man as passionately devoted to Dostoevsky's memory as his grandmother had been—her wish was carried out at last.

Acknowledgments can never adequately convey the quality of one's indebtedness, conscious and unconscious, to others. Nonetheless I shall try to express here my thanks to Ned Arnold, editorial director of Liveright, for unfailing patience, support, and perceptiveness; to Lily Feiler, first-class translator and good friend, for her conscientious reading of the translation and for valuable suggestions; to Bernard Koten, director of the Russian library at New York University, indefatigable and encyclopedic source of Russian lore; to Professor Robert Belknap of Columbia University, for accessibility and for warmth of spirit which lent me more support than he knew. And finally, to Rose Raskin of Columbia University, whose love and knowledge of Russian literature and whose double mastery of nuance have made her the mentor of half the Slavists in the United States, go my thanks for numberless hours of discussion, argument, guidance and enlightenment. Needless to say, deficiencies in translation and responsibility for error are mine alone.

New York
July, 1974

BEATRICE STILLMAN

Introduction

BY HELEN MUCHNIC

On the first of October, 1866, A. P. Milyukov, as he later recalled in his reminiscences, stopped in to see his friend Dostoevsky and found him pacing up and down the room in a state of obvious distress. "Why so gloomy?" he asked. "Who wouldn't be gloomy," Dostoevsky replied, "when he's being utterly destroyed?" He went to his desk, pulled out a paper and said, "Take a look!" It was a contract he had signed with the publisher Stellovsky, which stipulated that for the ridiculously small sum of three thousand rubles he sold all the writings he had done so far and also promised to deliver a new, full-length novel by the first of November, 1866, on penalty, in case of default, of forfeiting all compensation for whatever he might publish in the next nine years.

Only the direst financial necessity had made Dostoevsky agree to this swindle. For two years he had been struggling to support a good-for-nothing stepson, his late wife's offspring by a former marriage, as well as the family that his brother had left destitute at his death. Unable to make a go of the journal he and his brother had published together, he found himself bankrupt and heavily in debt. The money Stellovsky advanced had enabled him to pay off his most pressing debts and try his luck, with what was left, at the roulette tables in Wiesbaden, where he lost everything. His creditors were now pressing their claims and he was threatened with the debtors' prison.

What of the new novel, Milyukov asked; how much of it was

written? "Not a line!" said Dostoevsky. He had been absorbed in *Crime and Punishment,* which was being published serially, and as for Stellovsky's novel, he had only a plot in mind. Milyukov proposed that a group of their friends write it jointly, each one taking a chapter. But Dostoevsky refused. "I would never sign my name to someone else's work," he said. Milyukov's next suggestion was a better one. "Well, then, get a stenographer and dictate the whole novel yourself." Dostoevsky agreed—"I have never dictated before . . . but one can try. . . . Thank you" —and Milyukov sought out P. M. Olkhin, a well-known teacher of stenography, who recommended his best pupil, Anna Grigoryevna Snitkina. The rest of the story is hers, and it is told in this book.

She had taken up stenography as a means to independence, for as a "woman of the sixties"—so she thought of herself—she believed that women could and should be self-supporting. She was twenty years old. This was to be her first job. And so, untried, unsure of her ability, wanting desperately to make good, and very much in awe of her prospective employer, over whose works she had wept since girlhood and who had been her adored father's favorite author, she came on the morning of October 4, 1866, at precisely half-past eleven, "no earlier and no later," as Dostoevsky had directed, to the house that reminded her of the one Raskolnikov lived in. Every day for the next four weeks she took down Dostoevsky's dictation in shorthand and transcribed it at home each night; thanks to her faithful perseverance, the novel was finished in the nick of time. It was *The Gambler,* based on Dostoevsky's experience in Wiesbaden and his infatuation with Polina Suslova, but how much of this Anna Grigoryevna recognized at the time is unclear, nor is it important.

In the intervals of dictation Dostoevsky told her a great deal about his past—his arrest, the commuted death sentence, his exile in Siberia, something also about his marriage, of which he spoke reluctantly, and about his recent engagement, which had come to nothing. She found herself overwhelmed with pity for this gifted, tragic man, and became so absorbed in his life and in her work with him that all her former interests receded into insignificance. "Why is it," she asked him once, "that you remember only the unhappy times? Tell me instead about how you were happy."

"Happy?" he said. "But I haven't had any happiness yet. At least, not the kind of happiness I always dreamed of. I am still waiting for it."

The happiness he dreamed of was family happiness, and it seemed to him that now, perhaps, it might be possible. One night he dreamed that he had found a bright little diamond among his papers. But he was doubtful. After his unfortunate experiences with women—the unhappy marriage to Marya Isayeva, the tormenting affair with Polina Suslova, the unhappy courtship of Anna Korvin-Krukovskaya—he hardly dared hope that his sensible and helpful young secretary would accept a sick, poor, ugly man who was twenty-five years older than herself. She did, of course, accept him; and almost fifty years later, in a recollection that, like much of her narrative, is deeply moving, she described in detail his oblique, tremulous, eloquent proposal, couched in the form of "a plot for a new novel . . . a brilliant improvisation . . . an inspired tale." "The eighth of November, 1866," she wrote, "was one of the great days of my life. That was the day Fyodor Mikhailovich told me that he loved me and asked me to be his wife. Half a century has passed since then, and yet every detail is as sharp in my memory as if it had happened a month ago."

They were married the following February, and their life together, which ended only with Dostoevsky's death fourteen years later, is the subject of Anna Grigoryevna's *Reminiscences.* The main biographical events of these years are generally known: their travels abroad from 1867 to 1871; his obsession with gambling; the publication of his great novels *Crime and Punishment, The Idiot, The Possessed, The Brothers Karamazov,* as well as of several lesser ones and of *Diary of a Writer;* his triumphant speech at the Pushkin festivities in 1880; and the unprecedented, spontaneous tributes at his funeral in 1881 that first brought him to the attention of the public in the West. Anna Grigoryevna's memoirs fill in the general outline, bringing to life the circumstances of their journeys, the animosities and adulations that darkened or brightened their existence, the emotional and physical background of his writings and publications.

An unassuming, straightforward honesty is the special merit of her book. Without guessing at hidden motives or speculating about concealed significance, recording only what she had seen and felt, Anna Grigoryevna produced a document of rare fidelity. Her memory was aided by notes, letters, and, especially, a diary she kept for years, partly as an exercise in shorthand, in which she did not want to lose her skill, but mainly as a safeguard against forgetting and a device for setting her complicated experiences in order. "My husband was such an interesting and enigmatic person to me that I felt it would be easier to get to know and unriddle him if I wrote down his ideas and observations." The remark is touching, especially when one sees how little of Dostoevsky's "ideas" went into her annals. It is not for these one reads her reminiscences, but for the unique portrait of Dostoevsky the man that, stroke by stroke, emerges from this book, drawn with the kind of understanding that is given only to unremitting and truly selfless devotion.

Written some thirty years after Dostoevsky's death, the *Reminiscences* have an interest different from that of the diaries. No longer a day-to-day report but a remembrance of the past, its details, sifted through the experience of years, take on a value conferred on them by the passage of time and reflective judgment. The accounts are less circumstantial than a diary would be: minutiae and trivialities that seemed interesting at the moment have been excised, and only that is left which has remained noteworthy throughout the long interval between the living event and the memory of it. For this reason the very omissions and lapses in these memoirs are significant. There is no mention, for example, of Polina Suslova, who in the diaries figures in several troubled, jealous entries. And what of the moral, religious, political problems that agitated Anna Grigoryevna's contemporaries and were discussed in her husband's journals and dramatized in his novels? Perhaps late in life the memory of Dostoevsky's passion for Suslova was too painful to contemplate; perhaps it seemed incomprehensible; most likely, after the proof through many years of her husband's love and constancy, it was no longer important.

With regard to the disruptive national issues and fateful international events of the times, such as the theories and acts of Populists, Socialists, Anarchists, terrorists, the movement for Panslavism, the war of Italian liberation, the Paris Commune, Anna Grigoryevna was extraordinarily detached for "a woman of the sixties." Once she speaks of "squabbling" with Fyodor Mikhailovich "over a difference in views," when she expressed herself "quite sharply," and then, "vexed at having spoiled his affable mood," restored it with a pleasant joke; but what the quarrel was about we are not told. Another time, an argument about "the woman question" ends in her starting to collect stamps by way of proving to Dostoevsky that a woman is capable of sustained interest in an enterprise of her choice! She describes the triumphal reception of Garibaldi in September, 1867, at the Peace Congress in Geneva, mentions Dostoevsky's sympathy with "the idea of Slavic *rapprochement,*" speaks of his anguish, which she fears may provoke an epileptic seizure, at the news of a new attempt on "the life of the Emperor for whom he felt such deep esteem," acknowledges, in connection with "the woman question," that she herself is not a Nihilist. And that is about all. She entertains Dostoevsky's friends, is delighted that they talk way into the night, but gives no hint of the questions that absorb them. The fact is that there was nothing of greater importance to Anna Grigoryevna than her husband's peace of mind and the harmony of their relationship, nor indeed were there any fundamental disagreements between them. Both were of the Orthodox faith and profoundly devout, while political, social, philosophic problems were peripheral to Anna Grigoryevna's chief concerns.

The hours she worked with her husband, taking down his novels from dictation, Anna Grigoryevna remembers as some of the happiest of her life. She was proud to be "the first of his readers to hear the author's work from his own lips," and was sometimes so moved, as by the scene "of Alyosha's return with the boys after Ilyusha's funeral," from *The Brothers Karamazov,* that she "wrote with one hand and wiped [her] tears with the other." He valued her reactions, knowing them to represent those of the general reader, and always asked for her opinion, which she never falsified. But she did not pretend to understand his philosophic meanings, and considered that he "idealized" her and ascribed to her greater insight than she possessed. "The Legend of the Grand Inquisitor," for example, was beyond her. She said as much but he insisted, in spite of her disclaimer, that she did understand, and that it was only "from lack of training" that she would not express in words what she had understood.

Of her husband's feeling for her, Anna Grigoryevna speaks with gratitude and wonder. How was it that a man so extraordinary could care for a person so little educated as she, so inferior to him intellectually? But an onlooker does not have to strain to see that she possessed depths of wisdom beyond the reach of such clever and ambitious women as Polina Suslova or such brilliantly educated ones as Anna Korvin-Krukovskaya, the kind of wisdom that Tolstoy, with reference to someone else, once called "wisdom of the heart." It shines through Anna Grigoryevna's narrative in her infinite sympathy, forbearance, and sometimes, as she herself never recognized, true heroism. As far as she was concerned, she was simply protecting the man she loved against the encroachments of predatory relatives and the machinations of unscrupulous cheats—the Stellovsky affair was but the first of many—preserving his manuscripts, doing what she could to fashion a climate of emotional stability that might enable him to work and forestall his terrible epileptic seizures. She had no idea how remarkable she was.

There are episodes of stunning courage that she herself takes quite for granted, as for example the occasion soon after her marriage when, an inexperienced girl of twenty who had never witnessed an epileptic fit, she was left alone (as everyone else had fled the room in horror) with her stricken husband writhing and frothing at the mouth in an attack of exceptional severity. Terrified though she was, she tried vainly to keep him from falling and then supported his head as he slipped to the floor. Then, some years later, on their journey back to Petersburg from a remote country place, discovering that the suitcase which contained the manuscript of *A Raw Youth* was missing, she persuaded a reluctant, frightened cabby to drive her through the dark streets of a robber-infested town to a distant pier, on the right hunch that the suitcase might be there, roused the keeper of the baggage room, and dragged the heavy bag up the ramp to the cab, which the boy had not dared leave unattended. But here is how she concludes this chapter: "I cite the episode as an example of the difficulties and unpleasantnesses of making even so relatively short a journey as the one to Staraya Russa during those far-off days"!

Never, it seems, did she consider primarily her own safety or well-being. When Dostoevsky, yielding to the allurement of gambling, lost, bit by bit, everything they owned of value, far from reproaching him, she tried to assuage his despair and allay his sense of guilt; on one or two occasions, with extraordinary psychological acumen, she actually urged him to the gaming tables, in the knowledge that he would return cleansed of his passion and able to work again. When they were overwhelmed by tragedy, as in the deaths of two of their children—first a baby daughter, later an infant son—Anna Grigoryevna, muffling her own immeasurable sorrow, dwelt on her husband's grief. That makes her heartbreaking account of these days doubly affecting.

Dostoevsky adored her, she says in astonishment, remarking in a footnote that no one who has seen his letters to her (they have been published separately as well as in the complete collection of his correspondence) would accuse her of boasting. Indeed not! Away from her, he wrote every day, sometimes more than once. But even without the letters, which are but additional evidence, it is easy to see that Anna Grigoryevna must have seemed to him the very embodiment of the kind of self-abnegation and single-minded devotion he prized above all other human qualities, his ideal of virtue come to life. Nor is it difficult to understand the ferocious jealousy that accompanied his love. It was a marvel that he had found her at all, to lose her was unthinkable; and so he would fly into groundless rages if a man but kissed her hand politely or offered her some service. Her reports of these violent episodes are both harrowing and amusing. But understanding them for what they were, she was less pained by them than alarmed by their effect on his high-strung nerves. And so she soothed him and tried to preclude any further occasions for anxiety.

Meanwhile, Dostoevsky was filling notebooks with ideas for novels, essays, journalistic pieces. Anna Grigoryevna saw to their preservation. Her *Reminiscences* are a complement to them, and both are invaluable—the notebooks as a repository of Dostoevsky's thoughts at their inception and their evolution, her memoirs as a recreation of the atmosphere in which they arose and developed and of the man who dramatized them in fiction or articulated them in polemics, discussions, reviews.

The atmosphere was tense and turbulent, largely because of their chronic lack of funds. Dostoevsky was absurdly incompetent in matters of business, trusting to a fault, a prey to sharks. He borrowed, spent what he earned, increased his debts. Gradually, Anna Grigoryevna took their affairs into her own capable hands. She dealt with creditors, landlords, book dealers; she found out the cost of paper, printing, binding, and brought out her husband's books herself, advertising them in a newspaper and selling them in her own house. This is how *The Idiot, The Possessed,* and *The Brothers Karamazov* were first published in book form. Eventually, she inaugurated a very successful mail-order bookstore, and managed at long last to free them of debt. But this was just a year before Dostoevsky died. She is eloquently bitter about those who, unaware of the circumstances in which Dostoevsky was obliged to work, found fault with his lack of polish:

> Frequent comparisons are made, in literature and in society, between Dostoevsky's work and the work of other gifted writers, and Dostoevsky is criticized for excessive complexity, intricacy and accumulation of detail, whereas the work of others is polished. . . . And rarely does it occur to anyone to compare the circumstances in which other writers lived and worked and those in which my husband lived and worked. Almost all of them—Tolstoy, Turgenev, and Goncharov—were people in good health, financially secure and with full freedom to think their work through and refine it. Fyodor Mikhailovich, on the other hand . . . never had such a possibility—he needed money to live on, to pay debts! And therefore he was compelled to work even when he was ill, sometimes on the day after a seizure, to hurry, barely reading over his manuscript—just to send it off on time, so as to receive payment for it as soon as possible.

And she is equally bitter about those who, without understanding the man, condemned his behavior and attributed to him the characteristics of his villains. In one passage she speaks of the caviling rumors spread about Petersburg of his overbearing pride and snobbish deportment at parties, when he would sit silently in a corner of the room, turning away from the other guests or whispering with some special person he singled out. What these gentlemen did not know, Anna Grigoryevna explains, was that Dostoevsky, suffering from emphysema—the illness that was presently to cause his death—would climb the stairs laboriously to the apartment where he was expected, resting on each landing, and would arrive exhausted, unable to talk, struggling to catch his breath.

Worst of all were the "despicable slanders" in Strakhov's letter to Tolstoy, which, she wrote, "outraged me to the depths of my soul." This letter was written in 1883 but not published until 1913, when both Tolstoy and Strakhov were dead; Anna Grigoryevna herself did not see it until 1914, when she was already well on in her *Memoirs.* Nikolai Strakhov had been for years one of Dostoevsky's closest friends, a contributor to his journals—indeed, it was because of an article of his that *Time* was suppressed—a constant visitor in Dostoevsky's house, and after his death, co-author of the first biography about him. But now, at work on this biography, he wrote Tolstoy of his extreme aversion to Dostoevsky, whom he described as a malicious, envious, debauched, conceited man. Anna Grigoryevna refrained from publishing an immediate reply, but did so in an appendix to her *Reminiscences* in an indignant, meticulous refutation of Strakhov's calumnies.

But indeed her memoirs as a whole may be read as a rebuttal of all such slanders. The picture she draws of her "dear," her "cherished" husband is of a man as recklessly abused as he was wildly worshipped, an excessively kind, gentle, considerate being, shamelessly exploited because of his credulity and his total inability to refuse petitioners. Illness made him irritable and impatient, but though he would often lose his temper, he could not harbor a grudge. The moments of frenzy from which she herself had suffered—storms of rage, the madness of gambling, infatuation, jealousy—she recognized as elemental passions beyond his power to control. He was a compassionate, deeply suffering, large-souled man with nothing petty in him, and she remembered gratefully his great tenderness toward her and their children.

Writing of their first year together, when, because of the meddlesome intrigues of his relatives, their marriage was in danger of coming to a catastrophic end, Anna Grigoryevna described her feeling for Dostoevsky as follows:

> I loved Fyodor Mikhailovich without limit, but this was not a physical love, not a passion which might have existed between persons of equal age. My love was entirely cerebral, it was an idea existing in my head. It was more like adoration and reverence for a man of such talent and such noble qualities of spirit. It was a searing pity for a man who had suffered so much without ever knowing joy and happiness, and who was so neglected by all his near ones. . . .
>
> The dream of becoming his life's companion, of sharing his labors and lightening his existence, of giving him happiness—this was what took hold of my imagination; and Fyodor Mikhailovich became my god, my idol. And I, it seemed, was prepared to spend the rest of my life on my knees to him. . . .

In the course of time, her love became less diffident but did not change in essence, retaining to the end that quality of boundless admiration combined with fervid pity which characterized it from the start. And yet, though her happiness consisted wholly in alleviating his suffering and bringing him a measure of comfort, there was nothing abject in her self-forgetfulness. Strong and proud, she never surrendered her individuality and was doubtless right when in her "Afterword" she explained the success of her marriage by her own and her husband's ability to maintain their spiritual independence:

> But we always remained ourselves, in no way echoing nor currying favor with one another, neither of us trying to meddle with the other's soul, neither I with his psyche nor he with mine. And in this way my good husband and I, both of us, felt ourselves free in spirit.
>
> Fyodor Mikhailovich, who reflected so much and in such solitude on the deepest problems of the human heart, doubtless prized my noninterference in his spiritual and intellectual life. And therefore he would sometimes say to me, "You are the only woman who ever understood me!"

She did not pry into the solitary workings of Dostoevsky's mind, but sought to arrange his life so as to give his solitude the peace it needed. Emotionally, spiritually, materially, she shielded, supported and tended him. After his death, she busied herself with the posthumous publication of his works, including a collected edition, and only when poor health forced her to turn over her labors to someone else did she decide, as she tells it in her "Preface," to write her *Reminiscences.* Since the book's first publication in Russian, it has been consulted by every serious student of Dostoevsky as an indispensable, uniquely intimate and revealing source that, in addition to essential data about his life, throws a wonderfully suggestive light on the ambient circumstances and emotions, the pervasive atmosphere, in which his imaginative creations appeared. Best of all, perhaps, it is the simple, glowing history of a great love.

Chronology: Main Dates in the Lives of Fyodor and Anna Dostoevsky

1821	October 30: Birth of Fyodor Dostoevsky in Moscow in Hospital for the Poor, where his father was resident physician.
1837	February 27: Death of mother.
1838	January 16: Admitted to Military Engineering Institute in Petersburg.
1839	June: Father murdered by his own serfs at his estate, Chermashnya, in province of Tula.
1843	Graduated from engineering school as lieutenant, enrolls in Petersburg Engineers Corps as draftsman.
1844	October: Resigns from Army. Translates French novels into Russian: his translation of Balzac's *Eugenie Grandet* is published. Begins work on first novel, *Poor Folk*.
1845	Finishes *Poor Folk*. Acclaimed by Belinsky as a great writer. Meets Turgenev, becomes part of the literary group around Belinsky and Nekrasov.
1846	*Poor Folk* published in *A Petersburg Miscellany*. Second novel, *The Double*, appears two weeks later in *National Notes*. Belinsky's dislike of *The Double*

and later "The Landlady" plunges D. into depression and heightens strains with fellow-members of the group. Spring: First meeting with Mikhail Petrashevsky, host to group studying works of the French Utopian Socialists.

August 30: Anna Grigoryevna Snitkina is born in Petersburg.

October: "Mr. Prokharchin" published in *National Notes.* November: Rupture with Nekrasov and entire *Contemporary* circle.

1846–47 Various undiagnosed nervous ailments. Onset of epilepsy?

1847 "The Landlady" published in *National Notes.*

1848 Increasing intimacy with Petrashevsky circle, attraction to Socialist doctrine. "A Faint Heart," "An Honest Thief," "White Nights" in *National Notes.*

1849 D. comes under influence of radical wing of the Petrashevtsy: Speshnev and Durov, partisans of forcible seizure of government power. Participates in decision to organize a secret printing press. April 15: D. reads to the Circle Belinsky's letter denouncing Gogol for black reaction. April 23: D. arrested, imprisoned as a political criminal, sentenced to death. *Netochka Nezvanova,* an unfinished novel, published in *National Notes.* December 22: Last-minute reprieve; sentenced to an indefinite term in Siberia, including four years at hard labor. December 24: Deported to Siberia in irons.

1850–54 In Omsk as a convict serving at hard labor.

1853 Onset of periodic epileptic seizures.

1854 Released from penal servitude and sent as common soldier to Semipalatinsk, near the Mongolian border.

1856 Promoted to rank of ensign.

1857	Marries Maria Isayeva, a widow with a son, Paul. Rank of nobleman is returned to him. "A Little Hero" (composed in 1849 in prison) published anonymously in *National Notes.*
1859	Allowed to resign from Army and leave Siberia. August: Arrives in Tver. December 16: Allowed to return to Petersburg and literary career. "Uncle's Dream" in *Russian Word.* "A Friend of the Family" in *National Notes.*
1860	Chapter 1 of *Notes from the House of the Dead* in *Russian World.*
1860–65	Edits *Time* and *The Epoch* with his brother Mikhail. *The Insulted and Injured* published in *Time* in installments. *Notes from the House of the Dead* reprinted in *Time.*
1862	Summer: First trip to Europe (London, Paris, Geneva).
1862–63	Winter: Intimacy with Polina Suslova.
1863	"Winter Notes on Summer Impressions" in *Time.* April: *Time* is closed down by Imperial decree. August–October: Second trip abroad, part of the time with Suslova at the casinos of Wiesbaden, Baden-Baden, Homburg.
1864	Becomes editor of *The Epoch.* "Notes from Underground" published in *The Epoch.* April 15: Death of D.'s wife from tuberculosis. D. swears not to abandon his stepson Paul. July 10: Death of his brother Mikhail. D. assumes M.'s business and family debts. August and September: Publishes two stories by novice writer Anna Korvin-Krukovskaya.
1865	Demise of *The Epoch.* Unsuccessful courtship of Korvin-Krukovskaya. July–October: Third trip abroad, part of the time with Suslova. New two-volume collection of his writings.

1866 Publication of *Crime and Punishment* in *Russian Messenger* in installments. October 4: First meeting with Anna Snitkina, stenographer to whom he dictates *The Gambler*. October 30: Successful completion of *The Gambler*. Published in third volume of collected works. November 8: Proposes marriage to Anna Snitkina, and is accepted.

1867 February 15: The Dostoevskys are married in Izmailovsky Cathedral and settle down together with D.'s stepson Paul. April 14: The newlyweds go abroad "for three months" to escape debts and in-law problems, and remain for four years. Anna keeps a diary in shorthand for the first year and a half of her marriage. July 10: Encounter with Turgenev in Baden. Move to Geneva.

1868 February 22: Daughter Sonya is born, and dies suddenly at the age of three months. *The Idiot* published serially in *Russian Messenger*. Dostoevskys move to Vevey, Milan, Florence.

1869 To Prague, thence to Dresden, where daughter Lyubov is born September 26.

1870 "The Eternal Husband" published in *Dawn*.

1871 July 8: Return to Russia and Petersburg. July 16: Birth of son Fyodor (Fedya).

1871–72 *The Possessed* published serially in *Russian Messenger*. Anna Grigoryevna continues to serve as stenographer, copyist, secretary, and financial manager while seeking outside work to supplement the family income.

1873–74 Dostoevsky becomes editor of *The Citizen*, where his *Diary of a Writer* first begins to appear in form of a periodic column. Anna becomes a publisher and puts out *The Possessed* in book form.

1874 *The Idiot* published in book form. March 26: D. arrested and imprisoned for violation of censorship regulations. June: First of his four trips to Bad Ems for treatment of emphysema.

1875 *A Raw Youth* published serially in *National Notes.* August 10: Birth of son Alexey (Alyosha).

1876 *A Raw Youth* published in book form. D. founds *Diary of a Writer* as a one-man journal, and puts out eleven issues. "A Gentle Spirit" in November issue.

1877 Nine issues of *Diary of a Writer.* "The Dream of a Ridiculous Man" in April issue.

1878 May 16: Death of Alyosha at age three. June: Pilgrimage to Optina Pustyn with Vladimir Solovyov.

1879–80 Publication of *The Brothers Karamazov* serially in *Russian Messenger.* Anna opens a direct-mail book service.

1880 Period of public recognition and acclaim initiated with tumultuous reception of Dostoevsky's speech at the Pushkin festivities in Moscow in June. Enormous crowds and stormy emotional responses at D.'s public readings. August: Single issue of *Diary of a Writer.*

1881 January 28: Dostoevsky dies in Petersburg two days after a lung hemorrhage.

1881–1918 Anna Grigoryevna dedicates the remainder of her life to the perpetuation of her husband's work. Founds the Dostoevsky Museum, commissions the first biography of Dostoevsky, compiles bibliographic index of works by and about him, publishes an edition of his collected works.

1894 Begins deciphering and copying out the diary she had kept at the beginning of the marriage.

1911–16 Works on her *Reminiscences.*

1913 Daughter Lyubov settles abroad permanently.

1917 Anna Grigoryevna, in the Caucasus, is cut off from son Fyodor by war and revolution.

1918 June 9: Dies of acute intestinal inflammation from overeating after a period of semi-starvation.

1921 Death of Fyodor from heart disease.

1926 Death of Lyubov from leukemia.

DOSTOEVSKY
Reminiscences

A Preface to My Reminiscences

Never until now have I considered writing down my memoirs. Even if I ignored my awareness that I am utterly lacking in literary talent, I have been so intensively occupied throughout my life with the publication of my cherished husband's work that it was hard to find time for other matters connected with his memory.

In 1910 my failing health and strength forced me to give over to other hands the publication of my husband's works, with which I had been so vitally concerned. And when, at the insistence of the doctors, I was compelled to live far away from St. Petersburg, I began to feel a great gap in my life which had to be filled with some interesting kind of work—otherwise, I felt, I would not live much longer.

Living thus in total isolation and taking no part, or only the remotest part, in the flow of events, little by little I became immersed with all my soul and thoughts in the past—a past which had given me so much happiness; and this helped me forget the emptiness and aimlessness of the life I was leading. As I read and reread my husband's and my own notebooks, I kept finding such interesting details in them that I couldn't help wanting to put them down not in their shorthand form, as I had first written them, but in a language comprehensible to all, particularly because I was certain that these entries would be of interest to my children and grandchildren, and perhaps to some enthusiasts for my beloved husband's work who wanted to know what kind of person Fyodor Dostoevsky was in his own family setting.

Out of these reminiscences, written down at different times during the last five years between 1911 and 1916, several notebooks were compiled which I have attempted to bring into what order I could. Though I make no guarantee as to their interest, I can vouch for their truthfulness and their full objectivity in describing the acts of certain individuals. These memoirs are based mainly on entries in my notebooks, supported by references to letters and articles in newspapers and periodicals.

I freely acknowledge my numerous literary deficiencies—prolixity of narration, disproportion of chapter lengths, old-fashioned style and so forth. But it is not easy to learn new things at the age of seventy, and therefore I hope my flaws will be forgiven me in view of my deep and heartfelt wish to show Fyodor Dostoevsky to his readers in all his virtues and his faults—as the man he really was in his family and personal life.

CHAPTER ONE

My Childhood and Youth

Many memories important to me are associated with the Alexander Nevsky Monastery in Petersburg. My parents were married in the monastery's only parish church (now a monastery church), situated at its main entrance gates. And I was born on the thirtieth of August, the feast day of St. Alexander Nevsky, in a house which belonged to the monastery; and it was its parish priest who offered the prayer for me and christened me. In the Tikhvin Cemetery of the monastery my beloved husband lies buried, and if fate pleases I too shall find my own place of eternal rest next to him. It seems that everything has come together to make the Alexander Nevsky Monastery the dearest place for me in all the world.

I was born on August 30, 1846, on one of those splendid autumn days known as "Indian summer." Even today, the feast day of St. Alexander Nevsky is still considered to be almost the chief holiday of Petersburg, when the processional from Kazan Cathedral to Alexander Nevsky Monastery and back takes place, accompanied by great masses of people free from work for the day.

But in former times, now long past, August 30 was celebrated with even greater solemnity. A broad wooden elevated stage more than three versts[1] long was erected in the middle of Nevsky Prospect, along which the processional, separated from the crowd, slowly advanced with its gilt crosses and banners sparkling. Behind the long file of ecclesiastical dignitaries, arrayed in their gold and brocaded vestments, came the important civil personages and then the military men with their ribbons and orders, and behind them several gilded ceremonial carriages in which the members of the Tsar's household rode. The whole procession presented a picture of such rare beauty that the entire city would assemble there to see it.

My parents lived on the second floor of a house which still belongs to the monastery. The apartment was immense. It had eleven rooms, and its windows looked out on what is today Schlusselburg Prospect, and partly also on the square in front of the monastery.* Ours was a large family, consisting of my elderly grandmother and her four sons, two of whom were married and had children of their own. All lived together harmoniously and hospitably in the old-fashioned way. On namedays and birthdays, at Christmas and Easter all the relations, close and distant, came to my grandmother's in the morning and spent the day there in merriment till late at night.

But on the thirtieth of August the guests would assemble in even greater numbers since, when the weather was fine, the windows would be opened and the procession could be viewed in comfort as well as in a congenial, familiar setting. And so it was on that August 30 of 1846. My mother, quite well and cheerful, was happily greeting and looking after the guests together with other members of the family. A little while later she disappeared. Everyone was sure that the young hostess was in the inner rooms seeing to the refreshments. But actually my mother, who had not expected the "event" to be so imminent, suddenly felt unwell (probably as a result of excitement and fatigue) and went to her own room after sending for the person necessary in such circumstances. My mother had always enjoyed good health; she had given birth before; and therefore the coming event did not cause any chaos or upset in the household.

At about two in the afternoon the solemn mass in the cathedral came to an end. The sonorous monastery bells began to peal, and as the processional appeared from out of the main gates, the solemn strains of a military band in the square began to issue forth. Those who were standing at the windows began

*The house is still standing today the same as ever. (A.G.D.)

calling the other guests with exclamations of "It's started, it's started, the procession is moving!" And so it was to these exclamations, to the pealing of church bells and the sounds of music heard by my mother, that I too started moving on my own long road of life.*

The solemn procession passed, and the guests began getting ready to go home. But they were held back because they wanted to say goodbye to grandmother, who (as they had been told) had gone to lie down for a rest. At about three o'clock my father came into the drawing room with his old mother on his arm. Somewhat shaken by the event which had just taken place, he came to a halt in the middle of the room and solemnly announced, "Dear friends and family, congratulate me on my great happiness. God has given me a daughter, Anna."

My father was a man of very exuberant nature, nimble-witted and given to pranks, what is known as "the life of the party." Taking his announcement for a holiday joke, no one believed him, and exclamations were heard: "Impossible! Grigory Ivanovich will have his little joke! How could it be? Why, Anna Nikolayevna was here the whole time . . ." and so forth and so on.

Then grandmother herself turned to the guests. "No, Grisha is telling the truth. My granddaughter Nyutochka arrived an hour ago!"

Now there was a shower of congratulations, and a maid came in carrying brimming goblets of champagne. All drank to the health of the newborn girl child, to her parents and her grandmother. The women ran to congratulate the mother (in those days there were no medical precautions) and to kiss "the little one"; while the men took advantage of the ladies' absence to finish off the stores of champagne by proposing toasts to the newborn infant. This was the ceremonial manner in which my arrival in the world was greeted, and everyone said that it was a good omen for my future fate.

The prophecy came true. Despite all the material misfortunes and moral sufferings it has been my lot to bear, I consider

*Of the circumstances surrounding my birth I later heard many accounts in different versions, and with commentaries, from various uncles and aunts who were visiting us on that day. (A.G.D.)

my life to have been one of exceptional happiness, and I would not wish to change anything in it.

A few words about my parents. My father's family came from the Ukraine and my great-great-grandfather had the surname of Snitko. My great-grandfather sold his estate in the province of Poltava and moved to Petersburg, now calling himself Snitkin. Although my father was educated in the Jesuit school in Petersburg he did not become a Jesuit, but he remained all his life a good and open-hearted man.

He liked to tell about a strange episode from his childhood. When he was ten years old, he was going to school at about seven o'clock one winter morning along the Fontanka embankment. Near the Anichkov palace he was approached by a tall, well-dressed gentleman near whom a shabbily dressed woman was standing. The gentleman stopped my father and said, "If you want to do a good deed, come with me and be my son's godfather. And here," he added, pointing to the old woman, "is the godmother."

My father was a brave lad. Without hesitating for a moment he followed the old woman and the gentleman. They entered a sumptuous house where a priest was awaiting them. The christening of the infant began at once. After the child was baptized, tea and sweets were served to the priest, the godmother and the godfather, and the gentleman gave each godparent a ten-ruble gold piece.

Since papa was by then late for school, he went home again and told what had happened to him. It was explained to him that a popular belief exists that if all the children in a family have died, the newborn child—if it is to stay alive—must be christened by the first persons its father encounters. That was how the old woman had come to be the infant's godmother and my papa his godfather.

Afterwards my father used to receive gifts from his godchild at Christmas and Easter; and once he was summoned to come and bless the child when he was critically ill. (The belief also exists that the prayers and blessings of the godparents can save the infant from death.) The godchild recovered. Later my father lost touch with his godson; he told me his name, but I have forgotten it.

My father served in one of the magistracies or departments of the civil service. My mother was of Swedish extraction, a member of the estimable Miltopeius family. One of her ancestors was a Lutheran bishop, and her uncles were scholars. That fact is shown in the suffix of her name, *-eius,* which scholars used to affix to their names out of some kind of affectation, in the manner of the particles *de* or *von.*

My mother's forebears lived in Abo[2] and were buried inside the walls of its famous cathedral. Once, when visiting Abo on my way to Sweden, I thought I would try to locate the grave of my ancestors, but since I knew neither Swedish nor Finnish I was unable to obtain any information from the guard.

My mother's father, Nikolai Miltopeius, was a landowner in the province of Sankt-Mikhel[3] and the entire family lived on the estate except for a son Roman Nikolayevich, a student at the Moscow Geodetic Institute. When Roman finished his course of study and found a position in Petersburg he sold the estate of his father (who was by then deceased) and brought the family to Petersburg. Here my grandmother, Anna Maria Miltopeius, died soon afterward, and my mother and her two sisters went to live with their brother.

My mother was a strikingly beautiful woman with a tall, slim, graceful figure and perfectly regular features. She also had an extremely beautiful soprano voice which she retained almost up to her old age. She was born in 1812, and was engaged to an officer at the age of nineteen. They were not fated to marry, however: he enlisted in the Hungarian campaign and was killed. My mother's grief was terrible, and she resolved that she would never marry. But the years passed, and little by little the bitterness of her loss was assuaged.

There were amateur matchmakers in the circle of Russian society in which my mother moved (that was the custom of those days), and two young men in search of a bride were invited to a party arranged especially for my mother. Both of them liked her very much. But when she was asked how she liked them she replied, "No—I liked the old fellow better—the one who kept telling stories and laughing." She was speaking of my father. In former times people over forty were considered old, and papa was already forty-two (he was born in 1799).

Although my father had a gay and pleasurable youth, he kept

himself in restraint, under the supervision of a strict mother; and therefore at the age of forty-two he was a healthy, robust, pink-cheeked man with beautiful blue eyes and perfect teeth, although his hair was thinning noticeably. While his mother was living he did not intend to assume the responsibility of a family of his own; and therefore he used to appear in society as a pleasant companion and not as an eligible bachelor. He, too, had been introduced to my mother and had been much taken with her; but since she spoke Russian badly and his French was also poor their conversation did not develop very far.

But when he was told what my mother had said about him, his interest was piqued by the beautiful young lady's notice; and he began to make frequent visits to that house, where there was a possibility of meeting her.

It all ended with their falling in love with one another and deciding to marry. But there was a serious obstacle. Mama was a Lutheran. According to the precepts held by papa's Orthodox family, a wife must be of one faith with her husband. It reached the point where papa resolved to go against their will and to marry her, even if that meant breaking off with some of the members of his family.

My mother learned of this. Fearing to bring discord into so harmonious a family, she was in a dilemma for a long time: whether to convert to the Orthodox faith or to give up the man she loved.

And then an event occurred which influenced her decision. On the eve of her final answer to my father, late at night, she was on her knees for a long time in front of the crucifix, praying and asking God to come to her help. Suddenly she lifted her head and saw above the crucifix a lambent radiance which lit up the whole room and then faded. This phenomenon repeated itself twice more. My mother took it as a sign from heaven that she was to decide her perplexing problem in my father's favor.

That same night she had a dream in which she entered an Orthodox church and began to pray at the Shroud of Christ.[4] This dream she also interpreted as a sign from above. One can picture her astonishment when, two weeks later, standing inside the Simeonovskaya church (on Mokhovaya Street) for the ritual of anointing, she realized that she had been put next to the Shroud of Christ, and that the setting corresponded exactly to what she had seen in her dream.

This put her conscience to rest. Once having become Orthodox she began to fulfill the rites of the Church zealously, to fast and take communion. But she found it difficult to learn the prayers in Church Slavonic, and so she continued to use her Swedish prayerbook. She never regretted changing her faith. "Otherwise," she used to say, "I would have felt remote from my husband and children, and that would have been painful for me."

My parents lived together in harmony for about twenty-five years. Their characters blended very well. My mother had a strong will and was the real head of the house. My father yielded to her willingly, reserving for himself only one right—the freedom to go to the Apraksin and other antique markets (there was a profusion of them at that time) to hunt for and buy various rarities and curiosities, mostly rare porcelains, which he knew a great deal about.

In the first years of their married life they lived with my grandmother and her large family. But when in five years or so my grandmother died and the family fell apart, my mother persuaded my father to buy a house near Nikolayevsky Sukhoputny Hospital as well as a huge plot of ground (about two desyatinas[5]) occupying the space where Yaroslavskaya and Kostromskaya streets are now, overlooking Little Bolotnaya Street all the way to the Stieglitz factory.

My first conscious memory is of an incident that occurred in April of 1849—that is, when I was two years and eight months old. There was a tumbledown old barn in the courtyard of our house. My mother decided to have it torn down and a new one built. The workmen came and did what had to be done; it remained only to raze the old barn to the ground.

My mother went out on the glass-enclosed gallery to see from a distance how they were going to accomplish this. Behind her was my curious nurse, holding me in her arms. Unfortunately, some draymen who lived somewhere in the depths of the courtyard were dawdling about. The workmen shouted at them to drive through immediately, and they stretched out in a long line. It was believed that they had all left. But just at the moment when the men were exerting all their strength to level the barn, a belated drayman appeared.

Everyone realized that if he could not manage to gallop through in time, the collapsing barn would undoubtedly kill him and his horse together. The awful crash of the barn as it fell, mingled with the terror-stricken screams of the spectators, split the air. A column of dust rose up, and in the first few moments it was impossible to tell whether a catastrophe had occurred.

As luck would have it, everything turned out all right. The terrified cries of my mother and my nurse, however, affected me so that I started screaming at the top of my voice. When I asked him about it later, my father looked it up in his housekeeping accounts and established the fact that the new barn had been built in the spring of 1849.

My second conscious memory is of an illness when I was three years old. I don't know what my disease was, but the doctor prescribed several leeches to be applied to my chest. I remember vividly how repulsive these writhing worms were to me, how they terrified me, and how I tried to tear them off my chest. And I clearly remember my mother taking me to receive communion and to pray before the miraculous ikon of the All-Compassionate Mother of God in the church on Shpalernaya Street. When I saw that my mother and my nurse were praying and weeping, I too crossed myself and sobbed bitterly. The next day after the prayers came the crisis, and I began to recover quickly.

In general, the children in our family[6] were rarely ill. There were of course occasional coughs and head colds, but all these illnesses were treated with household remedies and passed satisfactorily.

It is with the happiest feeling that I remember my childhood and youth. My parents loved all of us very much, and never punished us without cause. Life in our family was quiet, measured and serene, without quarrels, dramas or catastrophes. We were well fed and were taken out for walks every day. In summer we played in our garden from morning to night, while in winter we used to go sledding from the ice hill which had been constructed there for us. We weren't pampered with toys, and therefore we valued them and cared for them. There were no children's books at all—no one tried to "develop" us.

Sometimes we would be told fairy tales, mostly by my father. After he had come home from work and had his dinner, he would lie down on the couch, call the children over and settle down to storytelling. He had only one fairy tale, "Ivan the Fool"; but there were countless variations on it. My brother and I could never understand it—why was it that they called Ivanushka a fool, when he managed to extricate himself so cleverly from all kinds of misfortunes?

Our special treats were rare. At Christmas, a fir tree which was lighted every evening. Dressing up in costumes at home. During Carnival week we would be taken to the show-booths and also for rides in the *veykas.*[7] Twice a year—before Christmas and at Easter—we went to the theatre, mostly to the opera or the ballet. But we cherished these rare pleasures enormously, and remained for months under their spell.

A few words about my education. Between the ages of nine and twelve I went to St. Anna's School, on Kirochnaya Street. All the subjects except religious instruction were taught in German, and my knowledge of that language was very useful afterwards, when my husband and I spent several years living abroad. The first gymnasium[8] for girls—the Mariinskaya—was opened in Petersburg in 1858; I entered it in the autumn and was enrolled in the second class. My studies came easily to me. When I was promoted to the third- and fourth-year classes I received books as prizes, and at my graduation in 1864 I was awarded a silver medal, first class.

In the previous year the Pedagogical Institute had been opened by N. A. Vyshnyegradsky for women wishing to continue their education. I enrolled there in the fall of 1864. At that time a passionate interest in the natural sciences had arisen in Russian society, and I too succumbed to the trend. Physics, chemistry and zoology seemed a revelation to me, and I registered in the school's department of mathematics and physics.

I soon realized, however, that I had chosen a field not really corresponding to my inclinations, and that my studies were showing merely pitiful results. During our experiments in the crystallization of salts, for example, I was busier reading novels than observing what was taking place in the flasks and retorts, and these suffered cruelly from my neglect. While the zoology lectures were being given, I was interested in them; but when we moved into practical work and a dead cat was dissected before my eyes, I fainted in revulsion—to my great embarrassment. Of my studies of that year, I retain the memory only of Professor V. V. Nikolsky's brilliant lectures on Russian literature, which were attended by students from both departments.

In the summer of 1865 a painful fact became clear to me: my father's illness was not responding to treatment, and he had not long to live. It was then that I, not wishing to leave my beloved invalid alone for days at a time, decided to drop out of school for a while. Papa suffered so from insomnia that I used to read to him from the novels of Dickens for hours on end, and I was very content when he was able to doze off for a bit to the sound of my monotonous reading.

At the beginning of 1866 an announcement appeared concerning courses in stenography to be given by P. M. Olkhin in the building of the Sixth Boys' Gymnasium. When I learned that the lectures were to be held in the evening, after my dear father had already retired for the night, I decided to enroll. My father put particular insistence on this, since he regretted keenly that I had dropped my studies because of his illness.

The stenography did not go at all well for me at first. After the fifth or sixth lecture I came to the conclusion that it was all gibberish as far as I was concerned, and that I would never manage to plough through it. But when I told this to papa, he was indignant. He reproached me with lack of patience and persistence and exacted my promise to continue with my studies. He expressed his confidence that I would eventually make a good stenographer. It was as though my good father had foreseen that it would be through stenography that I was to find my happiness.

My father died on April 28, 1866. It was the first real sorrow I experienced in my life, and my grief was stormy. I wept a great deal, spent whole days in the Great Okhta Cemetery at his grave and could not come to terms with this terrible loss. My mother was made distraught by my depressed state and begged me to settle down to some kind of work.

The stenography classes, unfortunately, had already ended. But our teacher, kindly Professor Olkhin, on learning of my grief and the fact that I had missed so many classes, suggested that I make them up by conducting a correspondence with him in shorthand. Twice a week I was to put two or three pages from a certain book into shorthand and send them to him. He would correct the errors in my work and return it to me. Thanks to this correspondence, which continued throughout the three summer months, I made great progress with my shorthand—especially because my brother, who was at home on vacation, used to give me dictation almost every day for an hour or more, so that little by little I not only learned the correct stenographic forms, but also mastered the speed of taking them down.

And that is why, when the courses reopened in September of 1866, I turned out to be the only student Olkhin had whom he could confidently recommend for literary work.

CHAPTER TWO

My Acquaintance with Dostoevsky and Our Marriage

On the third of October, 1866, at about seven o'clock in the evening, I went as usual to the Sixth Boys' Gymnasium, where my stenography teacher, P. M. Olkhin, held his classes. The lecture had not yet begun; they were waiting for the latecomers. I sat down at my usual place and had just started arranging my notebooks when Olkhin came over to me. He sat down next to me on the bench and said, "Anna Grigoryevna, how would you feel about doing some stenographic work? I have been asked to find a stenographer, and I thought you might want to take on the job."

"I'd like to very much," I answered. "I've dreamt about working for a long time now. My only doubt is whether my shorthand is good enough for me to take a responsible position."

Olkhin reassured me, saying that the work in question would not require greater shorthand speed than I had already mastered.

"But who is it who's offering the job?" I was curious to know.

"It's the writer, Dostoevsky. He's working on a new novel[1] and has decided to dictate it to a stenographer. He thinks it will come to about seven signatures[2] in large format, and he will pay fifty rubles for the entire job."

I was quick to agree. The name of Dostoevsky had been known to me since I was a child. He was my father's favorite author. I myself had been enraptured with his works and had wept over *Notes from the House of the Dead.* The very idea, not only of meeting this gifted writer, but also of helping him in his work, filled me with excitement and elation.

Olkhin handed me a small piece of paper folded over double, on which had been written "Stolyarny Lane, corner of Little Meshchanskaya Street, house of Alonkin, Apartment No. 13, ask for Dostoevsky."

"Please be there tomorrow at eleven-thirty, 'no earlier and no later,' as he himself put it."

Olkhin then told me his own opinion of Dostoevsky, which I shall mention later in my story. He glanced at his watch and went up to the lectern.

I have to admit that on this occasion his lecture was completely lost on me. I was too excited and happy to listen. My cherished dream had come true—I had a job! If even Olkhin himself, so strict and demanding, felt that I had learned enough stenography and could take it down fast enough, then it must be so. Otherwise he would not have given me the work. This realization filled me with jubilance and elevated me in my own eyes. I felt that I was setting out on a new road, that I would be earning money by my own labor, that I would become independent. And the idea of independence for me, a girl of the sixties,[3] was a very precious idea. But even more wonderful and important than the job itself, I felt, was the opportunity to work for Dostoevsky and to get to know him personally.

When I reached home I told my mother the whole story in every detail. She too was extremely pleased with my success. Because of my happiness and agitation I hardly slept all night, and kept imagining what Dostoevsky would be like. Since I thought of him as a contemporary of my father, I assumed that he was already quite middle aged. I pictured him sometimes as a fat, bald old man, sometimes as a tall, thin one; but in any case he would be gloomy and forbidding, as Olkhin regarded him. And so I grew even more apprehensive about how to talk to him. I thought of him as being so learned, so clever, that I trembled in advance over every word. I was also abashed by the thought that I couldn't remember very clearly the names of the characters in his novels, and I was positive that he would be certain to discuss them. Never having known any literary celebrities in my social circle, I imagined them as being exceptional creatures who had to be spoken to in a special way. As I recall those days I realize what a perfect child I was then, despite my twenty years.

On October 4, the memorable day of my first meeting with my husband-to-be, I woke up cheerful and in a state of happy excitement at the thought that today my long-cherished dream would come true—my transformation from a schoolgirl into an independent practitioner of my chosen profession.

I left the house a bit early so as to go first to the Gostiny Dvor[4] to lay in a supply of extra pencils and also to buy myself a small portfolio, which I felt would lend a more businesslike air to my youthful figure. By eleven o'clock I had completed my purchases. In order to get to Dostoevsky's house "no earlier and no later"* than the appointed time, I walked slowly along Great Meshchanskaya Street and Stolyarny Lane, looking constantly at my watch. By 11:25 I had reached the Alonkin house and asked the porter standing at the gate for Apartment 13. He directed me to the right, where the entrance to the staircase was located near the gates.

The house itself was a large one, with many small apartments occupied by merchants and artisans. I was immediately reminded of the house in *Crime and Punishment* where Dostoevsky's hero Raskolnikov had lived. Apartment 13 was located on the second floor. I rang, and the door was opened at once by a middle-aged maidservant with a green checked shawl wrapped about her shoulders. I had been reading *Crime and Punishment* so recently that I couldn't help wondering whether this might not be the prototype of the worsted shawl which had played so important a role in the life of the Marmeladov family.

To the maid's question I answered that I had been referred by Professor Olkhin and that her master was expecting me. I was only just taking off my hood when the door into the entrance hall was flung wide open. Against the background of a brightly lit room, a young man appeared—very dark, with hair

*This was a common expression of Dostoevsky's. He disliked wasting time waiting for people, and so would designate the exact hour of the appointment and invariably add, "No earlier and no later." (A.G.D.)

disheveled and shirt open at the chest, and wearing slippers. Seeing a strange face, he gasped and immediately disappeared behind a side door.

The maid led me into a room, rather modestly furnished, which turned out to be the dining room. Two large trunks covered with small rugs stood against the walls. A chest of drawers decorated with a white crocheted cover was standing near the window, and there was a sofa along another wall with a clock hanging above it. I noted with some satisfaction that the hands stood at exactly half-past eleven.

The maid asked me to have a seat and said that her master would be in presently. And indeed within a minute or two Dostoevsky appeared and asked me to go into his study, but went off himself (as I later found out) to order tea for us.

The study, a large room with two windows, seemed very bright on that particular sunny day, although at other times it left a gloomy impression. It was dim and hushed; and you felt a kind of depression in that dimness and silence.

Inside the room there was a soft divan draped in a rather shabby brown fabric. In front of it stood a round table covered with a small red cotton cloth, and on the table, a lamp and two or three albums. Soft chairs and armchairs stood about. Above the couch in a walnut frame hung a portrait of an emaciated woman wearing a black dress and cap. "Dostoevsky's wife, no doubt," I thought, being unaware of his family situation.

Between the windows stood a large pier glass in a black frame. Since the space was considerably larger than the mirror the latter, for convenience, had been moved closer to the right window, which produced a very unattractive effect. The window sills were adorned by two large, beautifully shaped Chinese vases. A large green morocco couch stood along another wall, and beside it a small table with a carafe of water. On the other side of the room a writing desk was drawn up, at which on later occasions I always sat when taking dictation from Dostoevsky. The furnishings of the study were of the most commonplace type, such as I had seen among families in modest circumstances.

I sat there and listened. I kept thinking that I would soon hear children shouting or the banging of a toy drum, or that the door would open and that very thin lady whose portrait I had just been examining would come into the room.

But it was Dostoevsky who came in. He apologized for being detained so long and asked, "Have you been studying stenography a long time?"

"Only half a year."

"And does your teacher have many pupils?"

"Over a hundred and fifty were registered for the course at the beginning but about twenty-five are left now."

"But why so few?"

"I suppose many of them thought that stenography was very simple to learn, and when they realized that you couldn't get anywhere with it in a few days, they dropped out."

"That's always the way in our country with every new undertaking," said Dostoevsky. "They start at fever heat, then cool off fast and drop it altogether. They see that you have to work—and who wants to work nowadays?"

At first glance Dostoevsky seemed rather old to me. But as soon as he began to speak he grew younger at once; and I decided that he could hardly be more than thirty-five or thirty-seven.[5] He was of medium height and very erect posture. His chestnut-colored hair, faintly tinged with red, was heavily pomaded and carefully smoothed. But it was his eyes that really struck me. They weren't alike—one was dark brown, while the other had a pupil so dilated that you couldn't see the iris at all.* This dissimilarity gave his eyes an enigmatic expression. His face, pale and sick-looking, seemed quite familiar to me, probably because I had seen portraits of him previously. He was dressed in a blue cotton jacket, rather worn, but with snow-white collar and cuffs.

In five minutes the maid came in carrying two glasses of very strong, almost black tea. Two rolls lay on the tray. I took a glass. I didn't really want it and the room was already overheated, but I drank it anyway, in order not to appear fussy. I was sitting near the wall at a small table, while Dostoevsky either sat at his desk

*During an epileptic attack Dostoevsky had once fallen against some sharp object and severely injured his right eye. He was treated by Professor Junge, who prescribed treatment with atropine drops, as a result of which the pupil had markedly dilated. (A.G.D.)

or walked around the room smoking, frequently putting out one cigarette and lighting another. He offered me a cigarette, too, but I declined it.

"Perhaps you're refusing just to be polite?" he said.

I was quick to assure him that I not only didn't smoke, but didn't even like to see other women smoke.

Our conversation was rather disjointed and Dostoevsky kept shifting to new topics. He looked exhausted and ill. Almost at the outset he announced that he suffered from epilepsy and had had an attack a few days before. I was astonished by this frankness. Of the work which lay ahead he spoke in a rather vague way: "We'll see how to work it out . . . we'll give it a try . . . we'll find out whether it's possible. . . ."

I began to think it very doubtful that our collaborative project would ever take place. It even came into my head that Dostoevsky had his doubts about whether he would be able to work in this fashion and was, perhaps, ready to drop the whole idea.

In order to help him with his decision I said, "Good, let's try it. But if it turns out to be inconvenient for you to work with me, you can tell me straight out. Please be assured that I won't hold it against you if the job doesn't come to anything."

Then he wanted to dictate a passage to me from the *Russian Messenger,* after which I was to transcribe my shorthand notes into ordinary script. He began reading extremely fast, but I stopped him and asked him to dictate no faster than the speed of normal conversation. Then I started transcribing, and finished rather quickly. But Dostoevsky kept hurrying me and seemed appalled that I was working too slowly.

"But you see, I'll be transcribing your dictation at home, and not here," I reassured him. "So isn't it all the same to you how much time it takes me?"

Looking through what I had written, he found that I had omitted a period and written a hard sign[6] unclearly. He made a rather sharp remark about it. He was obviously in an irritated state and unable to collect his thoughts. He kept asking me my name and would then forget it at once. Or he would walk about the room—pace about for a long time, as if unaware of my presence. I sat there without stirring, afraid to break into his reverie.

Finally he said that he was in no condition to dictate and

could I return that evening at about eight o'clock? He would then begin dictating the novel. For me it was very inconvenient to come back a second time; but not wishing to postpone the work, I agreed.

When he was saying goodbye Dostoevsky remarked, "I was glad when Olkhin suggested a female stenographer rather than a man; and do you know why?"

"Why, indeed?"

"Why, because a man would likely as not start drinking, while you—you won't fall into any drinking habits, I hope?"

I wanted terribly to burst out laughing; but I restrained myself. "I most certainly will not fall into any drinking habits—you may be sure of that," I replied, with perfect seriousness.

I left Dostoevsky's house in a very low mood. I didn't like him; he made me feel depressed. I strongly doubted that we would be working together, and my dreams of independence were threatening to crumble into dust. And this was all the more painful because only yesterday my good mother had so rejoiced in the start of my new career!

It was about two in the afternoon when I left Dostoevsky's house. To go home would be too much of a trip. I lived on Kostromskaya Street in a house owned by my mother near Smolny. I decided to go to some relatives on Fonarny Lane, dine with them and return to Dostoevsky in the evening.

My relatives were keenly interested in my new acquaintance and questioned me closely about him. Our talk made the time pass swiftly, and by eight o'clock I was approaching the Alonkin house again. I asked the maid, when she opened the door, the name and patronymic of her master (I already knew from the signature on his works that his first name was Fyodor, but I didn't know his patronymic).

Fedosya, the maid, again asked me to wait in the dining room and went to announce my arrival. When she returned she showed me into the study. I greeted Fyodor Mikhailovich and sat down at my old place near the little table. But he didn't like this arrangement and suggested that I change over to his desk, where it would be more comfortable for me to write. I must confess that I was terribly flattered by this invitation to work at the very desk where such a brilliant novel as *Crime and Punishment* had only recently been written[7].

I changed my seat and Fyodor Mikhailovich took my old place at the little table. Again he asked my name and inquired whether I was related to the talented young writer Snitkin, who had died not long before. I answered that we were not related. He then began to question me in detail about my family, my schooling, why I had taken up stenography and so forth.

To all these questions I replied simply, seriously, almost sternly, as Fyodor Mikhailovich later declared. I had long ago resolved that, if I should be working as a stenographer in private houses, I would from the very first put my relations with strangers on a businesslike footing, shunning any familiarity, so that no one might have the desire to say anything familiar or impertinent to me.

Apparently I never smiled even once while I was speaking with Fyodor Mikhailovich, and my seriousness pleased him very much. He confessed to me later that he had been pleasantly surprised by my knowledge of correct behavior. He was used to meeting Nihilist women socially and observing their behavior, which roused him to indignation. He was all the more pleased, therefore, to find in me the complete antithesis of the prevailing type of young woman of that time.

Meanwhile Fedosya had prepared tea in the dining room and brought in two glasses, two rolls, and some lemon. Again Fyodor Mikhailovich offered me a cigarette, and he urged me to eat some pears.

At tea the conversation took on a warmer and more sincere tone. All at once, it seemed to me that I had known Dostoevsky for a long time, and I began to feel more natural and at ease. For some reason our talk touched on the Petrashevsky circle[8] and the death penalty. Dostoevsky was carried away by his memories.

"I remember standing on Semyonov Square among my condemned comrades," he told me. "As I watched the preparations taking place, I knew that I had no more than five minutes left to live. But those minutes seemed years—decades—so much time, it seemed, still lay ahead of me!

"They had already dressed us in our death robes and divided

us into groups of three. I was number eight in the third row. The first three had been tied to the execution posts. In two or three minutes both rows would be shot, and then it would be our turn.

"My God, my God, how I wanted to live! How precious my life seemed to me, how much that was fine and good I might have accomplished! My whole past life came back to me then, and the way I had sometimes misused it; and I so longed to experience it all over again and live for a long, long time. . . .

"Suddenly I heard the drums sounding retreat, and I took heart. My comrades were untied and brought back from the execution posts. A new sentence was read. I was condemned to four years at hard labor. That was the happiest day of my life.[9] I walked back and forth in my cell in Alexeyevsky Ravelin and kept singing, singing out loud—so glad I was for the gift of life.

"Afterwards my brother was allowed to come and say goodbye to me; and on Christmas Eve we were sent off on our long journey. I still have the letter I wrote my dead brother on the day sentence was pronounced—my nephew returned it to me not long ago."

Fyodor Mikhailovich's story gave me an eerie feeling. I could feel the gooseflesh crawling along my skin. And I was quite astonished by his frankness with a young girl, hardly more than a child, whom he had met today for the first time in his life. This man, to all appearances withdrawn and severe, was telling me of his past life in such detail, so openly and naturally, that I couldn't help feeling amazed. It was only later, after I learned more about his family situation, that I understood the reason for his readiness to confide in me. At that time Fyodor Mikhailovich was utterly alone and surrounded by persons who were hostile to him. He felt too keenly the need to share his thoughts with those whom he sensed as kind and interested in him. His frankness with me on that day of our first meeting pleased me deeply and left me with a wonderful impression of him.

Our conversation shifted from one topic to the next—but we had not yet begun to work. I was worried by this: it was growing late and I had a long way to go to reach home. I had promised my mother to go home straight from Dostoevsky's house, and now I was afraid she would be upset. I felt awkward about reminding him of the purpose of my being there, and so I was very glad when he remembered it himself and asked me to begin taking dictation.

I got out my notebook, and Fyodor Mikhailovich began pacing about the room in swift strides, diagonally from the door to the stove and back. Every time he reached the stove he would invariably knock against it twice. On top of this he smoked one cigarette after another, throwing his unsmoked stubs frequently into the ashtray lying at the corner of his desk.

After he had dictated for some time he asked me to read back what I had written down; but he stopped me at the very beginning.

"What's that, 'she returned from Roulettenburg'?*[10] Did I mention Roulettenburg at all?"

"Yes, you did, Fyodor Mikhailovich, you dictated the word."

"Impossible!"

"Excuse me, but is there a city in your novel by that name?"

"Yes, the action takes place in a gambling town that I call 'Roulettenburg.' "

"But then you must have dictated the word to me—or else where would I have got it?"

"You're right," he admitted. "I've got something mixed up here."

I was very happy to have the misunderstanding cleared up. I think Fyodor Mikhailovich was too wrapped up in his thoughts or perhaps overtired by the day, and that was how the error came about. He himself realized this and said that he was not in condition to proceed with the dictation. He asked me to bring back my transcription the next day at about twelve, and I agreed to do this.

The clock struck eleven and I got ready to leave. Learning that I lived in the Peski section, he remarked that he had never been in that part of the city and hadn't the faintest notion where Peski might be. If it was far away he could have his maid take me home. Of course I declined his offer. He saw me to the door and told Fedosya to light my way down the stairs.

*Later the beginning of the novel was rewritten as follows: "At last I have come back after my absence of two weeks. Our party has already been in Roulettenburg for the past three days." (A.G.D.)

At home I ecstatically told Mama all about Dostoevsky's kindness and openness with me. But, so as not to upset her, I concealed from her the feeling of oppression which this day, spent so interestingly, had left with me, and which I had never felt before. It was a feeling that weighed me down heavily. This was the first time I had ever known such a man: wise, good, and yet unhappy, apparently abandoned by everyone. And a feeling of deep pity and commiseration was born in me. I was exhausted and went straight to bed; but I asked to be awakened early, so that I would have time to transcribe the whole dictation and bring it to Fyodor Mikhailovich at the appointed hour.

The next day I woke up early and set to work at once. Although relatively little had been dictated I wanted to make my copy of it as legible and attractive as possible, and that was time-consuming. Hurry as I might, I was still late by a full half hour.

I found Fyodor Mikhailovich in a state of great agitation. "I had already begun to think," he said in greeting, "that you had found working for me too burdensome and that you weren't going to come back. And, by the way, I didn't make a note of your address and ran the risk of losing what I dictated to you yesterday."

"I'm truly sorry to be so late," I apologized. "But I assure you that if I had had to decline the position, then of course I would have let you know and would have given you the original copy of what you dictated."

"The reason I'm so worried about it," he explained, "is that I must finish the novel by the first of November, and I haven't even worked out a plan for it. All I know is that it has to be no less than seven signatures long in Stellovsky's format."

I began to question him more closely, and he explained the truly outrageous way he had been entrapped.

When his elder brother Mikhail died, Dostoevsky had taken upon himself all the debts of the magazine *Time*,[11] which his brother had published. These debts were in the form of promissory notes, and the creditors were upsetting Fyodor Mikhailovich terribly by threatening to attach his property and to put him into debtors' prison. In those days it was still possible to do such a thing.

The immediately pressing debts amounted to about three thousand rubles. Fyodor Mikhailovich had explored all possible sources of funds without result. When all his efforts to dissuade the creditors proved futile and he was reduced to utter despair, the publisher Stellovsky came forward unexpectedly with an offer to buy the rights to his collected works in a three-volume edition, for the sum of three thousand rubles. But that was the least of it. In return for that same sum, Fyodor Mikhailovich would also obligate himself to produce a new novel.

His position was critical. To save himself from the threatened loss of his freedom, he agreed to all the terms of the contract. The agreement was concluded in the summer of 1865, and Stellovsky handed the money over to a notary. This money was paid out to the creditors the very next day, and so Fyodor Mikhailovich never even held a penny of it in his hands.

But the most galling thing of all was that all this money came back to Stellovsky again within a few days. It turned out that he himself had bought up Fyodor Mikhailovich's promissory notes for next to nothing and extracted the money from him through two intermediaries who were really figureheads. Stellovsky was a cunning, adroit exploiter of writers and musicians—Pisemsky, Krestovsky and Glinka, for example. He was clever at waiting for people to make a false step at difficult moments of their lives, and then catching them in his net. A price of three thousand rubles for the right to a complete edition of Dostoevsky was too paltry in view of the success of his novels!

The obligation to deliver a new novel by November 1, 1866, was the most difficult of all the conditions. If he failed to meet this deadline he would have to pay a heavy penalty; and if the novel was not completed by the first of December he would lose the rights to all his work, which would then pass to Stellovsky in perpetuity. That beast of prey, it goes without saying, was counting on this very eventuality.

In 1866 Fyodor Mikhailovich was deeply immersed in writing *Crime and Punishment* and needed the time to rewrite and finish it properly. How then could he, a sick man, possibly produce a new work of such length? By the time he returned to Moscow that autumn, he felt that it was impossible to fulfill the conditions of the Stellovsky contract in the space of a month and a half or two, and had reached a peak of desperation.

Hoping to rescue him from catastrophe, his friends Apollon Maikov, A. P. Milyukov, I. G. Dolgomostyev and others proposed to work out a plan for a novel. Each of them would undertake to write a part of it, and working collectively in that way they could finish it by the deadline. All that Fyodor Mikhailovich would have to do would be to edit it and smooth out the rough spots inevitable in a collaboration of that sort.[12]

But Dostoevsky turned down the proposal. He decided that it would be better to pay the penalty or lose the rights to his own work than to sign his name to the work of other people. It was then that his friends began urging him to turn to a stenographer for help.

Milyukov recalled the name of P. M. Olkhin, a teacher of stenography with whom he was acquainted. He went to him and asked him to see Dostoevsky who, despite strong reservations about whether he would be able to work in that way, decided to resort to stenographic assistance in view of the imminence of the deadline.

Limited as my knowledge of people was at that time, Stellovsky's behavior made my blood boil. Tea was served, and then Fyodor Mikhailovich began dictating. It was obviously difficult for him to get into the work. He stopped often, thought things over and asked me to reread what he had already dictated. Within an hour he announced that he was tired and wanted to rest.

Again we started to chat as we had done the day before. He was in an anxious frame of mind and kept shifting from one topic to the next. Again he asked my name and forgot it the next minute. Once or twice he offered me a cigarette, though he already knew that I didn't smoke.

I began asking him about our contemporary writers, and he brightened up. In answering my questions he seemed to throw off his obsessive thoughts and spoke calmly, even gaily. And some of what he said remained in my memory.

He considered Nekrasov the friend of his youth and had a high opinion of his poetic gift. Maikov he loved not only as a talented poet, but also as the finest and most intelligent of men. He mentioned Turgenev as a first-rate talent, but regretted that as a result of the latter's long residence abroad he had lost some of his understanding of Russia and the Russian people.

After a short rest we set to work again, and again Fyodor Mikhailovich began showing anxiety and irritation. His work was clearly going badly for him. I interpreted this as the awkwardness of having to dictate to someone he barely knew.

At about four o'clock I got ready to leave, promising to return with the finished work the next day at noon. At parting he handed me a packet of heavy writing paper ruled almost invisibly, the kind he habitually used, and showed me exactly what margins I was to leave on it.

So our work began and went on. I would come to his house at twelve and stay until four. During that time we would have three dictating sessions of a half-hour or more, and between dictations we would drink tea and talk. I began to notice joyfully that he was growing accustomed to his new way of working and was calmer each time I came. This grew particularly evident after I was able to determine, by calculating how many pages of my transcribed manuscript were equivalent to one signature of Stellovsky's edition, exactly how much of the total work we had already managed to complete.

The ever-growing number of completed pages cheered Fyodor Mikhailovich enormously. He would often ask, "And how many pages did we do yesterday? And how many do we have altogether? What do you think—will we finish in time?"

Each day, chatting with me like a friend, he would lay bare some unhappy scene from his past. I could not help being deeply touched at his accounts of the difficulties from which he had never extricated himself, and indeed could not.

At first it seemed peculiar to me that I never glimpsed any member of his family. I didn't know who they were or where they were. I had encountered only one—I think it was on my fourth visit. After work, I was going out of the house gate when I was stopped by a young man. I realized that this was that same young man whom I had seen in the vestibule of Dostoevsky's apartment on my first visit. From close up he looked even less attractive than at a distance. He had a sallow, almost yellow face, dark eyes with yellowish whites, and teeth yellowed with tobacco stains.

"You didn't recognize me?" he asked familiarly. "I saw you

at Papa's. I don't like to go in when the two of you are working, but I'm curious to know—what is this 'stenography' all about? I'm going to start studying it myself one of these days. Allow me —" And he unceremoniously took my portfolio out of my hands, opened it, and started examining my shorthand right there on the street. I was so taken aback by his familiarity that I wasn't even able to protest.

"Odd thing, that," he remarked casually, and returned the portfolio to me.

I thought to myself, how is it that such a good, fine man as Fyodor Mikhailovich could have such an ill-bred son?

With each passing day Dostoevsky was growing kinder and warmer toward me. He often addressed me as "golubchik"[13] (his favorite affectionate expression), "good Anna Grigoryevna," or "my dear," and I attributed these words to his graciousness toward a young girl hardly more than a child. It was so pleasant for me to be able to lighten his labor and to see how gladdened he was and how his spirits lifted with my reassurances that the novel was progressing well and would be finished in time.

Privately, I was very proud of the fact that I was not only helping my favorite author with his work, but also having a beneficial effect on his frame of mind. All this elevated me in my own eyes. I stopped being afraid of "the famous writer" and spoke with him freely and frankly, as if with an uncle or an old friend. I asked him about various events in his life, and he satisfied my curiosity very willingly. He told me about his eight months of imprisonment in the Peter and Paul fortress, of how he communicated with other prisoners by knocking on the wall. He spoke of his life as a convict, of the criminals working out their sentences while he was there. He reminisced about Europe, his travels and encounters abroad and his family in Moscow, whom he loved very much.[14]

Once he told me that he had been married and that his wife had died three years before, and he showed me her portrait. I didn't much care for it. The late Madame Dostoevskaya, as he told me, had been photographed when she was already very ill, a year before her death, and her appearance was terrible, almost corpse-like. It was then that I learned, with satisfaction, that the forward young man who had so displeased me was not Fyodor Mikhailovich's son at all, but his stepson—his wife's son by her first marriage to Alexander Ivanovich Isayev.

Fyodor Mikhailovich would also complain frequently about his debts, his penury and his financial straits. On a later occasion I was even a witness to these straits. Once as I was beginning my work I noticed the disappearance of one of the charming Chinese vases which his Siberian friends had given him.

"Surely the vase hasn't been broken?" I asked.

"No, not broken—taken to the pawnshop. I needed another twenty-five rubles and I had to pawn the vase."

About three days later, the other vase was overtaken by the same fate.

Another time, when I had finished taking my notes and was passing through the dining room, I noticed a wooden spoon in the place setting on the table, which had been laid for dinner. I laughed and said to Fyodor Mikhailovich, who was accompanying me, "Now I know you'll be eating buckwheat kasha[15] for dinner."

"What makes you come to that conclusion?"

"The spoon. They say kasha tastes better when eaten with a wooden spoon."

"Well, you're mistaken. I needed money, and I sent the servant to pawn the silver spoons. But they offer a good deal less for an odd lot than for a full dozen—so I had to give up my own spoon as well."

Fyodor Mikhailovich always spoke about his financial straits with great good nature. His stories, however, were so mournful that on one occasion I couldn't restrain myself from asking, "Why is it, Fyodor Mikhailovich, that you remember only the unhappy times? Tell me instead about how you were happy."

"Happy? But I haven't had any happiness yet. At least, not the kind of happiness I always dreamed of. I am still waiting for it. A few days ago I wrote my friend, Baron Wrangel, that in spite of all the grief that has come to me I still go on dreaming that I will begin a new, happy life."[16]

How painful to hear those words! It seemed strange that at his time of life, almost in old age, this kind and gifted man had not yet found the happiness he desired and was only dreaming about it.

On one occasion he told me the details of his engagement to Anna Korvin-Krukovskaya—how happy he was to receive the consent of this intelligent, kind, and gifted young woman, and how despondent when he had to release her from her promise, realizing that their antithetical political convictions precluded the possibility of mutual happiness.[17]

Once, when he was for some reason in a particularly anxious mood, he told me that he was standing at a crossroad at that moment and that three paths lay open before him: to go to the East—to Constantinople and Jerusalem—and remain there, perhaps forever; or to go abroad to play roulette and there to immolate himself in that game he found so utterly engrossing; or, finally, to marry again and seek joy and happiness in family life. He was troubled about the decision, which would radically change his unfortunate life, and seeing how well-disposed I was to him, he asked what I would advise.

I must confess that this very trustful question of his posed a dilemma for me, since his wish to travel to the East* as well as his desire to become a gambler seemed to me vague and somewhat fantastic. Knowing of many happy families among my acquaintances and friends, I advised him to marry again and find happiness in his family.

"So you think I can marry again?" he asked. "That someone might consent to become my wife? What kind of wife shall I choose then—an intelligent one or a kind one?"

"An intelligent one, of course."

"Well, no . . . if I have the choice, I'll pick a kind one, so that she'll take pity on me and love me."

While we were on the theme of marriage, he asked me why I didn't marry myself. I answered that I had two suitors, both splendid people, and that I respected them both very much but

*That he was *seriously* planning to go to the Far East is shown in the letter of introduction to A. S. Engelhardt, representative of the Imperial Russian Mission in Constantinople. This letter was given to Dostoevsky by the president of the Literary Fund, E. P. Kovalevsky, and was later found among his papers. It was dated June 3, 1863. (A.G.D.)

did not love them—and that I wanted to marry for love.

"For love, without fail," he seconded me heartily. "Respect alone isn't enough for a happy marriage!"

One day in mid-October while we were at work, Apollon Maikov appeared unexpectedly at the study door. I had seen portraits of him and so I knew him at once.

"Well, and what a patriarchal style of life you lead!" he remarked jokingly to Fyodor Mikhailovich. "The door to the staircase is open, there's no servant in sight—they could carry off your whole house!"

Fyodor Mikhailovich was obviously happy to see Maikov. He introduced us at once and called me his "zealous collaborator," which was very nice to hear. When Maikov heard my name he asked whether I wasn't related to the recently deceased writer Snitkin (the usual question when I met writers) and soon thereafter, saying that he was afraid of interfering with our work, started to leave. I suggested a short break, and Fyodor Mikhailovich took him into the next room. They talked for twenty minutes or so, and I transcribed the dictated material meanwhile.

Maikov came back into the study to say goodbye to me and asked whether Fyodor Mikhailovich wouldn't dictate something to me. At that time stenography was a novelty, and everyone was interested in it. Dostoevsky fulfilled his request by dictating half a page of his novel. I immediately read the dictation back aloud. Maikov examined my shorthand closely and kept repeating, "I can't make it out at all!"

I liked Maikov very much. Even before that I had loved him as a poet, but Fyodor Mikhailovich's praise of him as a splendid, kind person reinforced my favorable impression even more.

The more the time passed, the more deeply engrossed Dostoevsky grew in the work. He no longer dictated to me orally, improvising on the spot; now he worked at night and then dictated from his manuscript. There were times when he managed to get so much written that I had to sit up long past midnight to transcribe my notes. With what triumph I would announce the number of accumulated pages the next day! And how pleasant it was to see his happy smile in response to my assurances that the work was going successfully and that it would be finished by the deadline, without a doubt.

Both of us became involved with the lives of the characters of the new novel, and I began to have my favorites and my antagonists, just as he did. I was sympathetic to the grandmother who gambled away her fortune, and to Mr. Astley; but my contempt was aroused by Polina and by the hero himself, whose irresoluteness I could not forgive. Whereas Dostoevsky was wholly on the gambler's side, and told me that he had experienced many of his hero's emotions and feelings himself.[18] He maintained that it is possible to possess a strong character, to prove that fact by your own life, and nonetheless lack the strength to conquer in yourself the passion for roulette.

There were times when I was amazed by my own boldness in expressing my views about the novel, and still more amazed by the indulgence with which a brilliant writer used to listen to these almost childish remarks and opinions. During those three weeks of joint work all my former interests receded to the background. With Professor Olkhin's consent I had stopped attending my stenography lectures; I rarely saw my friends and concentrated wholly on work and on those utterly fascinating conversations we used to have while we were relaxing after our dictation sessions. I couldn't help comparing Dostoevsky with the young men I used to meet in my own social circle. How empty and trivial their talk seemed to me in comparison with the ever fresh and original views of my favorite writer!

Leaving his house still under the influence of ideas new to me, I would miss him when I was at home, and lived only in the expectation of the next day's meeting with him. I realized with sorrow that the work was nearing its end and that our acquaintance must break off. So that I was most surprised and happy when the very same thought that had been bothering me was put into words by Dostoevsky.

"You know what I've been thinking, Anna Grigoryevna?* You and I have been getting along so beautifully, we see one another every day in such a friendly way, we've grown so accus-

*Not until the end of the month did he remember my Christian name, and even then he kept forgetting it and asking me what it was. (A.G.D.)

tomed to our lively talks together—can it be true that all this will end when the novel is done? That would be a pity, truly! I shall miss you very much. And where will I ever see you again?"

"But, Fyodor Mikhailovich," I answered in embarrassment, "a mountain can't come to a mountain, as the saying goes, but people can meet without difficulty."

"But where, precisely?"

"Well—in society . . . at the theatre, at concerts. . . ."

"But you know that I rarely go out in society or to the theatre. And what kind of meeting would that be, anyway, when there's no possibility of saying what's on your mind? Why don't you invite me to your house to meet your family?"

"Please do come, we'll be very happy to see you. I'm only afraid that Mama and I will seem boring conversationalists to you."

"Then when may I come?"

"We'll set a date after we finish our work," I said. "That's the main thing now—the end of your novel."

The first of November was drawing near—the deadline for giving the novel to Stellovsky—and Dostoevsky began to be afraid that Stellovsky would contrive some kind of trick to get his penalty paid, and would therefore find a pretext for refusing to accept the manuscript. I reassured him as much as I was able to, and promised to find out what steps should be taken in the event that his suspicions proved justified.

That very evening I asked my mother to go to see a lawyer we knew. He advised that the manuscript be taken either to a notary or to the police officer of the district where Stellovsky lived, and that an official receipt for it of course be obtained. The same advice was given to Dostoevsky by Justice of the Peace Freyman, the brother of his former schoolmate, whom he consulted on the matter.

Our last dictation took place on the twenty-ninth of October. *The Gambler* was finished. From October 4 to 29, that is, in twenty-six days, Dostoevsky had produced a novel seven two-column signatures long in large format—the equivalent of ten normal signatures. He was hugely pleased, and announced that after the successful delivery of the manuscript to Stellovsky he was giving a dinner in a restaurant for his friends Maikov, Milyukov, and others, and was inviting me in advance to take part in the festivities.

"And have you ever been to a restaurant?" he asked me.

"No, never."

"But you will come to my dinner? I want to drink to the health of my dear collaborator! I would never have finished the novel in time without your help. So you will come?"

I answered that I would ask my mother's opinion; but privately I resolved not to go: my shyness would make me look stiff, and I would put a damper on the general merriment.

On the next day, October 30, I brought Fyodor Mikhailovich my transcription of the previous day's dictation. He greeted me with a special warmth, somehow, and even flushed when I walked in the door. We counted up the number of pages as usual, and were delighted to see that there were so many of them—more than we had anticipated. He said that he would reread the novel that day, make some corrections, and bring it to Stellovsky the next day. Then and there he handed me the fifty rubles, the pay we had agreed on; he shook my hand hard and thanked me warmly for my collaboration.

I knew that October 30 was his birthday and had decided, therefore, to change my usual black cotton dress for one of lilac silk. Fyodor Mikhailovich, who had always seen me dressed in mourning, was flattered by my attention, found that lilac became me and that I looked taller and more graceful in a long dress.

I was very pleased to hear these praises, but my pleasure was shattered by the entrance of Emilya Fyodorovna, the widow of his brother Mikhail, who had come to congratulate Dostoevsky on his birthday. He introduced us and explained that it was because of my help that he had succeeded in finishing the novel in time and had thereby escaped catastrophe.

These words notwithstanding, Emilya Fyodorovna behaved drily and haughtily toward me, which surprised and wounded me very much. Dostoevsky was displeased with his sister-in-law's ungracious tone and therefore began treating me with even greater kindness and cordiality. Inviting me to have a look at some book which had just come out, he took her aside and began to show her some papers.

Apollon Maikov came in. He bowed but evidently did not recognize me. Turning to Dostoevsky, he asked how the novel was progressing. But Fyodor Mikhailovich, who was engrossed in his conversation with his sister-in-law, didn't hear the question and so didn't answer. Then I decided to answer for him and said that the novel had been finished the day before and that I had just brought in the final chapter. Maikov quickly went over to me, held out his hand, and apologized for not having recognized me at once. He explained it by his being nearsighted and also by the fact that I had seemed shorter to him in my black dress.

He began asking about *The Gambler* and my opinion of it. I responded rapturously about this new work which had become so precious to me; I said that there were several remarkably vivid and well-brought-off types in it: the grandmother, Mr. Astley, and the lovesick general. We chatted for twenty minutes or so, and it was so easy for me to talk to this kind and good man. Emilya Fyodorovna was surprised and even a bit shocked at Maikov's attention to me, but the dryness of her tone did not alter. She probably considered it beneath her dignity to pay any notice to . . . a stenographer.

Maikov left soon afterward. I followed his example, not wishing to endure Emilya Fyodorovna's haughty manner to me any longer. Dostoevsky urged me very insistently to stay and tried in every possible way to soften his sister-in-law's ungraciousness. He accompanied me to the front hall and reminded me of my promise to invite him to our house. I confirmed the invitation.

"But when can I come, then? Tomorrow?"

"No, I won't be at home tomorrow, I'm invited to a school friend's."

"Day after tomorrow?"

"I have a stenography lecture."

"Then shall we say the second of November?"

"On the second of November I'm going to the theatre."

"My Lord! All your time is taken up! You know, Anna Grigoryevna, I have a suspicion that you're saying all this on purpose.

You simply don't want me to come. Tell the truth!"

"Not in the least—I assure you! We'll be glad to see you at our house. Come on November third, on Thursday, at about seven in the evening.

"Not until Thursday? How far off that is! I shall miss you so much."

I, of course, took these words as an amiable little joke.

And so the blissful time was done with, and the dreary days began. During that month I had grown so accustomed to that merry rush to work, the joyful meetings and the lively conversations with Dostoevsky, that they had become a necessity to me. All my old activities had lost their interest and seemed empty and futile.

Even his promised visit not only gave me no joy, but on the contrary weighed me down. I was aware that neither my good mother nor I was capable of being a fascinating conversationalist for a man as clever and talented as he. If up to now our talks had been so lively, that was only because, as I thought, they revolved around the matter that concerned us both.

But now he would be coming to us as a guest who would have to be "entertained." I began thinking up subjects for future conversations and tormenting myself with the thought that the long, tiring trip to our neighborhood and the evening spent in boredom would erase for him—exceptionally sensitive man that he was—the memory of our past meetings, and that he would regret his involvement in this dull acquaintance. Even while I dreamed of seeing him again, I was ready to wish he had forgotten his promise to visit us.

As a person of naturally buoyant spirits, I attempted to keep myself busy and so dissipate this depressed, or rather anxious, mood. I went to visit a girlfriend, and the next evening I went to the stenography lecture. Olkhin greeted me with congratulations on the successful completion of my work. Dostoevsky had written him about it and thanked him for recommending a stenographer with whose help he had brought his novel to a satisfactory conclusion. He had added that the new method of working had proved a convenient one for him, and that he was counting on using it in future.

On the morning of Thursday, November third, I began my preparations for receiving Dostoevsky. I went out to buy the kind of pears he liked and other sweets, such as he used sometimes to offer me. All day I worried, and by seven my anxiety had reached a peak.

But seven-thirty struck, then eight; and still he did not come. I was already deciding that he had changed his mind or forgotten all about it. At eight-thirty came the long-awaited peal of the bell.

I rushed to meet him and said, "So you managed to find me, Fyodor Mikhailovich?"

"That's a good one," he answered affably. "You say that in such a tone of voice, it seems you're displeased that I did find you. And here I've been searching for you since seven o'clock, driving all around the neighborhood and asking everybody. They all know that a Kostromskaya Street exists—but how to reach it—that they couldn't tell me.* Thank goodness I found a kind man who sat down on the box next to the cabdriver and pointed out the way."

My mother came in, and I was quick to introduce Fyodor Mikhailovich to her. He kissed her hand gallantly and said that he was very much obliged to me for my help in his work. While Mama was busy pouring tea, Fyodor Mikhailovich told me how many anxious moments the delivery of the manuscript to Stellovsky had caused him.

Just as we had foreseen, Stellovsky pulled a trick. He went off to the provinces, and his servant announced that it was not known when he would return. Then Dostoevsky went to his publishing house and tried to hand the manuscript over to the office manager, who flatly refused to accept it, saying that he had not been authorized by his employer to do so. By then it was too late to go to the notary; and at the police station none of the higher officials were present that day, and he was told to return in the evening. He spent the day in a state of anxiety; not

*Kostromskaya Street is located behind Nikolayevsky Hospital and the nearest way to it is through the hospital gates. In the evening these gates are locked, and the street can be reached either through Slonovaya Street (now Suvorovsky Prospect) or from Little Bolotnaya. (A.G.D.)

until ten o'clock that evening did he manage to hand over the manuscript in the police station of the X district and to obtain a receipt from the police inspector.

We settled down to drink our tea just as gaily and unconstrainedly as we always had. The conversational themes I had prepared had to be put aside, so many new and fascinating ones came up. My mother was enchanted with Dostoevsky, even though in the first few moments she had been a bit abashed by the visit of a "famous author." He knew how to charm, and on later occasions I was often to observe the way people, even those with prior prejudices against him, fell under his spell.

He told me among other things that he needed a week to rest, after which he was planning to tackle the final installment of *Crime and Punishment.*

"I would like to ask your help with it, kind Anna Grigoryevna. Working with you has been so easy. As a matter of fact, I would like to use dictation from now on, and I hope you won't refuse to be my collaborator."

"I'd do it gladly," I answered. "But I don't know how Olkhin will look at it. He may have another pupil of his in mind for this new job of yours."

"But I'm used to your way of working and I'm extremely satisfied with it. It would be strange for Olkhin to think of recommending a different stenographer who might not even suit me. But perhaps the truth is that you don't want to work with me any longer? In that case, of course, I won't insist. . . ."

He was obviously chagrined. I tried to reassure him; I said that in all probability Olkhin wouldn't have any objection to my doing this new work, but that in any case I really should consult him.

At about eleven he was ready to leave. During the goodbyes he extracted a promise from me to speak to Olkhin at the very first lecture, and write him about it. We parted in the friendliest possible way, and I returned to the dining room ecstatic that our talk had been so lively.

But not more than ten minutes had elapsed when the maid came in and said that in the dark someone had stolen a cushion from the special deluxe sleigh which had bought Dostoevsky to our house. The cabdriver was in despair, and only Fyodor Mikhailovich's promise to repay him for his loss could calm him down.

I was still so young that this episode embarrassed me horribly. I thought it would damage my relationship with Dostoevsky, and that he wouldn't want to come back to such a desolate neighborhood, where he might be robbed just as his cabby had been. I was on the point of tears over my fear that such a marvelous evening might be spoiled for him by this vexing incident.

On the day following Dostoevsky's visit I went to my sister Masha's house to spend the day. I told her and her husband, Pavel Grigoryevich Svatkovsky, all about my work with Dostoevsky. In spending my days taking his dictation and my evenings transcribing it I had seen Masha only sporadically, and lots of stories had been piling up. She listened with close attention, interrupting constantly and questioning me about every little detail. Having taken note of my extraordinary animation, she said to me at parting, "It's all for nothing, Netochka, your having such a crush on Dostoevsky. For your dreams can't ever come about, and thank goodness they can't—if he's that ill and overloaded with family and debts!"

With some heat I retorted that I didn't have the slightest "crush" on Dostoevsky, that I wasn't "dreaming" about anything, but was simply happy to chat with a clever, talented man and appreciative of his constant kindness and attention to me.

But my sister's words had upset me. When I was at home again I asked myself whether Masha was right. Was I really infatuated with him? Was it possible that this was the beginning of the love I had not as yet experienced in my life? What an insane dream that would be on my part! Was it possible at all? And on the other hand, if it was really the beginning of love, what on earth was I to do? Should I invent some convenient excuse to decline any further work with him, stop seeing him, stop thinking about him, try to forget him little by little, immerse myself in some other kind of activity and restore my former state of inner calm, which I had always prized so highly?

But possibly Masha was mistaken, after all, and no danger was threatening my heart. In that case what would be the point of depriving myself of my stenographic work, which I had been wanting to do for so long, as well as of those heartfelt, interesting talks that went together with the work? And anyway, it would be a terrible pity to leave him without stenographic help, now that he had adapted himself so well to it—all the more since I knew of no other student of Olkhin's (except for two who already had steady jobs) who were capable of replacing me fully, both in shorthand speed and in promptness of delivering the manuscript.

All these thoughts kept running through my head, and I was full of deep anxiety.

Sunday came, the sixth of November. I was supposed to go to my godmother's to congratulate her on her name day. I was not on close terms with her and visited her only on ceremonial occasions. Today there would be many guests, and I counted on being able to dissipate the oppressive mood that wouldn't leave me. She lived far away, at Alarchin Bridge, and I got ready to go before nightfall.

While I was waiting for the cabdriver I sat down at the piano, and so didn't hear the bell ring. The sound of a man's steps caught my attention. I looked around and, to my great amazement and joy, I saw that Dostoevsky was there. There was a timid and somehow embarrassed expression on his face. I went up to him.

"Do you know what I've done, Anna Grigoryevna?" he said, shaking my hand hard. "All these days I've missed you so much and all day today, ever since morning, I've been deliberating about it—should I come to see you or not? Would it be convenient for you? Wouldn't my coming again so soon seem strange to you and your mother? On Thursday I was here, and on Sunday I turn up again! And therefore I resolved not to come under any circumstances. And, as you see, here I am!"

"What are you saying, Fyodor Mikhailovich! Mama and I will always be happy to see you here!"

But despite my reassurances, our conversation couldn't seem to develop. I wasn't able to overcome my anxiety and could only answer his questions but was almost incapable of putting any of my own. There was also an external circumstance which was an embarrassment to me. The large drawing room in which we were sitting hadn't yet been heated, and it was very cold. He noticed this.

"But how cold your house is! And how cold you are yourself today!" Then, noticing that I was wearing a light gray silk dress, he asked where I was going. When he learned that I had to leave for my godmother's he said he didn't wish to detain me, and suggested taking me in his sleigh, since it was on the way. I agreed, and we left.

At a sharp turn in the road, he wanted to support me by putting his arm around my waist. But I, like all girls of the sixties, had a prejudice against any acts of male gallantry such as kissing the hand, putting a supportive arm around the waist, and things of that sort.

"Please don't trouble yourself—I won't fall out!" I said.

He was evidently offended and said, "How I wish you would fall out of the sleigh this minute!"

I burst out laughing, and peace was concluded between us. For the rest of the trip we chattered away gaily, and my despondent mood lifted as if a hand had taken it away. When we said goodbye he squeezed my hand hard and made me promise that I would come to his house the next day to set up a schedule for our work on *Crime and Punishment.*

The eighth of November, 1866, was one of the great days of my life. That was the day Fyodor Mikhailovich told me that he loved me and asked me to be his wife. Half a century has passed since then, and yet every detail is as sharp in my memory as if it had happened a month ago.

It was a brilliant, frosty day. I walked to his house, and therefore arrived half an hour later than the appointed time. He had apparently been waiting for me for a long time. When he heard my voice he appeared in the vestibule at once.

"So you're here at last!" he said happily and began helping me undo my hood and take off my coat. Together we went into his study. It was very bright there on this occasion, and I was surprised to notice that he was excited about something. The expression on his face was heightened, fervid, almost ecstatic, and made him look much younger.

"How happy I am that you've come! I was so afraid you'd forget your promise."

"What on earth made you think such a thing? Once I give my word I always keep it."

"Forgive me—I know you always keep your word. It's only that I'm so very glad to see you again!"

"And I'm glad to see you, Fyodor Mikhailovich, and in such a cheerful mood at that. Has something pleasant happened to you?"

"Yes, it has. Last night I had a marvelous dream."

"Oh, is that all!" And I started to laugh.

"Please don't laugh. I attribute great meaning to dreams. My dreams are always prophetic. When I dream about my dead brother Misha, or particularly when I dream of my father, I know it portends some catastrophe."

"In that case, tell me your dream!"

"Do you see that big rosewood box? That is a gift from my Siberian friend Chokan Valikhanov and I value it very much. I keep my manuscripts and letters in it, and other things that are precious to me for their memories. And so this is my dream: I was sitting in front of that box and rearranging the papers in it. Suddenly something sparkled among them, some kind of bright little star. I was leafing through the papers and the star kept appearing and disappearing. And this was intriguing to me. I started slowly putting all the papers to one side. And there among them I found a little diamond, a tiny one, but very sparkling and brilliant."

"And what did you do with it?"

"That's the pity of it—I can't remember! There were other dreams after that and I don't know what became of the diamond. But that was a good dream!"

"You know that dreams are usually explained as having the opposite meaning," I remarked, and instantly regretted my words. His face quickly changed, seemed to darken.

"So you think no happiness will ever come to me? All that—all that is only a vain hope?" he said pitifully.

"I'm not capable of interpreting dreams, and anyway I don't really believe in them."

I was very sorry that his cheerful mood had vanished, and I

began trying to cheer him up. In answer to his question about the things I dreamed about, I described my dreams in comic aspect.

"Mostly I dream about our former headmistress at school—a very majestic lady with old-fashioned ringlets at her temples. And she was always giving me a good scolding about something or other. I also dream about a tortoise-shell cat that once jumped at me from our garden fence and frightened me terribly."

"Oh, my child, my child!" he said, laughing and looking at me fondly. "What dreams you have! Well tell me, then, did you have a good time at your godmother's name day?"

"Oh, very good. After dinner the older people sat down to play cards, and we younger ones got together in our host's study and chattered away all evening. There were two very nice, amusing students there."

Fyodor Mikhailovich looked dark again. I was surprised by the rapidity of his changes of mood on this occasion. I thought this shifting mood might portend the onset of a seizure, and I felt terrified.

It had long been our custom, when I came to take his dictation, for him to tell me what he had been doing and where he had been during the time we weren't together. So I was quick to ask him how he had been keeping busy during the last days.

"I've been thinking up a plot for a new novel," he answered.

"You don't say! An interesting novel?"

"To me, quite interesting. The thing is, though, that I can't seem to work out the ending. The psychology of a young girl is involved in it. If I were in Moscow I would ask my niece, Sonechka, but as it is I shall turn to you for help."

Proudly I prepared to give my "help" to the brilliant novelist. "Who is the hero of your novel, then?"

"An artist, a man no longer young—well, in a word—a man about my own age."

"Oh tell me, do tell me about it," I begged, very curious about this new novel.

And now a brilliant improvisation poured out. Never, neither before nor afterwards, did I hear from him such an inspired tale as on that day. The further he went, the clearer it grew to me that he was telling about his own life, only changing names and situations. Here were all the things that he had previously spoken of to me in bits and fragments; but now his detailed, consecutive account explained a great deal about his relationships with his family and with his late wife.

The new novel also contained a harsh childhood, the early loss of a beloved father, some kind of fatal circumstance (a serious malady) which for ten years tore the artist away from life and from his beloved art. Then, his return to life (the artist's recovery from his illness), his meeting with the woman with whom he fell in love, the torments this love caused him, the death of his wife and of someone else close to him (a beloved sister), poverty, debt. . . .

The hero's inner state, his loneliness, his disenchantment with the people close to him, his hunger for a new life, his need for love, his passionate desire to find happiness again were depicted so vividly and with such fire that it was evident they were not merely the fruit of his imaginative power but had been experienced by the author himself.

Dostoevsky did not spare the darker shades in delineating his hero. By his own words his hero was a man grown old before his time, sick with an incurable disease (a paralyzed hand), gloomy, suspicious; possessed of a tender heart, it is true, but incapable of expressing his feelings; an artist and a talented one, perhaps, but a failure who had not once in his life succeeded in embodying his ideas in the forms he dreamed of, and who never ceased to torment himself over that fact.

Seeing Fyodor Mikhailovich himself in the hero of his novel, I could not keep from interrupting: "But why, Fyodor Mikhailovich, do you insult your hero so?"

"I see that you do not find him likeable."

"On the contrary, I find him very likeable. He has a splendid heart. Think how many sorrows have fallen to his lot, and how meekly he submits to them! Another man experiencing so much misery in his life would doubtless have grown hard, but your hero goes on loving people and helping them. No, you are being decidedly unfair to him."

"Yes, I agree that he has a kind and loving heart. And how happy I am that you understand him!"

He went on with his story. "And so, in that critical period of his life, the artist meets a young girl of your age, or perhaps a year or two older. Let's give her the name of Anya so as not to have to call her 'the heroine.' It's a nice name, Anya. . . ."

These words confirmed my conviction that by "the heroine" he was alluding to his former fiancée, Anna Korvin-Krukovskaya. It quite went out of my head at that moment that my own name was also Anna—so little did I feel that this story had any connection with myself. The theme of the new novel might have come into being (or so I thought) as the result of a letter he had recently received from her from abroad, which he had told me about a few days before.

The heroine's portrait was painted in different colors from the hero's. According to the author Anna was gentle, wise, kind, bubbling with life, and possessed of great tact in personal relationships. But I, who in those years attached much importance to feminine beauty, couldn't keep from asking, "And is your heroine pretty?"

"She isn't a real beauty, of course, but she is very nice-looking. I love her face."

Now I felt that he had let the cat out of the bag. Something pinched in my heart. A hateful feeling toward Anna Korvin-Krukovskaya took hold of me and I said, "But, Fyodor Mikhailovich, you are over-idealizing your 'Anya.' Can she really be all that?"

"She is just precisely 'all that'! I have studied her through and through!"

He went on with his story. "The hero used to meet Anya in art circles, and the more he saw of her the more he liked her and the stronger his conviction grew that he might find happiness with her. And still, his dream seemed to him almost impossible. For, as a matter of fact, what could this elderly, sick, debt-ridden man give a young, alive, exuberant girl? Wouldn't her love for him involve a terrible sacrifice on her part? And afterwards, wouldn't she bitterly regret uniting her life with his? And in general, would it be possible for a young girl so different in age and personality to fall in love with my artist? Wouldn't that be psychologically false? That is what I wanted to ask your opinion about, Anna Grigoryevna."

"But why would it be impossible? For if, as you say, your Anya isn't merely an empty flirt and has a kind, responsive heart, why couldn't she fall in love with your artist? What if he is poor and sick? Where's the sacrifice on her part, anyway? If she really loves him she'll be happy, too, and she'll never have to regret anything!"

I spoke with some heat. Fyodor Mikhailovich looked at me in excitement. "And you seriously believe she could love him genuinely, and for the rest of her life?"

He fell silent, as if hesitating. "Put yourself in her place for a moment," he said in a trembling voice. "Imagine that this artist is—me; that I have confessed my love to you and asked you to be my wife. Tell me, what would you answer?"

His face revealed such deep embarrassment, such inner torment, that I understood at long last that this was not a conversation about literature; and that if I gave him an evasive answer I would deal a deathblow to his self-esteem and pride. I looked at his troubled face, which had become so dear to me, and said, "I would answer that I love you and will love you all my life."

I won't try to convey the words full of tenderness and love that he said to me then; they are sacred to me. I was stunned, almost crushed by the immensity of my happiness and for a long time I couldn't believe in it. I remember that when Fyodor Mikhailovich—almost an hour later—began to talk of plans for the future and to ask my opinion, I told him, "How can I make any decisions about anything now? I'm too horribly happy!"

Since we did not know how circumstances would turn out and when our wedding could take place, we decided not to say anything to anyone except my mother for a while. Fyodor Mikhailovich promised to come to us the next day for the whole evening and said he would await our meeting with impatience. He took me to the door and solicitously fastened my hood. I was on the point of leaving when he stopped me with the words, "Anna Grigoryevna, now I know what became of the little diamond."

"Have you really remembered your dream?"

"No, I don't remember the dream. But I've found it at last, and am determined to keep it all my life."

"You've made a mistake, Fyodor Mikhailovich," I laughed.

"It's no diamond you've found, but just an ordinary little pebble."

"No," he said to me with great seriousness, "I'm convinced that this time I've made no mistake."

When I left him I was in an ecstatic state. I remember that all the way home, quite oblivious of the passers-by, I almost exclaimed out loud, "My God, what happiness! Can it really be true? Isn't it a dream? Is it possible he is going to be my husband?"

The hubbub of the crowds on the street sobered me down a bit, and I remembered that I was invited to a dinner party at the home of relatives, to celebrate the name day of my cousin Mikhail Nikolayevich Snitkin. I stopped in at a bakery (at that time, pastry shops were few) to buy a birthday cake. My heart was overflowing with joy, everyone seemed kind and dear to me and I wanted to say something to each one. I couldn't control myself, and remarked to the young German miss who sold me the cake, "What marvelous coloring you have, and what a lovely hairdo!"

I found many guests at my relatives' house, but my mother was not there, although she had promised to come for dinner. I was upset by this—I wanted so badly to tell her about my happiness at the first possible moment.

There was much merriment at dinner, but I behaved very strangely. Either I laughed at everything, or I withdrew into my own thoughts and heard nothing of what was said to me, or I responded irrelevantly; and I even addressed one gentleman as Fyodor Mikhailovich. They began making jokes about me and I excused myself by saying I had a terrible migraine.

At last my good mother arrived. I ran straight to the entrance hall to meet her, threw my arms around her and whispered in her ear, "Congratulate me—I'm engaged!"

There was no opportunity to say any more than this, since our hosts were coming toward us. I recall that Mama kept looking at me with great curiosity all evening, not knowing which of my suitors among those present was the one I was going to marry. Not until we reached home was I able to explain that I was marrying Dostoevsky.

I am not sure that my mother was happy about this: I think not. As a person with experience of the world, she could not help foreseeing that such a marriage had much torment and grief in store for me, as much because of my future husband's terrible disease as from lack of financial means. And yet she did not attempt to dissuade me (as others later did) and I was grateful to her for that. And who indeed could have persuaded me to refuse this great imminent happiness which later, despite the many difficult aspects of our life together, proved to be a real and genuine happiness for both of us?

The next day—November 9—stretched out unbearably. I wasn't capable of busying myself with anything: I kept thinking over every detail of what we had said to each other yesterday, and even wrote it all down in my shorthand notebook.

At half-past six Dostoevsky appeared and began by apologizing for being half an hour early.

"But I couldn't stand it, I wanted to see you so much!"

"Nous sommes logées a la même enseigne,"[19] I answered, laughing. "I haven't done a thing all day except think about you —and how awfully happy I am that you're here!"

He noticed at once that I was wearing a light-colored dress.

"All the way here I was wondering whether you'd have taken off your mourning, or whether you'd be wearing a black dress.[20] And here you are—in pink!"

"But how could it be any other way when I'm so full of joy! Of course I'll go on wearing mourning in public until we announce our engagement, but at home, for you, something bright."

"And pink becomes you very much. But it makes you still younger, and you look like a little girl."

My youthful appearance was evidently an embarrassment to him. Laughingly I began to reassure him that I would age very fast. And although this promise was meant as a joke, the circumstances of my life made it come true. Or rather, it was not that I aged but that I strove to become so sedate in my manner of dressing and speaking that the difference in age between my husband and myself soon grew almost imperceptible.

My mother came in. Fyodor Mikhailovich kissed her hand and said, "You already know, of course, that I have asked for your daughter's hand. She has consented to become my wife, and I am very happy. But I would wish you to approve her choice. Anna Grigoryevna has told me so many good things about you that I have already come to respect you. I give you my word that I shall do everything I can and more to make her happy. And to you I shall be the most devoted and loving son."

And it must be said in all justice to Fyodor Mikhailovich that throughout the fourteen years of our married life he was always extremely attentive and kind to my mother, and truly loved and respected her.

He made his little speech solemnly but somewhat haltingly, as he himself afterward remarked. But Mama was genuinely moved, embraced him, asked him to love me and care for me, and even cried a little. I hastened to cut short this scene, which was perhaps too onerous for him, with the words, "Dearest Mamochka, please give us tea right away—Fyodor Mikhailovich is terribly chilled!"

Tea was served; we sat down in the soft old-fashioned armchairs with our glasses in our hands and began to talk animatedly. About an hour later the bell rang and the maid announced the arrival of two young men who were in the habit of visiting us often. On this occasion, however, I was decidedly irritated by my uninvited callers and said to my mother, "You go out to them, please, and say that I apologize but I have a headache."

"Please don't refuse to see them, Anna Grigoryevna," Fyodor Mikhailovich interrupted and, turning to me, added in an undertone, "I feel like seeing you in the company of young people. After all, up to this point I've seen you only with us old folks."

I smiled and asked that the callers be shown in. I introduced them to Dostoevsky. When I pronounced his name they were a bit abashed by this unexpected encounter with a famous novelist. In order to explain the rather solemn nature of the occasion, I told my callers that they had happened on our celebration of the completion of our work together on his new novel. I badly wanted to get a general conversation started and to bring Dostoevsky into it, and utilized for this purpose a question put by one of the young men as to whether I had recovered from my migraine.

"It's your fault that I have a headache—you all smoked so much. Isn't that so, Fyodor Mikhailovich, that people shouldn't smoke too much?"

"I'm a bad judge of that, I smoke so much myself."

"But isn't that harmful to your health?"

"Of course it's harmful, but it's a habit that's very hard to shake off."

Those were the only words Dostoevsky said: I could not draw him into any further conversation. He kept smoking and looking the visitors and me over with curiosity. The young men were uncomfortable. The name of Dostoevsky had evidently over-awed them. They told me that yesterday, after my departure, they all had decided to go together to see Serov's opera, *Judith,* and that they had been given the mission of taking a loge after finding out when I would be free.

Very amiably but firmly, I explained that I wouldn't go to the opera because I was beginning an intensive stenography course so as to catch up with the rest of my classmates.

"But then you'll come to the concert on November 15? After all, you promised!" they said in chagrin.

"And not to the concert, either—and for the same reason."

"But you had such a good time at last year's concert!"

"Who cares about last year? Lots of water has flowed under the bridge since then," I remarked sententiously.

They felt superfluous and got up to go. I didn't try to keep them.

"Well, are you pleased with me?" I asked Dostoevsky after they had left.

"You chirped away like a little bird. I'm only sorry that you offended your admirers by rejecting so flatly everything that used to interest you."

"Who cares about them! What are they to me now? There's only one person I need—my precious, darling, wonderful Fyodor Mikhailovich!"

"Am I really so dear and precious to you?" he said. And again we began to speak from the heart, and went on that way all evening. What a happy time that was, and with what deep thankfulness to fate do I remember it!

Our decision to keep our engagement secret from relatives and friends lasted no longer than a week. Our secret was let out in the most unexpected way.

When Fyodor Mikhailovich came to visit us, he used to hire a cab by the hour, from seven to ten. Liking simple people as he did, he fell into the habit of conversing with the cabdriver during the long trips to our house and back; feeling the need to share his happiness with someone, he would talk about his forthcoming marriage.

After coming home from my house one evening, he couldn't find any change in his pocket and told the cabdriver that he would have the money brought out to him at once. This was done by his maid Fedosya. And she, not knowing which of the three cabbies standing at the gate was the one to pay, asked who it was who had just brought back "the old gentleman."

"You mean the bridegroom? I brought him."

"What bridegroom? My master is no bridegroom."

"Oh yes he is! He told me himself he's a bridegroom. And besides, I had a look at the bride when they opened the door. She came outside to say goodbye to him. Such a jolly one, smiles all the time!"

"And where did you bring the gentleman from?"

"From the Smolny district."

Fedosya, who knew my address, guessed the identity of her master's fiancée and hurried to convey this news to Fyodor Mikhailovich's stepson Paul.

Fyodor Mikhailovich, who had questioned Fedosya thoroughly, described the whole episode to me the next day. When I asked him how Paul had reacted to the news of our engagement his face darkened, and he obviously wanted to fend off any further questions. But I insisted on knowing all the details.

Then he started to laugh and told me that "Pasha" had appeared in his study that morning dressed in his best suit and wearing dark glasses, which he put on only for state occasions. He announced that he knew all about his stepfather's forthcoming marriage and that he was shocked, astounded and indignant that Fyodor Mikhailovich had not seen fit to ask the advice and consent of his "son" before making a decision in which the latter was so closely concerned. He asked his "father" to bear in mind that he was already an old man, and that neither in years nor in strength was he fit to begin a new life. And he reminded him that he had other obligations, and so on and so forth.

He was "pompous, bombastic and moralizing," according to Fyodor Mikhailovich, who grew so enraged at his stepson's tone that he lost control of himself, began to shout at him and ended by putting him out of the study.

Two days later, when I went to see Fyodor Mikhailovich after learning that he had had an epileptic attack, Paul did not come out to greet me. But with the aim of demonstrating to me that he was at home, he very noisily pushed something about in the dining room and angrily scolded the maid. At my next visit, a week later, he came into the study (as he had probably been ordered to do by his stepfather), congratulated me drily and officially, and then sat there in silence for ten minutes or so with an injured and offended expression on his face.

But Fyodor Mikhailovich was in marvelous spirits that day and my own mood was light-hearted. The two of us were so happy that we didn't pay the least attention to Paul's cold, severe tone. After that, seeing that his air of severity had no effect on us at all, but in fact only angered Fyodor Mikhailovich, he substituted amiability for wrath and grew polite and ingratiating with me—without, however, letting slip any opportunity to launch barbed remarks in my direction.

The joyful period of our engagement flew by with great speed. To outward appearance the days passed monotonously. Using the pretext of my intensive stenographic studies, I no longer went visiting, no longer invited anyone to my house, stopped going to concerts and to the theater. An exception to this was an evening spent at a performance of Count Alexey Tolstoy's play *The Death* of *Ivan the Terrible.*

Fyodor Mikhailovich had a very high opinion of this drama and wanted to see it with me. He took a loge and invited his sister-in-law Emilia Fyodorovna, with her daughter and sons, in addition to Paul. Although I found it very pleasant to share the experience with Fyodor Mikhailovich, the presence of others who were hostile to me was hard to bear. Emilia Fyodorovna displayed her antagonism so openly that toward the end I grew very depressed, and Fyodor Mikhailovich noticed this at once. He began asking me what was wrong, and I pleaded a headache.

But that unpleasant evening could not shatter my happy frame of mind. I felt myself in a state of perpetual holiday. I, a person who had always been occupied with something, now found myself doing nothing at all. For days at a time I would think about Fyodor Mikhailovich, would keep going over our conversation of the previous day and look forward impatiently to his arrival in the evening.

He would usually come at seven, sometimes at half-past six. The samovar would be boiling away on the table, ready for him. It was winter, and I was afraid he might catch cold during the long trip to our house. I would rush to give him a glass of hot tea the moment he came into the room.

I considered these daily visits a great sacrifice on his part. Taking pity on him, I tried to persuade him against his will to omit an evening now and then. In answer he would assure me that coming to us was sheer pleasure for him, that he felt revitalized and at peace when he was with me, and that he would not discontinue his daily visits until I myself told him that they were a burden to me. This last was said as a joke, for my joy in his presence was quite obvious.

After tea we would sit about in our old-fashioned easy chairs, and all kinds of sweetmeats would be set out on the table that stood between us. Every day he brought some delicacy from his favorite confectioner, Ballé. Since I was aware of his financial straits I tried to convince him to stop bringing sweets, but he considered that a bridegroom's presents to his fiancée constituted a good old-fashioned custom which should not be violated.

And for my part I always had ready for him his favorite pears, dried apricots and peaches, and a special sweet called *pastila*—all this in small quantity, but always fresh and tasty. I used to go myself to the shops just for this purpose, looking for something special to spoil him with. He marveled at me and declared that only a person with a sweet tooth like mine would be capable of turning up such dainties. But I would insist that he was the one with the sweet tooth. So we could not agree on which of us was the guilty party.

At the stroke of ten I would start urging him to go home. My mother's house was in a very desolate neighborhood, and I was afraid that something untoward might happen. At first, indeed, I suggested that our yard-keeper accompany him, but he refused to hear of this. He declared that he wasn't afraid of anything and that he was quite capable of coping with the situation if anyone should attack him. These assurances did little to calm me, and I ordered our yard-keeper to follow him secretly, keeping his sleigh fifteen or twenty paces behind, up to the turn into Slonovaya Street, which was livelier.

It sometimes happened that Fyodor Mikhailovich was unable to come to see me because he had been invited out to dinner, or because he was reading at a literary evening. On such occasions we would arrange in advance for me to come to his house at one and stay until five. I am still touched when I remember the way he used to beg me to stay "ten minutes more, one little quarter of an hour more" and say dolefully, "But just think, Anya, I won't be seeing you again for another whole day!"

Sometimes during an evening out he would slip away from the other guests, or give his reading and then come to us that same evening, arriving at nine or nine-thirty and announcing triumphantly, "I ran away like a schoolboy! We'll have half an hour together, anyway!"

And I, of course, was wildly happy to see him for the second time that day.

He would arrive at our house invariably good-humored, happy and gay. I often wondered how the legend of his morose and sullen personality came to be created—a legend that I often had to read and hear about from acquaintances. In this connection, I am reminded of an incident when Fyodor Mikhailovich, questioning me about my stenography teacher, P. M. Olkhin, remarked, "What a surly fellow he is!"

I burst out laughing. "Can you guess what he told me after meeting you? 'I can offer you a position with the writer Dostoevsky, but I'm not sure how you will get along with him—he seemed to me such a surly, gloomy man!' And here you are, expressing exactly the same opinion of him—and as a matter of fact neither one of you is the least bit surly or morose—you only appear that way."

Fyodor Mikhailovich was curious to know more. "And what did you tell Olkhin?"

"I said, what's the need for me to get along with Dostoevsky? I'll try to do his work the best way I know how, and as for Dostoevsky himself, I have so much respect for him that I'm even afraid of him!"

"So there it is! In spite of Olkhin's prophecy you and I did get along with each other, and now we're together for the rest of our lives, isn't it so, my darling Anechka?" he said, looking at me affectionately.

And if Fyodor Mikhailovich came to us in good spirits, then I too was gay, talkative and full of mischief. My voice rang out like a bell, I would laugh uproariously at every little trifle, and then he would clasp his hands together and exclaim in comic horror, "What am I to do with such a child, pray tell? And what has become of that strict, strait-laced Anna Grigoryevna who used to come to my house to take dictation? Someone must have made a substitution!"

I would immediately assume a pompous stance and start lecturing him and it would all end in general hilarity.

I didn't always feel gay, however. Whenever Fyodor Mikhailovich began playing the role of an old man trying to hold on to his youth, I was very ill-at-ease. He could speak for hours on end in the words and thoughts of one of his characters, the elderly prince of *Uncle's Dream.* He would express the most original and unexpected ideas, he would hold forth with gaiety and talent—and still I was always jarred by these anecdotes of his, told in the tone of voice of an old man no longer good for anything but trying to make himself younger than he was; and I would change the subject to something else.

Was there anything in the world that we didn't manage to talk about during those three happy months? I asked him all kinds of questions about his childhood and boyhood, about the Engineering Institute, about his political activity, his exile to Siberia, his return. "I want to know everything there is to know about you," I used to tell him, "to see your past clearly, to know you through and through!" And he was glad to reminisce with me about his tranquil, happy childhood,[21] and spoke of his mother with strong emotion. He especially loved his elder brother Mikhail and sister Varenka. His feelings toward his younger brothers and sisters were not as intense. I asked him about the women he had been in love with; and it seemed strange to me that, according to him, he had never in his youth experienced a really fervent, serious love for any woman. This I account for by the fact that he began too early to live a life of the mind. His writing consumed him wholly, and therefore his personal life receded into the background. And after that he committed himself utterly to the political episode for which he paid so dearly.

I tried to question him about his late wife, but he did not like to talk about her. It is a curious fact that during our later married life he never once spoke of her, except for a single instance which I shall relate at the appropriate time.[22]

With incomparably greater enthusiasm he used to reminisce about his former fiancée, Anna Vasilyevna Korvin-Krukovskaya. When I asked why their marriage plans had come to nothing he replied, "Anna Vasilyevna was one of the finest women I ever met in my life. She was exceptionally intelligent, cultivated and knowledgeable in literature, and had a wonderfully kind heart. She was a young woman of the highest moral qualities. But her convictions were diametrically opposed to mine and she wasn't capable of giving in—she was too inflexible. And under such circumstances our marriage could hardly have been happy. I released her from her promise, and wish for her with all my heart that she may meet a man of similar views and find happiness with him!"

Dostoevsky maintained the warmest relations with Anna Vasilyevna throughout his life, and considered her a true friend. When, six years after my marriage, I was introduced to her, we too became friends and were genuinely fond of one another. What he had said about her outstanding intelligence, warm heart and high moral qualities proved quite true; but no less true was his conviction that they could never have been happy together. She lacked that willingness to compromise which is indispensable to every good marriage, particularly marriage to such a sick, irritable person as Fyodor Mikhailovich, in consequence of his disease, often was. Moreover, she was then too committed to political party affairs to give much attention to her family. With the years, however, this changed, and I remember her as an excellent wife and tender mother.

The fate of Anna Korvin-Krukovskaya (who, incidentally, was the sister of the famous Sofya Kovalevskaya) was a tragic one. Soon after her break with Dostoevsky she went abroad and there became acquainted with a Frenchman, a Mr. Jaclard, whose political views were identical with hers. She fell in love with him and married him. In the aftermath of the Commune of Paris, Jaclard, an ardent Communard, was among those condemned to death; he was imprisoned in a fortress somewhere near the German border.

Anna's father bought Jaclard's freedom with a bribe of twenty thousand francs to the proper quarter, and he was permitted to flee to Germany.[23] Later, Jaclard-Korvin (who had joined his wife's name to his own, according to the foreign custom) took his family to Petersburg, where he found a position as teacher of French literature in a high school for girls. He and Anna lived a harmonious marital life, but still he longed for his homeland, and this caused Anna deep anxiety.

In a short while their material circumstances also underwent a change for the worse. Jaclard fell to speculating with the considerable sum he had received from Anna's dowry, and so unsuccessfully that within a few years all that remained to them was the heavily mortgaged house on Vasilyevsky Island. Anna, who had always been of fragile health, was so deeply affected by their financial ruin that she became seriously ill.

Then Jaclard received permission to return to France and took Anna to Paris. They had to return to Petersburg often in connection with business matters. During her last illness I was able to perform a service for her through K. P. Pobedonostsev: namely, to intercede on behalf of her husband, who, as a political suspect, had been ordered to leave the capital within two days, and to win for him a reprieve of several weeks to arrange his affairs and to accompany his sick wife and little son abroad.[24] Anna Vasilyevna died in Paris in 1887.

"Tell me, Anya, do you remember the day you first admitted you were in love with me?" said Fyodor Mikhailovich during one of our evening talks.

"You know, my darling," I answered, "the name of Dostoevsky has been familiar to me ever since childhood. I've been in love with you, or rather with one of your heroes, since I was fifteen years old."

He took my words for a joke and started to laugh.

"Seriously! I'm speaking seriously! My father loved to read, and whenever the subject of modern literature was brought up he would say, 'Well now, what kind of writers do we have nowadays? In my time we had Pushkin, Gogol, Zhukovsky. And of the younger writers there was the novelist Dostoevsky, the author of *Poor Folk.* That was a genuine talent. Unfortunately the man got mixed up in politics, landed in Siberia, and vanished there without a trace!'

"And later my father was so happy when he learned that the Dostoevsky brothers were going to publish a new magazine, *Time,* and he told us gleefully, 'You see, Dostoevsky did come back. Thank the Lord he didn't disappear!'

"I remember spending the summer of 1861 at Peterhof. Every time Mama went into town to shop, my sister and I would beg her to stop in at Cherkessov's bookshop for the latest number of *Time.* Our family kept to a patriarchal order of things, so that the magazine would land in Papa's hands first. The poor man was already in failing health and would often fall asleep in his armchair after dinner over his book or his newspaper. I used to sneak up to him and quietly take the magazine away from him, run into the garden, and sit down somewhere under a bush to revel in your new novel without anybody bothering me. But my cunning never succeeded, alas. My sister Masha would come and by right of seniority would take the new issue away from me, in spite of my pleading to let me finish my chapter in *The Insulted and Injured.*

"I was quite a daydreamer," I continued, "and the heroes of novels were always real people to me. I hated Prince Valkovsky and despised Alyosha for his weak will. I suffered with the old man, Ikhmenyev, pitied poor Nellie with all my heart, and . . . didn't like Natasha. . . . You see, I can still remember the names of your characters!"

"*I* don't remember them—and in general I have only a vague recollection of what the novel is about," said Fyodor Mikhailovich.

"You can't have forgotten!" I answered in astonishment. "What a pity! I was in love with your narrator, Ivan Petrovich. I simply couldn't understand how Natasha could prefer that worthless Alyosha to my dear Ivan Petrovich. While I was reading the novel I would think, 'She deserved what she got because she rejected the love of Ivan Petrovich.' It's strange—for some reason I always identified Ivan Petrovich, whom I liked so much, with the author of the novel. It seemed to me that it was Dostoevsky himself telling the sad story of his unsuccessful love. If you've forgotten it, you had certainly better reread that marvelous novel!"

My words piqued his interest, and he promised to reread *The Insulted and Injured* when he had some free time.

"By the way," I continued, "do you remember that once when you and I first met you asked me if I had ever been in love? And I answered, 'Never with a real person, but I was in love with the hero of a novel at the age of fifteen.' And you asked me, 'What novel?' and I quickly changed the subject. I felt awkward about naming the hero of your novel. You might have thought it was the flattery of a young lady looking for literary work. And I wanted to be completely independent.

"And how many tears I shed over *Notes from the House of the Dead!* My heart was full of sympathy and pity for Dostoevsky, who had to endure a horrible life in prison at hard labor. It was with those feelings that I came to work for you. I wanted terribly to help you, to lighten in some way the existence of the man whose work I so adored. I thanked God that Olkhin had chosen me and no one else to work for you."

When I realized that my remarks about *Notes from the House of the Dead* had put him into a melancholy mood, I hastily changed the subject with the joking remark, "You know, it was fate and nothing less that predestined me to be your wife. Ever since the age of sixteen I've had the nickname of 'Netochka Nezvanova.'[25] My name, Anna, was Netochka for short, and since I used to visit my relatives often without an invitation, they gave me the nickname of 'Netochka Nezvanova' to distinguish me from any other Netochka and at the same time hint at my passion for the novels of Dostoevsky. Please—you call me 'Netochka,' too."

"No!" he answered. "My Netochka had to bear a lot of sorrow in her life, and I want you to be happy. I would rather call you Anya—that's the way I fell in love with you."

The next evening I asked Fyodor Mikhailovich a question which had long been of interest to me, but which I was too shy to ask him up to then: when did he realize that he was in love with me, and when did he decide to propose?

He began thinking back and, to my great chagrin, confessed that during the first week of our acquaintance he wasn't even aware of what my face was like.

"What do you mean, you weren't aware? What does that mean?" I asked in surprise.

"If a new acquaintance is introduced to you and you exchange a few commonplaces with him—do you really remember his face? Surely you don't? At least I always forget it. And that was how it was then. I spoke with you, I saw your face, but you went away and I forgot it immediately. I couldn't have said whether you were a blonde or a brunette, if anyone had asked me. Not until the end of October did I notice your beautiful gray eyes and your lovely bright smile. But then I began to take pleasure in your whole face, and the more I saw of it the better I liked it. And now your face is the best in the whole world for me. To me, you're a beauty! Yes, and to everyone!" he added naïvely.

"On your first visit," he continued, "I was struck by your tact, by your serious, almost stern behavior. I thought to myself, what an attractive type of serious and efficient young girl! And I was glad that such a type had made its appearance in our society. Once I inadvertently said something clumsy, and you gazed at me with such a look that I began weighing my words, afraid of offending you.

"And then I began to marvel at you and be attracted to you because of the genuine warmth you showed about my interests, and your fellow-feeling for the catastrophe that was hanging over my head. Look here, I thought, my own relatives, my own friends also love me—apparently. They lament the fact that I might lose all the rights to my work, they're indignant with Stellovsky, they're furious, they reproach me for signing such a contract (as though I had any choice!), they offer me all kinds of advice, they console me. And I feel that all this is 'words, words, words'—and that none of them really takes to heart the fact that when I lose my civil rights I also lose my last shred of property rights!

"And here this outsider, this young girl with whom I'm barely acquainted, immediately puts herself in my position. Without moans and groans, without exclamations and shows of indignation she undertakes to help me out—not in words, but in deeds. When, in the space of a few days, you and I had established our pattern of working, I began to have a glimmer of hope—I, who was on the brink of despair—and I began to think, maybe if I can continue to work this way from this point on, then . . . perhaps . . . I'll finish the work in time! And your assurances that there was no doubt we would finish—do you remember how you and I used to count up the pages of manuscript you had already copied?—your assurances reinforced that hope, and lent me the strength to go on working. Often when I was talking to you I would think to myself: what a good heart that girl has! It isn't in words merely that she pities me and wants to save me from catastrophe, but in actual fact. I was so emotionally alone at that time that finding another person who genuinely felt for me was an enormous joy.

"I think it was then that I began to love you and only afterward that I began to take pleasure in your dear face. I often caught myself thinking of you; but it wasn't until then, when we were finishing *The Gambler*, and I realized that we would no longer see each other every day, that I became aware that I couldn't live without you. And it was then that I decided to propose."

"But then why didn't you propose to me straight out, the way other people do, instead of inventing that fascinating novel of yours?" I asked.

"You know, my darling Anya," he said in a voice full of emotion, "when I realized what you meant to me I felt desperate, and my plan to marry you began to seem like sheer lunacy. Just think how different we are! Take the difference in age alone.

I'm almost an old man, and you—you're almost a child. I'm ill with an incurable disease, I'm surly and irritable, while you're healthy, cheerful and full of life. I've almost lived out my life and there has been much unhappiness in it. Whereas for you things have always gone well, and your whole life lies ahead of you. And finally, I'm poor and in debt besides. And so what can be predicted, in the face of all this inequality? Either that we'll be miserable, we'll torment ourselves for a few years and then divorce—or . . . that we'll get along together for the rest of our lives, and be happy."

I couldn't bear to hear him denigrate himself in that way and retorted hotly, "My dear, you exaggerate everything! We aren't as unequal as you say. If we truly love one another we'll become friends and be happy forever. What worries me is something entirely different—how could you, so talented, so brilliant and educated, take as your life's companion such a foolish girl, so ill-educated in comparison with yourself—even though I did win a silver medal at the gymnasium" (at that time I took great pride in my medal). "I'm not sufficiently developed to be on your level—I'm afraid that you'll soon see through me and start getting irritated and upset because I'm not capable of understanding your ideas. And *that* inequality is worse than any unhappiness!"

He was quick to reassure me and said many flattering things. And we returned to that matter of his proposal which interested me so much.

"For a long time I hesitated as to the best way to go about it," he said. "An unattractive middle-aged man who proposes marriage to a young girl and doesn't meet any response on her part might appear ridiculous—and I didn't want to be ridiculous in your eyes. In the middle of my proposal you might tell me you were in love with someone else. And if you refused me there would be a coldness between us, and our old friendly relationship would no longer be possible. I would have lost you as a friend—the only person in the last two years who really cared about me. I'll repeat it—I felt so alone emotionally that losing your friendship and your help would have been too hard for me to bear.

"And so I invented a way of finding out what your feelings

were—by telling you my plan for a new novel. It made it easier for me to accept a refusal from you—for after all, we'd be talking about the characters in a novel and not about ourselves."

And then in my turn I told him all that I had felt while he was making his "literary" proposal: my failure to understand him, my envy and jealousy of Anna Korvin-Krukovskaya, and so forth.

"So it follows that I took you by surprise and extracted your consent by force! Now I see that the novel I told you was better than any I ever wrote—it had an instant success and produced the desired effect!"

In all the welter of joyful new experiences we had somehow forgotten about the completion of *Crime and Punishment,* the final third of which still remained to be written. Dostoevsky remembered this fact when the editor of the *Russian Messenger,* at the end of November, demanded the continuing installments of the novel. Luckily for us, journals rarely appeared on schedule in those years; and the *Russian Messenger* was actually famous for its delays. The November issue would come out at the end of December, the December issue at the beginning of February, and so on—so there was enough time ahead of us. Fyodor Mikhailovich brought me the editor's letter and asked for my advice. I suggested that he close his door to visitors and work from two to five in the afternoon, and then come to us in the evenings and dictate to me from his manuscript.

And that was how matters were arranged. After we had chatted for an hour or so I would sit down at the desk, he would seat himself next to me and the dictation would begin, punctuated with talk, jokes and laughter. The work progressed well, and the last installment of *Crime and Punishment,* comprising about a hundred and fifteen pages, was written in the space of four weeks. Fyodor Mikhailovich declared that his writing had never before come so easily to him and attributed his success to my collaboration.

His always gay and cheerful frame of mind had a beneficial effect on his physical health also. During the entire three-month period before our wedding he suffered no more than three or four epileptic attacks. This fact cheered me very much and gave me the hope that the disease might be alleviated with a calm and happy life. And so indeed did later events prove. His former almost weekly attacks grew rarer and less severe with each year that passed. A total cure for his epilepsy was not to be hoped for, particularly since Fyodor Mikhailovich himself had never received treatment for it, for he considered his illness incurable. But even a lessening of the frequency and severity of the seizures was a great grace of God for us. It freed him from that black, horrible state of mind which sometimes continued for an entire week, and which was the inevitable consequence of each attack. And as for me, I was spared the tears and pain I had felt in witnessing his paroxysms.

Our normally peaceful and jolly evenings together turned out on one occasion, quite unexpectedly, to be very stormy. It happened at the end of November. Fyodor Mikhailovich arrived at seven as usual, but chilled to the bone. After drinking a glass of hot tea he asked whether we had any cognac in the house. I told him that there was no cognac but that we did have a good sherry, which I brought at once. He swallowed three or four large glasses at a gulp, followed by more tea, and only then did he begin to thaw out. I expressed surprise at his being so chilled through, and couldn't understand how it had happened.

The answer was not long in coming. As I was going through the entrance hall to get something or other, I noticed a quilted fall coat on the hook instead of his usual fur greatcoat. I came straight back to the living room and said, "Can you possibly have come here today without your fur coat?"

"N-no," he faltered. "I wore my fall coat."

"What carelessness! Why ever didn't you put on your fur coat?"

"They said there would be a thaw today."

"Now I understand why you were so frozen! I'll send Semyon at once to take back your fall coat and bring your fur coat here."

"That's not necessary! Please, it's not necessary!" he said hastily.

"Whatever do you mean, my dear, 'not necessary'? You'll surely catch your death of cold on the way home—it will be even colder at night."

He didn't answer. But I persisted, and at last he admitted, "But I don't have my fur coat."

"How is that—you don't have it? Was it stolen?"

"No, it wasn't stolen. I had to pawn it."

I was astonished. To my insistent questions he told me, with obvious reluctance, that Emilya Fyodorovna had come to him that morning and begged him to help her out of trouble by paying some extra debt of hers amounting to fifty rubles. His stepson had also asked him for money, and his younger brother Nikolai needed some, too, and had sent him a letter to that effect. Since Fyodor Mikhailovich was unable to turn up any money, they had decided to take his fur coat to the nearest pawnbroker's while heartily assuring him that the thaw still continued, that the weather was warm and he could get by in his fall coat for a few days, until he received a remittance from the *Russian Messenger.*

I was outraged at the heartlessness of Dostoevsky's relatives. I said that I understood his desire to help them, but felt that he must not sacrifice his health to them and even, perhaps, his life.

I began quietly, but with each word my wrath and bitterness grew. I lost all control over myself and talked like a madwoman, without choosing my words. I pointed out that he had an obligation to me, his bride. I asserted that I would not survive his death. I wept, I exclaimed, I sobbed as if in a hysterical fit.

Fyodor Mikhailovich was terribly upset. He put his arms around me, kissed my hands and begged me to calm myself. My mother heard my sobbing and rushed in with a glass of sugar-water. This quieted me down a little. I started feeling ashamed of myself and I apologized to him. Then he began telling me, as a kind of explanation, that he had had to pawn his fur coat at least five or six times the winter before and go about in his fall coat.

"I'm so used to all this pawning that I didn't pay any special attention to it this time. If I had only known you would take it so tragically, I wouldn't have allowed Pasha to pawn it for anything!" he assured me with embarrassment.

I made use of his repentance to exact from him a promise that such a thing would never happen again. I offered him eighty rubles right then and there to redeem his fur coat from the pawnbroker, but he categorically refused. Then I began begging him to stay at home until the money arrived from Moscow. To this "house arrest" he agreed, first getting my promise to come to him every day at one and remain until dinner.

When we were saying good night I asked him again to forgive me for the scene I had made.

"There's no cloud without a silver lining!" he answered. "Now I'm really convinced of how much you love me. You couldn't have cried like that if I weren't dear to you."

I tied my white knitted scarf around his neck and made him throw our plaid over his shoulders. All the rest of the evening I tortured myself with the thought that he would fall out of love with me, now that he had found out I was capable of carrying on in that way. Then I began worrying that he would catch cold on the way home and fall dangerously ill. I hardly slept at all, got up early and by ten o'clock I was already ringing his doorbell. The maid calmed me down when she told me that her master was up and about, and had not become ill during the night.

I can say that this was the only "stormy" evening we had during the three months of our engagement.

Fyodor Mikhailovich's house arrest continued for a week, during which I came to him every day to take his dictation for *Crime and Punishment.* During one of these sessions he gave me another surprise. While we were hard at work we heard a barrel organ grinding out the well-known aria from *Rigoletto,* "La donna e mobile." Fyodor Mikhailovich left off dictating, listened, and suddenly started to sing the aria, substituting my name and patronymic, "Anna Grigoryevna," for the Italian words. He sang in a pleasant though somewhat muffled tenor. When the aria ended he went over to the casement window and threw out a coin, and the organ-grinder went away at once.

He then told me that the organ-grinder was evidently well aware of which song resulted in coins, since he came every day to the same spot under the window and played nothing but the aria from *Rigoletto.*

"And I walk back and forth, and I always sing your dear name to the melody!"

I laughed and pretended to be offended that he should associate such frivolous words with my name. I stated that fickleness was not in my nature and that, once having fallen in love with him, it was forever.

"We shall see, we shall see!" he laughed.

During the next two days I heard the organ-grinder's aria and Fyodor Mikhailovich's singing again, and was surprised at the accuracy with which he kept to the melody. Obviously he had a good musical ear.

No matter how diverse our daily talks were during that time, they never touched on anything improper or salacious. It would be difficult to have treated my girlish shyness and modesty with more restraint and delicacy than my fiancé did. His relationship to me can be characterized in a letter he wrote me after our marriage:

"God gave you to me so that none of the potentialities or riches of your spirit and your heart might be lost, but on the contrary, might grow and flower abundantly and luxuriantly. He gave you to me so that I might expiate my own great sins, might offer you to Him developed, put on the right path, preserved and saved from everything base and deadening to the spirit."[26]

And indeed Fyodor Mikhailovich set himself the goal of shielding me from all corrupting influences. Once, I remember, when I was at his house, I began leafing through a French novel lying on his desk. He came up to me and quietly took the book out of my hands.

"But I understand French," I said. "Let me read that novel."

"Not that particular one! Why soil your imagination?" he answered.

Even after we were married he wanted to direct my literary development and used to select books for me himself and not permit me to read frivolous novels on any account. I was sometimes offended by this supervision and would protest, "Then why do you read them yourself? Why soil your own imagination?"

"I'm hardened," he would answer. "Certain books are necessary to me as material for my work. A writer must know everything and experience much. But I assure you that I don't relish cynical scenes, and I often find them repulsive."

These were not mere phrases, but the truth.

He responded with similar distaste to the operettas which were then in fashion. He himself never attended *opéra bouffe,* nor did he allow me to attend. "If you have the opportunity to go to the theatre," he used to say, "then you should choose a play that can convey high and noble impressions to the spectators, and not choke the spirit with empty triviality!"

Out of the fourteen years of my married life with Dostoevsky, I carried the profound conviction that he was one of the purest of men. And how bitter it was to learn that one of my favorite authors, I. S. Turgenev, considered Dostoevsky a cynic and presumed to call him "the Russian Marquis de Sade."[27]

The main subject of our conversations and the one dearest to us both was of course our future life together. The idea that I would no longer be parted from him, would share in his work, could look after his health and shield him from persistent and irritating people seemed so attractive to me that there were times when I was ready to weep at the realization that all this could not soon come about.

Our marriage depended chiefly on whether some arrangement could be worked out with the *Russian Messenger.* Fyodor Mikhailovich prepared to go to Moscow over the Christmas holidays to offer the publisher, Katkov, his next novel. He had no doubt that the editorial staff of the magazine would wish to retain him as a contributor in view of the fact that their publication of *Crime and Punishment* in 1866 had made a considerable impact in the literary world and had attracted many new subscribers.[28] The only question was whether the journal would have sufficient resources available for an advance of several thousand rubles, lacking which we could not think of setting up a new household.

In the event of failure with the *Russian Messenger,* he proposed to start a new novel immediately after completing *Crime and Punishment,* to write the greater part of it and then offer it to another magazine. Failure in Moscow, however, threatened to postpone the wedding for a long period—perhaps as much as a year. At this thought, deep despondency took hold of me.

Fyodor Mikhailovich always shared his worries with me. He wished to conceal nothing from me, so that our future married life, full of the deprivations that seemed to lie in store, might not come to me as a painful surprise. I appreciated his frankness very much, and used to devise various means of decreasing his particularly pressing debts.

It didn't take me long to realize that it would be almost impossible to settle his debts completely under the present conditions. Even though I knew very little about practical affairs, having lived free from want in a rather well-to-do family, still, during the three months before our wedding, I had managed to take note of a very upsetting circumstance. The moment Fyodor Mikhailovich got hold of any money, all his relatives—his brother, sister-in-law, stepson, and nephews—would instantly put forward their sudden but urgent needs; and out of the three or four hundred rubles received from Moscow for *Crime and Punishment* no more than thirty or forty would remain to Fyodor Mikhailovich by the next day. Of this sum, moreover, nothing would be paid off on his promissory notes except the interest. And then his worries would begin all over again: where to find the money to pay the interest, to cover his living expenses, and to satisfy the requirements of his numerous relations.

This situation began to alarm me in earnest. I tried to comfort myself with the thought that after the wedding I would take the housekeeping into my own hands and would regulate the money paid out to relatives by providing each of them with a fixed sum per year. Emilya Fyodorovna had grown sons of her own, who were able to support her. Fyodor Mikhailovich's brother Nikolai was a talented architect who could have worked, had he so desired. And as for Paul, it was time for him, at the age of twenty-one, to settle down to some kind of serious work and stop relying entirely on the labor of a sick and debt-ridden stepfather.

I thought about all these idle people with a feeling of outrage when I saw how Dostoevsky's financial worries were ruining his disposition and damaging his health. His nerves were shattered by these continual unpleasantnesses, and his epileptic attacks were coming more frequently. That had been his situation before I entered his life—when, for a time, everything changed.

But I still dreamed that in the course of our future life he might find a real cure and might be able to maintain a cheerful and happy frame of mind.

In my distress over his financial situation I tried to console myself with the thought that very soon, within the year, I would be in a position to help him radically. On the day of my majority I was to receive a house which my father had willed to me. Since the end of the forties, my parents had owned two large plots of ground—approximately two desyatinas at the intersection of Yaroslavskaya and Kostromskaya streets. On one of these lots stood three wooden outbuildings and the two-storied stone house in which we lived. On the second lot two wooden houses had been constructed. One of these was part of my sister's dowry, and the other was intended for me. The sale of it would bring over ten thousand rubles, which I wanted to use to settle part of Fyodor Mikhailovich's debts. But to my great regret I could do nothing until I came of age. My mother tried to persuade him to become my trustee, but this he categorically refused to do.

"That house was meant for Anya," he said. "Let her get it in the fall when she turns twenty-one. I don't want to meddle in her financial affairs."

As my fiancé he always declined any financial help from me, although I used to tell him that if we loved one another, all that we had should be held in common.

"Of course, that's the way it will be after we're married," he would answer. "But until then I don't want to touch a ruble of yours."

I believe he well understood how fantastic the requirements of his relatives were at times; but lacking the strength to refuse them, he did not wish to satisfy them with my money. He did not want to touch even the two thousand rubles put aside by my parents for my dowry, but persuaded me to use the money to purchase whatever I wanted to set up housekeeping. I remember fondly how he inspected the silver knives and forks I had just acquired and packed away in their chests, and how he always approved of my choice. He knew that his praise would make me glow, and he took pleasure in my joy.

He especially loved to look at my new dresses. When they

were brought from the seamstress he made me try them on and show myself off to him. Certain dresses—a cherry-colored one, for instance—so took his fancy that he asked me to keep it on all evening. He would make me try on my hats as well and found them extraordinarily becoming. He always tried to say something pleasant and kind and to give me pleasure in that way. How much genuine goodness, how much tenderness there was in his loving heart!

The days before Christmas sped by. Fyodor Mikhailovich, who in the past few years had almost invariably spent the holidays in the household of his favorite sister Vera, decided to go to Moscow this time as well. The main object of the trip, of course, was to offer his new novel to Katkov and secure the money necessary for our wedding.

During the last days before his departure he was in a melancholy mood. By now he was really in love with me, and it was hard for him to leave me. I too felt very sad and imagined for some reason that I would never see him again. So as not to upset him even more, I hid my sadness and tried to be cheerful. In the railway station, where I had come to see him off, he was particularly despondent. He looked at me with great tenderness, squeezed my hand hard and kept repeating, "I'm going to Moscow with high hopes—and we'll manage to meet, somehow, my darling Anechka—somehow we'll see one another!"

His mood of dejection was much exacerbated thanks to a senseless act on the part of Paul, who had also come to the station together with Fyodor Mikhailovich's nephews. We all went into the railway compartment to see what his accommodations were like. Paul, in his desire to show his concern for his "father," suddenly said in a loud voice, "Papa, don't even dream of going to bed in the upper berth! You'll take a fit and dump yourself out on the floor, and they won't even be able to collect your bones!"

One can imagine the effect of these words on Fyodor Mikhailovich, on us, and on the other people in the car. One of the female passengers—a nervous person, evidently—asked a porter passing through the car a few minutes later to transfer her things to a ladies' compartment, since "it seems that people will be smoking here" (this, although it was a non-smoking car).

Fyodor Mikhailovich, who disliked any public mention of his dreadful disease, was horribly humiliated by the whole episode. And we too, who had come to see him off, were embarrassed and didn't know what to say, and were glad to hear the sound of the second bell so that we had to leave the car.

Outraged by Paul's clumsy act, I couldn't keep from saying to him, "What was the purpose of making poor Fyodor Mikhailovich angry?"

"What's it to me whether he's angry or not? I'm concerned for his health, and he should thank me for that!"

Paul's "concerns" were always of this nature and so, of course, he could not keep from irritating his stepfather.

From Moscow Fyodor Mikhailovich wrote me two beautiful letters which gave me great joy.[29] I reread them dozens of times and couldn't wait for his return. He remained in Moscow for twelve days and concluded negotiations with the *Russian Messenger* successfully. When Katkov learned of his marriage plans he congratulated him warmly and wished him happiness; and the requested advance of two thousand rubles was promised for the coming January, to be sent in two or three installments. And so the possibility arose of arranging the wedding before Lent.

The first remittance of seven hundred rubles from Moscow was somehow distributed in a twinkling between the relatives and the creditors. Every evening Fyodor Mikhailovich would mention with dismay that his money was "melting away." I began to feel worried; and when the second seven-hundred-ruble installment arrived I begged him to put at least some of it aside toward our wedding expenses. With a pencil in his hand he added up all the costs of the church and the reception after the ceremony. (He had unconditionally refused to allow my mother to undertake these expenses.) It all came to four or five hundred rubles. But how to hold on to them, when his numerous relations were putting new needs forward every day?

"You know what, Anya—you hold them for me," he said, glad of this convenient excuse for the relatives when they started asking for money, and he brought me five hundred rubles the very next day. While he was handing it over he said seriocomically, "Well, now, Anya, hold on to it tight—our future depends on it!"

Rush as we might with our marriage plans, we simply could not arrange the wedding for earlier than the middle of February. We had to find a new apartment because the old one with its four rooms was too small. Fyodor Mikhailovich gave up his apartment to Emilya Fyodorovna and her family, undertaking to pay fifty rubles a month for it. Its advantage lay in the fact that the wealthy merchant, Alonkin, who owned the house, esteemed Fyodor Mikhailovich highly as "a great one for working," as he used to put it.* He never bothered him with reminders of rent because he knew that Fyodor Mikhailovich would pay it himself when he had the money. And Fyodor Mikhailovich loved to chat with the venerable old man.**

Fyodor Mikhailovich found an apartment for us on Voznesensky Prospect, in the Toll house (now No. 27) directly opposite Voznesenskaya Church. The entrance to the apartment was inside the courtyard, but its windows overlooked Voznesensky Lane. It was on the second floor and consisted of five large rooms: living room, study, dining room, bedroom, and a room for Paul.

We had to wait until the apartment was decorated and then move our possessions into it—Fyodor Mikhailovich's things, my own furniture and so forth and so on. When everything was in readiness we set the wedding date for February 15, the Wednesday before Carnival, and sent out invitations to our friends and acquaintances.

On the day before the wedding I dropped in to see Fyodor Mikhailovich and to let him know that my sister Masha was coming at seven o'clock, to arrange all my possessions which had been shipped there in boxes, cartons and trunks, and to set out the various household articles necessary for the next day's wedding reception. Fyodor Mikhailovich, my sister told me

*"While I'm already on my way to morning mass he still has the light on in his study—that means he's at work," he used to say. (A.G.D.)

**It was from his likeness, in my opinion, that Dostoevsky drew the merchant Samsonov, Grushenka's protector in *The Brothers Karamazov.* (A.G.D.)

later, gave her a hearty welcome, helped her open the trunks and unpack the things, played host and charmed her utterly. She could not help agreeing with me that my future husband was a very genuine and dear person.

But I resolved to spend that evening with my mother. I pitied poor Mama with all my heart. She had lived her whole life surrounded by her family; and now my father was gone, my brother had moved to Moscow, and I too was leaving her house. She loved us all very much, we had lived together in harmony, and I understood how sad it was for her to be left alone.

All the evening we reminisced about the good life we had lived together. Now that we were alone, I asked her to give me her blessing for my new life. Thinking of my girlfriends' example, I said that when the bride is blessed in the presence of witnesses, during all the hubbub before the wedding party leaves for the church, the blessing is sometimes more official than real. She blessed me, and we cried a lot; but to make up for it we gave one another our word not to cry the next day at parting, since I didn't want to arrive at the church with my face all swollen and my eyes red with tears.

On the morning of February 15, I arose at dawn and went to Smolny Monastery to early mass, after which I went to see my confessor, Father Philip Speransky, to ask his blessing. Father Philip, who had known me since I was a child, blessed me and wished me happiness. From there I went to pray at my father's grave in Great Okhta Cemetery.

The day passed swiftly. By five my hair was done and I was dressed in my wedding gown of white moire, with a long train. Both my hairstyle and my dress were flattering to me, and I was very happy about that.

The wedding had been set for seven o'clock. Fyodor Mikhailovich's nephew, Fyodor Mikhailovich the younger, whom my fiancé had chosen as his best man, was to call for me at six. By six o'clock my relatives were all assembled, but the best man had not arrived. Nor had Professor Olkhin's little son Kostya, who was to carry the ikon in front of me, been brought to the house.

I was already starting to feel terribly upset. I imagined that Fyodor Mikhailovich had fallen ill and regretted that I hadn't sent to inquire after his health in the course of the day.

At last—just at seven—Fyodor Mikhailovich the younger rushed into the room and began urging me to hurry. "Anna Grigoryevna, you're ready—let's go! For goodness sake, let's start moving! Uncle is at the church already, and he's terribly worried that you might not come. We've been driving over an hour to get here, and it won't be any less going back. Just think how Uncle is suffering during these two hours!"

"But they haven't brought the little boy yet," I said.

"We'll go without the little boy. Just so we get Fyodor Mikhailovich calmed down as soon as possible!"

They blessed me. Mama and I put our arms around each other and my fur coat was wrapped around me. At the last minute pretty little Kostya also arrived, dressed up in his beautiful Russian suit.

We went out the door. A crowd of people was standing on the staircase. All the lodgers in our houses had come to see me off. Some of them kissed me, others shook my hand, all resoundingly wished me happiness, and on top of that someone sprinkled me with hops as an omen for "living it rich."

I was very much moved by this heartfelt send-off. We seated ourselves in the coach and quickly drove away. Not until then did my sister and I notice that little Kostya was sitting there without his fur coat and cap. We were afraid the child might catch cold, so I covered him with my own voluminous cloak, and he fell asleep a few minutes later.

The carriage drew near to Izmailovsky Cathedral. The best man wrapped sleepy Kostya from head to foot in his own warm greatcoat and carried him up the steep staircase into the cathedral. And I, with the help of a footman, alighted from the coach, covered the ikon with my veil and entered the church.

When he caught sight of me Fyodor Mikhailovich came over at once, grasped my hand hard and said, "Well, so you're here at last! Now you won't get away from me anymore!"

I wanted to tell him that I wasn't planning to get away, but when I looked at his face I was alarmed by its pallor. Without letting me say a word he hurriedly led me to the altar, and the wedding rite began.

The cathedral was brilliantly lit, a splendid choir sang, many elegantly dressed guests were there; but it was not until afterward that I learned all this from what others told me. For half of the wedding ceremony I was in a kind of fog. I crossed myself mechanically and responded to the priest's questions in a barely audible voice. Only after communion did my head clear, and I began to pray fervently. When the ceremony and the prayer of thanksgiving were done, the congratulations began. My husband took me to register our names in a book.

This time our small ikon-bearer was dressed in his fur coat, and we set out for our new home. The little miscreant stayed awake during the trip and told everyone later that "Uncle and Auntie kept kissing each other all the way home."

When we arrived, our guests were already there. Mama and my wedding sponsor gave us their solemn blessing. Then began the rounds of congratulations over goblets of champagne. All those who had witnessed the ceremony but who did not know me were very surprised when before them appeared not the pale, serious girl they had just seen in the cathedral, but a rosy-cheeked, exuberant bride radiant with happiness.

Fyodor Mikhailovich was also beaming. When he brought his friends over to me to be introduced he would say, "Look at that charming girl of mine! She's a marvelous person, that girl of mine! She has a heart of gold!"—and similar praises which embarrassed me terribly. Then he introduced me to the ladies, and was very pleased that I was able to say something amiable to each of them, and that they obviously liked me.

And I too introduced my husband to my friends and relatives, and I was happy to see how he charmed them all. Champagne, sweets and fruits were present in abundance, for he loved to shower hospitality on guests. They did not disperse until midnight, and for a long time after that the two of us sat there, thinking back over all the details of that wonderful day.

CHAPTER THREE

The First Stage of Married Life

About two weeks after the wedding, we were told by someone we knew that an article about Fyodor Mikhailovich had appeared in the February issue of *Son of the Fatherland* entitled "Marriage of a Novelist." We obtained a copy of the paper and read the following story:

The Petersburg correspondent of the newspaper *Nord* writes: People are talking about a certain marriage in our literary world, arranged in a rather peculiar fashion. One of our best-known novelists, a slightly absent-minded man not distinguished for great accuracy in fulfilling the obligations entered into with his publishers, remembered at the end of November that he had to produce a novel at least 200 pages long by December 1; otherwise he would be subject to a heavy penalty. What to do in such a case? True, the subject had already been found and the main scenes invented, but still not a line was yet written, and only one week remained to the fatal deadline.

Following the advice of a friend, our author, to lighten his labors, invited a stenographer to come to the house and started dictating to this stenographer, striding back and forth in his study and running his fingers through his long hair incessantly, as if in the hope of squeezing some new ideas out of it.

I have forgotten to mention that the stenographer invited by the author was a young lady, thoroughly saturated with modern ideas although not a Nihilist, who had achieved an independent position by her own labor. Agonized by his search for new ideas, Mr. X (we shall indicate our novelist's surname by that letter) hardly noticed that his collaborator was young and remarkably pretty. During the first few days the work could not have gone better, but as the *dénouement* approached, difficulties began to arise. The hero of the novel was a widower, no longer young and not handsome, in love with a young and pretty woman. The novel had to be brought to a conclusion with some natural *dénouement,* without suicides and trite scenes. No ideas came to the author's mind. His long hair was already beginning to suffer seriously from this situation, and meanwhile only two days remained in which to complete the novel.

He was already on the point of deciding that he had better pay the penalty, when suddenly his collaboratress, who up to that time had fulfilled her stenographic duties in silence, decided to advise the novelist to have his heroine become aware that she shared the feelings of love she had inspired.

"But that is completely unnatural!" exclaimed the author. "Just bear in mind that the hero is an elderly bachelor, like me, and the heroine is in the full flower of beauty and youth . . . like you, for example."

To this the lady stenographer replied that a man captivates a woman not by his outer appearance but by his mind, his talent, etc., etc. Finally the *dénouement* she had suggested was accepted, and the novel was completed on schedule. On the last day of work Mr. X, in a somewhat agitated voice, asked permission to visit the beautiful lady stenographer in order to express his gratitude. She consented.

"Then may I come tomorrow?" asked X.

"No, come the day after tomorrow if possible," she replied.

The novelist appeared at the appointed time, and after the second cup of coffee he risked a declaration of love. The declaration was favorably received.

"But why," asked Mr. X, "didn't you want to see me yesterday? You might have made me happy a day earlier."

"Because," replied the stenographer, blushing, "yesterday I was expecting my girlfriend, who is far better-looking than I, and I feared she might make you change your intentions."

The novelist was ecstatic over this naïve admission, which proved to him that he was truly loved.

Do not think, by the way, that this novel was concluded with the *dénouement* known in Russia as a *civil marriage.*[1] On the contrary, the pair were married a few days ago in a local parish church.

My husband and I had a good laugh over this little story, and Fyodor Mikhailovich said that, judging by its rather vulgar tone, Alexander Milyukov (who was quite familiar with his habits) had

had a hand in it.[2] It was true that Fyodor Mikhailovich really did like to walk around the room while dictating, and in the difficult spots he used to pull his long hair.

The period before Lent passed in a kind of merry chaos. We paid our "wedding visits" to my family and to Fyodor Mikhailovich's relatives and friends. They invited us to dinners and parties, and everywhere the "young couple" was toasted with champagne. That was the custom of those times, and it seemed to me that I drank more goblets of champagne during those ten days than I did all the rest of my life.

But these felicitations had a melancholy result and caused me the *first* great sorrow of my married life, namely, that Fyodor Mikhailovich suffered two epileptic attacks on the same day; and, even more striking, these occurred not at night, in sleep, as was almost always the case, but during the day when he was fully awake. This was how it happened.

On the last day of Carnival we dined at the home of relatives and then went to spend the evening at my sister's. Supper was gay (and accompanied again by champagne). The other guests left, but we stayed on for a while. Fyodor Mikhailovich was extremely animated and was telling my sister some interesting story. Suddenly he broke off in mid-syllable, turned white, started to get up from the couch and began leaning over toward me. I looked in amazement at his changed face. And suddenly there was a horrible, inhuman scream, or more precisely, a howl—and he began to topple forward. At the same moment my sister, who had been sitting alongside of him, let out a piercing scream, jumped up from her chair, and ran out of the room with hysterical sobs. My brother-in-law rushed after her.

In later years there were dozens of occasions when I was to hear that "inhuman" howl, common with epileptics at the onset of an attack; and that howl always shocked and terrified me. But on this occasion I was not the least bit frightened, to my own surprise, although it was the first time in my life I had ever seen an epileptic fit.

I grabbed Fyodor Mikhailovich by the shoulders and put him on the couch by main force. But I was appalled to realize that his unconscious body was sliding off it and that I did not have the strength to hold him back. I pushed aside a chair with a lighted lamp on it, and let him slide onto the floor. I too sat down on the floor and held his head in my lap all through his convulsions. There was no one to help me: my sister was in hysterics, and my brother-in-law and the maid were fussing over her.

Little by little the convulsions stopped and Fyodor Mikhailovich began regaining consciousness; but he did not know where he was at first, and had even lost the power of speech. He kept trying to say something, but instead of the word he wanted to say he would pronounce another, and it was impossible to understand him. Not for about a half hour did we succeed in lifting him up and putting him on the couch.

It was decided to let him have a chance to calm down before going home. But, to my extreme distress, he suffered a second attack an hour after the first one; and this time with such intensity that for two hours after regaining consciousness he screamed in pain at the top of his voice. It was horrible. In later years he did have some double attacks but these were relatively rare. On this occasion, however, the doctors explained it as a consequence of over-excitement produced by the champagne he had drunk at all the wedding visits and dinners and soirees arranged in our honor. Wine had a very bad effect on him and therefore he was not in the habit of drinking it.

We were compelled to remain at my sister's overnight, for Fyodor Mikhailovich was very weak. Moreover, we feared another repetition of the attack. What a dreadful night I spent! It was then that I realized for the first time the full horror of Fyodor Mikhailovich's disease. As I heard his cries and groans, which did not let up for hours, looked at his face distorted with suffering—completely unlike his own face—and his wildly staring eyes, as I listened to his incoherent speech which I was quite unable to understand, I was almost convinced that my darling, beloved husband was losing his mind—and what terror that thought inspired in me!

But, thank heaven, he recovered sufficiently to be able to go home after a few hours' sleep. The depressed and despondent mood which always descended on him after an attack, however, lasted over a week. "As if I had lost the most precious being in the world, as if I had buried someone," was the way he used to describe his state of mind after an attack. That double attack remained a dreadful memory forever after.

In the course of that very same week there also began those troubles and misunderstandings which so poisoned the first weeks of our marriage and made me remember our "honeymoon" with feelings of vexation and sorrow. To make my point clear I shall describe the order of my new life. Fyodor Mikhailovich, who was accustomed to working at night, could not fall asleep early and used to read at night, and therefore got up late in the day. Whereas I would be ready by nine in the morning and would go to Sennaya Square with the cook to do the marketing. To be quite candid, I was a terrible housekeeper at the time of my marriage. Seven years at the gymnasium, then college courses followed by my stenographic studies—when during all this could I have learned how to manage a household? Having become Fyodor Mikhailovich's wife, however, and knowing his material circumstances, I gave my word to him and to myself that I would master the housekeeping. Laughingly I assured him that I myself was going to bake the pies he loved so much. I even persuaded him to hire an "expensive" cook for those times, for twelve rubles, so that I might learn the culinary art from her.

On returning from Sennaya Square at about eleven I nearly always found Katya Dostoevskaya, Fyodor Mikhailovich's niece, at our house. She was an extremely pretty girl of about fifteen, with beautiful dark eyes and two long flaxen braids hanging down her back. Her mother, Emilya Fyodorovna, had told me several times that Katya loved me, and had expressed the hope that I would have an influence over her daughter. To such a flattering opinion I could answer in no other way than by an invitation to Katya to come to see me as often as possible. Since she had no regular occupation and found it boring at home, she would come to our house straight from her morning walk. And this was the more convenient for her because we lived only five minutes away.

At about twelve Misha Dostoevsky, Fyodor Mikhailovich's nephew, would stop by to see Paul. He was a seventeen-year-old youth who was studying the violin at that time, and he used to drop in to see us on his way home from the conservatory. I, of course, would ask him to stay for lunch. Fyodor Mikhailovich the younger, an excellent pianist, also came frequently.

From two o'clock on, Fyodor Mikhailovich's friends and acquaintances began arriving. They knew he had no urgent work at the moment and therefore considered it quite all right to visit more often. And sister-in-law Emilya Fyodorovna often came to dinner, as well as brother Nikolai, sister Alexandra Golenovskaya, and her good husband Nikolai Ivanovich. The dinner guests would usually remain all evening, until ten or eleven o'clock. This was the order of things day in, day out—there was always an abundance of visitors at our house, both family and friends.

I too had grown up in a patriarchal and hospitable family; but our guests used to come on Sundays and holidays. This onset of continuous hospitality, however, when I had to "be a hostess" and to "entertain" from morning to night, was very burdensome to me, all the more since the young Dostoevskys and my stepson were not suited to me either in age[3] or in my interests of that time.

It was just the opposite with Fyodor Mikhailovich's literary friends—Maikov, Averkiev, Strakhov, Milyukov, Dolgomostyev, and the others—whom I found extremely interesting. The literary world was an unknown quantity to me up to then, and I was fascinated by it. I so wanted to talk with these people, to discuss things perhaps, but mainly to listen, to listen. Unfortunately, that pleasure was mine only rarely. Seeing the bored faces of our young people, Fyodor Mikhailovich would whisper to me, "Anna darling, you can see they're bored, take them away, amuse them." And I would think up some excuse to take them out of the room and would grudgingly set about "amusing" them.

I was also irritated by the fact that, owing to the constant presence of guests, I had no time for my favorite occupations, and that was a great deprivation for me. I would realize with vexation that I hadn't read a book for a whole month, hadn't worked systematically at my stenography, which I wanted to master to the last fine point.

But the most galling thing of all was the fact that because of these continual visitors there was no opportunity at all to be alone with my dear husband. If in the course of the day I contrived to wrest a minute to come sit with him in his study, someone or other would come in right away, or I would be called away on some housekeeping matter. We were forced to forget about those evening chats we used to cherish so much. By evening, because of the senseless manner in which we had spent the day and the profusion of visitors and conversations, both Fyodor Mikhailovich and I would be very tired; I would be drawn toward sleep, and he to an interesting book that he could relax with.

It is possible that in time I might have adjusted to the structure of our life and might have managed a degree of freedom and time to do what I liked best, if it had not been for my troubles with Fyodor Mikhailovich's family.

His sister-in-law, Emilya Fyodorovna Dostoevskaya, was a good but not very bright person. When she saw that after her husband's death Fyodor Mikhailovich had taken the responsibility for her and her family upon himself, she came to regard that as his obligation; and she was stunned to learn that he was planning to marry. This was the source of her hostility to me during the period of our engagement.

After the wedding, however, she accepted the fact and her attitude toward me became more affable, particularly when she saw how much attention I was devoting to her children. Since she was at our house almost daily and considered herself an excellent housekeeper, she was constantly giving me advice on the running of the house. It is possible that this arose out of the goodness of her heart and the desire to be useful to me. But since her homilies were always delivered in the presence of Fyodor Mikhailovich, it wasn't altogether pleasant for me to have my incompetence and lack of thriftiness constantly thrust before his eyes. And even less pleasant was the fact that she was constantly holding up to me, in every little thing, the example of his first wife, which was rather tactless on her part.

But if Emilya Fyodorovna's ceaseless admonitions and mildly patronizing tone were unpleasant, the insolence and boorishness to me in which Paul indulged himself seemed really unbearable. When I married I knew, of course, that Fyodor Mikhailovich's stepson would be living with us. Besides the fact that there were not sufficient means for him to live separately, Fyodor Mikhailovich wanted to have an influence on him before his character became fully formed.

I was still so young that I hadn't foreseen the presence of a complete stranger in my new family as something unpleasant. And besides, I felt that Fyodor Mikhailovich loved his stepson, was used to his presence, and would find it difficult to be separated from him. Therefore I did not wish to insist on Paul's living separately. On the contrary, it seemed to me that the presence of someone my own age* could only liven up the household, that he would help me become familiar with Fyodor Mikhailovich's habits (many of which I did not know) and that in this way I would not have to disrupt the normal course of his life very much.

I cannot say that Paul Isayev was a stupid or unkind person. His chief trouble was that he could *never* understand his position. Accustomed from childhood to receive nothing but kindness and help from all of Fyodor Mikhailovich's family and friends, he took this as his due, and he never understood that this friendly behavior was being shown him not so much for his sake as for Fyodor Mikhailovich's. Instead of valuing and earning the love of the kindly people around him, he behaved so brashly, treated everyone so thoughtlessly and arrogantly that he only upset and antagonized them.

I shall cite a typical instance. When we returned from abroad Paul began begging Fyodor Mikhailovich to get him a job in the Volga-Kamsky Bank. My husband spoke to E. I. Lamansky about the matter and Paul was given a position, first in Petersburg and later in Moscow. There he boasted to many people at the bank that his "father" Dostoevsky was a friend of Lamansky's, and that he himself was a man of important connections.

Lamansky once happened to be passing through Moscow and visited the Volga-Kamsky Bank. As director of the Imperial State Bank, Lamansky was an important financial power and was therefore given a very ceremonious reception. When Paul learned of his arrival he went into the hall where the directors

*Paul was a few months younger than myself. (A.G.D.)

were all assembled, walked up to Lamansky, extended his hand and said, "Hello, Evgeny Ivanovich, how are you? I guess you didn't recognize me? I'm Dostoevsky's son, you've seen me at papa's."

"Excuse me, I did not recognize you—you have changed a great deal," answered Lamansky.

"We're none of us getting any younger," laughed Paul. "And you've changed quite a bit, too, old man!" And with this, he clapped Lamansky on the shoulder in the very friendliest fashion.

Lamansky was taken aback, but as a courteous person he asked after Fyodor Mikhailovich's health. "Not bad," was the answer, "the old gent is creaking along!"

At this Lamansky couldn't restrain himself any longer and turned away. It is easy to imagine the effect of this unmannerly act on Paul's employers and on their opinion of him.

Apollon Maikov, that estimable man, had to put up with particularly frequent unpleasantness from Paul (for Fyodor Mikhailovich's sake, of course) when he attempted to direct his thoughts and acts into good channels—unfortunately, without success. Paul's behavior toward his stepfather (he always called him "father" and himself "son") was equally careless and arrogant. He could not have been Fyodor Mikhailovich's son because he had been born in Astrakhan in 1845,[4] and Fyodor Mikhailovich did not leave Petersburg until 1849.[5]

Living with Fyodor Mikhailovich from the age of twelve and knowing his kindness, Paul became deeply convinced that his "father" should live exclusively for him, work for him, and furnish him with money. He himself, however, not only did not help Fyodor Mikhailovich in any way nor do anything to make his life easier, but on the contrary often irritated him intensely with his rash actions and frivolous behavior and could even drive him to the point of a seizure, as his intimates used to tell me.

Paul considered his stepfather an "obsolescent old man," and his desire for personal happiness seemed to him an "absurdity," as he openly told the family. And he looked upon me as a usurper, as a woman who had broken into their family by force

—a family where he had been in complete charge up to then, since Fyodor Mikhailovich, occupied with his literary work, was naturally unable to take charge of the housekeeping. Seeing me in that light as he did, his malice toward me was understandable.

Since he was unable to prevent our marriage, he determined to make it unbearable for me. It is quite possible that with these continual unpleasantnesses of his, his squabbling and the tales he carried to Fyodor Mikhailovich, he was counting on embroiling my husband and myself in quarrels and forcing us to separate. Each of these unpleasantnesses was trivial in itself. But there were countless numbers of them; and since I knew that they were perpetrated with the specific intention of infuriating and insulting me, I could not avoid paying notice to them and feeling vexed by them.

To give an example: Paul picked up the habit of sending the maid away somewhere or other every morning—either to buy cigarettes, or to deliver a letter to a friend and wait for an answer, or to take something to the tailor's and so on. For some reason it was always necessary to send her very far away from our apartment, so that poor Fedosya, even though she was quick-moving, was always late for Fyodor Maikhailovich's getting up, and didn't have time to tidy his study.

Fyodor Mikhailovich was a great lover of cleanliness and order and would therefore be angry if he found his study in disarray. There was nothing else to do—I myself had to pick up a brush and clean the study. When Fyodor Mikhailovich discovered me at this occupation he reprimanded me, saying that it was Fedosya's job and not mine. But when Fedosya begged off going on a distant errand for Paul and told him she had to clean Fyodor Mikhailovich's study or else "the mistress will probably give me a scolding," he would say—not in the least inhibited by the fact that I was sitting in the next room—"Fedosya! Who's in charge here, Anna Grigoryevna or me? Is that clear? Well then, get going where you're sent!"

This Fedosya was a dreadfully cowed person. She was the widow of a clerk who used to drink himself into delirium tremens and thrash her unmercifully. After his death she was left with three children, in a state of terrible destitution. One of

Fyodor Mikhailovich's relatives told him about it and he took her in as his maid, together with all the children (the oldest was eleven years old, the little girl seven, and the younger boy five).

With tears in her eyes she told me, when I was still engaged to him, what a good human being Fyodor Mikhailovich was. She said that when he was sitting over his work at night and heard a child coughing or crying he would go in, cover the child with a blanket and try to comfort it; and only if he couldn't manage to do it himself would he awaken her. I myself noticed this concern for her children on his part after we were married.

Since Fedosya had happened to witness Fyodor Mikhailovich's epileptic attacks on several occasions, she was terribly frightened both of the attacks and of him. She was afraid of everyone, incidentally: of Paul when he shouted at her, and even of me, who was feared by no one. When she went outside she always wore a green worsted shawl, the very one which is mentioned in *Crime and Punishment* as the common property of the Marmeladov family.

Paul's petty tricks were inexhaustible. Sometimes he would drink up all the cream before Fyodor Mikhailovich came into the dining room, so that we would have to rush to the shop to buy more, which of course would be rancid, and so Fyodor Mikhailovich would have to wait for his coffee. Or he would eat a grouse just before dinnertime, so that two were served instead of three, and there wouldn't be enough. Or all the matches in the house would disappear, although there had been several boxes of them only the day before. All these shortages were a terrible annoyance to Fyodor Mikhailovich and he would shout at Fedosya; and Paul, who had been the cause of all the trouble, would shrug his shoulders and say, "Well, papa, such things didn't happen when I was in charge of the housekeeping!"

So it would end by being my fault, or rather the fault of my slipshod housekeeping.

Paul had a strategy of his own. In Fyodor Mikhailovich's presence he behaved toward me with exceptional courtesy: passed me the plates, ran to summon the maid, lifted my napkin if I dropped it, and so forth. Fyodor Mikhailovich even remarked once or twice that the presence of the feminine element and my presence in particular (Paul was on hail-fellow-well-met terms with the Dostoevsky women, Emilya Fyodorovna and Katya) was having a beneficial influence on him, and that his manners were gradually showing improvement.

But the moment Fyodor Mikhailovich left the room, Paul's manner toward me would change. He would make unflattering remarks on the subject of my housekeeping in the presence of outsiders, and would declare that everything had been in order before I came. Or he would say that I spent too much money, and that our money, after all, was "for all of us." Or he would depict himself as the victim of familial despotism. He would start talking about the difficult position of an "orphan" who up to then had lived happily in the household and was regarded as its chief member. And then, out of the blue, an alien (that was me—the wife) bursts into the house and counts on acquiring influence and taking the number one position in the family. The new mistress of the house starts persecuting the "son," making things difficult for him, making his life miserable. He can't even eat his dinner in peace, knowing that the mistress' resentful, suspicious gaze is following every bite he takes. And he thinks back on the happy years of old and hopes they will return once more, says that he will not give up his influence on his "father," and so on.

The younger Dostoevskys weren't able to stand up for me, and the older ones would laugh at Paul, but that was the extent of their defense of me.

So as not to yield his influence on "father" to me, Paul started coming into Fyodor Mikhailovich's study almost every morning the moment he would begin reading his newspaper. Sometimes Fyodor Mikhailovich's outcry would be heard immediately, and Paul would dart out of the study a bit abashed, saying that "father" was busy and he didn't want to disturb him. On other occasions he would stay there for a long while, exit with a triumphant expression, and instantly start giving orders to the cowering Fedosya.

And Fyodor Mikhailovich would always say to me after these talks with Paul, "Anechka, that's enough fighting around with Pasha, don't hurt his feelings—he's a good boy!"

And when I asked in what way I had hurt "Pasha's" feelings

and what was his complaint about me, Fyodor Mikhailovich would answer that it was all such nonsense that it made him sick to listen to it, but that he begged my indulgence to "Pasha."

People sometimes asked me why it was that I—hearing Paul's rude remarks and daily insolences, experiencing his boorishness, knowing that he was slandering me to Fyodor Mikhailovich—how was it possible that I held my tongue and was incapable of putting Paul in his rightful place? Yes, held my tongue and was incapable!

It should not be forgotten that even though I was already past twenty, I was a complete child in the worldly sense. I had spent my few years of life in a kindly, harmonious family where there were no complications and no struggles. For this reason Paul's improper actions toward me astonished, insulted and wounded me, but I was at first incapable of doing anything to prevent them. And on top of that Paul had a special trick. He would say all kinds of nasty things and then run away immediately without giving me a chance to answer; and when he reappeared I would have calmed down and wouldn't feel like starting a quarrel again.

On top of that, I am a peace-loving person by nature, and quarreling has always been painful to me. And anyway, what could I have done—complained to Fyodor Mikhailovich? But Paul was already complaining constantly about me—so that if I started making complaints against him, what would my darling husband's life have turned into? It was my desire, after all, to preserve his peace of mind, even though that might present difficulties for me.

And then, too, I could understand Paul's chagrin at the change in his untrammeled existence; and I imagined that he would eventually get tired of being nasty to me, that he would come to realize the indelicacy of his behavior or, if he himself couldn't understand it, it would be pointed out to him by Fyodor Mikhailovich's family.

And so it was under such inauspicious circumstances as these that the first two weeks of our married life went by: Paul's rudeness and insolence, Emilya Fyodorovna's homilies, the constant irksome presence of people who bored me and prevented me from being alone with my husband, the eternal anxiety about our tangled affairs.

And it even seemed to me that Fyodor Mikhailovich himself was feeling a kind of estrangement from me, stemming from the way our life was being lived. All this oppressed and tormented me, and I used to ask myself how it would all end. As I recall my character at that time, I see that it might have ended in disaster. I loved Fyodor Mikhailovich without limit, but this was not a physical love, not a passion which might have existed between persons of equal age. My love was entirely cerebral, it was an idea existing in my head. It was more like adoration and reverence for a man of such talent and such noble qualities of spirit. It was a searing pity for a man who had suffered so much without ever knowing joy and happiness, and who was so neglected by all his near ones, whose duty it should have been to repay him with love and concern for everything he did for them all his life.

The dream of becoming his life's companion, of sharing his labors and lightening his existence, of giving him happiness—this was what took hold of my imagination; and Fyodor Mikhailovich became my god, my idol. And I, it seemed, was prepared to spend the rest of my life on my knees to him. But all that was exalted feelings, dreams which could be crushed by the onset of harsh reality.

Because of the circumstances in which we lived there gradually came upon us a time of misunderstandings and doubts. There were times when I thought that Fyodor Mikhailovich had already fallen out of love with me, that he understood how empty I was, how foolish, and how completely unsuited to him, and that he was probably repenting of having married me but did not know how to correct his mistake. Although I loved him ardently, my pride would not have allowed me to remain with him if I believed that he had ceased to love me. I even imagined sometimes that I had to make that sacrifice for him, to leave him, since our married life had obviously become a burden to him.

Or I would notice with real sorrow that I was feeling outraged by him because he, "the great master of the heart," failed to see how difficult my life was and kept pressing his boring relatives on me and defending Paul, who was so hostile to me. Or I would mourn over the fact that those marvelous evenings together he and I had spent before our wedding, so filled with enchantment, were over for us; and that the happy life we had dreamed of would never come about.

There were even times when I felt a flash of regret for my old peaceful life at home, where there was no misery and I didn't have to feel depressed or irritated. In a word, I was agitated by a mixture of the most childish fears and most genuine griefs; many unresolved doubts presented themselves to my still immature mind. I did not as yet possess either a correct view of life or a fully formed character, and that prefigured disaster.

I might have given way to this domestic unpleasantness, might have exploded, vexed Fyodor Mikhailovich with baseless reproaches and suspicions, and evoked a counter-explosion from him. We might have had a serious quarrel after which I, so proud a person, would of course have left him. It should be borne in mind that I belonged to the generation of the sixties, that like all women of that time I valued my independence above all. I would hardly have made the first overture toward him, despite all my love for him. I was still childishly vain and couldn't bear the thought of Paul's sneers if I should be the one to admit guilt.

And it is possible that neither would Fyodor Mikhailovich have wanted to make the first overture to me. At that time he did not love me nearly so much as he did in later years. His wounded pride, his sense of his own dignity, and in particular Paul's slanders might at first have swayed him against a reconciliation.

The misunderstandings between us would of course have grown, and reconciliation would in the end have proved impossible. When I think back to that time I am appalled by what might have occurred. For Fyodor Mikhailovich could not have divorced me, inasmuch as divorces were enormously expensive then. And so he would not have arranged his future life happily, would not have had the family and children he had dreamed of having his whole life long. And my future life would have been wretched as well. I had set too high hopes of happiness on our union—and how bitter it would be if that golden dream were not realized!

But it was not the will of fate to deprive us of that immense happiness which was to be ours for the next fourteen years. I remember as if it were today that Tuesday in the fifth week of Lent when things unexpectedly took a turn for the better.

The day had begun with its usual unpleasantness. Some lapse in my housekeeping, cunningly engineered by Paul, came to light (there wasn't a pencil or a match to be found throughout the whole house) and Fyodor Mikhailovich was enraged and shouted at poor Fedosya. The guests I was so tired of seeing arrived, and I had to "entertain" and "amuse" them. Paul said impertinent things to me, as usual. And Fyodor Mikhailovich was particularly withdrawn and downcast and hardly said a word to me, which upset me very badly.

We had been invited to spend the evening at the Maikovs. Knowing that fact, our guests left immediately after dinner. But because of all that day's troubles my head had begun to ache severely and my nerves were strung so tight that I was afraid of bursting into tears in front of the Maikovs if there should be any mention of our family life. So I decided to stay at home. Fyodor Mikhailovich tried to talk me out of it and seemed put out by my refusal.

He had barely left the house when Paul appeared and reproved me for irritating his "father" with my caprices. He said he didn't believe I had a headache at all and had decided against going with Fyodor Mikhailovich just so as to vex him. He said that Fyodor Mikhailovich had committed a "colossal folly" in marrying me, that I was "a terrible housekeeper" and was spending too much of "the funds intended for all of us." And he stated, in conclusion, that Fyodor Mikhailovich's attacks had grown worse since our marriage, and that I was responsible. Having delivered himself of all this insolence, he disappeared from the house at once.

This time his astounding effrontery was the straw that broke the camel's back. He had never before insulted me quite so cruelly, attributing even Fyodor Mikhailovich's worsened health to me. I was wounded and offended to the highest degree. My head started to ache even worse; I flung myself on the bed and began to sob uncontrollably.

Perhaps an hour and a half had elapsed when Fyodor Mikhailovich returned. It seems that after staying with the Maikovs for a little while he had begun to miss me and therefore went home. When he saw that the house was dark he asked Fedosya where I was.

"The mistress is in bed crying, sir!" Fedosya informed him portentously.

He was alarmed and asked me what was the matter. I would have hidden the truth, but he entreated me so, spoke so kindly that my heart melted and I began telling him, weeping and sobbing, how hard my life was, how I was being insulted in his house. I said I could see that he had fallen out of love with me, had stopped asking my opinion about things the way he used to; I told him how mortified I was and how I was suffering from it, and so on.

For me to weep in that fashion was rare. The more he tried to console me, the more copiously my tears flowed. I expressed with the most utter frankness everything that was lying heavy on my heart, all my doubts and misunderstandings. My poor husband listened and gazed at me in the greatest astonishment. Seeing Paul's exceptional obligingness toward me, he hadn't had the slightest suspicion, it seems, that his stepson had presumed to insult me.

He began by chiding me gently for not having been frank with him, for not having complained about his stepson, for not having put myself on such a footing that Paul would not dare to be impertinent. He reassured me of his fervent love, and showed astonishment that I could have gotten it into my head that he had stopped loving me. And then he finished by confessing in his turn that our present chaotic life was terribly hard on him, too. Even in former times his young relatives came to visit, but seldom, because they found it boring. Whereas now he had been explaining the frequency of their visits by my cordiality toward them, and by the fact that they enjoyed themselves at our house. And as a matter of fact he had been under the impression that I found these young people with their lively conversation and discussion terribly interesting. He told me that he too missed our old talks and regretted the fact that the continual presence of guests was an impediment. He added that he had been thinking a good deal during the past few days about making a trip to Moscow; and that now, after this talk of ours, he had definitely decided to go ahead with it.

"We'll go together, of course," he said. "I want to show you to my Moscow family. Both Verochka and Sonya know you already from the things I've told them about you, and I want you to get to know each other and love each other. And besides, I have the notion of trying for another advance from Katkov, and using the money to take you abroad. Why, that used to be our dream, yours and mine, remember? And perhaps it will come true! And anyway, I wanted to talk to Katkov about my new novel. It's hard to discuss things by mail, much better face to face. And even if we don't manage to go abroad, it will still be easier for us to set up a new order of things after we come back from Moscow, without all this hustle and bustle that we both find so unpleasant. Well then—on to Moscow! What about it, Anechka, are you agreed?"

It wasn't at all necessary to ask my consent. Fyodor Mikhailovich was as tender with me, as kind and dear as he had been when we were engaged. All my fears and doubts of his love disintegrated like smoke. It was almost the first time since our wedding that we had the opportunity to be alone together for a whole evening, deep in the friendliest and most heartfelt kind of talk. We decided not to put off the trip but to leave the very next day.

The next day the relatives—and Paul in particular—were unpleasantly surprised by the news of our departure. But since they were aware that his funds were running out and assumed that it was for money he was going, they did not attempt to dissuade us. Paul did not spare his barbs at parting, and announced that he was going to "take my neglected household affairs into his own hands and straighten things out." I didn't contradict him and didn't take offense. I was too glad of the chance for even a temporary deliverance from his harassment.

We arrived in Moscow on Thursday of the fifth week of Lent and stopped at the Hotel Dussot, which Fyodor Mikhailovich particularly liked. Fatigued after the journey, we decided not to try to get any business accomplished that day, but to go to the Ivanovs.

The thought of this visit perturbed me a good deal. Of all his relatives, Fyodor Mikhailovich loved his sister Vera Ivanova and her family the most. While we were still in Petersburg he told me how happy it would make him if the Ivanovs liked me and I made friends with them. I myself wanted that very much, and I was afraid that the first impression I made on them would not be to my advantage. I dressed with special care, selecting my best lilac-colored dress and elegant hat. Fyodor Mikhailovich seemed satisfied with my appearance and said that I looked my best. The praise was doubtless exaggerated, but it pleased me and helped my morale.

The Ivanovs lived near the Geodetic Institute and one had to traverse the whole city to reach them—at first by way of Myasnitskaya Street and then along Pokrovka. As we were driving past the Church of the Assumption of the Virgin (which is on Pokrovka) Fyodor Mikhailovich said that next time we would get out of our sleigh and walk some distance away, so as to view the church in its full beauty. He had a high opinion of the architecture of this church and invariably went to look at it whenever he was in Moscow. A few days later, when we were going past it, we did view it, both inside and out.

The closer we drew to the Ivanovs, the more uneasy I became. What if I make a bad impression? I thought anxiously. How that will upset Fyodor Mikhailovich!

The servant who opened the door to us said that Alexander Pavlovich (his sister Vera's husband) and Sofya Alexandrovna (their daughter) were not at home, but that he would inform Vera Mikhailovna of our arrival right away. We entered a vast drawing room furnished with antique mahogany furniture. Fyodor Mikhailovich picked up a copy of the *Moscow Gazette* from a table and I began looking through a photograph album that was lying there.

Vera did not come out for a long while. She probably didn't consider it appropriate to appear before a new member of the family in her dressing gown and so changed her clothes, which took quite a little time. In about a half hour the door into the drawing room suddenly burst open with a clatter, and a little boy of about ten shot into the room like a whirlwind.

"Vitya, Vitya!" shouted Fyodor Mikhailovich. The child did not stop, however, but ran into the next room exclaiming loudly, "She's young, she's all dressed up, and she has no spectacles!"

He was hushed up at once, and fell silent. Fyodor Mikhailovich, who was thoroughly familiar with the family's habits, guessed right away what was going on.

"They couldn't wait!" he said, laughing. "They sent Vitya to see what my wife looks like."

Vera Mikhailovna appeared at last and was very warm to me. She kissed me and put her arms around me, and she asked me to love and cherish her brother. Her husband and eldest daughter Sonechka [Sofya Alexandrovna] also came in. Alexander Pavlovich congratulated us in official phrases and wished us happiness. Sonechka gave me her hand and smiled nicely, but was very quiet and kept looking closely at me.

Alexander Pavlovich opened the door to the next room and said, "Children, come in and congratulate Uncle and meet your new auntie."

One after the other, the young Ivanovs began to come out. There were seven of them: Sonechka, who was twenty, Mashenka (nineteen), Sasha (seventeen), Yulenka (fifteen), Vitya, and [two] other children. They all greeted Fyodor Mikhailovich with affection but behaved coolly toward me—the boys bowed and the girls curtsied, and then they all sat down and started looking me over, all eyes.

Immediately, I felt intuitively that the young people were prejudiced against me. And I was not mistaken. As later events proved, a whole cabal had been created against me. All the Ivanovs dearly loved their aunt on their father's side, Elena Pavlovna. Her husband had been incurably ill for many years, and it had been decided within the family that after his death Elena Pavlovna was to marry Fyodor Mikhailovich and settle permanently in Moscow.

He was their favorite uncle. It was therefore not surprising that all these young people should take a dislike to me, who had disrupted their cherished dream. Nor did they much care for the praises he had showered on me when he was in Moscow for Christmas. When they found out that I was a stenographer they decided that I was old, a Nihilist, with bobbed hair and spectacles. On learning that we were in Moscow they had agreed to make fun of me, to put me in my place and thereby demonstrate their independence right from the start. But when, instead of an old lady, an erudite "Nihilist," they saw a young woman, hardly more than a girl and, what is more, one who practically trembled before them, they were astonished and couldn't take their eyes off me.

I was embarrassed by this concentrated attention. Although it was my habit to speak simply and without affectation, I now began talking in a more literary fashion and kept inventing eloquent phrases, and my speech was very unnatural. When I tried to talk to my young relatives they answered with "yes" or "no" and obviously did not wish to sustain any conversation.

We sat down to dine at about five. Champagne was served, and they began to toast us. It was noisy but I didn't feel gay although I joked and laughed and tried to be animated. After dinner, things went even worse for me. Several young friends arrived. Many of them were fond of Fyodor Mikhailovich, who had spent the previous summer at the Ivanovs' summer house in Lublin, near Moscow, where all these friends of the Ivanov children used to come to visit. They all wanted to get a look at Fyodor Mikhailovich's wife.

They organized some parlor games, quite intricate ones demanding a sharp eye and quick thinking. In this respect a friend of Vera Mikhailovna's elder daughters, Maria Sergeyevna Ivanchina-Pisareva, was particularly excellent. She was a young lady of about twenty-two, not pretty but lively, pert, quick-witted, always ready to make fun of someone. (She was later depicted very graphically as the pert girlfriend of Maria Nikitishna in Dostoevsky's novel *The Eternal Husband,* in which the Ivanov family was portrayed under the name of "the Zakhlebinins.")

The young people had assigned to Marya Sergeyevna the mission of discomfiting me and making me look ridiculous in my husband's eyes. They began playing forfeits. Each of the players was to put together a bouquet (a verbal one, of course) for various occasions: for someone's eightieth birthday, for a young girl's first ball, and so forth. It fell to me to gather a bouquet of field flowers. Since I had never lived in the country I knew only cultivated flowers and could name no more than poppies, cornflowers, dandelions, and something else; and therefore my bouquet was unanimously, and rightly, censured. I was asked to put together another, but foreseeing failure, I refused.

"No, please let me off!" I laughed. "I can see for myself that I have no taste at all."

"We don't doubt that for a moment," Maria Sergeyevna retorted. "You have just demonstrated that fact brilliantly!"

And with these words she looked meaningfully at Fyodor Mikhailovich who was sitting next to me and listening to our games. She said these words so caustically and at the same time so amusingly, that everyone burst out laughing, including Fyodor Mikhailovich and myself. The general laughter broke the ice of hostility, and the evening ended more pleasantly than it had begun.

On the way home Fyodor Mikhailovich questioned me about my reactions. I told him that I liked Vera Mikhailovna and Sonya very much, but had not yet formed any opinion about the rest of the family. Seeing my downcast expression, he took pity on me.

"My poor Anechka!" he said. "They've pecked at you thoroughly. It's your own fault—you should have parried their thrusts and that would have made them bite their tongues at once! You'll have to be bolder, my dear friend! My sister and Sonechka liked you very much, and indeed you were so charming all day that I couldn't stop looking at you!"

These words had a very consoling effect on me, but just the same it was a long time before I could fall asleep that night. I alternated between reproaching myself for my inability to get along in society and wondering why all these nice young people were behaving so inimically to me. It was not until afterwards that I found out I had ruined their hopes of arranging a union between their favorite uncle and their favorite aunt.

The Ivanovs invited us to spend whole days with them, but on the following day, a Friday, we decided not to go there until evening. During the day Fyodor Mikhailovich went to see Katkov but did not find him at home. We dined at the hotel and set out for the Ivanovs' in the evening. Friday was their "at home" day, and we found many callers there. The group was divided: the older people were playing cards in the living room and study, and the young people, myself included, stayed in the drawing room. They began to play the then fashionable card game called *stukolka*. Next to me a young man, a friend of Sasha Ivanov's, was sitting. Seeing that he was not infected with the general prejudice against me, I started chatting and laughing with him, especially since he turned out to be a witty and lively young person.

A funny incident occurred at *stukolka*. During the sixties, there was little small change in silver; copper coins were circulated more freely. The Ivanovs sent their servant to change ten or twelve rubles, and the entire sum was brought in heavy five-kopeck coins. There was a maiden lady of about forty among the guests, dressed in a brilliant pink sheer wool dress and with a profusion of bows on her head, shoulders and bodice. After a few plays, she began complaining about her losses. Other people complained too, and for a long time we couldn't figure out who was winning.

At eleven we were called in to supper. We got up and suddenly heard the ringing of coins scattering over the floor and a scream from the rose-colored maiden lady, whose pockets evidently could not sustain their weight. We all rushed to pick up the coins, which had rolled all over the floor, but the lady bent down to the floor and covered her winnings with her wide skirt, screaming, "No, no, don't touch it! I'll pick it all up myself!"

She looked so comical, her fright that we would take away her five-kopeck pieces was so absurd, that all of us began laughing with all our might and I, apparently, more than anyone.

Fyodor Mikhailovich, who was playing preference in the study, came out often to have a look at us, and it seemed to me that he was growing more and more serious and downcast. I attributed this to fatigue. At supper I sat next to my *stukolka* partner and Fyodor Mikhailovich sat opposite us, not taking his eyes off me and trying to listen to our conversation. I felt very gay. I addressed comments to my husband a few times to try to draw him into the conversation but was unsuccessful.

We went home immediately after supper. Fyodor Mikhailovich was stubbornly silent all the long way home and made no response to my questions. When we reached our hotel he started pacing the room, and was obviously in a state of extreme irritation. This worried me, and I went up to him to give him a caress and try to dissipate his mood. He pushed my hand away roughly and gave me such a hostile and furious look that my heart stood still.

"Are you angry with me, Fedya?" I asked timidly. "What are you angry about?"

At this question he burst out in a terrible rage and said many hurtful things. According to him I was a heartless coquette and had flirted all evening with my companion simply to torment my husband. I started justifying myself, but that only put the fat in the fire. He was beside himself. Forgetting that we were in a hotel, he started shouting at the top of his voice.

Knowing how groundless his accusations were, I was deeply wounded by his unfairness. His shouting and the awful expression on his face terrified me. I began to imagine that he was going to have a seizure right then and there, or else that he would kill me. I couldn't maintain my self-control, and burst into tears.

He regained his self-possession in a flash and began to soothe me, comfort me, beg my forgiveness. He kissed my hands, cried and swore at himself for the scene he had made.

"I suffered so terribly all evening," he said, "when I saw how animated you were, talking to that young man. I imagined that you were falling in love with him and I was in a frenzy of jealousy and ready to say all kinds of nasty things to him. Now I see how unfair I was to you!"

He was truly repentant, begged me to forget the wounding things he had said and gave me his word never to be jealous again. His face expressed deep suffering. I began to feel real pity for my poor husband. I sat up with him almost all night, comforting and calming him. Our talk came to an end with the church bells for matins. We went to bed, but could not fall asleep for a long time.

I awoke the next day at one in the afternoon. Fyodor Mikhailovich had awakened earlier and sat there without stirring for about two hours, fearing to disturb my sleep. He complained comically that I had almost starved him to death, since, being afraid to wake me, he hadn't rung for coffee. He was extremely tender with me.

The memory of that nocturnal scene printed itself permanently on my heart. It forced me to think about our future relationship. I understood how terribly he suffered from jealousy, and I promised myself then and there that I would shield him from such painful experiences in future.

Of the balance of our stay in Moscow I remember with special vividness my trip to Petrovskoye-Razumovskoye, where my brother Ivan, a student at the Agricultural Academy, was living. He was just past seventeen, very handsome and pink-cheeked, with curly blond hair. He was exceptionally kindhearted and gay but as shy as a girl. He was the youngest student at the Academy, and everyone was fond of him.

I wrote to him as soon as we arrived in Moscow, asking him to come any day at all—the sooner the better—at about eleven in the morning; and that if he didn't find us at home he was to wait for us in the hotel reading room. He received the letter on Friday and was at our hotel at eleven the following morning. Learning from the valet that we were not yet up, he went to visit a sick friend and stayed a long while. By the time he came back we were no longer there. Assuming that we would soon return, he waited at the hotel till dusk, and then left us a note saying he would return again on Monday.

But Fyodor Mikhailovich had already decided that in the event of failure with Katkov we would leave for home on Sunday evening; and so there was a risk of not seeing my brother at all. I pleaded with Fyodor Mikhailovich to let me go myself to see my brother. He was unable to accompany me because Katkov had asked him to come during the day. He therefore hired a cab to take me to the Agricultural Academy, taking note of the cabby's number, and I left at about one in the afternoon, promising to return toward four and bring my brother with me.

I was in a marvelous mood. Fyodor Mikhailovich had behaved very tenderly and kindly to me all the morning—our recent quarrel had evidently left no painful trace on him. The weather was glorious, the road was beautiful, and I was jubilant at the thought of the forthcoming meeting with my beloved brother.

It was Sunday and there were relatively few students left at the academy except for those who lived there permanently. I entered an immense reception room and asked a student I encountered there whether I might see my brother, the student Snitkin. Everyone at the academy knew that Snitkin's sister was newly married because on my wedding day my brother—who never took part in drinking bouts—got dead drunk for the first time in his life and sobbed noisily all evening. When his comrades tried to console him he said, "Everything is done for! I have no more sister. My sister is dead to me!"

The student sent at once for someone to take me to my brother's room. Vanya greeted me ecstatically and even cried when he threw his arms around me. We sat down to talk. Within five minutes a waiter came in carrying a samovar, a tray with a teapot, two glasses and French rolls. Almost simultaneously another waiter brought in a second samovar with a coffeepot, cream and rusks. These had been ordered by my brother's friends, who assumed that his guest had got chilled on the way to see him. Each sent to Vanya's room what was on his own table.

Little by little Vanya's friends, some of whom were admirers of my husband's, began drifting in to have a look at the wife of their idol Dostoevsky. About nine young men crowded into the room—some sat on chairs, some on the bed, some on the window sill. I poured out tea for them since the first waiter, thinking that the samovar he had brought wasn't hot enough, brought in a third samovar, still boiling. Such a plethora of samovars on our table delighted everyone and gave the students, who had been a bit shy with me at first, something to joke about.

The conversation turned to literature and the students divided into two groups: the pro- and anti-Dostoevskyites. One of the latter began arguing heatedly that Dostoevsky had slandered the younger generation by making Raskolnikov, a student, the hero of *Crime and Punishment.* I, of course, came to my husband's defense. Others supported me and a youthful debate flamed up, the kind where no one listens to his opponent but simply restates his own opinion.

During this fervid debate we failed to keep track of the time, and instead of an hour I had stayed at my brother's for over two hours. I was in a hurry to get home. All my companions of both persuasions went in a body to see me off. But the cabdriver who had brought me there and whom I had been rash enough to pay had disappeared, alas. The students scattered in all directions looking for him and returned with the news that he had waited for me about an hour and had finally taken one of the professors into the city.

What to do? One of the students volunteered to lead us by the shortest route to Butyrki, where it was always possible to find a cabby. The whole company set out for Butyrki. The shortest route, as always happens, turned out to be the longest route—we had to go through piled-up drifts, getting deep into the snow. We all laughed, but my heart was uneasy at the thought of how worried my poor husband would be.

It took us almost an hour to reach Butyrki at last, and once there we searched a long while for a cabby. It was not until half-past six that my brother and I were approaching the Hotel Dussot. It was already almost dark. I ran inside and asked the doorman whether my husband was at home.

"He's been standing at the street-crossing for three whole hours and keeps coming back to find out whether you have returned."

I went outside and saw Fyodor Mikhailovich, who was indeed standing on the corner and peering closely at all the passing carriages. I was terrified at the sight of him, he looked so white and upset.

"Darling Fedya, I'm back, let's go home," I said, walking up to him.

He was terribly glad to see me and grabbed my hand with a look on his face as though he had despaired of ever seeing me again. I led him to the hotel entrance and introduced my brother. I admit that I was very much afraid he might pour out his anger on innocent Vanya, and that my dream that he would love Vanya would be shattered. Luckily, that did not happen; my husband behaved very amicably with him.

Dinner was very gay. Fyodor Mikhailovich wanted to know all the details of our adventures, and I described them humorously. In view of the lateness of the hour my brother left immediately after dinner, and my husband and I spent a beautiful evening alone together, like the wonderful evenings before our wedding. I asked him prankishly, "Well, tell the truth, now—you must have thought I ran off with somebody today?"

"Now, now, what kind of an idea have you cooked up!" he replied. But his eyes looked guiltily at me, and I understood that my guess was not entirely without foundation.

It is with pleasure that I recall the rest of our stay in Moscow. Every morning we would set out to see the sights of the city—the Kremlin churches, the Palace, the Armory, the house of the Romanov boyars. One bright morning Fyodor Mikhailovich took me to Lazarevskoye Cemetery, the resting place of his mother, for whose memory he retained a heartfelt tenderness. We were very pleased to find that the priest was still in the church and could recite a memorial prayer at her grave.

We also went to the Sparrow Hills. Fyodor Mikhailovich, a Muscovite by birth, was an excellent guide, and he told me many interesting things about the chief sights of our ancient Russian capital.

After the sightseeing we would usually repair—tired and starving—to Testov's for lunch. My husband loved Russian cooking and would order specially for me—a Petersburger—such local delicacies as *selyanka,* a thick, spicy soup; the special open-faced pastries called *rasstegai;* and hearth-baked *pirozhki;* and he would pretend to be horrified at my youthful appetite.

Afterward we would return to the hotel to rest and would go on to the Ivanovs' for dinner. While I was at their house I didn't let Fyodor Mikhailovich stir a step away from me, so as to avoid any outbursts of jealousy. With his help, I really made friends with his sister Vera, with Sonechka and the rest of the young people. I became friendly even with the treacherous Maria Sergeyevna. They all told me in the minutest detail how and why they had taken a dislike to me even before meeting me, and what techniques they had been intending to use to anger and infuriate their unwanted new relative.

We would go home toward eleven and didn't go to bed until two in the morning, exchanging our reactions to the day spent so pleasantly. The feelings of estrangement from my husband which had begun to grow during the last weeks in Petersburg vanished completely in Moscow, and I became again the high-spirited, responsive person I had been during our engagement. Fyodor Mikhailovich declared that he had found here his "old Anya," whom it seemed he had begun to lose in Petersburg, and he would say that for him, this was "our honeymoon."

It was only now that I became fully aware of how happy our married life could become if it were not for some of my husband's hostile relatives who were standing between us. My memories of our trip to Moscow stayed with me forever, and in later years I always felt happier, calmer, and more satisfied in Moscow than anywhere else.

The editor of the *Russian Messenger* agreed to a new advance of a thousand rubles to Fyodor Mikhailovich. The matter was settled on Friday and we left for Petersburg the following day. I remember that our train, for some reason, stopped at the Klin station for a whole hour. It was about seven o'clock in the evening, and a vespers service was going on in the main hall for Palm Sunday Eve. All were standing with lighted candles and palms. We joined the worshipers and I remember the fervor with which I prayed, standing side by side with my dear husband; and with what sincerity, with what a full heart, I thanked God for the happiness He had sent me! Moments like those are not forgotten.

We returned to Petersburg, and that style of life so irksome to me began all over again. The usual guests turned up for lunch and then the rest of the family began to arrive, since they knew from Paul that we would be back by Sunday. Again it fell to my lot to "amuse" and "be a hostess" to our relatives. But this time I performed my role willingly, hoping that all this would be changed very soon.

Fyodor Mikhailovich had gone off somewhere and I, to avoid any unpleasantness, decided not to say anything for the time being about our plans to go abroad. The subject did not come up until dinner, when the whole family, including my mother, were assembled. There was talk of the fine, almost spring-like weather they had been having all week. Emilya Fyodorovna said that we ought to take advantage of these sunny days to hunt for a summer house, or else all the good ones would be taken. She added that she knew of an excellent house in Tyarlevo, near Pavlovsk, with a large garden—a house ample enough, in fact, to hold the entire Dostoevsky family as well as ourselves.

"It will be jollier for Anna Grigoryevna to be in the company of young people. And I—so be it!—I will make the sacrifice and take over the housekeeping, which isn't going too well for our dear hostess."

Fyodor Mikhailovich frowned at this innuendo about my bad housekeeping and also, perhaps, at her remark about my being happier in the company of young people.

"There isn't any point in our looking for a summer house," he announced. "Anya and I are going abroad."

All the relatives took these words as a joke. But when he began to expound our plans for the trip in detail, they understood that it was real and were evidently quite displeased, since they suddenly stopped talking. I tried to liven up the conversation by telling about the Ivanovs and about our Moscow adventures, but no one helped me out.

Coffee was served and Fyodor Mikhailovich, irritated by this silent protest, went off to his study. Emilya Fyodorovna followed him a little later, while the rest went into the living room and I stayed behind in the dining room with Paul.

"I see perfectly well that this is some trick of yours, Anna Grigoryevna!" he began angrily.

"What trick?"

"You don't un-der-stand me? Why, this absurd trip abroad, that's what! But you are very much mistaken in your calculations. If I *permitted* your trip to Moscow, it was only because *papá* had to go there to get money. But a trip abroad—that's a whim of yours, Anna Grigoryevna, and I do not intend to allow it under any circumstances."

I was outraged by his manner but I didn't feel like starting a quarrel, so I said ironically, "But perhaps you'll have mercy on us?"

"Don't count on it! After all, this whim of yours is going to cost money, and the money isn't for you alone, you know, it's for the whole family—our money is held in common."

And this from a person indebted to his good stepfather for everything, and incapable of earning a kopeck on his own! So as not to give him a piece of my mind for his effrontery, I quickly walked out of the room.

After a half hour or so Emilya Fyodorovna came out of the study, evidently irritated. She ordered her daughter to get ready to go home and left after saying goodbye to me very drily. Her place in the study was taken by my husband's brother Nikolai, and then the rest of the family went in to say good night. Paul went in last of all. As was his habit, he began speaking with such vehemence and in such a didactic tone of voice that Fyodor Mikhailovich lost patience and sent him out of the room; and he immediately went away somewhere.

After everyone had left I went into the study and found my husband irritated and furious. He told me that the relatives were unanimously opposed to our trip abroad—but that if we did go, they were *demanding* that money be left for them for several months in advance.

"But how much would that come to?" I asked.

"Emilya Fyodorovna promised to speak to her children and give me an answer tomorrow."

His words alarmed me badly. Out of the thousand-ruble advance from the *Russian Messenger,* Fyodor Mikhailovich was proposing to give two hundred to Emilya Fyodorovna, a hundred to Paul for living expenses, and a hundred to his brother Nikolai. Another hundred would go for our own living expenses up to the time of our departure. That would leave about five hundred for the trip. We were counting on the fact that after a month's rest in Europe, Fyodor Mikhailovich would set to work on his article on Belinsky. He estimated that it would be no less than fifty or sixty pages long, and that he would receive three or four hundred rubles for it within a comparatively short space of time to take care of his family's needs during the summer months. And we were intending to return to Petersburg by the beginning of August.

My gloomy forebodings turned out to be justified. Emilya

Fyodorovna arrived the next morning and announced that she must have five hundred rubles for her family and an additional two hundred for Paul's keep during our absence. Fyodor Mikhailovich tried to get her to agree to three hundred all-inclusive, and promised to deliver the rest of the money within two months. But she would not agree to this, and he did not have the strength to refuse her. Since his brother's death, he had grown too accustomed to concerning himself with the interests of his brother's family.

In the middle of the day Fyodor Mikhailovich had another unpleasant experience. A young man appeared out of the blue—the son of a Madame Reisman, who was holding several court orders on Fyodor Mikhailovich for approximately two thousand rubles. Since he was paying her a high interest rate, she had never bothered him about it. Now, however, her son declared that Madame Reisman was asking for a payment of five hundred rubles on one of the court orders, and that if he refused to pay, she intended to go to the bailiff and have our furniture attached. Fyodor Mikhailovich was dumbfounded by this unexpected demand, but in view of Reisman's insistence he promised to pay him three hundred rubles by the next day.

In the course of the day letters came from the relatives. It turned out that Fyodor Mikhailovich was to pay eleven hundred rubles over to them and an additional three hundred to Reisman. And a thousand rubles was all we had to our name.

I have to say frankly that this sudden demand from Madame Reisman, always heretofore a very easygoing creditor, seemed somewhat suspicious to me, but I did not express my feelings to my husband.

Late that evening, after totaling up all the immediate payments, Fyodor Mikhailovich said to me sadly, "Fate is against us, my darling Anechka! You can see it for yourself. If we go abroad now, in spring, we'll need two thousand rubles and we scarcely have one. If we stay in Russia we can live comfortably on that money for two months and even perhaps rent the summer house Emilya Fyodorovna is recommending. Out there I can set to work and perhaps we'll have some money again in the fall, and we can go abroad for two months. If you only knew, my darling, how badly I feel that this cannot happen now! How I've dreamed of this trip, how needed I felt it was, for both of us!"

When I saw how downhearted he was I tried to hide my own vexation and said cheerfully, "Well now, don't take it so hard, my darling. We'll wait till fall. And perhaps we'll have better luck then!"

I pleaded a headache and hurried out of the study, afraid of bursting into tears and upsetting him even more. But there was a dead weight on my heart. All those melancholy feelings and doubts which had caused me such anguish, and which had dissipated only during our stay in Moscow, now returned with redoubled force. Seeing that the dream which had so possessed us both could not be realized, I fell almost into despair. I thought to myself, only the constant spiritual contact with my husband—which I had so cherished in those blessed weeks before our wedding, and which had made our life in Moscow so beautiful—could create the strong, close-knit family we both dreamed of having. If we were to save our love, we needed to be alone together if only for two or three months, and I must calm down from the agitations and unpleasantnesses I had suffered. I was deeply convinced that then the two of us would come together for the rest of our lives, and that no one could separate us again. But where to get the money for this trip so vital to both of us? And suddenly a thought flashed through my mind—why couldn't I give up my whole dowry for the sake of the trip, and save our happiness that way?

Little by little this idea took hold of me, although certain complications stood in the way of carrying it out. In the first place, it was hard for me to bring myself to make the sacrifice. I have already mentioned that despite my twenty years I was a child in many ways. Possessions—furniture, fancy clothes—have great importance when one is young. I was extremely fond of my piano, my charming little tables and whatnots, all my lovely things so newly acquired. What a pity it would be to lose all that and risk never getting it back again!

I also feared my mother's displeasure. Such a recent bride, I was still under her influence and was afraid of upsetting her. A part of my dowry had been bought with her money. What, I thought, if mama accuses my husband of excessive favoritism toward his own family and doubts his love for me? How she'll suffer, who always put her children's happiness above her own!

In such doubts and vacillations I passed a sleepless night. At five the bells rang for morning mass, and I decided to go to pray in the Church of the Ascension, which was located across the street from our house.

The service moved me, as always. I prayed fervently, wept, and left the church with my resolve strengthened. I went straight from church to my mother's house without going home. My arrival at that early hour, and moreover with eyes all red with weeping, alarmed my poor mother. Of all our intimates, she was the only one who knew about the troubles in my family life. She often chided me with my inability to make Paul treat me with respect and to change the atmosphere in the house. She was also indignant over the fact that I, who had always been busy before and who found moral satisfaction in work, now did nothing for days at a time except to amuse and entertain dull visitors. She was a Swede, her view of life was Western, more cultured; and she feared that the good habits inculcated by my upbringing would vanish thanks to our Russian style of living with its disorderly hospitality. Realizing that I lacked both the strength and experience to bring things within the necessary bounds, Mama was counting very heavily on our European trip. She was planning to invite Fyodor Mikhailovich to move into her house in the autumn after our return from abroad. We would have a good apartment free of charge. In view of the distance, moreover, the relatives wouldn't be paying their daily visits to us. Neither would Paul care to live "in the wilderness," as he contemptuously called our neighborhood, and he would stay, naturally, with Emilya Fyodorovna. In that way our separation from him would not have the appearance of a family quarrel and would occur by his own wish.

When she learned that the trip was off and that the prospect of spending the summer in the same house with the Dostoevskys lay ahead of me, my mother took fright. She knew my independent nature and youthful intransigence, and feared that I wouldn't be able to keep control of myself, and that a family disaster would be the result.

Right then and there she approved my plan of pawning all my possessions, to my great joy. And when I asked her whether she didn't feel badly about the dowry she had given me, she replied, "Of course I do, but what else is to be done when your happiness is at stake? You and Fyodor Mikhailovich are so different from each other that if you don't become close now, as married people should, then you never will. But you must leave as soon as possible, before the holidays, before new complications come up."

"But will we have time to pawn our things and get the money before the holidays?" I asked.

Fortunately, my mother knew one of the directors of the "Heavy Properties" Company and she promised me to go to see him at once and have him send an appraiser to us tomorrow. The lease on our apartment was up on May 1, and the furniture could be taken to the warehouse after Easter. My mother undertook to hand over to Fyodor Mikhailovich's relatives the money received from the pawn, in accordance with the amount he would set for each. And as for our gold and silver things, our bonds and fur coats, there would be time enough to pawn them before our departure.

Joyously I returned home and arrived before Fyodor Mikhailovich was up. Paul, who was very curious to know where I had been all morning, came immediately into the dining room where I was preparing coffee for my husband, and started taunting me, as was his habit.

"I am pleased to see that you are so devout, Anna Grigoryevna," he began, "that you stay not only for the morning service but also for midday, as I found out from Fedosya."

"Yes, I was in church," I answered.

"But why are you so pensive today? May I inquire in which European spas your burning imagination is dwelling?"

"But you know that we are not going abroad."

"What did I tell you? Now you have learned by experience that I know how to get my way, and I don't allow any European trips!"

"Oh, I know, I know! Why even talk about it?" I answered, not wishing to start a quarrel, although in my heart I was outraged by his insolence.

Ahead of me was the great task of persuading Fyodor Mikhailovich to agree to the plan I had contrived. To talk to him at home was impossible. Someone might interfere at any moment, and moreover Paul was at home, stubbornly waiting for the arrival of the young Dostoevskys, our regular morning visitors. Luckily my husband had to go out on some errand. I volunteered to accompany him to the nearest apothecary. As we left the house I suggested to him that we stop in to the chapel of the Church of the Ascension. Together we prayed before the ikon of the Virgin and then walked along Voznesensky Prospect and the Moika embankment. I was highly agitated and didn't know how to begin.

He helped me. Seeing my excitement, he said, "How happy I am, Anya, that you're taking it so well—the cancellation of our trip that we've both been dreaming about!"

"But it can still take place if you agree to the plan I'm proposing to you," I answered, and began explaining it right away. As I might have predicted, he instantly rejected my plan because he did not want me to sacrifice my possessions. We began to argue and, not noticing where we were going, we wandered (still walking along the Moika embankment) into a quite deserted part of the city where I had never been before.

For the second time in our married life I confessed to my husband that it was very hard for me to live this way, and I begged him to let me have at least two or three months of calm and happy life. I assured him that under present conditions we not only would never become friends, as we used to dream, but would perhaps separate forever. I implored him to save our love, our happiness; losing control of myself, I burst into such violent sobbing that poor Fyodor Mikhailovich was quite nonplused and didn't know what to do with me.

He hastily agreed to everything. I was so happy that I kissed him hard, ignoring the passersby, of whom there were few in that locality. Right then and there, without losing any further time, I suggested that we go straight to the Governor-general's office to find out when we could get our foreign passport. There were always complications for my husband in regard to that passport. As a former political criminal he remained under police surveillance, and in addition to the usual formalities he had to obtain preliminary permission from the military Governor-general.

In the office a clerk my husband knew, a great admirer of his work, suggested that he write out his application on the spot, and promised to make a report of it to his superior the very next day. He promised also that the passport would be ready by Friday.

I remember how boundlessly happy I was that day. Even Paul's ridiculous badgering didn't upset me. I knew there would soon be an end to it. That day we said nothing about our departure to anyone but my mother, who came in the evening and took away with her our gold trinkets, the silver and the bonds, in order to pawn them on the following day.

The day after that, a Wednesday, the company appraiser came and estimated the sum we would receive for our furniture. That same evening, when almost the entire family was at our house for dinner, Fyodor Mikhailovich announced that we were leaving for abroad the day after tomorrow.

"Permit me, *papá,* to make an observation," Paul began immediately, taken aback by the news.

"No observations!" Fyodor Mikhailovich exploded. "All of you will receive the amount you have stipulated and not one kopeck more."

"But that's impossible! I forgot to tell you that my summer coat is completely out of style and I must have a new one, and there are other expenses. . . ."

"You will receive nothing except what was stipulated. We are going to Europe on Anna Grigoryevna's money, and I have no right to dispose of it."

Paul tried two or three times to put demands forward, but Fyodor Mikhailovich refused even to listen to him.

After dinner the family filed into my husband's study, one after the other. There he gave each one a part of the sum due in cash, and the rest in IOU's due on May 1, which my mother was to pay out of the money received from the pawning of our possessions.

I persuaded Fyodor Mikhailovich to give Paul the money for a summer coat, so that he wouldn't put obstacles in our way. This sacrifice did not propitiate him, and at parting he told me that my treacherous act would not go unrequited, and that in the autumn he would "measure swords with me and we will see whose side the victory will be on."

I was so happy that I paid no attention to the barbs aimed at me from all directions.

We packed quickly. Believing that we were going for a short time, we took along only the indispensables and left the pawning of our furniture and the safekeeping of the rest of our household possessions to my mother. Paul thrust his assistance on her, but he hindered more than he helped. He took Fyodor Mikhailovich's books and part of his study furniture to his own quarters, saying that he wanted to complete his education by reading.

We left for three months and returned to Russia more than four years later. During this time many joyous events occurred in our lives, and I shall be eternally grateful to God for giving me strength in my decision to go abroad. There a new, happy life began for Fyodor Mikhailovich and me which strengthened our mutual friendship and love and continued up to the day of his death.

CHAPTER FOUR

Living Abroad

The eighteenth of April. A light rain, but the kind that promises to last all day. The windows of Berlin are open. Beneath the window of our room a linden tree has come into leaf. Although it was still raining, we decided to go out to have a look at the city. We went over to Unter den Linden, saw the Schloss, the Bauakademie, the Zeughaus, the Opernhaus, the university, and Ludwigskirche.

My dear Fedya remarked that I was dressed as if for winter (in my white beaver hat) and that my gloves were shabby. I was very much offended and replied that if he considered me so badly dressed it would be better for us not to walk together. Then I turned on my heel and began walking quickly in the opposite direction.

Fedya called to me a couple of times and made as if to run after me, but then reconsidered and continued on his way. I was extremely hurt; his remark seemed horribly indelicate to me. Almost at a run, I crossed several streets and found myself at the Brandenburg Gate. It was still raining. The Germans were looking at me in surprise: a girl without an umbrella, walking in the rain and paying no attention to it.

But I calmed down little by little, and then I realized that Fedya had not had the slightest intention of offending me with his remark and that I was all worked up over nothing. My quarrel with Fedya worried me very much, and I began imagining goodness knows what. I decided to go home right away, thinking that he had returned and that I could make up with him.

But what was my chagrin to learn on arriving at our hotel that Fedya had already been there, remained a few minutes in the room, and then gone out again! My Lord, what I went through! I imagined that he had stopped loving me and, convinced that I was such a spoiled and unstable person, had found it all too much and thrown himself into the Spree.

Then I imagined that he had gone to our Embassy in order to get a divorce, have a separate passport made out for me, and pack me off to Russia again. This conviction grew even more persistent when I noticed that he had unlocked the suitcase (it wasn't in the same place as before, and the straps were undone). It was obvious that Fedya had taken our documents and gone to the Embassy.

All these miserable thoughts tormented me so that I began to weep bitterly, upbraiding myself for capriciousness and a foolish heart. I vowed to myself that if Fyodor Mikhailovich should leave me I wouldn't return to Russia for anything, but would hide myself in some little European village where I would bemoan my loss forever after.

In this manner two hours went by. Every minute I jumped up from my chair and went over to the window to see whether Fedya was coming. And just at the point when my despair had reached its final limit, I looked out of the window and caught sight of him walking down the street with both hands thrust into the pockets of his coat, and with the most independent air.

I was overjoyed. When he came into the room I threw myself on his neck, weeping and sobbing. He was quite alarmed when he saw my tear-reddened eyes and asked what had happened to me. When I described my fears to him he was very much amused and said, "A person would have to have a very low opinion of himself to drown himself in the Spree—such a little trickle of a river."

And he was also amused at my idea about the divorce, and told me that I evidently still didn't know how much he loved his "darling little wife." And that the reason he had stopped at the hotel and opened up the suitcase was to take out some money to order a coat. And so the air was cleared, we made peace, and I was terribly happy.[1]

After spending two days in Berlin we moved to Dresden. Since Fyodor Mikhailovich had difficult literary work ahead of him, we decided to remain there at least a month. My husband was very fond of Dresden, chiefly because of its famous art gallery and the lovely parks surrounding the city. He invariably stopped there in the course of his travels. Since the city contains many museums and cultural treasures, Fyodor Mikhailovich, knowing my eagerness to learn, thought I would find these interesting and would not be homesick for Russia—something he feared very much at first.

We stopped in Neumarkt at one of the best hotels of that day, the Stadt Berlin. After changing our clothes, we set out immediately for the art gallery he wanted to show me before all the rest of the city's treasures. He assured me that he remembered the shortcut to Zwinger perfectly, but we immediately lost our way in the narrow streets. Then that episode occurred which he quotes in one of his letters to me[2] as an example of the heaviness and stolidity of the German mind.

"If you please, *gnädiger Herr,* where is the picture gallery?"

"The picture gallery?"

"Yes, the picture gallery."

"The Royal Picture Gallery?"

"Yes, the Royal Picture Gallery."

"I don't know."

We were amazed that he kept questioning us when he didn't know where the gallery was in any case. We soon found it, however, and decided to go in even though only an hour was left to closing time. My husband went past all the rooms and took me straight to the Sistine Madonna—the painting he considered the highest manifestation of human genius. On later occasions I saw him standing for hours at a time in front of this strikingly beautiful work, deeply touched and moved.[3] I must say that I was stunned by my first impression of the Sistine Madonna: it seemed to me that the Virgin with the Infant in her arms was floating in the air toward the passersby. (I experienced a similar sensation on a later occasion when, during the vespers service on October 1, I entered the brilliantly lit Cathedral of Saint Vladimir in Kiev and viewed the painter Vasnyetsov's work of genius. That same impression of the Virgin as coming toward me with a gentle smile of good will on Her divine countenance moved me and touched my heart.)

We rented an apartment on Johannesstrasse that very day. It consisted of three rooms: a living room, study and bedroom, and our landlady was a recently widowed Frenchwoman. The next day we went to buy me a hat to replace my Petersburg hat. My husband made me try on at least ten of them before deciding on one which, he said, was "amazingly becoming." I remember it as if it were today—it was a white Italian straw with roses and with long black velvet ribbons hanging down to my shoulders, called, in the mode of that time, *suivez-moi.*

Then for two or three days the two of us went to buy me some summer outerwear, and I marveled at the fact that Fyodor Mikhailovich did not grow bored with choosing and examining fabrics from the point of view of the durability, pattern and cut of the article we were buying. Everything he chose for me was of good quality, simple and elegant, and after that I had complete confidence in his taste.

Once we had settled in, a time of serene happiness came for me. We had no financial cares (these were not anticipated until autumn), there were no persons standing between my husband and myself, I had the full opportunity to revel in his company. My memories of that marvelous time remain vivid in my heart in spite of all the decades which have passed since then.

Fyodor Mikhailovich loved order in everything, including the allocation of his time. Therefore we soon worked out a daily routine permitting each of us to utilize our time as we wished. Since my husband liked to work at night he would not get up before eleven. I would take breakfast with him and then set straight out to have a look at some *Sammlung,* after which my youthful curiosity would be completely satisfied. As I recall, I did not miss a single one of those numberless *Sammlungen:* I inspected with utter conscientiousness the mineralogical, geological, botanical, and other collections. But by two o'clock I would invariably be in the art gallery (located in that same Zwinger as all the science collections). I knew that my husband would be coming to the gallery at about this time and that we would go to admire his favorite paintings, which naturally also became my favorites.

Fyodor Mikhailovich prized the works of Raphael more highly than anything else in painting and considered the Sistine Madonna his greatest work. He deeply admired the genius of Titian, particularly his famous painting *The Tribute Money,* and would stand for a long time without taking his eyes off that masterly depiction of the Saviour.[4] The other works of art which gave him intense pleasure, and which he always went to every time he visited the gallery, bypassing the other treasures, were Murillo's *Maria with the Child,* Correggio's *Holy Night,* Annibale Carracci's *Christ,* Pompeo Batoni's *Magdalene Repentant,* Ruisdael's *The Hunt,* Claude Lorraine's *Coastal Landscape: Morning and Evening* (my husband used to call these landscapes "The Golden Age" and speaks of them in his *Diary of a Writer*),[5] Rembrandt von Rijn's *Rembrandt and His Wife,* and Van Dyke's *King Charles I of England.* Of the water colors and pastels he highly prized Jean Liotard's *The Chocolate Seller.*

At three o'clock the gallery would close and we used to go to the nearest restaurant to dine. That was the so-called Italienisches Dörfchen ("Italian Village"), whose covered portico hung directly over the river. The restaurant's enormous windows opened out on a view of both sides of the Elbe, and in fine weather it was extremely pleasant to dine there and watch all the river activity. Eating there was relatively cheap and quite good, and every day Fyodor Mikhailovich would order his portion of *blauer Aal,* which he was very fond of and knew could be had here fresh-caught. He loved to drink the white Rhine wine which at that time cost ten groschen a half-bottle. The restaurant subscribed to many foreign newspapers, and he used to read the French ones.

After resting at home we would go out at six for a walk in the Grossengarten. Fyodor Mikhailovich loved this vast park, chiefly for its charming lawns in the English style and for its lush vegetation. It was at least six or seven versts from our house to the park and back and my husband, who loved walking, placed great value on this walk and used to take it even in rainy weather, saying that it had a beneficial effect on us.

In those days there was a restaurant in the park, Zur grossen Wirtschaft, where a military brass band or sometimes an instrumental group used to play. Sometimes there was a serious concert program. Although he was no connoisseur, Fyodor Mikhailovich was very fond of the musical works of Mozart, Beethoven's *Fidelio,* Mendelssohn-Bartholdy's *Wedding March,* and Rossini's *Air du Stabat Mater,* and felt genuine pleasure when he listened to these favorites of his. He did not at all care for the works of Richard Wagner.[6]

During these walks my husband would usually relax from all literary and similar preoccupations and was always in the most genial of moods, laughing and joking. One of the numbers in the concert program, I remember, was the "Variations and Potpourri" from Franz von Suppé's opera *The Poet and the Peasant.* Fyodor Mikhailovich came to love these variations because of a special circumstance. Once during a stroll in the Grossengarten we fell to squabbling over a difference in views, and I expressed my opinion quite sharply. Fyodor Mikhailovich broke off our conversation, and we walked to the restaurant in silence. I was vexed at having spoiled his affable mood, and in an effort to bring it back I said to him, when the "Potpourri" from von Suppé's opera was struck up, that it had been "written about us"—that he was the poet and I was the peasant—and I started quietly humming the peasant's part. This notion took his fancy, and he began to hum the poet's aria. In this fashion, von Suppé reconciled us.

From that time on we fell into the habit of softly humming along with the music during the duet of the two heroes. My husband would sing the poet's part and I the peasant's. This was inconspicuous because we always sat a distance away under "our" oak tree. There was much laughter and hilarity, and my husband would declare that with me he had grown younger by as many years as the difference in our ages.

Little incidents occurred also. Once a twig fell from "our oak" into Fyodor Mikhailovich's big mug of beer, and together with the twig a large black beetle. My husband was squeamish and didn't want to drink from the mug, so he gave it back to the waiter and asked him to bring another. After the waiter had left, Fyodor Mikhailovich was sorry he hadn't thought to ask for a clean mug first, for now in all likelihood the waiter would simply fish out the beetle and then bring back the same mug of beer.

When the waiter appeared again, Fyodor Mikhailovich asked him, "Well then, did you empty that mug?"

"What do you mean, empty it? I drank it up!" he answered, and one could rest assured from his satisfied look that he had not let the opportunity slip to get an extra drink of beer.

These daily walks recalled and replaced those marvelous evenings during our courtship—so much merriment, frankness and openheartedness did they hold.

At nine-thirty we would come home and drink tea, and then Fyodor Mikhailovich would sit down to read the works of Herzen, which he had just bought, while I would settle down with my diary. I kept it in shorthand during the first year and a half or two of our married life, with brief interruptions during illness.[7]

I had thought up the idea of keeping a diary for several reasons. Amid the welter of new impressions, I was afraid of forgetting details; moreover, the daily practice was a reliable way of keeping up my shorthand and perhaps even improving it. But the main reason was a different one. My husband was such an interesting and enigmatic person to me that I felt it would be easier to get to know and unriddle him if I wrote down his ideas and observations. On top of that, I was quite alone abroad; there was no one for me to share my observations with, let alone the doubts that sometimes arose, and my diary was a friend to whom I confided all my thoughts, hopes and fears.

My diary interested my husband very much, and he would often say to me, "I'd give a lot, Anechka, to find out what it is you're writing in those little squiggles of yours—you're saying bad things about me, no doubt?"

"That's as it may be. I both praise you and find fault with you," I would answer. "You get what you deserve. And anyway, why shouldn't I scold you—who wouldn't do it in my place?" I would finish with the same facetious questions he sometimes addressed to me when he wanted to chide me.

One of the causes of our ideological differences was the so-called "woman question." Since I belonged in age to the generation of the sixties, I would stand up firmly for women's rights and independence, and was indignant with my husband for what I considered his unfair attitude toward these. I was even ready to regard his attitude as a personal insult and sometimes expressed this feeling to my husband.

I remember that once, seeing me upset, he asked me, "Anechka, what's wrong with you? Have I offended you in some way?"

"Yes, you have. We were talking about Nihilist women and you said such awful things about them."

"But you're no Nihilist, after all, so why were you offended?"

"No, I'm not a Nihilist, it's true, but I am a woman, and I don't like to hear a woman being disparaged."

"What kind of a woman are you?"

"What do you mean by that—what kind of a woman am I?"

"You're my charming, wonderful Anechka, and there's no other in the world like her, that's who you are—not 'a woman'!"

Because of my youth I was ready to reject his excessive praise and to be angry that he didn't consider me a woman, as I considered myself.

I must say in this connection that Fyodor Mikhailovich really did not like the Nihilist women of that period. Their denial of any femininity, their slovenliness, their coarse, affected tone aroused his revulsion, and it was precisely the opposite qualities he valued in me. Later, in the seventies, he held an entirely different attitude toward this matter, when from their number evolved many intelligent, well-educated women who viewed life with seriousness. It was then that my husband stated in *Diary of a Writer* that he had great expectations of Russian women.[8]

One of the things that annoyed me in my husband's arguments with me was his denial of any firmness of character in the women of my generation, of any persistent, sustained striving toward the attainment of a stated goal. He once said to me, for example, "Take such a simple thing as—what shall I say? Say, even collecting stamps. . . ." (Just at that moment, we were passing a shop in whose window an entire stamp collection was displayed.) ". . . If a man takes this up systematically he collects, he saves, and even if he doesn't give too much time to it, and even if he loses interest in it, he still doesn't drop it, he keeps the collection for a long time, perhaps even to the end of his life, as a reminder of the interests of his youth. But a woman? She'll burn with the desire to collect stamps, she'll buy an expensive stamp album, she'll pester all her relatives and friends and wheedle stamps out of them and spend piles of money buying them. And then the desire will cool off, the sumptuous album will lie around on all the bookstands, and in the end it will be thrown away as an outworn and useless object. That's the way it is in everything, in serious things and trivial things alike. Very little strength of character. In the beginning, a burning desire; but never a persevering, stubborn effort to achieve solid results toward a set goal."

This argument for some reason provoked me, and I announced to my husband that I was going to prove by my personal example that a woman is capable of pursuing for years an idea which has attracted her.

"And since at this moment I don't foresee any important task ahead of me," I said, "I'll begin with the trivial one you've just mentioned. From today on, I shall collect stamps."

No sooner said than done. I dragged Fyodor Mikhailovich into the first stationery store we came across and bought—with my own money—a cheap stamp album. At home, I pasted in the stamps from three or four letters we had just received from Russia, and laid the foundation of the collection with it. When our landlady learned of my intention she rummaged through her own letters and gave me several old stamps of Thurn-und-Taxis and the kingdom of Saxony. And so began my stamp collecting, which has been going on for forty-nine years. I never made any special effort to collect the stamps, of course—I simply amassed them. At the present time I have [. . .]*pieces, some of which are rarities. I can give my word that not a single one of my stamps was purchased for money. They either came from letters or were given to me. My intimates know this weakness of mine. My daughter, for instance, sends me letters with stamps of different denominations. From time to time I used to boast to my husband about the quantity of stamps I had accumulated, and he would sometimes tease me about my foible.

*A gap in the manuscript.

During those weeks in Dresden an episode took place which confronted me once again with an unpleasant trait in Fyodor Mikhailovich's character. That was his quite groundless jealousy.

What happened was that my old stenography professor, P. M. Olkhin, on learning that we would be living in Dresden for some time, had given me a letter of introduction to Professor Zeibig, vice-president of the group of stenographers who followed the Gabelsberger System—the shorthand method I had studied. Olkhin had written me that Zeibig was a fine person and that he might be useful to us in visiting art galleries and so forth.

I didn't call on Zeibig for a long while after our arrival. But since it would have been awkward not to give him Olkhin's letter, I decided, finally, to pay him a visit. I did not find him at home and left my letter. The very next day the professor returned my visit, found us both at home, and invited us to attend the next meeting of the group, which was just about to take place.

We accepted the invitation, but then my husband decided that I should go along with Zeibig without him, assuring me that such a specialized assembly would be boring for him. And so we did it that way. The stenographers' meeting was being held at the Hotel [. . .]*on Wildrüferstrasse. The session had already begun, and a report was being read by some elderly gentleman. Although Zeibig invited me to sit next to him, I sat off to one side and was bored stiff for the next half hour.

During the intermission, the professor brought me up to meet the president and announced to all present that I had come from Russia with a letter from a specialist in their field. The president extended greetings to me, and I was so embarrassed that I didn't say a word in answer but merely bowed. There were no more reports. All the members of the group sat at a long table, drank beer, and chatted. One after the other they began coming up to me to be introduced, and I grew so brave that I began chattering away as though I were at home.

*A gap in the manuscript.

I spoke in German, making mistakes of course, but very glibly, and soon I had "recruited into the ranks of my admirers" (as my husband later chided me) all the members of the circle, young and old. All drank to my health and offered me berries and pastries.

By the time Professor Zeibig offered to take me home at nine o'clock, I even managed to make a little speech in German in which I thanked them for their cordial reception and invited them to come to Petersburg, assuring them that the followers of the Gabelsberger System would be received just as warmly by the Russians as they had received me. In a word, I was jubilant over my triumph, all the more because I read the following news story the next day in the *Dresdener Nachrichten:* [. . .][9]

But Fyodor Mikhailovich reacted differently toward my "triumph." While I was recounting to him all the details of my reception I noticed an expression of hostility on his face, and he was very downcast for the rest of the evening. And when, two or three days later, we met one of the members of the circle while we were out for a walk—a young man as plump and rosy as a piglet, with whom we exchanged greetings—Fyodor Mikhailovich made a scene.

After that I no longer felt like taking part in those social outings to the city outskirts that Zeibig kept inviting us to. This new outbreak in Fyodor Mikhailovich of a disturbing and hurtful character trait forced me to be more careful, so as to avoid any such complications in future.

During our stay in Dresden an event occurred which deeply disturbed us both. Fyodor Mikhailovich found out from someone that rumors were circulating through the city that our Emperor had been shot while attending the World's Fair in Paris (the Berezowski attempt), and that the villainous deed had succeeded.[10] One can imagine how stricken my husband was. He was a warm admirer of Emperor Alexander II because of his emancipation of the serfs as well as for his later reforms. Besides that, he considered the Emperor his benefactor, for it was on the occasion of his coronation that my husband's status of hereditary nobleman, which he so treasured, was restored to him. And it was the Emperor who granted permission for my husband to return to Petersburg from Siberia, thereby making it possible for him to engage once again in the literary work so dear to his heart.[11]

We resolved to go to our Consulate at once. Fyodor Mikhailovich "looked like death," as they say. He was highly upset and almost ran the whole way, and I feared that there would be an immediate epileptic attack (which did indeed occur that very night).

To our great joy, our fears turned out to have been exaggerated. At the Consulate, they comforted us with the news that the villainy had failed. We immediately asked permission to register our names in the list of visitors to the Consulate, in order to express our indignation at this odious attempt.

My husband was very distressed and sad all that day. This new assault, following so swiftly after the Karakozov attempt,[12] clearly demonstrated to him that the network of political conspiracy had penetrated deep, and that danger threatened the life of the Emperor for whom he felt such deep esteem.

We had been living in Dresden for about three weeks when my husband first brought up the subject of roulette (he and I often reminisced about the way we wrote *The Gambler* together). He said that he would certainly go to play a game or two if he were alone in Dresden. He returned to this idea a few times after that and then I, who did not wish to stand in his way in anything, asked why he couldn't go now?

He pleaded the impossibility of leaving me alone but said that it would be too expensive for both of us to go. But I began urging him to go to Homburg for a few days, assuring him that nothing would happen to me in his absence. He offered a few demurrers, but since he himself was really very anxious to try his luck, he finally agreed and went off to Homburg, leaving me in the care of our landlady.

I tried to put on a cheerful face, but when the train pulled away I felt so alone that I couldn't hold back my misery and burst into tears. After a few days I began receiving letters from Homburg in which my husband told me about his losses and asked me to send him money. I did so, but as it turned out he lost that money as well and asked me to send more, which I of course did. But since these gambling passions were an unknown quantity to me, I exaggerated their effect on my husband's health. I imagined from his letters that he was feeling upset and distressed in Homburg. I feared a new epileptic attack and was in despair at having let him go by himself, and asked myself why I wasn't with him so that I could comfort and console him. I felt myself to be a terrible egotist, practically a criminal, for not being in a position to give him any help during these trying times.

Eight days later Fyodor Mikhailovich returned to Dresden,[13] terribly glad and happy that I not only didn't reproach him and complain about the lost money, but even consoled him and begged him not to feel too unhappy over it.

The unfortunate trip to Homburg had a bad effect on his frame of mind. He returned often to the subject of roulette, expressed regret over the wasted money, and blamed himself alone for losing. He told me that often the lucky chances were actually in his hands but he hadn't been able to hold on to them. He was too impatient—he changed his bets and tried out different systems, and as a result he lost. It had happened because he was in too much of a hurry, because he had come to Homburg alone and was constantly worried about me. And also, his previous visits to the tables had always been for no more than two or three days and always with paltry sums of money, so that it was hard to hold out through an unfavorable turn of the wheel.

But if he could only manage to go to a roulette town and stay there for two or three weeks with a certain sum of money in reserve, then he would surely be successful. Without any necessity to hurry, he would apply that temperate system of playing in which it is impossible not to win—if not an enormous sum, then at least enough to cover your losses.

He spoke so persuasively, cited so many examples in proof of his theory, that he convinced me, too; and when the question came up of whether we should stop in Baden-Baden for a week or so on our way to Switzerland, I willingly agreed, counting on the fact that my presence during his play would provide a certain restraining influence. And for my part it was all the same to me where we lived, as long as I didn't have to part with my husband.

When at last we decided to go to Baden-Baden for two weeks

after the money arrived, Fyodor Mikhailovich calmed down and began to rewrite and finish the work he was having so much trouble with. This was an article on Belinsky in which my husband wanted to express everything in his heart on the subject of that famous critic.

Belinsky was a man dear to Fyodor Mikhailovich, who had a high regard for his ability even before meeting him personally and wrote about this in an issue of *Diary of a Writer* in 1877. Nonetheless, despite his high estimate of Belinsky's critical acumen, and sincerely grateful as he was for Belinsky's encouragement of his literary gift, still he could not forgive Belinsky's mocking and almost blasphemous attitude toward Fyodor Mikhailovich's religious views and beliefs.[14]

It is possible that many of the unhappy feelings Fyodor Mikhailovich retained from his contacts with Belinsky were a result of the gossip and innuendoes of those "friends" who, at first, acknowledged Dostoevsky's talent and praised it to all and sundry, but later, for reasons not altogether comprehensible to me, began to persecute the modest author of *Poor People*, to invent fables about him, to compose epigrams, and to try his patience in every possible way.[15]

When it was proposed to Fyodor Mikhailovich that he write an article on Belinsky, he undertook this interesting theme with pleasure. He planned to express, not superficially but in a serious article on the subject, his most basic and sincere opinion of this writer who in the beginning was so dear to him, and in the end treated him with such hostility.

It became evident that there was much in Fyodor Mikhailovich's thinking that had not yet ripened; many things needed to be thought through and resolved, many doubts remained. So that the article had to be rewritten at least five times, and in the end Fyodor Mikhailovich was dissatisfied with it.

In a letter to Maikov dated September 15, 1867, he wrote:

> . . . The thing is that I'm finally done with that confounded article, "My Acquaintance with Belinsky." There was no way of delaying it or putting it aside. Actually, I worked it out last summer but it gave me so much trouble and was so hard for me to write that I've been drag-

ging it out up to this moment; and at last, gritting my teeth, I've finished it. The joke was in taking on an article of that sort, like a fool. The moment I came to grips with writing it, I realized that there was no possible way of doing it from the *censorship* point of view (since I wanted to put down the whole story). A hundred and fifty pages of a novel would have been easier to do than those thirty-two pages! And the final result of all this was that I rewrote this triple-damned article —taking everything together—*five times* at least; and then crossed it all out and put it all together again. And finally, I have produced an article, somehow—but such a rotten one that it makes me sick. How much valuable material I was forced to throw out! As I ought to have known, what was left was the most worthless "golden mean." Crap!

This article suffered a deplorable fate. Fyodor Mikhailovich had been asked to do it for a volume of collected articles by the writer K. I. Babikov, who paid him an advance of two hundred rubles for it. The article was to be finished by autumn and forwarded to the Hotel Rome in Moscow. Fearing that Babikov might have moved to other quarters, Fyodor Mikhailovich asked Maikov to do him a favor and send the manscript to the Moscow bookseller I. G. Solovyov to hand over to Babikov. Maikov carried out my husband's instructions, as he later informed us in a letter of November 3, 1867.

Living abroad, we did not know whether or not the article had appeared in print. Not until 1872 did Fyodor Mikhailovich receive a request from some bookseller to let him have the article commissioned by Babikov. This man informed us that Babikov had died and that the volume had never come into being.[16]

My husband was very perturbed over the loss of the article, particularly since he had expended much labor on it—and even though he was not satisfied with it, it did have value for him. We began making inquiries as to where it could have disappeared —we even asked the Moscow bookseller to help us in this—but the result of our quest was disappointing. The article had vanished into thin air. I still feel sorry about it because, judging by my impression of it at that time and by the comments in my stenographic notebook, it was a brilliant and extremely interesting article.[17]

At the end of June we received the money from the editor of the *Russian Messenger* and began at once getting ready to leave. It was with genuine regret that I left Dresden, where my life had been so good and so happy, and I had a cloudy presentiment that our new circumstances would bring with them a good deal of change in our feelings. My forebodings were justified. As I recall the five weeks we spent in Baden-Baden and read again what I wrote in my shorthand diary, I come to the conclusion that it was all some kind of nightmare which took complete possession of my husband and would not release him from its heavy shackles.

All of Fyodor Mikhailovich's rationalizations about the possibility of winning at roulette by using his gambling system were entirely correct. His success might have been complete—but only on condition that this system was applied by some coolheaded Englishman or German and not by such a nervous and impulsive person as my husband, who went to the outermost limits in everything. In addition to coolheadedness and perseverance, moreover, the roulette player must have substantial means in order to be able to hold out through unfavorable turns of the wheel. And this was exactly what Fyodor Mikhailovich was lacking. We had little money, relatively speaking, and we had absolutely no way of getting any more from anywhere in case of bad luck.

And so not a week had passed when Fyodor Mikhailovich lost everything he had on hand. And then began the anxiety as to where to get more money to go on gambling. We had to resort to the pawnshop. But even after pawning things he could not hold himself in check, and would sometimes lose all the money he had only just received for an item he had pawned.

There were times when he was almost down to his last thaler, when suddenly luck would be on his side again, and he would bring home several dozen gold Friedrichsdor. I remember that once he brought home a tightly stuffed purse in which I counted two hundred and twelve Friedrichsdor (each worth twenty thalers)—in other words, about four thousand three hundred thalers.

But this money did not remain in our hands for very long.

Fyodor Mikhailovich could not hold out. Even before calming down after the excitement of the play, he took twenty coins and lost them, then came home for another twenty and lost those. And so in the course of two or three hours, coming home for money a few times, he lost it all in the end. Then to the pawnshop again. But since our valuables were few, this source of funds was quickly exhausted.

And meanwhile our debts were growing and were making themselves felt. We were forced to run up a bill with our landlady, an aggressive woman who, seeing us in difficulties, didn't hesitate to treat us slightingly and deprive us of various comforts which were ours by virtue of our arrangement with her.

We wrote letters to my mother and impatiently waited for funds to come in. These would be put into play that very day or the next. And we, after paying off only a small part of our pressing debts (for the apartment, for meals and so forth), were penniless once again and trying to think what to do—how we could get a substantial sum together and, forgetting any thought of winning, get out of this hell once and for all.

As for myself, let me say that it was with great coolness that I received these blows of fate which we had brought voluntarily on ourselves. After a certain period following our initial losses and upsets, I formed the firm conviction that Fyodor Mikhailovich could never win. That is, even if he did win, and win a considerable sum, this sum would be gambled away that same day or no later than the next; and none of my prayers, entreaties, or efforts to persuade him to stay away from the gaming tables, to stop gambling, would have any effect on him.

It seemed strange to me at first. How was it that Fyodor Mikhailovich, who had so courageously endured so many and such diverse sufferings in his life—imprisonment, the scaffold, banishment, the death of his beloved brother, of his wife—how was it that he did not have enough will power to keep himself in check, to stay inside a definite limit of losses, not to risk his last thaler? This seemed to me even rather degrading, unworthy of his lofty character! And I found it painful and wounding to acknowledge this weakness in my dear husband.

But I soon understood that this was not a simple weakness of will but an all-consuming passion, an elemental force against which even a strong character could not struggle. One had to come to terms with it, to look at his gambling passion as a disease for which there was no cure. The only means of struggle was flight. But we could not flee Baden before receiving a considerable sum of money from Russia.

In fairness to myself, I never reproached my husband for his losses and I never quarreled with him over them (he prized this aspect of my character).[18] I handed over the last of our money to him without a murmur even though I knew that my things would certainly be lost if they were not redeemed in time* (which did indeed happen), and even though I had to suffer the unpleasantness of our landlady and our petty creditors.

But it wounded me to the depths of my soul to see how Fyodor Mikhailovich was suffering. He would come back from the roulette tables (he never took me with him, considering a young, respectable woman out of place in a gambling hall) white, exhausted, barely able to stand on his feet. He would ask me for money (he had handed over all our funds to me), go away and come back again for more within a half hour, even more distraught. And this would go on until he had lost every penny we had.

When there was nothing to go to the roulette hall with, and nowhere to get money from, Fyodor Mikhailovich would be so crushed that he would start sobbing, fall on his knees before me and beg my forgiveness for torturing me with his behavior. He would fall into utter despair. And it cost me much effort, much convincing and exhortation to comfort him, to picture our position as not so hopeless, to think of ways out of it, to direct his attention and his thoughts elsewhere.

And how satisfied and happy I was when I managed to accomplish this! I would go with him to the reading room to have a look at the newspapers, or take him on a long walk, which always had a beneficial effect on him. During the long intervals between remittances the two of us tramped around the outskirts of Baden for many dozens of versts. Then his kindly,

*In gambling towns, pledges are accepted not for months, but for weeks or days. If not redeemed in time the item is lost, since the voucher states that it has been sold. (A.G.D.)

good-humored frame of mind would be restored, and we would talk about the most varied things for hours on end.

Our favorite walk was to Neues Schloss and from there by the lovely wooded paths to Altes Schloss, where we always drank milk or coffee. We would walk also to the distant Schloss Ehrenbreitstein, about eight versts from Baden, where we would dine and return home when the sun was already setting. These walks were so good and our talks so interesting that, despite our lack of funds and the aggravations with our landlady, I was ready to wish that the remittance from Petersburg would be longer in coming. But the money would come, and then this so pleasant life of ours would turn once again into some kind of nightmare.

We had no friends at all in Baden. Once, while walking in the park, we met the writer Goncharov, to whom my husband introduced me. His appearance reminded me of a Petersburg official, and his conversation also seemed so commonplace to me that I was a bit disappointed in this acquaintance and didn't even want to believe that this was the author of *Oblomov,* a novel I greatly admired.[19]

Fyodor Mikhailovich also went to visit Turgenev, who was living in Baden-Baden at that time. My husband came back from there in an extremely irritated state and told me in detail about his talk with Turgenev.[20]

With our departure from Baden-Baden the stormy period of our life abroad came to an end. Our good genie, the editor of the *Russian Messenger,* came to our aid as usual. But we had accumulated many debts and pawn pledges during the time of scarcity, and almost all the money we received from him went to pay these off. The thing that hurt the most was that I couldn't redeem my husband's wedding present—so precious to me—a diamond and ruby brooch and earrings. They were lost forever.

At first the two of us dreamed of going from Baden to Paris or making our way to Italy. But after figuring out what we had on hand, we decided to settle in Geneva for a while and counted on moving south after our circumstances had improved.

On the way to Geneva we stopped overnight in Basel, with the object of viewing a painting in the museum there which someone had told Fyodor Mikhailovich about. This painting, by

Hans Holbein, depicts Jesus Christ after his inhuman agony, after his body has been taken down from the Cross and begun to decay. His swollen face is covered with bloody wounds, and it is terrible to behold.

The painting had a crushing impact on Fyodor Mikhailovich. He stood before it as if stunned. And I did not have the strength to look at it—it was too painful for me, particularly in my sickly condition[21]—and I went into other rooms. When I came back after fifteen or twenty minutes, I found him still riveted to the same spot in front of the painting. His agitated face had a kind of dread in it, something I had noticed more than once during the first moments of an epileptic seizure.

Quietly I took my husband by the arm, led him into another room and sat him down on a bench, expecting the attack from one minute to the next. Luckily this did not happen. He calmed down little by little and left the museum, but insisted on returning once again to view this painting which had struck him so powerfully.[22]

On the very day of our arrival in Geneva we set out immediately to find a furnished room. We tried all the main streets and inspected many *chambres garnies* to no avail. Either the rooms were beyond our means, or there were too many people living in the apartment, which was awkward in my condition. Not until dusk did we locate a completely suitable apartment, on the corner of rue Guillaume Tell and rue Bertellier, on the second floor. It was rather spacious, and from its middle window we could see the bridge across the Rhone and the island of Jean-Jacques Rousseau. We liked our two spinster landladies as well—the Mlles. Raymondin. They welcomed us with such warmth and showed me so much kindness that we decided without hesitation to move in with them.

Our life in Geneva began with the scarcest means possible. Having paid our landladies for a month in advance, we had only eighteen francs left by the fourth day after our arrival, although we expected to receive fifty rubles. But we were already accustomed to getting along on small sums and, when these were exhausted, to live by pawning our things. So that our life, especially after our recent vicissitudes, seemed most pleasant to us at first.

Here also, as in Dresden, we established a daily routine. Fyodor Mikhailovich worked at night and so did not get up before eleven in the morning. After breakfasting with him I would go for a walk, as the doctor had prescribed for me, and he would work. At three we would go to a restaurant to dine. Then I would rest while my husband, after taking me home, would drop into the café on the rue du Mont Blanc, where Russian newspapers were available, and spend a couple of hours going through the *Voice*, the *Moscow Gazette* and the *Petersburg Gazette*. He would look at length through the foreign newspapers as well. In the evening at about seven we would go for a long walk during which, so that I wouldn't become overtired, we would stop often in front of the brightly lighted windows of the smart shops, and Fyodor Mikhailovich would point out the jewels he would give me if he were rich. To give him his due, my husband had an artist's taste, and the jewels he pointed out were lovely.

The evening would be spent either in dictating his new work or in reading French books. My husband saw to it that I read and studied systematically the work of one writer at a time, without allowing my attention to be distracted by other writers. He especially valued Balzac and George Sand,[23] and gradually I read all their work. During our walks we used to discuss my reading, and he would expound to me all the merits of the books I was going through. I was amazed at the fact that Fyodor Mikhailovich—who forgot what had happened only a short time ago—remembered graphically the plots and characters' names in the works of these two favorite writers of his. I recall that he particularly liked *Pere Goriot*, the first part of the epic *Les parents pauvres*. And he himself reread Victor Hugo's celebrated novel, *Les humiliés et les offensés*, during the winter of 1867–68.[24]

We knew almost no one in Geneva. Fyodor Mikhailovich always had great difficulty in making new acquaintances. And of his old ones, he met only N. P. Ogaryov, the well-known poet and friend of Herzen, at whose home they had met at one time. Ogaryov came to see us often, bringing books and newspapers, and would even sometimes lend us ten francs or so, which we would return to him as soon as we got some money. Fyodor

Mikhailovich had a high regard for many of the verses of this warm-hearted poet,[25] and we were always very glad when he visited us.

Ogaryov, then already a very old man, made special friends with me, showed me great warmth, and, to my surprise, treated me almost like a girl, which indeed I was then. But after about three months the visits of this good and kind man came to an end, to our deep regret. An accident happened to him on the way home to his villa in the suburbs. He had an epileptic attack, fell into a ditch, and broke his leg. The poor man lay there in the ditch until the next morning and caught a severe cold. His friends took him to Italy for treatment and in this way we lost our only friend in Geneva, with whom it had been so pleasant to meet and to talk.

The Peace Congress took place in Geneva at the beginning of September, 1867,[26] and Guiseppe Garibaldi came for the opening. His coming was considered extremely important, and the city organized a brilliant reception for him. We too went to the Rue du Mont Blanc, along which he was scheduled to drive from the railroad station. The houses were decorated lavishly with flags and greenery, and throngs of people had assembled along the way he was to come. Garibaldi, dressed in his original style, rode in his carriage standing up and waving his cap in response to the enraptured greetings of the crowd. We managed to get a glimpse of him from very close, and Fyodor Mikhailovich thought the Italian hero had a very sympathetic face and a kindly smile.

Since we were interested in the Peace Congress, we attended its second session and listened for a couple of hours to the speeches of the orators. These speeches left Fyodor Mikhailovich with a painful impression which he described in a letter to his niece, Sonya: "They began by saying that for the attainment of peace on earth it is necessary to destroy Christianity, annihilate the large states and divide them up into small ones. Down with all capital, so that everything will be held in common by edict. And so on. And all of this without a shred of evidence, all of it learned by heart twenty years ago, and so it has remained. And first and foremost is fire and sword; and after everything is destroyed—then, they think, we shall have peace."

Unfortunately, we soon came to regret choosing Geneva as our place of permanent residence. In the autumn the sharp winds set in, the so-called *bises,* and the weather would change two or three times a day. These changes had an oppressive effect on Fyodor Mikhailovich's nerves and his epileptic seizures grew much more frequent. This circumstance alarmed me very much, but Fyodor Mikhailovich was depressed chiefly by the fact that it was time to settle down to write, and these frequent attacks interfered with his work.

In the autumn of 1867 he was engaged in working out a plan for and writing his novel *The Idiot,* intended for the first issues of the *Russian Messenger* for 1868. The idea of the novel was "an old and cherished one—to depict a positively good man"; but this task seemed "immeasurable" to him. All of this irritated him intensely. And on top of it all was added, alas, an anxious but totally groundless concern that I might be bored, living alone with him in total isolation "on a desert island," as he wrote Maikov.

Try as I might to dissuade him, to assure him that I was completely happy and didn't need anything except to live with him and for him to love me, my reassurances had little effect, and he would worry about not having enough money to go to Paris and provide me with amusements like the theatre and the Louvre. My husband didn't know me very well then!

In a word, Fyodor Mikhailovich was in very low spirits. In order to distract him from his glum thoughts I suggested the idea of making a trip to Saxon les Bains to try his luck at roulette once more. (Saxon les Bains is about five hours away from Geneva. The roulette rooms existing at that time have long since been closed down.) Fyodor Mikhailovich approved of my suggestion and went to Saxon for a few days at the end of October or the beginning of November.

As I had expected, no financial advantage accrued from his gambling, but there was a different and beneficial result. The change of scene, the traveling, and the violent reactions he experienced radically altered his frame of mind. When he came back to Geneva he settled down to his interrupted work with fervor, and wrote about ninety-three pages for the January issue of the *Russian Messenger* within twenty-three days.

He was not satisfied with the part of *The Idiot* he had finished, and used to say that Part One was not a success. I should say in this connection that he was always extremely demanding with himself and rarely found anything to praise in his own work. He would at times be quite excited about the underlying ideas of the novels, he would love them and gestate them for a long time in his mind—but he was almost always—with very rare exceptions—dissatisfied with their actual realization in his work.

I remember that during the winter of 1867 he became extremely interested in the details of the Umetsky trial, which was causing a good deal of comment at that time—so interested that he intended to make Olga Umetskaya, the chief figure in the trial, the heroine of his novel (in the first plan for it). Her name is designated that way in his notebook. He was very sorry that we weren't living in Petersburg, since he would certainly have written about the trial.[27]

During that same winter he was extremely interested in the operation of the jury system (which had recently been established in Russia). There were times when he was actually thrilled and ecstatic over a jury's just and intelligent decisions, and he always kept me informed about all the important newspaper accounts he was reading which related to what was going on in court.[28]

Time was passing and we had a new concern: whether there would be a successful outcome to the much-awaited event in our lives—the birth of our first child. It was on this forthcoming event that our thoughts and dreams were chiefly focused, and both of us already loved our future child tenderly. By mutual consent we decided that if it should be a daughter, we would name her Sofya (after Fyodor Mikhailovich's niece and also in memory of Sonya Marmeladova in *Crime and Punishment*, whose misfortunes I had so lamented). But if it should be a son we proposed to name him Mikhail, for my husband's beloved brother.

It is with feelings of heartfelt gratitude that I remember the tenderness and solicitude Fyodor Mikhailovich showed me in my sickly condition, how he guarded me and cared for me, warning me at every step against quick movements which might be harmful, and which I in my inexperience did not consider very important. The most loving mother could not have watched over me more than my dear husband did.

He insisted that we visit the best gynecologist in Geneva as soon as the first remittance of funds arrived, and asked him to recommend a *sage-femme* who would take me under her care and visit me every week.

A month before the birth something happened which touched me deeply and showed me the minute details my husband's heartfelt concern for me encompassed. During one of Mme Barraud's visits she asked which of our friends lived on the same street that she did, since she often met my husband there. I was surprised at this but thought she must have made a mistake.

I began questioning Fyodor Mikhailovich. He denied it at first, but then he told me that Mme Barraud lived on one of the many streets ascending the hill from Geneva's main commercial artery, the rue Basses. These streets, inaccessible to carriages because of their steepness, all look very much alike. And so Fyodor Mikhailovich, thinking that this lady's help might be needed suddenly, perhaps at night, and not wishing to rely on his visual memory, made Mme Barraud's street the goal of his walks. Every day after visiting the reading room he would walk past her house and five or six houses further on, and would then come back. He had been making this walk during the last three months of my pregnancy, although climbing the steep hill was a considerable sacrifice for him in view of the asthma which was then just beginning to develop.

I begged him not to tire himself with this walk, but he continued to do it. And how triumphant he was afterwards that during the most trying moments of the actual event his knowledge of Mme Barraud's street and house was such a help, and that he found her so quickly in the half-dark of early morning and brought her to me!

Worried about my condition and wanting to please me, Fyodor Mikhailovich decided to ask my mother to come and spend a few months with us. My mother, who had been missing me very much and was very anxious about me, gladly agreed to come, but asked for time to arrange her affairs in the management of her houses, which were presenting certain difficulties.

In mid-December of 1867, in anticipation of my delivery, we moved to another apartment on the rue du Mont Blanc, next to the English church. This time we took two rooms, one of them very large, with four windows and a view of the church. The apartment was better than the first one, but we were later to regret often the loss of the kind old women who had been our first landladies. The new landlords were never at home, and only a servant girl was left in the house—a native of German Switzerland who understood little French and was not able to be of the slightest help to me. Fyodor Mikhailovich therefore decided to hire a *garde-malade* to care for the infant and me during the period of my illness.

The winter passed swiftly for us in unremitting mutual work on the writing of the novel and in other cares as well. February of 1868 arrived, when the greatly desired and anxiously awaited event was to take place. The weather in Geneva had been glorious at the beginning of the year, but there was a sudden break in mid-February, and daily storms set in. This sudden change of weather, as always, had an irritating effect on Fyodor Mikhailovich's nerves, and he had two epileptic attacks within a very short space of time.

The second, a very severe one, struck on the night of February 20. He became so weak that he could barely stand on his feet when he got up in the morning. He was in a kind of fog all day. Seeing him so feeble, I persuaded him to go to bed earlier, and he fell asleep at seven. Not an hour after his going to bed I felt a pain, small at first but growing stronger with each hour. Since the pains were characteristic ones, I realized that labor was beginning.

I endured the pains for about three hours, but toward the end I began to be afraid I would be without help, and sorry as I was to disturb my sick husband, I decided to awaken him. And so I quietly touched him on the shoulder. He quickly raised his head from the pillow and asked, "What's the matter, Anechka?"

"I think it's started—I'm suffering so!"

"How sorry I am for you, my darling!" my husband said in the tenderest voice, and suddenly his head bent down to the pillow and he was asleep.

I was terribly touched by his deep tenderness combined with absolute helplessness. I realized that his condition was such that he was unable to go for the midwife, and that if he weren't allowed to strengthen his shattered nerves through prolonged sleep, he might have a fresh attack.

Our landlords, as usual, were not at home (they used to attend some meeting or other every night until morning), and calling on the servant would be useless. Luckily my pains abated a bit and I resolved to bear them as long as I could. But what a dreadful night I spent then! The trees around the church were rustling violently; wind and rain rattled at the windows. There was deep darkness on the street. I have to admit that I was oppressed by the feeling of being completely alone and helpless. How bitter it was for me that during those trying hours of my life there was no close relative near me, and that my only guardian and defender, my husband, was himself in a helpless state. I began to pray with fervor, and prayer sustained my failing strength.

Toward morning the pains grew sharper. At about seven I decided to awaken Fyodor Mikhailovich. He woke up feeling much stronger. When he found out that I had been in agony all night long he grew terribly alarmed, reproached me for not waking him earlier, dressed in a second, and ran to get Mme Barraud.

It was a long time before anyone answered the door at her house. The servant did not want to wake her mistress, saying that she had just returned from a visit. Then Fyodor Mikhailovich threatened that he would go on ringing or break the glass. The mistress was awakened and my husband brought her to me within the hour.

I had to listen to her reprimands for much that I had done in my ignorance, and she declared that my carelessness would retard my labor. She asserted also that the birth would not take place in less than seven or eight hours and promised to return at that time.

Fyodor Mikhailovich went to fetch the *garde-malade.* Then

he and I, in terrible despondency and fear, began to await further developments. Mme Barraud did not arrive at the promised hour, and again my husband went to get her. It turned out that she had gone to dine with friends somewhere near the station. He went to the address and insisted on her coming back to check on my condition. In her opinion, labor was progressing badly and delivery was not to be expected before late evening. After giving me several pieces of advice, she went out to have her dinner. I went on suffering and Fyodor Mikhailovich was in torment looking at me.

After nine o'clock he couldn't stand it any longer and went again to Mme Barraud's friends to fetch her. He found her at a game of family lotto and told her that I was in too much pain, that if she wouldn't come and remain constantly at my bedside without leaving me, then he would ask the doctor to recommend another midwife more attentive to her responsibilities.

The threat worked. Mme Barraud was obviously displeased at being torn away from her absorbing game and expressed her dissatisfaction to me, adding several times, *"Oh, ces russes, ces russes!"*

To console her, Fyodor Mikhailovich arranged a fine supper for her, purchasing the most varied array of hors d'oeuvres, sweets and wines. I was very pleased that his tormented concentration on my condition was distracted, even if only for a short while, by running for the midwife, rushing around to the shops, and setting out the supper.

In addition to the usual pangs of childbirth I was anguished by the effect my suffering was having on my husband, already distraught from his recent attacks. His face showed such torment, such desperation! At times I saw him sobbing, and I myself began to fear that I might be on the threshhold of death. Remembering my thoughts and feelings then, I have to say that it was not so much myself I pitied as my poor husband, for whom my death might prove catastrophic. It was then that I realized what burning hopes and expectations he was concentrating on me and on our future child. The sudden crushing of all those hopes, in view of the impetuosity and unrestraint of Fyodor Mikhailovich's nature, might finish him.

It is possible that my fears for my husband and my agitation retarded the course of the labor. Mme Barraud felt the same way, and toward the end she forbade my husband to come into my room, declaring that his desperate expression was upsetting me. He obeyed, but I grew even more worried, and in the intervals between the pains I would ask either the midwife or the nurse to go and see what my husband was doing.

With each hour my pains increased. Sometimes I lost consciousness, and as I regained it and saw the dark eyes of the strange nurse fixed on me, I was afraid and did not know where I was or what was happening to me.

At last, at about five in the morning of February 22 (our style), my torments ceased and our Sonya was born. Fyodor Mikhailovich told me afterward that he was praying for me all the time, when suddenly in the midst of my groans he seemed to hear some kind of strange cry like a child's. He could not believe his ears; but when the cry was repeated he realized that the child was born. Beside himself with joy, he jumped up from his knees, ran over to the door, which was hooked shut, pushed it open with all his strength and, throwing himself on his knees beside my bed, began kissing my hands.

I too was immensely relieved that my suffering had stopped. We were both so shaken that for the first five or ten minutes we didn't know whether we had a boy or a girl. We heard one of the women say, *"Un garcon, n'est-ce pas?"* and the other replied, *"Fillette, une adorable fillette!"*

For us, it was equally thrilling whoever it was—we were both so happy that our dream was fulfilled, that a new being was in the world, our first-born!

Meanwhile Mme Barraud tended the baby, congratulated us on the birth of our daughter, and brought her to us like a big white package. Fyodor Mikhailovich reverently made the sign of the cross over Sonya, kissed her tiny wrinkled face and said, "Anya, look, what a beauty we have!"

I too blessed and kissed the little girl and rejoiced in my dear husband as I saw on his tender, transported face such overflowing happiness as I had not seen up to that moment. In an upsurge of joy, he embraced Mme Barraud and shook the nurse's hand hard several times. The midwife told me that in all her many years of practice she had never seen a newborn's father in such a distraught and agitated state as my husband's, all through the delivery. Once again she repeated, *"Oh, ces russes, ces russes!"* She sent the nurse to the apothecary's for something and sat Fyodor Mikhailovich down to watch me so that I wouldn't fall asleep.*

Mme Barraud informed Fyodor Mikhailovich that, according to Swiss law, the father of a newborn child must personally report this fact to the police and obtain a legal birth certificate. She warned him that he must do this as quickly as possible or else he might be subject to a fine or even arrest.

The very next day, he set out for the proper institution and was gone for about four hours, which frightened me very much. Because of my sickly condition I pictured various horrors that might have happened to him. At last he returned and gaily recounted his adventures. It seems that upon appearing at the police station he found out that the father of the newborn child must bring with him two witnesses to attest to the identity of the parents as well as to the event itself. He began to explain to the clerk that he was a foreigner and knew no one in Geneva; but the clerk wouldn't even listen to him, and turned to the next applicant.

In the greatest perplexity, Fyodor Mikhailovich left the building and appealed to the sergeant on duty at the door for advice. The latter helped my husband out of his difficulty in a twinkling by offering to appear as a witness for him. He added, however, that he would not be available until the relief sergeant arrived at the change of shift, in another hour and a half. And when Fyodor Mikhailovich asked him where he might find a second witness, the sergeant offered him *"un camarade á moi."*

So the matter was settled, but it was necessary to wait. Fyodor Mikhailovich took the sergeant's advice and went to sit on a bench on the boulevard, thinking in consternation of how long it would be before he was at home again.

At the appointed hour the sergeant finished his shift and went to get the second witness, bringing another sergeant back with

*Fyodor Mikhailovich described many of his own sensations during the birth of our first daughter in *The Possessed,* in the scene where Shatov's wife gives birth. (A.G.D.)

him. All three of them—my husband and the two sergeants—appeared before the official in charge of receiving applications. A rather large amount of time was consumed in writing down the statements of the father and of the witnesses, in registering the application in several different books and writing out the birth certificate.*

After it was all over Fyodor Mikhailovich asked his sergeant benefactor how much he owed him and his friend for the time they had lost. The sergeant answered, *"Mais rien, monsieur, rien!"* Then it occurred to Fyodor Mikhailovich to invite both the sergeants to a café to drink some wine to the health of the new baby. To this the sergeants agreed with pleasure, and they led Fyodor Mikhailovich to the nearest restaurant. There, in a private room, my husband ordered three bottles of the local red wine.

This loosened the merrymakers' tongues, and the sergeants began telling him all kinds of stories about the things that happened in the course of their work. He told me he was sitting on pins and needles when he thought of how worried I would be over his long absence. But it would have been awkward to leave his companions, all the more because two additional bottles followed on the heels of the first three, and the sergeants, who had grown very merry indeed, kept toasting my health, as well as *la petite Sophie* and the man who was responsible for her coming into the world.

Fyodor Mikhailovich asked Apollon Maikov to be godfather to our Sonya and my own mother to be her godmother. She had planned on being present for the birth but fell ill, and the doctor would not allow her to undertake such an extensive journey before spring. My mother arrived in Geneva at the beginning of May, and it was then that Sonya's christening took place.

Although I recovered rather quickly after my illness, I had lost all my strength as a consequence of the difficult thirty-three-hour labor. And so, although I started breast-feeding my little daughter gladly, I soon realized that we wouldn't be able

*A copy of which should be appended here. (A.G.D.)

to manage without supplementary milk, for the child was large and healthy and required much nourishment.

To take Sonya to a wet-nurse was impossible. In Switzerland infants are usually fed artificially with cow's milk from a bottle plus nutritional powders. Some mothers, as a matter of fact, send their newborn infants as much as sixty versts away to the mountains to be breast-fed by peasant women. To part with Sonya and give her over to a stranger's hands was unthinkable, and indeed the doctor did not advise it, inasmuch as the unsupervised peasant women used to take several infants at a time, and many of them would die.

After a certain order had been established in our house, a life began of which the most blissful remembrances remained with me forever after. To my great joy, Fyodor Mikhailovich proved to be the tenderest possible father. He was always present for the baby's bath and he used to help me—he himself wrapped her in her little piqué blanket and fastened it with safety pins, carried her around and rocked her in his arms and, putting his work aside, would rush to her the moment he heard the tiny sound of her voice.

When he woke up or came home, his first question would be, "How's Sonya, is she all right? Did she sleep well? Did she eat?" He would sit by her crib for hours on end, now singing songs to her, now talking to her, and was convinced that she recognized him in her third month. On May 18 he wrote Maikov: "This tiny three-month-old being, so helpless, so minuscule, was to me already a person and a personality. She was beginning to know me and love me, she smiled when I came near her. When I sang songs to her in my ludicrous voice she loved to listen. She didn't cry and didn't wrinkle up her face when I kissed her; she would stop crying if I approached her."

It was not given us for long, however, to bask in this unclouded happiness of ours. During the early days of May the weather was glorious. Following the doctor's insistent counsel, we used to take our precious little one to the Jardin des Anglais every day, where she would sleep in her little carriage for two or three hours.

One ill-fated day during such a stroll the weather suddenly changed. A *bise* sprang up and the child evidently caught a chill, for her temperature went up that same night and she started coughing. We went immediately to the best children's doctor. He visited her daily and assured us that our little girl would recover. Three hours before her death, he was still telling us the patient was much better.

Despite these reassurances, Fyodor Mikhailovich wasn't able to concentrate on anything and hardly stirred away from her cradle. We were both terrified; and our gloomy presentiments came true. Our darling Sonya died during the day of May 12 (our style).

I cannot express the desolation that took hold of us when we saw our lovely daughter lying dead. Profoundly shaken and afflicted by her death as I was, I was even more afraid for my broken-hearted husband. His grief was stormy. He sobbed and wept like a woman, standing in front of the body of his darling as it grew cold, and covering her tiny white face and hands with burning kisses. I never again saw such paroxysms of grief.

It seemed to us both that we would not survive this anguish. For two days the two of us, not parting from each other for a minute, went around to different government offices to get permission to bury our little one. Together we ordered everything necessary for the funeral, together we dressed her in her little white satin dress, together we put her into her small white-satin-upholstered coffin, and we cried, cried uncontrollably.

Fyodor Mikhailovich grew so thin and hollow-cheeked during the week of Sonya's illness that he was almost unrecognizable. On the third day we took our treasure to the Russian church for the funeral service, and from there to the cemetery at Plain Palais, where she was buried in a section set aside for children. In a few days her grave was planted with cypresses and a white marble cross was put up in their midst. Every day we went to that little grave, put flowers on it, and cried. It was just too bitter to part with our priceless little one, so deeply and utterly had we come to love her, and so many dreams and hopes were connected with her life.

To stay in Geneva, where everything reminded us of Sonya, was unbearable, and we decided to carry out our old plan at once and move to Vevey, on that same Lake Geneva. We deeply regretted that—because of lack of means—we could not leave Switzerland altogether. It had become almost hateful to Fyodor Mikhailovich: he blamed Sonya's death on the changeable climate of Geneva, on the arrogance of the doctor, the incompetence of the baby nurse, and so on. The Swiss themselves had always been an object of dislike to him; but the coldness and heartlessness shown by many of them during the time of our most acute grief exacerbated this dislike even more.

As an example of heartlessness, let me mention the fact that our neighbors, even though they knew about our loss, sent their maid to ask me not to cry so loud, because it was getting on their nerves.

I shall never forget that everlastingly sad day when we, after sending our things to the steamer, went for the last time to say goodbye to the grave of our little girl and to put a farewell wreath on it. For a whole hour we sat at the foot of the monument and cried as we remembered Sonya, and then we went away bereft, looking back often at her last resting place.

The steamship on which we were traveling was a freighter and there were few passengers at our end of the ship. The day was warm but overcast and matched our state of mind. Still shaken by his farewell to Sonechka's small grave, Fyodor Mikhailovich was in an extremely anguished state. Now, for the first time in my life with him (he rarely complained) I heard him cry out bitterly against the fate that had persecuted him all his life. Remembering back, he told me about his dismal, lonely youth after the death of his tenderly beloved mother. He recalled the gibes of his literary friends, who first praised his talent and then later cruelly wounded him. He remembered back to his prison term at hard labor and how much he had suffered through the four years of it. He spoke about his dream of finding that much-longed-for family happiness through his marriage to Maria Dmitrievna—and this was never realized. He had no children with her, and her "strange, mistrustful and sickly-fanciful character"[29] was the reason he had been so unhappy with her.

And now at last, when "this great, this *only* human happiness—having a child of your own"—had come to him, and he had the opportunity to know and appreciate this happiness, evil fate did not spare him, but took away this being so precious to him! Never again, neither before nor afterwards, did he dwell in such minute and sometimes touching detail on those bitter insults he had had to endure in his life from people dear and close to him.

I tried to comfort him, pleaded with him to accept with submission the ordeal visited upon us. But his heart was evidently full to overflowing with grief, and he had to relieve it even if by crying out against the lifelong persecution of fate. With all my heart I felt for my despairing husband, and I wept with him over his hapless life. Our deep mutual sorrow and the heartfelt talk in which he laid bare to me the intimate recesses of his wounded heart seemed to draw us still closer together.

In all the fourteen years of our married life I cannot recall a summer more wretched than the one my husband and I spent in Vevey in 1868. Life seemed to have stopped for us. All our thoughts, all our talks focused on our memories of Sonya and the happy time when her presence lighted our life. Every child we met reminded us of our loss. So as not to lacerate our hearts, we used to go for walks somewhere off in the mountains, where we might avoid such upsetting encounters.

I too took our sorrow very hard, and shed many tears over our little girl. But deep down there was a tiny flicker of hope that a merciful God would take pity on us and send us another child, and I prayed fervently for that. My mother, too, who missed her granddaughter very much, tried to comfort me with the hope of becoming a mother again.

Thanks to prayer and hope, the sharpness of my grief was assuaged little by little. But it was different with Fyodor Mikhailovich. His emotional state began to alarm me very seriously. This is what I read in a letter of his to Maikov of June 22, when I had occasion to add a few words of greeting to his wife:

. . . the more time passes, the more corrosive my memory becomes and the more vividly do I see the image of my dead Sonya. There are moments which are impossible to bear. She already recognized me. On the day of her death, when I went out of the house to read the newspapers, having no inkling that she would be dead in two hours, she followed me so attentively with her eyes, she gazed at me so hard that

I still go on picturing her ever more and more vividly. I shall never forget and never stop tormenting myself! Even if there is another child, I don't understand how I can love it, where I will find the love. It's Sonya I want. I cannot take it in that she is no more and that I will never see her again.[30]

He responded to my mother's words of solace in similar language. I was very worried about his depressed state and thought in distress, is it possible, if God should bless us once again with the birth of a child, that Fyodor Mikhailovich won't love it and won't be as happy as he was when Sonya was born? It was just as though a black curtain had been drawn in front of us, so dismal and gray had our family life become.

Fyodor Mikhailovich continued to work on his novel, but work was no comfort to him. To our already despondent state a new worry was added: letters addressed to us were getting lost, and so our contact with family and friends was hampered; and this contact was our only source of consolation. We felt especially badly about losing Maikov's letters, always full of palpitating interest. Our misgivings about the loss of our letters were strengthened by an anonymous letter we received, in which we were informed that Fyodor Mikhailovich was under suspicion and that an order had been given for his mail to be opened and for him to be thoroughly searched at the border, on his return home to Russia.[31]

And just then, as fate would have it, a forbidden book came into Fyodor Mikhailovich's hands: *Secrets of the Tsar's Palace (in the Reign of Nicholas I).* Dostoevsky and his wife figure as characters in the book; among the novel's many other absurdities it is stated that Dostoevsky dies and that his wife enters a nunnery. Fyodor Mikhailovich was outraged and even wanted to write a refutation (a rough draft of a letter survives), but he decided later that it wasn't worth while to pay attention to a trashy little book.[32]

By autumn, it was clear to us that we had to bring about a change in our depressed state at all costs. And so at the beginning of September we decided to move to Italy and to begin by staying in Milan. The nearest pass through the mountains was the Simplon. We did part of it on foot, walking, my husband and I, alongside an enormous mail coach which was climbing the mountain. We went in front of it, climbing the footpaths and gathering Alpine wildflowers along the road. We made the descent to the Italian side in a cabriolet.

I remember a comical episode when I went to buy fruit in the little hamlet of Domo d'Ossola and to try out my knowledge of Italian acquired during the summer. Noticing that Fyodor Mikhailovich had gone into some shop and thinking I would help him out with the conversation, I hurried to join him. It turned out that he, in his wish to give me some pleasure, was inquiring about the price of a chain he had seen in the window. The merchant, taking us for "eminent foreigners," asked the exorbitant price of three thousand francs, assuring him that the chain dated back practically to the time of Vespasian. Fyodor Mikhailovich had to laugh at the gap between the price named and the amount of money we had on hand, and this was almost his first cheerful reaction since our loss.

The change of setting, the impressions of the journey and the new people (Lombardy peasants, very similar in appearance to Russian peasants, in Fyodor Mikhailovich's opinion)—all this had an effect on his frame of mind, and he was very lively during the first days of our stay in Milan. He took me to see the famous Cathedral of Il Duomo, which had always been an object of deep and genuine admiration for him. He expressed regret only over the fact that the square in front of the cathedral was built up, with the houses too close to it (it has since been considerably widened), and that caused the architecture of Il Duomo to lose its majesty. One clear day we even climbed up to the cathedral roof to have a look at the surrounding area and to examine at closer hand the statues adorning the cathedral.

We lived near the Corso, on such a narrow street that the neighbors could talk back and forth from window to window. I began to rejoice in my husband's revived spirits, but they did not last long, to my sorrow, and he fell into a sadness again. One thing that served to distract him a bit was his correspondence with Apollon Maikov and Nikolai Strakhov. The latter told us about the issuance of a new journal, *Dawn,* published by V. V.

Kashpiryov. Fyodor Mikhailovich was curious about it chiefly because Strakhov, a former contributor to *Time* and *The Epoch,* was editor-in-chief; and therefore, as my husband wrote him, "Our way of thinking and our mutual work are not dead. *Time* and *The Epoch* have borne fruit in spite of everything, and the new enterprise had to start where we left off. That is too comforting."[33]

Fyodor Mikhailovich, who was in complete sympathy with the new journal, was interested in the contributors as well as in the articles they produced (in particular, one by N. Y. Danilevsky, author of the important work *Russia and Europe,* whom my husband had known when he was still in his youth as a follower of the teachings of Fourier).

Strakhov strongly urged Fyodor Mikhailovich to become a regular contributor to *Dawn.* He accepted with pleasure, but not until finishing *The Idiot,* which was giving him so much trouble and which he was very dissatisfied with. Fyodor Mikhailovich maintained that he had never had a better and richer poetic concept than the one which unfolds in the novel and that he had not expressed even a tenth part of what he wanted to say in it.

The autumn of 1868 in Milan was cold and rainy, and it became impossible to take the long walks my husband loved so much. There were no Russian newspapers or books in the reading rooms there, and it was very tedious for him to be without news from home. After two months in Milan, therefore, we decided to move to Florence for the winter. Fyodor Mikhailovich had been there at one time and had retained good impressions of the city, chiefly of its art treasures.

And so we moved to the then capital of Italy at the end of November, and settled down near the Palazzo Pitti. The change of scene again had a beneficial effect on him, and we began exploring churches, museums and palaces together. I remember his ecstatic reaction to the Cathedral, the church of Santa Maria del Fiore, and the small Chapel dei Battistero, in which infants are usually christened. The bronze doors of the Baptistery (especially the Delta del Paradiso), the work of the renowned Ghiberti, enchanted my husband and, passing the chapel often, he always stopped to look at them. He assured me that if he should happen to get rich he would certainly buy photographs of these doors, in their actual size if possible, and hang them in his study where he could admire them.

Often the two of us would go to the Pitti Palace, where he was entranced by Raphael's painting *Madonna della Sedia.* The same artist's other painting, *Saint John in the Desert,* which hangs in the Uffizi gallery, also enchanted him, and he always stood before it for a long time. After visiting the art gallery he would invariably go to see the statue of the Medici Venus, located in the same building, the work of the noted Greek sculptor Cleomenes.[34] My husband considered this statue a work of genius.

To our great joy, the city of Florence had an excellent library and reading room which subscribed to two Russian newspapers, and my husband went there every day to read for a while after dinner. He borrowed from the library the works of Voltaire and Diderot, which he knew fluently in French, and read them at home all winter.[35]

The year 1869 brought us happiness. We soon learned that God had blessed our marriage and that we might hope to have another child. Our joy was boundless, and my dear husband began showing as much concern for me as he had during my first pregnancy. His solicitude reached the point where, after reading the volumes of Count Leo Tolstoy's novel *War and Peace,* which had just come out and been sent to us by Strakhov, he concealed from me that part of the novel in which the death of Prince Andrey Bolkonsky's wife in childbirth is so masterfully described. Fyodor Mikhailovich feared that this picture of death might have a powerful and painful effect on me.

I searched everywhere for the missing volume and even upbraided my husband for losing such an interesting book. He apologized profusely and assured me that the book would turn up, but he did not give it to me until after the expected event had come to pass. Waiting for the child to be born, Fyodor Mikhailovich wrote to Strakhov: "I wait with excitement, and with fear, and with hope, and timidity." We both dreamed of having a girl, and since we loved her already in our dreams with a burning love, he gave her the name of Lyubov[36] in advance, a name no one in my family or my husband's family had.

The doctor had prescribed a lot of walking, and every day Fyodor Mikhailovich and I went to the Boboli Gardens (the park surrounding the Pitti Palace) where the roses were in bloom although it was January. Here we warmed ourselves in the sunlight and dreamed of our happiness to come.

Our financial circumstances were very bad in 1869, just as before, and we were often in need. Fyodor Mikhailovich was receiving 150 rubles per signature of sixteen pages for *The Idiot,* coming to a total of about seven thousand. But out of this, three thousand had been advanced before our departure abroad to pay for our wedding. And of the remaining four thousand, we had to pay interest on the articles we had pawned in Petersburg and we had to give frequent help to our stepson and to Emilya Fyodorovna's family, so that relatively little was left for us. But we bore this comparative poverty not only without a murmur, but sometimes even with light hearts. Fyodor Mikhailovich used to call himself "Mr. Micawber" and me "Mrs. Micawber."[37] We lived together in true harmony, and now in view of our hopes for a new happiness, everything would have been perfect if it had not been for the threat of a new trouble.

During the past two years Fyodor Mikhailovich had lost his ties with Russia and was beginning to be very concerned about this. In a letter to his niece Sonya on March 8, 1869, telling her about his forthcoming novel, *Atheism,*[38] he said: "I cannot write here. For that I must be in Russia without fail, must see, hear and take direct part in Russian life; whereas here I am losing even the possibility of writing, since I lack both the essential material, namely, Russian reality (which produces the ideas) and the Russian people."

But it was not only Russian people but people in general that we were lacking. We did not know a single soul in Florence with whom we could talk, argue, joke, exchange reactions. Around us, all were strangers, and sometimes hostile ones; and this total isolation from people was sometimes difficult to bear. I remember that it occurred to me then that people living in such complete solitude and isolation might, in the final analysis, either come to hate each other or else draw close together for the rest of their lives. Fortunately, it was the latter which happened to us. Our enforced isolation compelled us to come even closer to one another and to value each other even more.

During our nine months' stay in Italy I learned to speak a little Italian—that is, enough to speak to the servant or go to the shops. I could even read the newspapers *Piccola* and *Secola* and understood everything. Fyodor Mikhailovich, engrossed in his own work, could not learn the language, of course, and I served as his translator. Now, in view of the approaching event, it was necessary to move to a country where French or German was spoken, so that my husband could talk freely with the doctor, the midwife, the shopkeepers and so forth.

For a long time we discussed the question of where to go so that Fyodor Mikhailovich might find an intellectual milieu. I suggested that we settle for the winter in Prague, as a country akin and close to Russia. There my husband might get to know the outstanding political leaders, and through them enter the local literary and art circles. He approved of this idea, since he had more than once regretted not being present at the Slavic Congress of 1867. Sympathetic to the idea of a Slavic *rapprochement* emerging in Russia at that time, he wanted to get to know the Slavic peoples better. Therefore, we finally made the decision to go to Prague and stay there all winter. In my condition traveling was cumbersome, and we decided to stop in several cities to rest on the way to Prague.

Our first move was to Venice but we stopped in Bologna between trains and went to the museum to look at Raphael's painting *St. Cecilia.* Fyodor Mikhailovich valued this work of art very highly, but up to that time had seen only copies and was very pleased now to see the original. It was very hard to tear him away from his contemplation of that marvellous painting, but I was afraid of missing our train.

We stayed in Venice for several days. Fyodor Mikhailovich was enchanted by the architecture of St. Mark's Cathedral and would gaze for hours on end at the mosaics adorning its walls. We went together also to the Palazzo Ducale, whose amazing architecture my husband admired very much. He was entranced as well with the striking beauty of the ceilings in the Palace of the Doges, painted by the finest artists of the fifteenth century. I can say that we didn't stir away from St. Mark's

Square throughout those four days—so completely did it charm us, by day and by night.

The steamship journey from Venice to Trieste was extremely rough. Fyodor Mikhailovich was very concerned for me and didn't move a step away; but luckily everything went well. After that we stopped for two days in Vienna, and so reached Prague only after a ten-day journey.

There a great disappointment awaited us. It turned out that furnished rooms were available in those days for single people only. Furnished rooms for families—that is, quiet and comfortable rooms—simply did not exist. In order to remain in Prague we would have to rent an apartment, pay for six months in advance, and on top of that provide our own furniture and all our household necessities. That was beyond our means. After a three-day search we were compelled, to our great regret, to leave Golden Prague, which we had come to like very much in the course of those days.

Thus crumbled my husband's dream of making contact with the leaders of the Slavic world. There was nothing left for us but to settle in Dresden, where we were familiar with living conditions. And so we moved to Dresden at the beginning of August and rented three furnished rooms in the English quarter of the town *(englischer Viertel)* at No. 5, Victoriastrasse. (My mother had returned in order to be present at the birth of my baby.)

And it was in that house, on September 14, 1869, that a happy family event took place—the birth of our second daughter, Lyubov. In a state of extraordinary happiness, Fyodor Mikhailovich informed Maikov and invited him to be the godfather. "Three days ago a daughter, Lyubov, was born to me. Everything is fine, and the child is big, healthy and a beauty."[39] Only an infatuated and ecstatic father's eyes, of course, could see "a beauty" in that tiny pink morsel of flesh.

With the arrival of our child in the world, happiness glowed in our house once again. Fyodor Mikhailovich was uncommonly tender with his daughter, fussed over her, bathed her himself, carried her about in his arms, sang her to sleep and felt so happy that he wrote Strakhov, "Oh, why aren't you married and why don't you have a child, esteemed Nikolai Nikolayevich? I swear to you that ¾ of life's happiness lie in that, and one-quarter at most in the rest."[40]

This time again Maikov was the godfather, but as godmother my husband chose his favorite sister, Vera Ivanova; my mother was the substitute. The christening did not take place until December—I was not well at first, and later the priest of the Dresden church left for Petersburg on business.

We located an excellent reading room in Dresden, with many Russian and foreign newspapers. We also came to know some people among the Russian permanent residents of Dresden who used to come after mass to the home of the priest's family, who were very hospitable. Among these new acquaintances were several intelligent and cultivated people with whom my husband found it interesting to converse. That was the good side of our Dresden life.

Upon completing *The Eternal Husband* Fyodor Mikhailovich sent it to the journal *Dawn,* where it appeared in the first two issues for 1870. This novel contained autobiographical elements. It was an echo of a summer spent in Lublin, near Moscow, in 1866, where he lived in a summer house next door to the one occupied by his sister Vera. It was the Ivanov family which Fyodor Mikhailovich depicted as the Zakhlebinins. There were the father, totally absorbed in his large medical practice, the mother eternally fatigued with household cares, and the light-hearted young people, Fyodor Mikhailovich's nieces and nephews and their young friends. In the character of Marya Nikitishna's girlfriend a family friend, M. S. Ivanchina-Pisareva, is portrayed, and Alexander Lobov is my husband's stepson, Paul Isayev—in highly idealized form, of course. Even the character Velchaninov contains certain aspects of Fyodor Mikhailovich himself, for example in the description of the different kinds of games he thought up. N. N. von Vocht, one of those who took part in those summer evenings and diversions during his stay there, recalls Fyodor Mikhailovich as being just such a gay and ready-witted person in the company of young people.

In the winter of 1869–70 Fyodor Mikhailovich was occupied with the writing of a new novel which he intended to call *The Life of a Great Sinner.* This work, according to my husband's plan, was to consist of five long stories (about two hundred and fifty pages apiece), each of which would comprise an independent work which might be published in a magazine or appear as a separate book. He proposed to pursue throughout all five stories the all-important and agonizing question which had tormented him all his life—namely, the question of the existence of God.[41] The action of the first story was to take place during the 1840's. Both the material and the character types of that period were so real and familiar to him that he was able to write that story even while continuing to live abroad. That was the story he wanted to place in *Dawn.*

But to write the second story, which was set in a monastery, it would be necessary for him to return to Russia. My husband proposed to make the holy bishop Tikhon Zadonsky the protagonist of that story, under another name, of course.[42] Fyodor Mikhailovich had great faith in this projected novel and considered it the culmination of his literary career. His prevision proved correct, since many of the characters of this novel figured later in *The Brothers Karamazov.* But at that particular time he did not succeed in carrying out his intention, because he became engrossed in another theme of which he wrote to Strakhov: "I have high hopes for a piece I'm writing now for the *Russian Messenger,* although from a tendentious rather than an artistic motivation. I want to express certain ideas even though its artistic merit dies in the process; I am possessed by the things that have accumulated in my mind and heart. Even though nothing more than a pamphlet comes out of it, I *will* speak my mind."

That was his novel *The Possessed,* which appeared in 1871. The emergence of this new theme was influenced partly by the arrival of my brother. The thing was that Fyodor Mikhailovich's reading of various foreign newspapers (which contained much news not printed in the Russian papers) had brought him to the conclusion that political disturbances would very shortly break out in the Petrovskaya Agricultural Academy.[43] Fearing that my brother, through youthfulness and weakness of will, might take an active part in them, my husband persuaded my mother to invite her son to stay with us in Dresden. Fyodor Mikhailovich counted on my brother's coming to provide some cheer for me, who had already begun to long for home, as well as for my mother, who had been living abroad for two years now, either with my sister's children or with us, and who missed her son very much.

My brother had always dreamed of a trip abroad, and he took advantage of his vacation to come to us. Fyodor Mikhailovich had always liked my brother and was interested in his work and his friends, as well as in the mood and way of life of the student world in general. My brother used to discuss these subjects in detail and with enthusiasm. It was then that the idea came to Fyodor Mikhailovich of depicting the political movement of that period in a story and of using as one of his main characters (under the name of Shatov) a real person, the student Ivanov, who was later murdered by Nechayev. My brother spoke of Ivanov as an intelligent man of outstandingly firm character who had drastically altered his former [radical] views. And how deeply shaken my brother was when he learned later in the newspapers of the murder of Ivanov, for whom he felt a real affection! Fyodor Mikhailovich's description of the Agricultural Academy park and the grotto where Ivanov was murdered was taken from my brother's words.[44]

I should add that my brother's coming to Dresden turned out to be a major event in his life. In the Russian colony there, he met the young woman who became his wife within the year.

Even though the material for the new novel had been taken from real life, still my husband found it extremely difficult to write. He was dissatisfied with his work as always, rewrote it many times, and destroyed about two hundred and forty pages of it. A tendentious novel was evidently not in the spirit of his work.[45]

As our little Lyubochka grew and no longer needed my constant presence, I was able to go with Fyodor Mikhailovich to the art galleries and the inexpensive concerts at Brülow Terrace, or out walking. On one of these occasions an incident occurred which shows the ever-present impetuosity of my husband's character. It was announced in the winter of 1870 that there was to be an auction of the furnishings and possessions of some deceased German duchess. They were selling diamonds, dresses, linens, furs, and so forth, and the drawing rooms of her house were full to overflowing with people.

During the last days of the auction we were walking past the house and I suggested going in to have a look at the way the Germans handle these public sales. Fyodor Mikhailovich agreed, and we went up to the hall. There were comparatively few things left, and these were largely luxuries for which there were few takers among the thrifty Germans. The articles therefore were now being sold not at their former valuation, but to the highest bidder.

Suddenly, Fyodor Mikhailovich noticed on the shelves of the buffet a charming dinner set of elegant Bohemian crystal in a dark red color decorated in gilt. There were eighteen items in all: two large serving bowls on stands, two medium-sized, six a little smaller, four jam dishes, and four plates, all of the same design.

Fyodor Mikhailovich, who loved elegant things, admired the bowls and said, "Wouldn't it be nice to buy these lovely bowls? What about it, Anechka, shall we buy them?"

I laughed, knowing that even though we had some money at that moment, there wasn't very much of it. Next to us, some Frenchwoman was admiring the crystal; she was telling her companion that she was sorry there were so many pieces—otherwise she would have liked to buy some of them. Fyodor Mikhailovich heard that and turned to her right away and said, "Madame, let's buy them together." Not five minutes later the articles were offered to the public at a price of eighteen thalers, or one thaler per piece.

Economical as the Germans are, such a paltry price for so many articles seemed cheap even to them, and takers appeared, each raising the bid by five groschen. Only Fyodor Mikhailovich would raise the bid by a thaler. His zeal was growing by the minute; the price was going up and I thought, horror-struck, what if the Frenchwoman refuses her part and we have to take all the things? The auctioneer, who had brought the price up to forty-one thalers and was afraid of losing his buyers, closed the sale, and the articles were our property. The Frenchwoman did not refuse the purchase and we divided the pieces honorably.

And now we had to transport our purchase home. Fyodor Mikhailovich stayed with the things while I set out for home with two porters, each carrying a bowl in each hand. They had to come back twice. One can picture my mother's astonishment when she saw the collection of bowls in my husband's room.

Her first question was, "How on earth are you going to take all that to Russia? You don't even have trunks, only suitcases—and that is all going to be smashed on the way."

This consideration had not occurred to either one of us—and even if it had, Fyodor Mikhailovich, in the fever which had taken hold of him, would not have turned down the opportunity. Everything turned out well, however. Russians often made trips from Dresden to Petersburg, and I asked some people I knew to take a bowl apiece and give them to my sister. That table set is still intact today and comprises our family treasure.

As I have mentioned, my husband and I used to visit the Russian priest N. F. Rozanov. My husband did not have a particularly high opinion of him; due to the liveliness of his personality and a certain levity of judgment he did not embody the ecclesiastical type as my husband conceived it. The priest's wife was very kind and hospitable, and they had darling little children who brightened up the household.

Among the Russian ladies living in Dresden at that time were several ardent admirers of my husband's work. They used to bring him flowers and books, but mainly they indulged and pampered our Lyubochka with toys, with which, of course, they attracted Fyodor Mikhailovich's attention.

At the end of October, 1870, the Russians in Dresden assembled at the home of the priest and decided, on their own initiative, to send an address to the then Chancellor on the occasion of the dispatch of the nineteenth of October to the Russian representatives [in foreign countries].[46] All those present begged Fyodor Mikhailovich to write this address, and although he was extremely busy then with urgent work, he agreed to do so. The address is as follows:

> We, Russians in temporary residence abroad in Dresden, have learned with joy and gratitude of the Sovereign's will, which you have expressed in the dispatch of the 19th of October to the representatives of Russia among the powers, signatories to the Treaty of Paris. Assembled in fraternity and unanimity, we are happy that even from here we can express to your Excellency the feelings of joy experienced by

each of us in reading your dispatch. It was like hearing the voice of all our great and glorious Russia. Each of us, taking pride in the name of Russian, has read those words full of truth and of the highest merit. We pray God for the happiness of our beloved Motherland and that He may long preserve her from affliction. We pray that He continue to preserve our adored Sovereign and Liberator for long years, and that he may always have such valiant servitors as yourself.

This address was covered with a multitude of signatures (almost one hundred) and sent to the Chancellor.

Even though I missed Russia during the first three years of living abroad, still there were constant new impressions, good or bad, which served to dissipate my homesickness. But in the fourth year I no longer had the strength to struggle against it. Although I was surrounded by the creatures most beloved and precious in the world to me—my husband, my child, my mother and brother—still something fundamental was lacking—Russia, my motherland. Gradually, my homesickness grew into an illness, into a nostalgia, and our future seemed quite hopeless to me. I believed we would never return to Russia again, that inconquerable obstacles would continue to arise. Sometimes we had money, sometimes not, but still we could not leave because of my pregnancy or because of the fear that our child might take cold, and so forth. Living abroad seemed like a prison in which I was trapped and from which I could never free myself. No matter how my family tried to convince me, no matter how they consoled me with the hope that circumstances would change and that we would return home, all these efforts at consolation were in vain. I had ceased to believe in these promises and was convinced that fate had condemned me to remain forever in an alien land.

I knew full well that my longing caused pain to my dear husband, who himself found it terribly hard to live so far from his own country. I tried to control myself in his presence—not to cry, not to complain—but my sometimes melancholy expression would give me away. I would say to myself that I was prepared for any misfortune, for poverty, even for destitution, if only I could live in my homeland, so precious to me and in which I took such pride. Thinking back on my state of mind at that time, I have to say that it was unbearably low at times and that I would not have wished it on my worst enemy.

At the end of 1870 a circumstance occurred thanks to which the possibility arose of our receiving a considerable sum of money. Stellovsky, who had bought from Fyodor Mikhailovich the rights to a complete edition of his work in 1865, now published the novel *Crime and Punishment* in a separate edition. According to their agreement, Stellovsky owed my husband over a thousand rubles. And yet, although the novel was already published, the publisher did not wish to pay anything, even though my husband's stepson had informed him that he had the power of attorney to receive the money.

Not relying on his stepson's business experience, Fyodor Mikhailovich asked Maikov to undertake the task of obtaining payment—that is, not to do it personally, but to turn the matter over to an experienced attorney.

It is with deepest gratitude that I recall the endless kindness of our highly valued friend Apollon Maikov during the four years of our residence abroad. Once again he took up our cause wholeheartedly, and not only retained a lawyer but even tried to negotiate with Stellovsky himself. That publisher, however, was an arrant swindler, and Maikov, fearful of being cheated by him, decided to summon Fyodor Mikhailovich himself to Petersburg.

Since he knew that we were always penniless, he resorted to an extreme measure: he sent my husband a telegram advising him to request a loan of one hundred rubles from the Literary Fund and to use this money to travel to Petersburg alone, without his family. Unfortunately, the telegram arrived on April 1—April Fool's Day. At first we took this summons to Petersburg as somebody's joke or as the cunning scheme of one of his creditors or perhaps even Stellovsky himself to get Fyodor Mikhailovich to Petersburg and there, by threatening to put him into debtors' prison, to pay for *Crime and Punishment* with our promissory notes, which he had bought up for next to nothing.

The good Maikov did not confine himself to a telegram but put out feelers on his own initiative to the committee of the Literary Fund on the subject of extending a loan of *one hun-*

dred rubles to the writer Dostoevsky. But once again they responded negatively to this request, as Maikov mentions in his letter of April 21, 1871.[47] (At a later point I intend to clarify my husband's friendly attitude toward the Literary Fund, his repeated readiness to give readings for its benefit evenings, and the ever hostile treatment of him by the Literary Fund.)[48]

Fyodor Mikhailovich was very perturbed by that letter and wrote in answer: ["But you see how arrogantly the Fund treated my request for a loan (i.e., your request on my behalf), what guarantees they demanded and so forth, and how arrogant was the tone of their answer. If it had been a Nihilist asking, they wouldn't have answered him in such a fashion."][49]

Time was passing; April of 1871 marked four years since we had been living abroad, and our hope of returning to Russia sometimes appeared close and sometimes disappeared. Finally, we firmly resolved that we must without fail return to Petersburg soon, no matter how difficult the consequences of our return might be.

But our calculations hung by a thread. We were expecting a new addition to the family by July or the beginning of August; so that if we didn't manage to make the move to Russia a month before the event we would have to remain for another whole year until the following spring, since it would be out of the question to transport a newborn infant in late fall. When we contemplated the prospect of having to wait another whole year before seeing Russia again, both of us plunged into total despair, so unbearable had it become for us to live in a foreign country. Fyodor Mikhailovich would repeat often that "it would be the end of him" if we stayed abroad; that he was no longer able to write, that he had no material, that he felt he was losing his memory and understanding of Russia and the Russian people, since our Russian friends in Dresden were in his opinion not Russians but voluntary émigrés, who did not love Russia and had left it forever.

And that was the truth. These were all members of the landed gentry who could not adjust to the abolition of serfdom and the changed conditions of life, and who had left their own country to luxuriate in the civilization of Western Europe. They were for the most part people resentful of the new order of things and of the reduction in their standard of living, who supposed that they would find life easier in a foreign country.

Fyodor Mikhailovich spoke so often of the inevitable "destruction" of his talent, tormented himself so with the problem of how he was going to feed his beloved and ever-growing family, that I sometimes felt desperate as I listened to him. In order to soothe his anxiety and dispel the somber thoughts which prevented him from concentrating on his work, I resorted to the device which always amused and distracted him. In view of the fact that we had some money on hand (about three hundred thalers) I once brought the conversation around to roulette and asked him if he didn't want to try his luck again—he had won a few times, after all, why not hope that this time luck would be on his side, and so forth.

Of course I did not believe for a moment that he would win, and I very much regretted the hundred thalers which would have to be sacrificed. But I knew from my experience of his previous visits to the roulette table that after undergoing some intense emotions and satisfying his craving for risks, for gambling, he would return assuaged. And, having convinced himself of the futility of his hope of winning, he would settle down to his novel with new energy and make up for all the lost time and work in two or three weeks.

My suggestion about roulette was only too close to my husband's heart, and he did not raise any objections. Taking with him one hundred and twenty thalers with the agreement that in the event of loss I would send him the fare home, he left for Wiesbaden, where he stayed for a week.

The roulette playing had lamentable results, exactly as I had surmised. Including the cost of the trip, Fyodor Mikhailovich spent one hundred and eighty thalers—a very considerable sum for us at that time. But the cruel torments he went through in the course of that week, when he kept upbraiding himself for taking the money away from his family, from me and his child, weighed so heavily on him that he resolved that he would never again in his life play roulette.

This is what he wrote me on the 28th of April, 1871:

A momentous thing has happened to me: the disappearance of the base fantasy that *tormented* me for almost ten years (or, rather, since my brother's death, when I was suddenly overwhelmed by debt). I used to dream perpetually of winning; I dreamed passionately, in earnest. But all that is over and done with! This was really the *last* time. Can you believe it, Anya, that my hands are untied now? I was shackled to gambling, body and soul; henceforth I will think about my work and not dream for nights on end about gambling, as I used to.[50]

Naturally I could not all at once believe in such an enormous joy: that Fyodor Mikhailovich would cool toward roulette. After all, he had promised me many times not to gamble and had not had the strength to keep his word. But this happiness did come about, and it was actually the last time he played. Subsequently, during his trips abroad in 1874, 75, 76, and 79, he never once considered going to a gambling resort. True, the tables were closed down in Germany soon afterwards, but they still existed in Spa, Saxon-les-Bains and Monte Carlo. The distance would not have prevented him from going there if he had wanted to. But he was no longer drawn to gambling. It seems that his fantasy of winning at roulette was a kind of obsession or disease from which he recovered suddenly and forever.

Fyodor Mikhailovich returned from Wiesbaden calm and in good spirits. He settled down right away to the continuation of *The Possessed,* realizing that the move to Russia and the process of getting settled in a new place and then the expected birth would not give him much opportunity to work. All of his thoughts were directed toward the new page of life which was opening for us, and he began to wonder how he would get along with his old friends and relatives, who he thought might have changed a good deal in the course of the past four years. He was aware of a change in some of his own views and opinions as well.

In the last days of June the money due him for his novel was received from the editor of the *Russian Messenger.* Without losing a single day we went about winding up our affairs in Dresden (or rather, redeeming our things from pawn and settling our debts) and packing our possessions. Two days before our departure, Fyodor Mikhailovich called me into his study, handed me several thick packets of large-sized paper, closely written, and asked me to burn them. Even though he and I had spoken about this previously, still I felt so badly about [destroying] the manuscripts that I began imploring him to let me take them along. But he reminded me that he would undoubtedly be searched at the Russian border and that the papers would be confiscated, and then they would be lost just as all his papers had been lost at the time of his arrest in 1849. It might be assumed that we would be detained in Verzhbolovo until the papers were inspected, and that would be hazardous in view of the approaching event.

Sad as I was to part with the manscripts, still I had to yield to Fyodor Mikhailovich's insistent arguments. We lit a fire in the fireplace and burned the papers. Thus perished the drafts of *The Idiot* and *The Eternal Husband.* I felt particularly sad at losing that part of *The Possessed* which was the early variant of that tendentious work. I succeeded in saving only the notebooks to the above-mentioned novels and gave them to my mother, who was planning to return to Russia in late autumn.[51] She would not agree, however, to taking a whole suitcase full of manscripts with her. Such a large quantity was sure to arouse suspicion, and the papers would have been taken away from her.

Finally, on the fifth of July, we managed to leave Dresden for Berlin, where we changed to a train bound for Russia. We had a good deal of trouble on the journey with our playful Lyubochka, then twenty-two months old. We were traveling without a nurse, and in view of my sickly condition my husband took care of her through the whole sixty-eight-hour trip: he took her out to walk on the platform, brought milk and food to her, played games with her—in short, he behaved like the most experienced nanny and in this way greatly lightened the long-drawn-out journey for me.

Things turned out just as we had surmised. All our bags and suitcases were ransacked at the border, and the papers and a packet of books were put aside. All the other passengers were released from the customs hall, but the three of us remained, in addition to a cluster of officials crowding around a table and looking at the books and a slim packet of manuscripts they had confiscated. We began to feel afraid we might miss our train for Petersburg, when we were rescued from our troubles by our Lyubochka. The poor little thing was hungry by this time and began to scream "Mama, give me a roll!" so hard that the officials soon grew sick of her crying and decided to let us go in peace, returning both the books and the manuscripts with no further remarks.

We still had to endure another twenty-four hours on the train, but our consciousness of the fact that we were riding on Russian soil, that all around us were our own people, Russian people, was so comforting that it made us forget all about the troubles of our journey. My husband and I were gay and happy and kept asking one another if it was really true that we were in Russia at long last. That was how wondrous the realization of our long-cherished dream seemed to us.

In summing up the European period of our life I would like to say that I recall it with deepest gratitude to fate. It is true that in the course of the more than four years spent in voluntary exile terrible ordeals befell us: the loss of our first daughter, Fyodor Mikhailovich's illness, our constant financial need and insecurity in work, my husband's unhappy passion for roulette, and the impossibility of going home; but these ordeals proved useful to us: they drew us closer together, forced us to understand and value one another more, and created that solid mutual attachment thanks to which we were so happy in our marriage.

For me personally, the memory of those years is a beautiful and vivid picture. We lived in and visited many charming cities and places: Dresden, Baden-Baden, Geneva, Milan, Florence, Venice and Prague; before my admiring eyes a whole world hitherto unknown to me was revealed, and my youthful curiosity was completely satisfied with visits to cathedrals, museums and art galleries, especially when I was able to see them in the company of the person dear to me, every conversation with whom revealed something new to me in art or in life. For Fyodor Mikhailovich, all these places presented nothing new, but as the possessor of a highly developed artistic taste he visited the galleries of Dresden and Florence with genuine pleasure and explored St. Mark's Cathedral and the palaces of Venice for hours on end.

It is true that we had no social life abroad except for chance and fleeting encounters. But during the first two years Fyodor

Mikhailovich was even glad of this total isolation from society. He was too exhausted after his brother's death by his struggle with the failures and troubles which had befallen him, and he had had too many bitter experiences with members of the literary world. He felt, moreover, that it is sometimes extremely useful for a thinking man to live for a time in solitude—far from always disturbing current events—and to give himself up completely to his own thoughts and dreams. Later, after he had returned to the hubbub of the capital, Fyodor Mikhailovich more than once recalled how good it had been for him abroad when he had complete leisure to think through the plan of a work or to read a particular book without hurry, surrendering fully to the feeling of delight or emotion aroused by it.

And how much vivid joy our life abroad gave us, apart from the beauty of our surroundings! The birth of our children, the start of the family Fyodor Mikhailovich had always dreamed of, filled and illuminated our life, and I say with gratitude to fate: bless those wonderful years I was lucky enough to spend abroad, in close company with this man, so remarkable for his lofty qualities of spirit!

In concluding this summation of our sojourn abroad I would like to speak of the inner meaning of our life, so long solitary. Despite numberless cares, constant financial embarrassments, and sometimes oppressive boredom, so protracted a life of solitude had a fruitful effect on the appearance and development in my husband of the Christian ideas and feelings which had always been present in him. All the friends and acquaintances who met us again after our return from abroad told me that they did not recognize Fyodor Mikhailovich, so strikingly had his character improved, so much milder, kinder, and more tolerant to others had he grown. His customary obstinacy and impatience had almost entirely disappeared.

To quote from the reminiscences of Nikolai Strakhov:

> I am completely convinced that the more than four years which Fyodor Mikhailovich spent abroad were the best time of his life, that is, the time which yielded the most profound and the purest thoughts and feelings. He worked with great intensity and was often in need; but he had the peace and joy of a happy family life and lived almost

exclusively in total solitude, that is, remote from all occasion to deviate from the straight path of development of his thinking and his profound spiritual work. The birth of children, concern for them, the sharing of man and wife in one another's suffering, even the death of his first-born —all these were pure, sometimes exalted experiences. There is no doubt that it was precisely abroad, in that setting, amid those long, serene reflections, that the particular revelation of the Christian spirit which had always dwelt in him was consummated.

This fundamental change was revealed very clearly to all those who knew him when Fyodor Mikhailovich returned from abroad. He would constantly bring the conversation around to religious themes. Not only that: his manner changed, acquired greater mildness sometimes verging on utter gentleness. Even his features bore traces of that frame of mind, and a tender smile would appear on his lips. . . . It was evident that the highest Christian feelings dwelt in him, those feelings which were expressed in his works ever more often and more distinctly. This was the man who returned from abroad.[52]

Fyodor Mikhailovich himself recalled our life abroad with gratitude in later years.

Our family and friends noticed a great change in me too. I had developed from a timid, bashful girl into a woman of decisive character, no longer frightened by the struggle with life's misfortunes, or rather with the debts which, by the time of our return to Petersburg, amounted to twenty-five thousand rubles. I retained my gaiety and exuberance but exhibited them only in my own family, among my intimates and friends. In the presence of strangers and particularly in male company I behaved with utmost reserve, limiting myself in my relations with men to cold courtesy, holding my tongue and listening carefully rather than expressing my own ideas.

My women friends declared that I had aged terribly during those four years and reproached me for not paying attention to my appearance, for not dressing well and not doing my hair fashionably. Even though I agreed with them, I did not want to change. I was firmly convinced that Fyodor Mikhailovich loved me not for my appearance only, but also for the good qualities of my mind and character, and that during that period "our hearts had knitted together," as he used to say. And my old-fashioned appearance and obvious avoidance of male society could only act beneficially on my husband, since it gave no occasion for him to display the unfortunate side of his character —his groundless jealousy.

CHAPTER FIVE

In Russia Once Again

On the hot, clear day of July 8, 1871, we came back to Petersburg after living in Europe for four years. From the Warsaw station we drove along Izmailovsky Prospect past the Cathedral of the Holy Trinity, where our wedding had taken place. As we went past it my husband and I said a prayer to the church; looking at us, our little daughter also crossed herself.

"Well, now, Anechka," said Fyodor Mikhailovich, "we've lived these four years abroad happily, even though things were a bit hard at times. But what will Petersburg have in store? Everything is foggy ahead. I foresee plenty of trouble, plenty of problems and worries before we get on our feet. It's only God's help I'm counting on!"

"Why worry about it in advance?" I tried to comfort him. "Let's hope God won't abandon us! The main thing is that our old dream has come true, and you and I are in our own country again!"

We stopped at a hotel on Great Konyushennaya Street, but stayed only two days. Because of the imminence of the birth it was inconvenient to stay on there, and beyond our means as well. We rented two furnished rooms on Ekaterinhof Prospect, on the third floor of house No. 3. We chose that neighborhood so that our daughter could spend the hot days of July and August in Yusupov Park nearby.

We were visited by Fyodor Mikhailovich's relatives in the very first days after our arrival, and our reunion with all of them was very friendly. In the course of those four years Emilya Fyodorovna's position had changed for the better. Her elder son Fyodor was an excellent musician and was giving many well-paying piano lessons. Her second son Mikhail worked in a bank. Her daughter Katya, a stenographer, also worked; so that the family lived in comparative comfort. And during this period, moreover, Emilya Fyodorovna had become accustomed to the idea that Fyodor Mikhailovich, having a family of his own, could help her out only in special cases.

It was only Paul who simply could not give up the notion that "father," as he stubbornly called Fyodor Mikhailovich, was *obliged* to support not only him but also his family. Still, this reunion too was cordial, mostly because I very much liked his wife, Nadezhda Mikhailovna, whom he had only just married that April. She was a pretty young woman, not very tall, modest, and quite intelligent. I couldn't understand at all how she had come to marry such an impossible person as Paul. I was genuinely sorry for her; I foresaw how difficult her life would be.

Our first son, Fyodor, was born eight days after our arrival, early in the morning of the sixteenth of July. I had begun to feel unwell the day before. Fyodor Mikhailovich, who had been praying all day and all night for a successful delivery, told me afterwards that he had decided that if it was a boy—even if he was born only ten minutes before midnight—he would name him Vladimir, after Prince Vladimir, the saint co-equal with the apostles, whose name day is celebrated on July 15. But the infant was born on the sixteenth and was named Fyodor for his father, as we had decided long ago. Fyodor Mikhailovich was terribly happy, both because we had a boy and because a family event which had caused him so much worry was successfully over.

When I began to recover, our baby was christened. His godfather, just as with our two daughters, was Fyodor Mikhailovich's friend Apollon Maikov. As godmother my husband chose our daughter Lyubochka, who was not yet two years old.

At the end of August[1] my husband made a trip to Moscow and received from the *Russian Messenger* a part of the honorarium due for his novel *The Possessed,* published in 1871. The sum received was not very large; still, it permitted us to move from our furnished rooms to an apartment for the winter. Our chief problem was that we had no furniture. I got the idea of going to the Apraxin Arcade and asking the furniture dealers there whether they wouldn't agree to sell us furniture on the installment plan at the rate of twenty-five rubles a month, with the condition that the furniture would be considered the property of the seller until the entire sum was paid.

We found a merchant who agreed to these conditions and gave us some pieces right away for four hundred rubles. But what pieces they were! They were new, but made entirely of alderwood and pine. Not to mention their clumsy design, they were constructed so badly that within three years they all came unglued and fell apart, and had to be replaced with new furniture.

But I was glad to have even that sort of furniture, for with it we could set up our own apartment. It was out of the question to remain in furnished rooms. Besides all sorts of inconveniences, the close proximity of little children who sometimes yelled and cried kept my husband both from sleeping and from working.

After working out an agreement on the furniture, I started hunting for an apartment. Paul volunteered to help me. That very evening he announced that he had found an excellent eight-room apartment for the very cheap rent of one hundred rubles a month.

"But what do we need with such a large apartment?" I asked in amazement.

"It's not a bit large. There will be a sitting room, study, bedroom, and nursery for you; we'll have a sitting room, study, and bedroom; and the dining room will be used jointly."

"Surely you aren't thinking of living with us?" I was astounded by his effrontery.

"How else then? That's just what I told my wife—when father comes, we'll all live together."

At that point I had to talk with him seriously and explain to him that circumstances were now changed, and that I would not consent under any conditions to live in the same apartment with him. As was his habit, he began making insolent remarks and threatened to complain to Fyodor Mikhailovich. But I wouldn't even listen to him. Four years of independent living had not been in vain for me.

Paul carried out his threat and went to Fyodor Mikhailovich, but received this answer in reply: "I have turned over the entire household management to my wife; so however she decides, that's the way it will be."

For a long time after that Paul could not forgive me for the breakdown of his plans.

After a long search I located an apartment on Serpukhovskaya Street in the house of Madame Arkhangelskaya, near the Technological Institute. I rented it in my own name so as to relieve my husband of household responsibilities. The apartment consisted of four rooms: a study where Fyodor Mikhailovich worked and slept, a sitting room, a dining room and a large nursery, where I slept as well.

As I looked at my shoddy furniture, I consoled myself with the thought that at least we would not have to buy household necessities and warm winter clothing, since these had been left in the care of several different persons. But alas—bad luck awaited me here too. The dinnerware, pots and pans and kitchen utensils had been stored with an elderly spinster friend who lived in our house. While we were abroad she died and her sister took away to the country all the things she had left, without stopping to figure out what belonged to her and what belonged to someone else. The pawn payments on our fur coats had been allowed to lapse by a certain lady who had promised to see that the interest was paid, although we sent her money for that very punctually. The glassware and porcelain left in my sister Masha's care was broken by the maid who was supposed to wash them; she had slipped and dropped a tray loaded with our porcelain on the floor.

I was particularly upset by this last loss. My father had been a connoisseur and collector of porcelain, loved going to the antique shops, and had acquired many beautiful things. After his death I inherited several charming turn-of-the-century Vieux-Saxe and Sevres teacups and also some finely-faceted antique cut crystal. Even today I still regret losing my charming cups with their shepherdesses and the drinking-glass with a fly painted on it in such a life-like manner that all who drank from it would try to catch it as though it were alive. I would give a great deal to get back those dear reminders of my childhood!

The same sad fate befell Fyodor Mikhailovich's things as well.

He had a fine library which he missed very much while we were living abroad. It contained many books given him by writer friends and inscribed by them; many were serious works on history and on the sect of the Old Believers, in which he took a keen interest. At the time we went away Paul had asked my husband to leave this library in his care, assuring him that it was necessary for his education, and promising to return it intact. But it turned out that he had sold it off to the second-hand book dealers because he needed money. When I rebuked him for this he answered insolently and asserted that we ourselves were to blame for not sending him money on time.

Fyodor Mikhailovich was extremely upset by the loss of his valuable library. He was no longer able to spend large sums as he used to do to buy the books he needed so badly. And on top of that his library had contained a number of rarities which were impossible to replace.[2]

A pleasant surprise was a large woven basket containing papers which had been stored with relatives of mine. In looking over the contents I found several of Fyodor Mikhailovich's notebooks for *Crime and Punishment* and some of the shorter stories, several record books connected with the journals *Time* and *The Epoch,* left by his deceased brother, and a good deal of very varied correspondence.[3] These documents were extremely useful in our later life, when there was occasion to confirm or refute data relating to Fyodor Mikhailovich's life.

In September, 1871, some newspaper informed the public that the writer Dostoevsky was back from abroad, and did us a disservice thereby. Our creditors, who up to now had been quiet, suddenly turned up with demands for the settlement of our debts. The first of these, and the most formidable, was Hinterstein. The debt was not connected with Fyodor Mikhailovich personally nor with the journals [*Time* and *The Epoch*] but with the tobacco factory of his late brother.

Mikhail Mikhailovich, a very enterprising person, had owned a tobacco factory in addition to his journal. In order to increase tobacco sales he had devised the idea of premiums such as scissors, razors, penknives and so forth, which were put inside the cigar boxes. These surprises attracted many buyers. Mikhail

Mikhailovich purchased the above-mentioned metal articles from the wholesale dealer G. Hinterstein, who supplied them on credit at a high rate of interest.

As *Time* developed a good circulation Mikhail Mikhailovich gradually settled with Hinterstein, whom he regarded as the most demanding of his creditors. A few days before he died he joyfully told his wife and Fyodor Mikhailovich, "At long last I've shaken off that leech Hinterstein." When, after his brother's death, all his debts were transferred to Fyodor Mikhailovich, Madame Hinterstein came to him and said that Mikhail Mikhailovich still owed her approximately two thousand rubles. Fyodor Mikhailovich remembered his brother's remark about the settlement of the Hinterstein debt and told her so; but she maintained that this was a separate matter and that she had given the money to Mikhail Mikhailovich without obtaining any receipt for it.

She begged Fyodor Mikhailovich either to pay her in cash or to give her promissory notes, sobbed, got down on her knees, and swore that her husband would be the death of her. Fyodor Mikhailovich, who always trusted other people's honesty, took her word and gave her two promissory notes for a thousand rubles apiece.

The first note was paid even before 1867, but on the second one (which had gone up to twelve hundred rubles, including five years' interest) Hinterstein demanded payment shortly after our return. He sent a threatening letter, and Fyodor Mikhailovich went to see him to ask for an extension until New Year's day, by which time the payment for his novel would have been received.

He came back in despair. Hinterstein had said he had no intention of waiting any longer and was going to attach all Fyodor Mikhailovich's moveable property. And if that was not sufficient to cover the debt he would have him put into debtors' prison.

"But how could I do any literary work in debtor's prison among all kinds of strange people, far away from my family? And what will I pay you with, if you take away my possibility of working?"

"Oh, you're a prominent writer and I'm sure the Literary

Fund will buy you out of prison right away," Hinterstein replied.

Fyodor Mikhailovich did not care for the then leaders of the Literary Fund. He was doubtful that they would offer to help, and even if help were proffered, as he informed Hinterstein, he would rather stay in prison than accept it from them.

The two of us had a long discussion about the best way to resolve the matter and decided to offer Hinterstein a new arrangement: namely, to give him one hundred rubles now and fifty rubles a month thereafter, so as to settle the balance of the debt after New Year's. My husband went to Hinterstein a second time with this proposal and came back very incensed. It seems that Hinterstein, after a long discussion, had told him, "Here you are, a talented Russian writer, while I'm just a little German merchant; and I want to show you that I can have a prominent Russian author put in jail. Be assured that that is just what I am going to do."

This was after their victory in the Franco-German war, when all the Germans grew arrogant and haughty.

I was outraged by such behavior toward Fyodor Mikhailovich, but I realized that we were in the scoundrel's hands and that we had no way of getting rid of him. Foreseeing that Hinterstein would not confine himself to threats, I decided to make an attempt to work the matter out on my own. I went to see him without saying a word to my husband (who would, of course, have forbidden me to do it).

He greeted me arrogantly and declared, "It's either money on the table, or inside of a week your property will be attached and sold at public auction and your husband will be sitting in Tarasov's house." That was the way the debtors' section was referred to, because it was located in the Tarasov house, in the first company of the Izmailovsky Regiment.[4]

"Our apartment was rented in my name and not Fyodor Mikhailovich's," I replied coolly. "And as for the furniture, that was bought on credit, on the installment plan, and it belongs to the furniture dealer until the final payment is made, so it can't be attached."

And in proof of this I showed him the apartment rent-book and a copy of my agreement with the furniture dealer. "And as far as your threat of debtors' prison is concerned," I went on, "I'm warning you that if that happens I'll beg my husband to stay in prison until the term of your debt expires. I'll settle nearby myself and visit him with the children, and help him with his work. So that way you won't get a single penny, and on top of that you'll have to pay his keep.* You'll be punished for your stubbornness, I promise you!"

Hinterstein started complaining of Fyodor Mikhailovich's ingratitude in not wishing to repay a debt which had been permitted to run on so magnanimously.

"No, it's you who should be grateful to my husband," I answered hotly, "for the fact that he gave your wife a promissory note for a debt which may have been paid off long ago. If Fyodor Mikhailovich did that, it was only out of generosity and pity. Your wife cried and said you would be the death of her. And if you dare to carry out your threat, I'll write up this whole story and publish it in *Son of the Fatherland*. Let everybody see what the honest Germans are capable of!"

I was beside myself and spoke without choosing my words. This time my vehemence was an advantage. The German backed down and asked, what exactly did I want?

"Just exactly what my husband asked you for yesterday."

"Well, all right then—hand over the money!"

I demanded a detailed receipt outlining our agreement, since I was afraid Hinterstein might change his mind later and start tormenting us all over again. I returned home victorious, knowing that—for a time at least—I had gained some peace of mind for my dear husband.

Before describing our struggle with our creditors, which continued for another ten years, almost up to my husband's death, I should like to explain just how these debts, so agonizing to us both, arose.

Only the tiniest part of them—two or three thousand—were

*The debtor's term of imprisonment canceled the debt. To cancel a debt of twelve hundred rubles, it was necessary to stay in prison between nine and fourteen months. The creditor was obligated to pay the keep of the debtor he had put in jail. (A.G.D.)

incurred by Fyodor Mikhailovich personally. Mainly, they were Mikhail Mikhailovich's debts for the tobacco factory and the journal *Time.* After his sudden death (his illness lasted only three days) his family, his wife and four children, who were accustomed to a life of security and even ease, were left without any means at all. Fyodor Mikhailovich, then a widower with no children of his own, considered it his duty to pay his brother's debts and support his family. It is possible that he might have succeeded in carrying out his noble intention if he had possessed a cautious and practical nature. Unfortunately, he trusted too much in people's honesty and honor.

When later I heard stories from people who had witnessed the way my husband handed out promissory notes, and after learning many details from old letters, I was struck by his positively childlike impracticality. All those people who weren't too ashamed or too lazy cheated him and took promissory notes from him. Fyodor Mikhailovich had had nothing to do with the financial side of the journal while his brother was alive, and did not know the state of its affairs. And when he had to take responsibility for publishing *The Epoch* after his brother's death, he also had to accept all the outstanding bills for *Time:* for printing, paper, binding, etc.

But in addition to *Time*'s contributors, whom Fyodor Mikhailovich knew, other people began coming to him—for the most part completely unknown to him—who maintained that the late Mikhail Mikhailovich owed them money. Hardly anybody furnished any proof of this, but Fyodor Mikhailovich, trusting in people's honesty, didn't even ask them for it. He (as I was told) would usually say to the claimant, "I have no money just now, but I can give you a promissory note if you wish. I only ask you not to present it too soon. I'll pay you when I can."

People would take the notes, promising to wait; and of course they didn't keep their promises, but presented the notes for payment immediately. I shall describe an instance whose authenticity I happened to trace through documents.

A certain hack writer, X, who had placed his work in *Time,* came to Fyodor Mikhailovich and asked for two hundred and fifty rubles in payment for a story which had appeared in the journal while Mikhail Mikhailovich was still alive. As usual, my husband had no money and offered a promissory note. X, thanking him profusely, promised to wait until my husband's affairs were going better, but asked that the note be undated so as not to have to claim payment by its expiration date.

What was Fyodor Mikhailovich's amazement when a demand for payment was made within two weeks, with a threat to attach his property! He went to X for an explanation. The latter was embarrassed and began justifying himself, alleging that his landlady was threatening to throw him out of his apartment. Driven to extreme measures, he had given her Fyodor Mikhailovich's note after first extracting her promise that she would wait before demanding the money. He said he would talk to her again, would convince her, and so forth. Naturally nothing came of these negotiations, and Fyodor Mikhailovich was forced to borrow money at a high rate of interest to settle this debt.

About eight years later, having occasion to go through Fyodor Mikhailovich's papers for some reason, I found the editorial records for *Time.* Picture my amazement and indignation when I discovered in it a voucher from the writer X in receipt of payment from Mikhail Mikhailovich for that very story! I showed the voucher to my husband and heard in reply, "I never thought X would be capable of swindling me! Look what necessity can drive people to do!"

In my opinion, a large part of the debts Fyodor Mikhailovich had assumed were of similar character. They amounted to about twenty thousand rubles. With accumulated interest, they totaled twenty-five thousand by the time we returned from abroad. We had to pay them back for thirteen years. Not until the year before my husband died did we settle them at last, so that we could breathe freely without fear of being hounded by reminders, explanations, and threats of attachment and sale of our possessions.

In order to pay off these fictitious debts Fyodor Mikhailovich had to work beyond his strength and still deny, both to himself and to our whole family, not only pleasures and comforts but even our most essential needs. How much happier, more content and serene the fourteen years of our married life might have been if the worry about paying off debts had not been eternally hanging over our heads!

And how my husband's work would have gained in the artistic sense if he had not had those self-imposed debts and could have written without hurry, looking over and rewriting his work before handing it over to the printer. Frequent comparisons are made, in literature and in society, between Dostoevsky's work and the work of other gifted writers, and Dostoevsky is criticized for excessive complexity, intricacy and accumulation of detail,[5] whereas the work of others is polished—in Turgenev's case, for example, chased almost like jewelry.

And rarely does it occur to anyone to compare the circumstances in which other writers lived and worked and those in which my husband lived and worked. Almost all of them—Tolstoy, Turgenev, and Goncharov—were people in good health, financially secure, and with full freedom to think their work through and refine it. Fyodor Mikhailovich, on the other hand, suffered from two serious diseases,[6] was burdened with a large family and with debts and preoccupied with oppressive thoughts of tomorrow, of earning his daily bread. What possibility was there of polishing his work under such circumstances? How many times did it happen in the last fourteen years of his life that two or three chapters [of a novel] had already been published in the journal, the fourth was in process of being set up in type, the fifth was in the mail on its way to the *Russian Messenger*, and the rest had not yet been written down and existed only in his head. And how often Fyodor Mikhailovich, in reading through a chapter of a novel which had already appeared in print, would suddenly see his mistake clearly and feel desperate when he realized that he had spoiled his work in progress.

"If only I could bring it back!" he used to say sometimes. "If only I could correct it! Now I see where the difficulty was, I see why the novel isn't going right. And my mistake may have killed my idea altogether."

And it was genuine grief, the grief of an artist who sees clearly where he has gone wrong and has no possibility of correcting the error. Yes, unfortunately, he never had such a possibility—he needed money to live on, to pay debts! And therefore he was compelled to work even when he was ill, sometimes on the day after a seizure, to hurry, barely reading over his manuscript—just to send it off on time, so as to receive payment for it as soon as possible. And never once in his life, except for his first novel, *Poor Folk*, did it fall to his lot to write a novel unhurriedly, without pressure, taking the time to think his plan through thoroughly and to work out all its details. Fate did not bestow that great happiness on him although it was always his cherished but, alas, unattainable dream!

These self-imposed debts harmed Fyodor Mikhailovich in an economic sense as well. At a time when financially secure writers such as Turgenev, Tolstoy, and Goncharov knew the journals would be vying with each other to print their novels, and while they were receiving five hundred rubles per signature of sixteen pages, Dostoevsky, who lacked such security, had to *offer* his work to the journals. And since the one who makes the offer is always the loser, he would be paid much less by the very same journals. Thus, for his novels *Crime and Punishment, The Idiot* and *The Possessed,* he received one hundred and fifty rubles per signature; for *A Raw Youth* two hundred and fifty, and not until his last novel, *The Brothers Karamazov,* did he receive three hundred rubles per signature.

Bitterness rises in me when I remember how my personal life was ruined by *other people*'s debts, by the debts of a person I never met in my life, and on top of that by fictitious debts for which my husband gave promissory notes to conscienceless people who swindled him. My entire life then was darkened by the never-ending preoccupation of where to get such-and-such an amount by such-and-such a date; where and for how much to pawn such-and-such an article; how to manage so that Fyodor Mikhailovich wouldn't find out about some creditor's visit or about some possession which had gone to the pawnshop. On this my youth was wasted, my health was impaired and my nerves were shattered.

And I feel even more wounded when I reflect that half these misfortunes might have been eliminated if there had been some kind persons among my husband's friends to guide him in the unfamiliar business of putting out a magazine. It has always seemed incomprehensible and cruel to me that the people he regarded as his best friends,[7] who knew his completely childlike impracticality, his excessive credulousness, and his sensitivity, could have left him alone to deal with all the claims and bills remaining after Mikhail Mikhailovich died. Couldn't they have helped him examine all these claims and require proof of each debt? I am convinced that many claims would never have arisen if it were generally known that they would be examined by others besides the trustful Fyodor Mikhailovich. Alas—not a single kind person could be found among my husband's friends and admirers who felt like giving him some time and performing a real service. All of them pitied him, all of them sympathized with him, but it was only "words, words, words."

Some may say, perhaps, that Fyodor Mikhailovich's friends were poets and novelists who understood nothing of practical life. To that I must reply that all these persons were able to arrange their own personal affairs beautifully. It will be objected, perhaps, that Fyodor Mikhailovich wanted to be independent and would not have accepted direction from outsiders. But this objection too is invalid. He willingly turned over all his affairs to me, listened to my advice and followed it, although at the beginning, of course, he could not regard me as an experienced businesswoman. He would have responded with the same trustingness to help from his friends, if it had been offered. It is with a feeling of bitter hurt for my husband that I reflect on such friends and such friendships.

During the first period after our return to Russia, I hoped to pay off part of our debts by selling the house which had been my dowry. Impatiently I waited for my mother to come home from Dresden, where she had gone for my brother's wedding, and for my sister to return from Rome (she was managing all our houses in my mother's absence). She had promised to render a full account of her management when she came home in the spring. But in the spring she fell ill with typhus, and she died in Rome on May 1, 1872.

After her death we learned that she had long ago given her husband a power of attorney for the management of all our affairs, and that he in turn (since he often traveled with her outside of Petersburg) had transferred the management to some friend of his. This gentleman, who enjoyed the income from our houses over a period of three or four years, did not find it necessary to pay the government taxes. Large arrears piled up, and the houses were designated for sale at public auction.

We did not have the means to settle these arrears and save the houses from being auctioned off, but we hoped they would be bought at a good price and that my mother would receive the money, which she would then give me instead of the promised house.

My hopes, unfortunately, were not justified. The gentleman who had been managing our houses made a fictitious arrangement with intermediaries to whom he allegedly rented the houses for ten years, receiving all the rent money in advance. This transaction did not come to light until the auction and so, understandably, there were no buyers for the houses. Then this scoundrel acquired them for himself by paying the tax arrears. In other words, for a few thousand rubles he acquired three houses with two large outbuildings and an enormous plot of land. And nothing was left for my mother, my brother and myself.

We could, of course, have initiated a lawsuit, but we did not have the means to carry it through. And on top of that, a suit would have necessitated a court action against my sister's husband. This would have set us at odds with him, and we would have lost contact with the orphaned children we loved. It was very painful to me to relinquish my only hope of putting our wretched situation to rights!

At first, I used to allow creditors to negotiate with Fyodor Mikhailovich. But these negotiations produced bad results. Creditors would be insolent with my husband, would threaten him with attachment of the furniture and with debtors' prison. After conversations of that sort Fyodor Mikhailovich would feel desperate and pace the room for hours, pulling the hair at his temples (his usual gesture when he was intensely agitated) and saying over and over, "Now what in the world, whatever in the world are we going to do?"

And the next day he would have an epileptic seizure.

I was terribly sorry for my poor husband. Without saying anything to him, I decided to take these negotiations with creditors upon myself alone. What amazing character types used to visit me during that period! They were for the most part dealers in promissory notes: widows of government clerks, landladies of furnished rooms, retired officers, legal hangers-on of the lowest class. They had all bought up the notes for pennies and wanted to redeem them in full. They used to threaten me with both attachment and prison, but I knew by then how to handle them. My arguments were exactly the same as they had been with Hinterstein. When they realized the futility of threats the creditors would come to terms, and we would sign a special agreement in exchange for Fyodor Mikhailovich's promissory note.

But how difficult it was for me to pay the promised sum on time! What contrivances I had to resort to: borrowing from relatives, pawning our things, denying myself and my family the most basic necessities! Our income was not regular but depended entirely on the success of Fyodor Mikhailovich's work. We were compelled to run up arrears for the rent and with the shops; and when we did receive some funds, four or five hundred rubles in a lump sum (which my husband always handed over to me) there would be only twenty-five or thirty rubles left by the next day.

There were times when my husband could not fail to notice creditors' visits. He would question me as to who had come and on what business, and seeing my reluctance to discuss it, would start reproaching me for my secretiveness. These complaints were reflected in some of his letters as well. But I could not always be frank with him. Peace of mind was indispensable for him to be able to work; and these unpleasantnesses frequently brought on attacks which kept him from working. I had to conceal from him painstakingly anything that might cause him upset or chagrin, even at the risk of appearing furtive. How painful all that was—and it was the life I was forced to lead for almost thirteen years!

It is with bitterness also that I think back on the unceremonious demands put forward by Fyodor Mikhailovich's relatives. No matter how small our means were, my husband could not bring himself to refuse help to his brother Nikolai, to his stepson, and, in special cases, to other relatives as well. In addition to his fixed stipend of fifty rubles a month "brother Kolya" received five rubles every time he paid us a visit.[8] He was a nice man and a pathetic one, I loved him for his kindness and his tact. And all the same, I resented it when he multiplied his visits under various pretexts: to congratulate the children on their birthdays or name days, to express his concern for our health, and so forth. This was not stinginess on my part but the agonizing realization that we had only twenty rubles in the house while some payment was due the next day, and that I would be forced to pawn something again.

I was particularly irritated by Paul. He did not ask—he *demanded,* and was fully convinced that he had the right to do that. Fyodor Mikhailovich invariably gave a considerable sum to his stepson whenever a large payment came in. But special needs used to arise constantly with Paul, and he would come to his stepfather for money even though he was perfectly well aware of how hard our life was financially.

"Well, how's *papá,* how's he feeling?" he would ask as he came in the door. "I have to talk to him—I need forty rubles desperately."

"But you know that Katkov hasn't sent anything yet and that we have no money at all. I pawned my brooch today for twenty-five rubles. Here's the receipt—have a look!"

"So what? Pawn something else."

"But everything I have is pawned already."

"There is something I simply have to buy," he would persist.

"Buy it after we get some money."

"I can't put it off."

"But I have no money!"

"What's that to me! Get it somehow."

I would try to persuade him to ask his stepfather not for the forty rubles I didn't have, but for fifteen, so that five at least would be left for myself for the next day. After long entreaties he would compromise, feeling evidently that he was doing me a great favor thereby. And I would give my husband fifteen rubles for his stepson, thinking ruefully that we could have lived peacefully on that money for three days; and now I would have to go and pawn something again. I cannot forget how much unpleasantness and grief that rude individual caused me!

Amazement may be felt, perhaps, at the fact that I did not protest such unceremonious demands for money. But if I bickered with Paul he would complain to Fyodor Mikhailovich right away, manage to distort the whole thing, and make himself out as the injured party. There would be a row, and the effect of all this on my husband would be extremely oppressive. Wishing to spare his peace of mind, I preferred to bear it all myself and deny myself everything to keep the peace in our family.

Notwithstanding the harassments of our creditors and our eternal lack of funds, I remember the winter of 1871–72 with pleasure. The mere fact that we were in our own country again, surrounded by Russians and everything Russian, was the highest happiness for me. Fyodor Mikhailovich too was very happy to be back, to see his friends, and, most important, to observe the mainstream of Russian life, from which he had been feeling somewhat remote. He renewed contacts with many of his old friends and he met many men of the scholarly world at the home of his relative, Professor M. S. Vladislavlev; he took particular pleasure in his conversations with one of them, the orientalist V. V. Grigoryev. At the home of Prince Vladimir Meshchersky, publisher of *The Citizen,* he was introduced to T. I. Filippov and to the whole circle which used to dine at Meshchersky's on Wednesdays. And it was there that he became acquainted with Konstantin Pobedonostsev, who later became his close friend—a friendship which endured to the day of his death.

I remember that Nikolai Danilevsky, whose permanent residence was in the Crimea, came to Petersburg that winter. Fyodor Mikhailovich, who had known him in their youth as an ardent disciple of Fourier and who deeply admired his book *Russia and Europe,* wanted to renew this old friendship. Since Danilevsky was going away shortly, my husband invited him right then and there to dine with us on the following day. When Danilevsky's friends and admirers learned of this, they invited themselves as well. My horror can be imagined when my husband counted up the number of guests expected and they came to approximately twenty. Despite my limited facilities for entertaining I managed to arrange everything properly, dinner was lively and the guests stayed long past midnight, deep in stimulating talk.[9]

During that same winter P. M. Tretyakov, owner of the celebrated art gallery in Moscow, asked my husband's permission to have his portrait painted for the gallery. With this aim in mind the eminent artist Vasily Perov came from Moscow and came to see us every day for a week before beginning work. He found Fyodor Mikhailovich in the most varied of moods, chatted with him, drew him into discussion, and succeeded in noting his most characteristic expression, namely, the one he had when he was absorbed in thought about his work. One might say that Perov's portrait captures the "Dostoevskian creative impulse." I often noticed that expression on his face when I went into his study. I would see that he seemed to be "looking inside himself" and go away without saying anything. Afterwards I would learn that he had been so absorbed in his own thoughts that he hadn't noticed my entrance and refused to believe I had been there.

Perov was an intelligent and pleasant person, and Fyodor Mikhailovich loved talking with him. I was always present at the sittings and have very fond remembrances of Perov.

Winter flew swiftly by. The spring of 1872 arrived, and with it a whole chain of misfortunes and calamities which left a trail of consequences we could not wipe out of our memories for a long time.

There is a proverb that says, "Troubles don't come singly." And there is a time in the life of almost everyone when he is overtaken by a whole succession, a train of different and unexpected misfortunes and reverses. This happened to us too.

Our troubles began at the end of [April], 1872, when our daughter Lyuba stumbled and fell before our very eyes while she was running about the room. She burst into loud screams. We rushed to her, picked her up and tried to comfort her, but she went on crying and wouldn't let her right hand be touched.

This made us suspect that the injury was serious. Fyodor Mikhailovich, the children's nurse and the maid rushed out to find a doctor. Fyodor Mikhailovich found out the address of the nearest surgeon from the apothecary and brought him back within a half hour. Almost simultaneously, Nanny brought another doctor from Obukhov Hospital.

After examining the injured arm the surgeon said that a dislocation had occurred. He set the joint immediately and bandaged the wrist in heavy cardboard. The second doctor confirmed the surgeon's opinion as to the dislocation and assured us that the wrist would knit quickly now that it was set.

We were reassured by the opinion of two competent physicians. We asked the surgeon to visit the patient and he came every morning for two weeks, undid the bandages, and said that everything was progressing properly. Both Fyodor Mikhailovich and I pointed out that there was a dark purple-red bump about three inches above the palm of the child's hand. He maintained that it was the entire hand which was swollen and that this was the usual hemorrhaging after a dislocation, which should gradually disappear.

In view of our imminent departure for Staraya Russa, the surgeon advised us not to undo the dressing on the hand until we arrived at our destination, for safety on the journey. Completely reassured on the score of the accident, we left on May 15. We had chosen this resort as our summer residence on the advice of Professor Vladislavlev, the husband of Fyodor Mikhailovich's niece Marya Mikhailovna. Both husband and wife had assured us that life there was quiet and cheap, and that their own children's health had much improved the previous summer because of the salt baths. And so Fyodor Mikhailovich, who was extremely concerned about the children's health, had decided to take them to Staraya Russa to take advantage of the bathing.

Our first trip to Russa imprinted itself vividly on my mind as one of the joyous memories of our family life. Although the winter had been a good and interesting one we had been dreaming ever since Lent of going away somewhere in early spring to some remote spot where we could work and live together—not always among other people, as in Petersburg, but the way we used to live in Europe, content with one another's company. And now our dream had come true.

We left on a glorious warm morning. After a trip of about four hours we arrived at Sosninka Station, from which the steamers to Novgorod sail down the Volkhov River. There we learned that our steamer would depart at one o'clock in the morning and that we would have to wait all day. We stopped at an inn, and since the room was stuffy we took the children and their elderly nanny with us for a walk in the village.

At this point a comical incident occurred. We hadn't gone halfway down the street when we met an old woman and a child whose face was covered with red spots and swellings. We walked on and came upon three or four little boys who also had bumps and red spots on their faces. This disquieted us very much and made us fear that there might be smallpox in the village and that our children could catch it.

Fyodor Mikhailovich briskly ordered us home and asked our landlady whether there was any sickness in the village and why the children's faces were covered with spots. The woman took offense at this and answered that there were "no sickenings there and never been any" and that it was only the mosquitoes "picking on the children." As to the question of smallpox, we were quickly reassured. Not an hour had gone by before we were convinced that it was indeed mosquitoes, since our own children's hands and faces were much disfigured by their bites.

At midnight we transferred to the steamer and put the children to bed, while we ourselves sat on deck till three, admiring the River Volkhov and the trees along its shore, which had just come into leaf. It grew cold before dawn and I went into our cabin, but Fyodor Mikhailovich remained outside—he loved the white nights so!

At about six in the morning I felt someone touching my shoulder. I got up and heard Fyodor Mikhailovich saying, "Anya, come out on deck and look at this fantastic view!"

And truth to tell, the view was fantastic and one might indeed sacrifice sleep for it. Whenever I thought of Novgorod afterward, it was that scene I pictured. It was a glorious spring morning: the sun shone bright on the river's far shore from which the crenellated white walls of its kremlin[10] rose up, the gilded cupolas of the Cathedral of St. Sophia were ablaze, and in the chilly air the bells were loudly calling to matins. Fyodor Mikhailovich, who loved and understood nature, was in a tender mood which I unconsciously absorbed. We sat in silence for a long time side by side, as though afraid to break the spell. But our joyful humor lasted all the rest of the day. It was a long time since we had felt so happy and so much at peace!

When the children woke up we transferred to another

steamer sailing to Staraya Russa. There were few passengers, and we settled down comfortably. And indeed it was a wonderful journey. Lake Ilmen was smooth as a mirror. The cloudless sky made it look dove-blue, and one might imagine that we were sailing on a Swiss lake. During the last two hours of the trip, the steamer went along the Pola River which is very winding, so that Staraya Russa with its church steeples visible from afar seemed at times to be drawing near us, at times receding.

At three in the afternoon, the steamer approached port at last. We collected our luggage, took seats on the *lineykas*[11] and set out to look for the summer house belonging to the priest Father Rumyantsev, rented for us by our relative, Professor Vladislavlev. It did not take very long to find it, however. We had just turned from the embankment into Pyatnitskaya Street when the cabby said to me, "There's Father Rumyantsev standing at the gate. Looks like he's waiting for you."

The priest and his family, knowing we were to arrive about May 15, were indeed expecting us and were now sitting and standing by the gate. All of them greeted us cordially, and we felt at once that we had come to good people.

After saying hello to my husband, who was driving with the first cabby, the priest walked up to the second one in which I was sitting with Fedya in my arms. And behold, my little fellow, who tended to shy away from people and would never let anybody pick him up, stretched out his arms very amiably to the priest, tore his wide-brimmed hat off his head, and threw it on the ground. We all burst out laughing; and from that minute on began our friendship with Father Ioann Rumyantsev and his worthy wife Ekaterina Petrovna, which lasted for decades and ended only with the death of these fine people.

We were all very tired after our journey and finished this first day of our Russa life in a good and happy frame of mind. But Lord! How little we are given to know what the next day will bring!

And this is what happened the next day. After breakfast, at about eleven o'clock, wanting to let the children go out into the garden and embarrassed because the bandage on my little girl's arm was very dirty, I decided to undo the cardboard into which the surgeon had stitched her injured wrist and remove the bandage, as he had given me permission to do.

And what did I see! During the past few days the swelling had greatly subsided and therefore the bump above her palm which my husband and I had pointed out to the surgeon in Petersburg was clearly defined. This bump no longer seemed soft as before, but hard. And when you looked down at the arm you could see a hollow one finger deep, so that there was no doubt that the wrist was crooked. I was struck very hard by this and called Fyodor Mikhailovich right away. And he was terribly alarmed and assumed that something bad had happened to our little girl's wrist during our long journey.

We called Father Ioann and asked him to recommend a doctor.[12] The latter lived close by and came very soon. Carefully examining the arm, he announced to our horror that the child's problem was not a dislocated wrist but a broken bone; and since it had been set incorrectly and not put into a plaster cast, it had knit improperly. In answer to our question as to what would happen to the arm later, the doctor replied that the crookedness would grow worse and the arm would be deformed. There was also a possibility that the left arm would grow normally while the right one would be retarded in growth—in other words, that the child would have a shriveled arm.

How we felt on hearing that our darling little girl, so loved and cherished, would be a cripple! At first we could not believe it and asked whether there wasn't a surgeon in the town. The doctor said there was an Army physician-surgeon who had come with the soldiers sent to Russa for the baths, but he did not know this man and could not vouch for his competence.

We decided to call the surgeon and asked the doctor to wait. Good Father Ioann went to fetch him. Within a half hour he brought back to us an Army doctor, quite tipsy, whom he had turned up at billiards somewhere in the town. It did not occur to this doctor, accustomed to dealing with soldiers, to be more gentle with a small patient. In examining her arm he pressed the barely-knit bone so hard that she began to scream horribly and burst into sobs.

To our great grief, the Army doctor confirmed the opinion of his colleague that the problem was not a dislocation but a break in the bone. And since approximately three weeks had elapsed since the accident, there had been enough time for the bone to knit, and it had knit wrong. When we asked the doctors what to do now, both said it would be necessary to re-break the knit bone, set the parts, and put the arm into a plaster (immobile) cast, and that then the bone would knit properly. And they warned us that the operation must be performed without losing any time, before the bone was finally knit. To our question as to whether this was very painful, the doctors replied in the affirmative, and the surgeon even added that he could not guarantee that our daughter, who looked so fragile and pale, could stand such a painful operation.

"But isn't it possible to perform the surgery under chloroform?" asked Fyodor Mikhailovich.

They replied that administering chloroform to small children was dangerous, since they might go to sleep forever.

I remember with heartache how stunned my husband and I were by this disclosure, and how crushed. We didn't know what to do and asked the doctors, who were hurrying us, to give us another day to think it all over. Our situation was genuinely tragic. On the one hand it was unthinkable to leave the child crippled, without making an attempt to straighten her wrist. On the other—how could we entrust this operation to a surgeon who might even be inexperienced (we had so recently paid cruelly for our trust!) and a man, moreover, who was fond of drinking?

And on top of that the surgeon's uncertainty ("I can't guarantee, after all, that the arm will knit properly—it may be necessary to repeat the operation"—those were his exact words); his uncertainty even as to whether our darling little one could withstand such an agonizing operation—all this made us completely desperate.

My God, what we lived through on that unhappy day, deciding what to do! My husband, beside himself with misery and worry, paced rapidly back and forth on the garden terrace, tearing his hair at the temples—always a sign of extreme agitation in him; while I waited from minute to minute for him to have a seizure. As I looked at him and at our little sick daughter, I wept. Our poor little one, who wouldn't stir a step away from me, wept also. In a word, it was sheer horror.

We were rescued by Father Rumyantsev, our friend forever after. Seeing our desperation, he said to us, "Drop both of those local doctors. They don't understand anything and can't do anything. They'll only torture your daughter. Better take her back to Petersburg, and if an operation is necessary, have it done there."

Father Ioann spoke so persuasively and furnished so many convincing arguments that he helped us make the decision to go to Petersburg. But there were also some strong arguments against making the trip. Just think of it: we were counting on spending our summer in solitude and peace and storing up good health for the winter; we had found a good summer house and completed an exhausting journey. And now suddenly we would have to take the whole family back to stifling Petersburg, where we didn't even have an apartment (we had given up ours before our departure for Russa). After paying a hundred and fifty rubles for the summer house, we would have to look for another one somewhere in the outskirts of the capital—and this in our modest circumstances, when we had to observe the strictest economy. Besides that, it was a pity to leave both the country house we liked so much and the people who were so kind to us.

Father Rumyantsev proposed a different solution: that Fyodor Mikhailovich and I should leave with Lyuba and return after the operation, but leave Fedya with his nurse and cook in Russa meanwhile. Both Father Rumyantsev and his wife promised to look after the child and his nurses all the time we were away. Both of them, the priest and his wife, felt for us so genuinely in our grief and volunteered in such a heartfelt way to watch over Fedya that we could rest assured they would take good care of our little fellow.

But there was another circumstance which gave us a good deal of anxiety. Our son was only ten months old, and I was still breast-feeding him. Both he and I were quite well and I was planning to wean him when his eyeteeth came through. And now suddenly we had to leave a boy who had never known anything but mother's milk. We thought he might react badly to this abrupt change in his regime and that he might get sick; and then, too, the sudden end to the breast-feeding might have a bad effect on me as well. All this troubled us both very much, but our anxiety and pity for our little girl overrode all the rest and we decided to leave for Petersburg the very next day.

I have to remember the Rumyantsev family with heartfelt gratitude. Thanks to their concern everything turned out all right. I was told afterwards that when my son felt hungry he kept looking for me, showed his nurse the door with his finger, and said "there." The old woman carried him from room to room. When he didn't find me anywhere the child broke into tears, pushed away the milk that was offered him, and didn't sleep the night through. Then he grew used to drinking from a bottle and was quite well. But to me the most wounding thing was the fact that when I—who had so longed for my Fedya—returned to Russa three weeks later, he didn't recognize me, his mother, and didn't come into my arms—in other words, he had managed to forget me completely.

Our voyage to Petersburg was a sad one, and the view of Lake Ilmen and the River Volkhov before our eyes did not hold our attention. That was focused entirely on the problem of how to keep our little girl from hurting herself further. In order to keep her from lying on her injured arm at night and disturbing it, my husband and I worked out a guard duty. We changed shifts every two hours and waited impatiently for the long trip to be over.

As I have already mentioned, we had no apartment. Therefore we decided to stay in the empty city apartment belonging to my brother Vanya, who had moved with his wife and mother to a summer house in the suburbs. It was a stifling hot day. The first words of the servant who answered the door were, "But our old mistress is ill."

"Good Lord, what's wrong with her? Where is she? At the dacha?"

"No, here in the apartment."

I ran into my mother's room and saw her, very white and hollow-cheeked, sitting on the couch with her leg all bound up. I began questioning her and learned that she had had an accident the day our furniture was moved to the Kokorev warehouse. She wasn't sufficiently watchful and a workman, probably drunk, dropped a full trunk on her foot. The big toe of her left foot was crushed. The doctor had told her that an inflammation had set in, forbade her to move, and could not promise recovery in less than a month.

Immediately upon our arrival Fyodor Mikhailovich went to see Ivan Martynovich Barch, the chief physician at Maximilian Hospital. He was one of the best surgeons in Petersburg at that time. He was an old friend of Fyodor Mikhailovich's, but my husband had not yet paid him a visit after returning from abroad. We had wanted to go to him when our daughter first had the accident with her wrist, but my husband knew that Barch would refuse to take any payment for the visit, and that would have embarrassed us very much; to repay him with some gift, however, was beyond our means. And then too, the surgeon treating her arm had seemed competent to us and had described the problem as such a trivial dislocation that we felt awkward at going to such a celebrity as Barch then was. Fyodor Mikhailovich upbraided himself bitterly for that and could never forgive either himself or me for "this negligence of ours," as he later wrote.

Dr. Barch received Fyodor Mikhailovich with great friendliness, chided him for not coming to him from the very beginning, and promised to pay us a visit that evening. He arrived at the appointed hour, managed to get the little girl interested in his watch and the ornaments on his watch chain, unobtrusively unbound the wrist, didn't even palpate it, so as not to cause her needless pain, but said straight out that the Staraya Russa doctors had made a correct diagnosis and that the bone was improperly knit together. In his opinion there was very little possibility that the child's right hand would be shorter than her left, but he warned us nonetheless that the hollow on one side of the arm and the small bump on the palm side would be visible. In order to correct the damage it was necessary to break the bone again and let it knit in a plaster cast.

Fyodor Mikhailovich said that he knew how terribly painful such an operation was and feared the child could not endure it.

"But she won't feel a thing—the operation will be performed under chloroform."

"The doctors in Staraya Russa told us that chloroform is not used on small children," said my husband, "because that is too dangerous."

The surgeon smiled at that. "The Russa doctors can do as they please, but we use chloroform even on young infants and everything goes perfectly well."

As he questioned us in detail, Barch kept looking at me closely. My flushed appearance did not escape his expert notice.

"But are you well yourself?" he asked, turning to me. "Why is your face so red? Why, you have a fever!"

At that point I had to admit that I had been feeling feverish all night and that my head had been spinning and aching terribly all day, and I explained the reason.

Fyodor Mikhailovich was deeply alarmed and began reproaching me for concealing my condition from him.

"Look here, Madame," said Barch, "we'll cure your daughter, but I won't undertake any surgery until you are well yourself. Your milk might go to your head, and that is no joke. Here, send to the apothecary for the medicine I'm going to prescribe for you, and try to have a good sleep."

When he learned that we were living in a strange apartment and had another sick person with us as well, Barch suggested that we move to Maximilian Hospital, where we could take a private room, for three weeks. He did not think the bone would knit before that time and would not undertake surgery unless we remained in Petersburg throughout the period of convalescence. It is understandable that as a first-class surgeon he did not wish to take responsibility for an operation which might turn out a failure because of the incompetence of the doctor in Staraya Russa who would supervise the course of treatment and remove the cast.

My husband and I decided immediately that we would move to the hospital the next day, and Barch promised to perform the operation that very day, if possible.

The day came, so painful, so filled with doubt. We arrived at the hospital at about noon and Apollon Maikov, our daughter's godfather, joined us shortly afterward. Barch had requested the day before that one of our relatives or friends be present during surgery, and Fyodor Mikhailovich had asked Maikov to do it.

It was decided that the chloroform would be administered to the child while she was having her usual nap after lunch. But she was overexcited by the trip through the city and the unfamiliar surroundings, and she could not fall asleep. Then the decision was made to administer the chloroform while she was awake.

Barch and his assistant, Dr. Glama, came into the room. When Barch found out that my husband and I were planning to be present during the operation, he forbade it.

"Look here," he said, "one of you will faint and the other one will have an attack, and we'll be bringing you both back to consciousness—and there goes the operation! No, you both have to leave, and I'll send for you if it becomes necessary."

We made the sign of the cross over our little girl several times and kissed her, and since she was falling asleep under the effect of the chloroform, Barch took her out of my arms and put her gently down on the bed. My husband and I walked out of that room feeling like death, not expecting to see our daughter alive again. A servant led us to a distant room and left us alone. Fyodor Mikhailovich was white as a handkerchief. His hands were shaking; I too, in my agitation, could barely stand up.

"Anya, let's pray, let's ask God's help, the Lord will help us!" he said in a breaking voice, and we got down on our knees and prayed as fervently during those moments as perhaps we had ever prayed in our lives before. And then we heard hurried footsteps, and Maikov came into the room.

"Go there, Barch is calling for you," he said.

The same thought came to both Fyodor Mikhailovich and me: that our Lyubochka had not survived the anesthetic and that Barch was summoning us to be present during her last moments. I had never before experienced a horror like that. Before my eyes I vividly pictured my first child's death. My husband took me by the arm and squeezed it convulsively, and we went down the corridor as fast as we could, almost at a run.

As we entered the room we saw Barch obviously excited, without his jacket and with his white shirtsleeves rolled up. He indicated to us by a gesture that we were to approach the bed on which our little girl was peacefully asleep. Her broken wrist, now perfectly *straight,* without the earlier lump which had given us so much anxiety, was flung out and was lying on a little pillow.

"Now take a look," said Barch. "You can see that the wrist is perfectly straight—and I think you didn't believe me. And now move away and let me finish up."

Right then and there in front of the three of us Barch tied up her wrist and wrapped it in a plaster cast, and did it all with such speed (seven minutes) that the operation was over before we realized it. Dr. Glama kept track of the child's pulse throughout the precedure. Then Barch felt it was time to rouse her and had me call her loudly by name. For a long time she couldn't wake up, but when she recovered consciousness she was surprised at her bound-up wrist and announced that she had a "sugar wist" (because of the color of the plaster).

My Lord, how insanely happy we were when it was all over, when the doctors had left and we were alone with our dear little one! It seemed to us that all our griefs and cares had disappeared and would never return. Unfortunately, however, things did not turn out that way in reality.

Fyodor Mikhailovich stayed in Petersburg for one more day. Since the result of the operation (that is, whether the bone had knit properly this time) could not be ascertained before three weeks, he decided not to wait but to go at once to Russa, to his Fedya, for whom he had been longing all this while.

But when I was left alone with Lyuba in Petersburg, I didn't realize the torments I would still have to go through. In the first place, I developed a terrible anxiety that she might fall on her injured wrist when running about the room or might knock it against something. The plaster might break at any clumsy movement, the bandages might come apart, and then the bone would knit improperly again. I watched her every second; but since she was a lively child my nerves grew terribly strained from constant fear and over-anxious attention. On top of that I slept badly at night, waking up every minute to see whether she was lying on the injured arm in her sleep.

And the child was accustomed to living in a family, to seeing people around her, that is, her father, brother, nanny, and so forth; whereas here she was doomed to complete solitude and was therefore understandably bored and capricious, and used to cry. The city was hot and stifling and the hospital rooms smelled of medicine. One simply had to go out into the air, and moreover I wanted to visit my mother, who still could not seem to recover. And in going out, how many chances of falling, of injuring the child! I wasn't strong enough to carry her, she couldn't walk very far, and riding in carriages was a genuine torment—it was so easy to injure the child's wrist while climbing into or getting out of the drozhky.

In addition to my fear for Lyuba, I couldn't shake off my worry for my husband. Might he have had an attack? I saw from his letters that he missed us and worried about us, and there was no way for me to help him. I tormented myself also with longing for my dear little boy; I worried because the wound on my mother's foot was not only not healing but growing even worse. Thanks to all this my nerves became so impossibly overstrained that I had fits of weeping and sobbing several times a day.

But trouble continued to pursue us. A few days after my husband's departure for Russa my brother Ivan (who was awaiting the birth of a child at any moment and could therefore leave his country house only for a very short time each day to visit my mother and me) came to me looking so miserable and broken up that I noticed it at once.

I began questioning him closely as to whether something had happened. He answered that everything was all right: his wife was well, Mama was even a little better. Then why was he looking so woebegone, and why did there sometimes seem to be tears in his eyes? I thought to myself.

He left soon afterward, but it occurred to me that some accident might have happened to Fyodor Mikhailovich or to my son and that my brother was concealing this from me. My anxiety reached the ultimate limits. All night long I could not sleep, picturing various horrors. Early in the morning I telegraphed my brother to come to me without fail.

And he came, looking just as crushed and miserable as the day before. I told him my suspicions about some accident to my family in Russa and added that I couldn't bear this anxiety any longer and was therefore planning to set out for home this very day together with my daughter, taking the risk of ruining her recovery.

My brother started reassuring me that there was no bad news from Russa and that the cause of his sadness was something different. In view of my insistence my brother, fearing that I might really leave, dared at last to tell me about the new sorrow which had befallen us. Our only sister, Masha, was dead.

She had gone abroad with her husband and her two older children in November, 1871, leaving the two younger ones in Petersburg. They settled in Rome in February, 1872. While out walking there she contracted malaria or, in the opinion of some doctors, typhus. She was ill for two months and died on May 1. Her husband for some reason did not find it possible to inform us of her death and told his sister (who was living with his children) only that they would be returning home soon.

My brother and I loved our sister Masha very dearly, and the news of her untimely death was a dreadful blow to us. She was a very beautiful, healthy, and high-spirited woman, and she had only just reached thirty. On top of our deep grief for her we were worried about the fate of her four children, to whom she had been a very loving mother. There were no bounds to our despair and my poor little daughter, seeing us weep, also burst into tears. I shall never forget the sadness of that day.

And a painful task lay before us. We had to tell my mother that our sister was dead. It was her eldest child, her favorite; and my brother and I feared she would not survive the blow and would suffer a stroke or go out of her mind.

We decided to conceal the news of our sister's death from our mother for a time. I planned to persuade her to come to Russa with me and to tell her there, preparing her gradually for the sad news. In that case I counted on the help of my husband, who always got along very well with my mother and had an influence over her. But Fyodor Mikhailovich opposed our plan with all his might[13] and felt that it would only deepen her grief if we carried it out. He convinced us that we must tell her at once while she could share her sorrow with her orphaned grandchildren.

Our task was complicated by still another consideration. When my mother's doctor heard of our loss, he asked me to conceal it from her until her foot was healed. He declared that the inflammation (a consequence of excitement and tears) would doubtless grow worse, and then they would have to amputate the toe.

What decision to take? That was the terrible question my

brother and I had to resolve. And my brother, moreover, had his own heavy cares. His wife was due to give birth any day, and since this was her first child they were both terribly worried about whether the confinement would go well. And I too had my heart's pangs: about my dear little son, Fyodor Mikhailovich, the success or failure of my daughter's operation, my mother's illness. And now we were stricken by a fresh, heavy grief. That is when you see plainly that a merciful God in sending us ordeals grants us also the strength to endure them!

And so we resolved to conceal the news of our sister's death from my dear mother for a time. But how difficult that was! For Mama spoke about her daughter as if she were alive, wrote letters to her, prepared presents for her arrival. How dreadful it was for us to listen to her talk about Masha and guard our every word so as not to blurt it all out, for the very mention of her name produced anguish in us. Mama often noticed that I was crying, but I assured her that I was worried about the success of the operation or about my family in Staraya Russa.

Time passed, and we kept postponing the decision to reveal our secret. Suddenly, however, my dear mother, distressed because she had had no news of her sick daughter, decided to visit her younger grandchildren. No matter how hard my brother and I tried to dissuade her or suggest that the trip might cause further damage to her injured foot, she insisted on having her way.

What my brother and I went through that day! We drove slowly so as not to disturb my mother's injured foot, and I felt as though I were being taken to my execution.

We drew up to my sister's house on Italyanskaya Street, and the doorman and porter carried my mother in their arms to the second floor. The elder children, Lyalya and Olya, ran to meet my mother on the staircase. But my poor mother was struck by the fact that my sister didn't come out with them. She *suddenly* (as she told us afterwards) felt convinced that her daughter was no longer in the world.

"Masha is dead! My dear Masha is dead!" she screamed hysterically, and burst into sobs. The children began crying, my brother and I also cried, and Pavel Grigoryevich, my sister's husband, also came out, very upset. Then a harrowing scene of grief and despair took place which words cannot convey. Perhaps two hours passed before we gained some control over ourselves. We had to think about taking my mother home. My brother had to hurry to his sick wife, I had to return to Lyubochka in the hospital, and meanwhile our tears and anguish went on.

Finally, my mother gave in to our urging and our promise to bring her to the orphans again in a few days; and we took her back home, just as slowly as we had come. From her house I rushed to the hospital. There, fortunately, everything was all right. I found both Lyuba and the nurse sleeping soundly on the bed. I dressed my daughter at once and took her to my mother's for the balance of the day, since I couldn't bring myself to leave my mother alone in her deep grief. We cried together a lot, and there was a certain relief for me in not having to hide any longer the secret weighing so heavily on my brother and myself.

When Lyuba and I returned to Staraya Russa there was a period of calm and quiet, but it did not last very long. Following a severe chill (the summer was cold and rainy) I developed an abscess in my throat and had a temperature of about 104 degrees for a few days. The chief Army doctor, N. A. Schenk, who was there for the season and was treating me, deemed it necessary one sad day to warn Fyodor Mikhailovich that if the abscess did not burst within twenty-four hours he would not answer for my life, for my strength was failing and my heart was weak.

When he heard those words Fyodor Mikhailovich fell into utter despair. So as not to frighten me he did not cry in front of me, but went to Father Ioann, sat down at the table, covered his face with his hands, and burst into sobs. The priest's wife came over to him and asked what the doctor had said.

"Anna Grigoryevna is dying!" he said in a voice breaking with sobs. "What will I do without her? How can I live without her —she is *everything* to me!"

The good woman put her arms around his shoulders and began to comfort him. "Don't cry, Fyodor Mikhailovich, don't feel so badly. God is merciful, he won't leave you and the children orphans!"

Her heartfelt sympathy and words of comfort had a beneficial effect on him and lifted his failing spirits. He always remembered her sympathy with gratitude and respected her deeply.

My own despair during my illness can be imagined. I saw that my condition was growing worse. For several days I had not been able to speak a word, but only wrote what I wanted on little pieces of paper. As I looked at the temperature chart the doctor marked twice a day (Fyodor Mikhailovich had hidden the chart, but the children's nurse, not understanding what it meant, showed it to me when I asked her to) I understood clearly the way things were going.

I made signs first to Fyodor Mikhailovich and then to the children to come over to me. I kissed them, blessed them and wrote down for my husband my instructions as to what he was to do in the event of my death. But a kind of dumb indifference settled on me in the last two days before the crisis. Somehow I felt no pity either for Fyodor Mikhailovich or for the children; it was as though I had already left the world.

The crisis occurred that same night. The abscess in my throat burst and I began to recover. In two weeks or so there was another throat abscess, but this time in milder form. So ended that phase of the calamities which befell us in the year 1872.

I have undergone many bitter experiences in my life. There were terrible losses—my husband, my son Alyosha—but such a time of catastrophes never repeated itself again.

CHAPTER SIX

The Years 1872 and 1873

By the autumn of 1872 we had recovered somewhat from the painful experiences of that unhappy summer. After our return from Staraya Russa we moved into the house of General Meves at the second company of the Izmailovsky Regiment. Our apartment was on the second floor of a detached house deep inside the court. It consisted of five rooms, not large but comfortably laid out, in addition to a sitting room with three windows. Fyodor Mikhailovich's study was medium-sized and was far away from the nursery, so that the children with their hubbub and running about could not disturb him while he was at work.

Although my husband had been working on *The Possessed* all summer, he was so dissatisfied with it that he discarded his former plan completely and revised all of Part Three. He had been in Moscow in October and had arranged with his editor for Part Three of the novel to appear in the last two issues of the *Russian Messenger.* I must say that *The Possessed* had an enormous success with the reading public, but at the same time it brought my husband a great many enemies in the literary world.[1]

As I reflected on our distressing financial situation, I began to think about ways of augmenting our income through my own labor and taking up my stenographic work again, for I had made considerable progress in it during the past few years. I began asking my family and friends to find me work as a stenographer in some institution.

My old stenography teacher, P. M. Olkhin, obtained a position for me through an acquaintance at a forestry conference. N. S. Shafranov, editor of a forestry journal, had written on July 17, asking me to come to Moscow between August 3 and 13. Unfortunately, I was so depressed by the painful events of that summer that I turned down the work.

In the winter of 1872 my brother, who had moved to Petersburg with his young wife not long before, told me that a conference (I do not recall in what government department) was to take place soon in one of the cities of the western provinces, and that a stenographer was being sought for it. I wrote immediately to the chairman of the conference, on whom the choice of stenographer depended. Naturally I did this with Fyodor Mikhailovich's consent, although he maintained that I was doing enough for the family by caring for the children and the household, and helping him with his work besides. Seeing my fervent wish to earn some money by my own labors, however, he could not bring himself to oppose me. (He admitted to me later that he was counting on a rejection from the chairman of the conference.)

The latter, however, agreed to hire me and told me the conditions. I cannot say they were tempting: the greater part of my salary would go toward train fare and the cost of living in a hotel. But it was not so much the money as the start of my employment which was important. If I performed my job well I might find other and more profitable work through a recommendation from the chairman of the conference.

Fyodor Mikhailovich had no serious objections to my taking the trip, since my mother had promised to come and look after both the children and the household during my absence. Nor did Fyodor Mikhailovich have any work for me to do, since he was then in the process of revising *The Possessed.* But just the same, he was not a bit happy about this proposed trip of mine. He contrived every possible pretext to keep me from going. He asked how I, as a young woman, could think of traveling alone to a Polish city where I did not know a single soul, what kind of living arrangements I would make, and so forth.

On hearing objections of this sort, my brother recalled that one of his old school friends was traveling to the conference, a man who knew the western provinces well, and he invited

Fyodor Mikhailovich and me to come for tea to meet his friend and receive all the information from him.

On the appointed evening we went to my brother's house. Fyodor Mikhailovich, who had not had an attack for a long time, was in an excellent mood. We chatted quietly with my brother and his wife while waiting for his friend to arrive. I had never seen him but had heard a good deal about him from my brother. He was a goodhearted but not very bright young man from the Caucasus, nicknamed "the wild Asian" by his school friends because of his hotheadedness and rashness. This sobriquet made him very indignant, and to prove that he was a "European" he set up idols for himself in every field of art. In music, his god was Chopin, in painting, Repin, and in literature, Dostoevsky.

My brother went out to the vestibule to greet his guests. When the poor young man learned that he was about to meet Dostoevsky and even, perhaps, do him a service, he was first ecstatic but then took fright. As he entered the drawing room and saw his idol, he was so abashed that he nodded awkwardly to his hostess and to my husband without saying anything. He was about twenty-three, tall and curly-haired, with prominent eyes and bright red lips.

Seeing his friend's embarrassment, my brother hastened to introduce him to me. The "Asian" seized my hand, kissed it, shook it hard several times, and said, burring his *r*'s: "How happy I am that you are going to the conference and that I can be of service to you!"

His enthusiasm amused me but angered my husband deeply. Fyodor Mikhailovich, who used to kiss women's hands himself (though seldom) and never ascribed any special significance to this act, was always displeased when anyone kissed my hand. My brother, noticing that Fyodor Mikhailovich's mood had changed (my husband's mood swings were always sharp ones) hastened to start a businesslike conversation on the subject of the conference. The "Asian," very shy as before and not daring to look at Fyodor Mikhailovich when answering questions, directed his remarks mostly to me. I remember some of his polite but absurd answers.

"Is it difficult to get to Alexandria?" I asked him. "Are there many changes?"

"Don't worry, Anna Grigoryevna, I myself will accompany you. And I can even ride in the same compartment with you if you like."

"Is there a decent hotel in Alexandria where a young woman can stop?" my husband asked.

The young man looked at him enraptured and exclaimed fervidly, "I was planning to stay with a school friend, but if Anna Grigoryevna wants me to, I can stop at the same hotel with her."

My husband cried out loudly, "Do you hear that, Anya? The young man is ready to move in with you!" And he banged on the table with all his might.

A glass of tea standing in front of him fell to the floor and broke. Our hostess rushed to steady a lighted lamp, rocking with the force of the blow, and Fyodor Mikhailovich jumped up from his seat, ran into the front hall, threw on his coat, and ran outside.

I quickly put on my things and dashed after my husband. Out on the street I caught sight of him running in the opposite direction from where we lived. I ran after him and caught up with him very soon. He was panting hard by that time but refused to stop despite my entreaties. I ran in front of him, grabbed with both hands the edges of the coat he had thrown over his shoulders, and exclaimed, "Fedya, you're out of your mind! Where on earth are you running? This isn't even the way home! Stop—put your arms into your coat sleeves—you can't go about like this, you'll catch a chill!"

My excited face took effect on my husband. He stopped running and put on his coat. I buttoned him up, took him by the arm, and led him back in the opposite direction. He remained silent in his embarrassment.

"What is this—you're having a jealous fit again, aren't you?" I said indignantly. "Do you think I've managed to fall in love with 'the wild Asian' in the space of a few minutes? And he with me? And we're getting ready to run away together, isn't that right? Well, now, aren't you ashamed of yourself! Can't you understand that you are insulting me with your jealousy? We've been married for five years—you know how much I love you and how I treasure our family happiness—and yet you are capable of being jealous of the first man I meet, and putting me and yourself into a ridiculous position!"

My husband apologized, tried to justify himself, and promised never to be jealous again. I couldn't be angry with him for long. I knew that he was incapable of maintaining his self-control during a fit of jealousy. I began to laugh as I recalled that rapturous young man and Fyodor Mikhailovich's sudden fury and flight. Seeing the change in my mood, my husband also began chaffing himself, asked how many things he had broken at my brother's house and whether he had by any chance knocked down his enthusiastic admirer as well?

It was a glorious evening and we went home on foot, a long walk which took more than an hour. At home we found my brother waiting. He had taken fright at our abrupt departure, had rushed to our house, and was terribly upset not to find us at home. He had been waiting for us for a whole hour filled with the gloomiest forebodings, and was astonished to see us in a peaceful mood. We made him stay to have tea with us and laughed a lot as we talked over what had happened. When we asked how he had explained our odd flight to his friend from the Caucasus, my brother replied, "He asked me what was wrong and I said to him, 'Well go to hell if you can't understand it yourself!' "

After this episode I realized I would have to decline my new work. I might have talked my husband into letting me go even now, of course. But the moment I was gone he would get excited and worry about me. And then, unable to contain himself, he would go to Alexandria to fetch me back. There would be a scandalous scene and the money we had so little of anyway would go for nothing.

So ended my effort to earn some money by stenography.

The following curious incident occurred in our family on Christmas of 1872.

Fyodor Mikhailovich, a very tender father, was constantly thinking of ways to entertain his children. He always made a special fuss about setting up the tree—insisted that I buy a tall, bushy one, decorated it himself (the decorations were kept over from year to year), and would climb up on a stool to attach the candles at the top and affix the star firmly.

Our Christmas celebration for 1872 was a very special one. It was the first time our elder son Fedya was "consciously" present. The candles on the tree had been lighted earlier and Fyodor Mikhailovich solemnly led his two nestlings into the drawing room. The children, of course, were wonderstruck by the glowing lights, the decorations, and the toys all around the tree. Their papa handed out their gifts to them: for his daughter, a charming doll and a set of tiny dishes; for his son a big trumpet that he started blowing immediately, and a drum.

But the thing that produced the greatest effect on both children was a pair of bay horses with luxuriant manes and tails, made of pasteboard and harnessed to a basswood sleigh, a broad double-sized one. The children dropped their toys and sat down in the sleigh; and Fedya grabbed the reins and began shaking them and urging the horses on. The little girl soon grew bored with the sleigh and began playing with other toys. It was quite different with the boy, however. He was beside himself with glee, shouted at the horses and smacked them with the reins, probably remembering the way the peasants had done it when they drove by our country house at Staraya Russa. Only by some ruse or other did we manage to get him out of the sitting room and into his bed.

For a long time Fyodor Mikhailovich sat there talking over the details of our little celebration. He was, if anything, happier about it than his children. I went to bed at midnight, but my husband showed me a new book bought that day at Wolf's, which he was very interested in and was planning to sit up and read that night.

That was not the way things turned out, however. At about one he heard frenzied sobbing in the nursery, rushed there and found our little boy red in the face with screaming, trying to squirm out of his elderly nurse Prokhorovna's arms and mumbling some kind of unintelligible words (he was not yet a year and a half old, and he still spoke unclearly).

I too was awakened by the child's cries and ran to the nursery. Since his screaming might awaken his sister, asleep in the same room, Fyodor Mikhailovich carried him into his study. When we were passing through the sitting room and Fedya caught sight of the sleigh by the light of the candle, he stopped crying at once and stretched out toward it with all the strength of his robust little body, so that Fyodor Mikhailovich wasn't able to hold on to him and had to sit him down in the sleigh.

Though the tears still went on rolling down his cheeks, he was already laughing; he grabbed the reins and began shaking them again and making a smacking sound with his lips as though urging the horses on. When he seemed quite pacified Fyodor Mikhailovich tried to take him back into the nursery, but the child broke into bitter sobs and cried until he was put back into the sleigh.

At that point his father and I (who had been alarmed at first by this mysterious illness that had befallen the child and had already decided to call the doctor, despite the lateness of the hour) realized what the matter was. It was evident that the child's imagination was fired with the Christmas tree, the toys, and the pleasure he experienced while sitting in his sleigh; and when he awoke in the night he remembered his horses and wanted his new toy. And when his demands were not met he raised the shout which achieved his objective.

There was nothing to be done. The little boy was wide awake and would not go to bed. So as not to keep all three of us up, it was decided that Nanny and I would go to bed while Fyodor Mikhailovich sat up with the little fellow, and would put him into his crib when he grew tired. And that was what we did.

The next morning, my husband complained to me cheerfully, "My, and didn't Fedya wear me out last night: I didn't let him out of my sight for two or three hours, worrying that he would fall out of the sleigh somehow and hurt himself. Nanny came twice to take him "bye-bye" but he just waved his little arms at her and got ready to burst out crying all over again. So we stayed there together till about five in the morning. Then he evidently tired and started leaning over to the side. I lifted him up and saw that he was fast asleep, and carried him into the nursery. So I couldn't even open the book I bought," he laughed, obviously very pleased that an episode which frightened us so at first had ended so well.

After finishing *The Possessed* Fyodor Mikhailovich was very undecided for a while as to what to take up next. He was so exhausted by his work on the novel that it seemed impossible to him to set to work right away on a new one. And yet, the realization of the idea conceived while we were still living abroad[2]—namely, the publication of a monthly journal, *Diary of a Writer*—presented problems. Quite substantial means were needed for putting out a journal and maintaining a family, not to mention the settlement of our debts. And there was also the question of whether such a journal would have much success, since it was something entirely new in Russian literature up to that time, both in form and in content. And if the *Diary* proved a failure we would be put into a hopeless position.

Fyodor Mikhailovich felt very uncertain about it; and I do not know what decision he would have taken if just at that time Prince Vladimir Meshchersky had not offered him the position of editor of the weekly journal *The Citizen.*[3] It had been founded only a year before under the editorship of G. K. Gradovsky; and a group of people holding similar ideas and views had formed around the new publication. Some of them—K. P. Pobedonostsev, Apollon Maikov, T. I. Filippov, Nikolai Strakhov, A. U. Poretsky, E. A. Belov—were men whom Fyodor Mikhailovich found congenial, and working with them appealed to him. No less attractive was the opportunity to share more closely with his readers those hopes and doubts which were ripening in his mind. The idea of *Diary of a Writer* might be realized in the pages of *The Citizen,* even though in a different format from the one given it subsequently.

From a material point of view the matter was arranged comparatively well. Fyodor Mikhailovich's editorial duties would be compensated at three thousand rubles in addition to separate payment for the column "Diary of a Writer" and later for his political articles. All in all we would receive about five thousand a year. There was another advantage to a regular monthly salary. It allowed Fyodor Mikhailovich not to be distracted from his work by concern with living expenses, which so oppressively affected his health and frame of mind.

Having given in to the urgings of congenial people to edit *The Citizen,* however, Fyodor Mikhailovich did not conceal from them the fact that this undertaking was temporary, a kind of respite from fiction writing which would also bring him into closer touch with current events; but that he would leave this field, so foreign to his nature, when the need for creative work arose once again.

The beginning of 1873 is particularly memorable because it marked the appearance of the first novel published by my husband and myself—*The Possessed.* This book was the cornerstone of our joint publishing activity and, after his death, of my own work, which continued for thirty-eight years.

One of our hopes (and perhaps our main hope) for putting our financial situation to rights was the possibility of selling the publishing rights to *The Idiot,* and after that *The Possessed,* as separate books. While we were living abroad it was difficult to negotiate such a sale; and it did not grow any easier even after we returned to Russia and were able to hold personal discussions with publishers. No matter whom we turned to, we were offered very unfavorable prices. Thus, the bookseller A. F. Bazunov paid us one hundred fifty rubles for the right to publish *The Eternal Husband* as a separate book (in two thousand copies). For the rights to *The Possessed* we were offered only five hundred rubles, and even that in installments spread over two years.

Even as a youth Fyodor Mikhailovich had dreamed of publishing his own work, and he had written his brother on the subject and discussed it with me while we were still abroad. I too was very much taken with the idea, and little by little I tried to learn all I could about the publication and distribution of books. When ordering visiting cards for my husband I had a talk with the owner of the printing shop and inquired about terms for book publishing. He explained to me that most books were published on a cash basis; but that if the author had a big literary name and his books were good sellers, any printer would willingly extend a six-month credit on condition that a certain percentage of interest be levied on the unpaid balance after six months. The same credit could be obtained on paper also, and he gave me a rough estimate of the cost of the publication I was planning, that is, the cost of paper, printing, and binding.

By his estimate, publication of *The Possessed* in thirty-five hundred copies might come to about four thousand rubles. For a three-volume edition printed in large, elegant type on satiny white paper, the printer suggested a price no lower than three rubles fifty kopecks. Out of the total sum of 12,250 rubles received for all the copies sold, about 30 percent would go to the bookseller. But even so, taking all additional expenses into consideration, we would net a considerable sum for ourselves if sales went well.

In those days no writer published his own work, and even if such a bold fellow did appear he would inevitably pay for his daring by taking a loss. There were several book firms in existence—Bazunov, Wolf, Isakov and others—who bought book rights and printed and distributed books throughout Russia. Books published by learned societies or private persons, however, were taken by the booksellers either for stock or on consignment at a 50 percent discount. This was done under the pretext that the storage and promotion of books (which they actually did on a very niggardly scale) was a large expense to them. Moreover, the unsold books given for stock or on consignment were returned to the publisher, sometimes even in bad condition.

Since we wished to publish *The Possessed* ourselves, I tried to make inquiries in the bookshops as to discount, but received vague answers: that the discount depended on the book, that it might be 40 or 50 percent or even more. Once, when I was buying a book for my husband which cost three rubles, I checked on this. I asked them to let me have the book for two rubles since they themselves received a 50 percent discount, so that the cost of the book to them was a ruble and a half. The salesman was indignant at this proposal and stated that they themselves received a discount of 20 or 25, or in a few cases 30 percent, and then only on condition that they purchase a large quantity. Through questions like these I was able to clarify the relationship between the quantity of copies and the discount one had to extend to the booksellers.

When we told our friends and acquaintances that we wanted to publish the novel ourselves many objections were raised, and we were advised not to embark on so unfamiliar an enterprise which, due to our inexperience, would inevitably ruin us, so that we might pile up a few thousand in new debts on top of our old ones. But these remonstrances had no effect on us, and we decided to carry our plan through.

We bought our printing paper from the firm of A. I. Vargunin, the best manufacturer of rag paper then as now. And we gave the printing to the firm of Zamyslovsky, just then transferred to the Panteleyev brothers. The end of 1872 and the beginning of the following year passed in work connected with the book. I read the first and second proofs and Fyodor Mikhailovich read the page proofs.

The book was bound about the twentieth of January and part of the stock was delivered to our house. Fyodor Mikhailovich was very pleased with its appearance, and I was enchanted with it. The day before publication Fyodor Mikhailovich took a copy to show to a very prominent bookseller, from whom he bought books all the time, in the hope that he might wish to buy a certain number of copies. The bookseller turned the book over in his hands and said, "Well, all right, send me two hundred copies on consignment."

"But at what discount?"

"No less than 50 percent."

Fyodor Mikhailovich did not reply. Downcast, he came home and told me about his failure. I too was worried, and the bookseller's proposition of two hundred copies on consignment didn't make me happy at all. I knew that even if he sold the books we would have a long wait for our money.

The great day in our lives came on January 22, 1873, when our advertisement of the publication of *The Possessed* appeared in the newspaper *The Voice.* At about ten in the morning a messenger arrived from the bookshop of M. V. Popov, located under the Galleries. I came out into the vestibule and asked what he wanted.

"It's about your advertisement—I need ten copies."

I brought him the books and said in some agitation, "The price for ten copies is thirty-five rubles with a 20 percent discount—that's twenty-eight rubles."

"Why so little? Can't you make it 30 percent?" asked the messenger.

"Impossible."

"Then 25 percent, at least?"

"Really no, impossible," I said, inwardly very worried and thinking, what if he goes away and I lose my first customer?

"Well, if it's impossible, then take it." And he handed me the money.

I was so pleased that I even gave him thirty kopecks for a cab. A little later a boy came from an out-of-town bookshop and bought ten copies, also at a 20 percent discount, and also after bargaining with me. The messenger from Glazunov's bookshop wanted twenty-five copies if I would give him 25 percent off. In view of the large quantity I had to give in.

Several more people came. All took ten copies apiece and all tried to bargain with me, but I would not let them have any more than 20 percent off. At about noon a very elegantly dressed salesman arrived from the bookseller Fyodor Mikhailovich had approached at the beginning, and announced that he was there to take two hundred copies on consignment. Emboldened by my success with the morning's sales, I replied that I did not give books on consignment but sold them for cash.

"But how can that be? Fyodor Mikhailovich promised to send them to us on consignment, and that's why I'm here."

I said that my husband was the publisher but I was in charge of sales, and that such-and-such booksellers had bought the book for cash.

"But then can't I talk to Fyodor Mikhailovich himself?" the salesman asked, evidently relying on my husband's more yielding nature.

"Fyodor Mikhailovich worked all night, and I will not awaken him before two o'clock."

The salesman asked me to let him take the two hundred copies with him and "give the money direct to Fyodor Mikhailovich."

I remained firm on this point also and, after explaining what discount I allowed for how many copies, I said that we had only five hundred copies on hand and expected to sell them all that day. The salesman hesitated and went away with nothing for his pains. But within an hour another messenger, a bit less grand, came from the same shop and bought fifty copies for cash at a 30 percent discount. I wanted terribly to share my glee with

Fyodor Mikhailovich, but I had to wait till he came out of his room.

Apropos of this, I must mention that my husband had a strange trait. When he woke up in the morning he seemed to be still completely under the spell of the dreams and nightmares which sometimes tormented him. He was very taciturn and very much disliked being spoken to then. Therefore, I acquired the habit of not bothering him with anything in the morning, no matter how important. I would wait until after he had drunk two cups of scalding hot coffee in the dining room and had gone into his study. Then I would go to him and tell him all the news, pleasant and unpleasant. At that point he would be in the most benign of moods, show an interest in everything, ask about everything, call the children, and play and joke with them.

So it was on this occasion as well. When he was talking to the children I sent them back to the nursery and sat down at my usual place near his desk. Seeing that I was silent Fyodor Mikhailovich asked, looking at me teasingly, "Well, Anechka, how is our business going?"

"Marvelously," I answered in the same vein.

"And you—you've managed, perhaps, to sell a book?"

"Not 'a' book, but a hundred and fifteen."

"You don't say! Congratulations, then," he continued his teasing, assuming that I was having a joke.

"And I'm telling you the truth," I said, vexed. "Why don't you believe me?" And I took out of my pocket the piece of paper with my notation on the number of books sold, and together with it a wad of banknotes, about three hundred rubles in all.

Since he knew we didn't have much money at home, the sum I showed him convinced him that I wasn't joking.

And after four o'clock there were more rings at the door. New buyers came, and the morning buyers returned for a new supply of books. It was evident that the book was having a great success, and I felt a rare sense of triumph. I was happy about the money, of course, but mainly because I had found myself an interesting business—the publication of my dear husband's work. I was pleased also with the fact that the enterprise had come out so well in defiance of the warnings of my literary advisors.

Fyodor Mikhailovich was also very pleased, particularly when I told him one salesman's remark that "the public has been asking for the novel for a long time." Public support was always very precious to him, since it alone had sustained him with its attention and sympathy throughout his literary career; whereas the critics (with the exception of Belinsky, Dobrolyubov and Burenin) did very little at that time to interpret his talent to readers. They either ignored his work or treated it with hostility.[4] Now, more than thirty-five years after his death, I even find it strange to reread the critics' reviews of my husband's work —their judgments were so shallow, superficial, and frivolous, and often so deeply hostile.

But my triumph was complete when the bookseller Kozhanchikov came to us with an offer to buy three hundred copies right away on a four-month promissory note. He asked for the regular discount, that is, 30 percent. Kozhanchikov's offer was tempting, since he was taking the books for the provinces and therefore wouldn't interfere with our city trade. What troubled us was that he would be taking them on notes, and Fyodor Mikhailovich came to ask my opinion about this. I had no idea what a commercial note was at that time and therefore suggested to my husband that he should chat for a while with the buyer while I would drive over to the printer, who lived not far away.

Luckily I found one of the Panteleyevs at home, and he advised me not to lose such a solid sale. He assured me that Kozhanchikov's notes were good and that he would be willing to accept them in payment of our printing debt. I returned home with this news. Kozhanchikov immediately wrote out three notes for seven hundred thirty-five rubles (as an experienced businessman he always had blanks on him); and Fyodor Mikhailovich gave him a voucher so that he could obtain the books from the printer.

In a word, our publishing business began brilliantly, and three thousand copies were sold before the end of the year. The sale of the remaining five hundred copies extended over the next two or three years. As a result, after deducting the booksellers' discount and paying all our expenses we were left with a net profit of four thousand rubles, which made it possible for us to pay off some of our most urgent debts.

I cannot say we had no losses the first time. Two or three swindlers took advantage of my publishing inexperience. But our losses taught us to be more cautious and not to yield to flashy propositions which later turned out to be losing ones.

The novel's title, *The Possessed,* gave buyers occasion to refer to it by all sorts of names to the girl who gave out the copies. Sometimes they called it "the Evil One," sometimes they would say "I came for the devils," sometimes "Let me have a dozen demons." Our old nanny, who often heard the book referred to that way, even complained to me about it, maintaining that ever since we started breeding the powers of darkness in our apartment, her nursling (my son) was more restless during the day and sleeping worse at night.

At the start of his editorship of *The Citizen,* Fyodor Mikhailovich took a great interest both in the novelty of his editorial duties and in the great variety of character types he had occasion to meet at the editorial office. I also was glad at first of the change in my husband's occupation, since I assumed that editing a weekly journal would not present any special difficulties and would give him the opportunity to rest, at least a little, after his almost three-year-long labor on *The Possessed.* But little by little we came to understand that he had made a mistake in undertaking work so unsuitable to his nature.

Fyodor Mikhailovich was extremely conscientious in his attitude toward his editorial duties and not only read all the articles submitted to the journal but also revised some poorly written articles (such as those written by the publisher himself).[5] A great deal of his time was consumed by this. I have saved two or three rough drafts of poems clumsily written but with sparks of talent evident in them, and how elegant these poems turned out after being revised by Fyodor Mikhailovich!

But in addition to reading and editing other people's articles he was overwhelmed by correspondence with authors. Many of them fought for every sentence of theirs, and if he cut or changed anything they would write him sharp or sometimes even insolent letters. He would pay them back in the same coin, and in answer to the caustically worded letter of a dissatisfied contributor would send one no less biting, which he would regret by the next day.

Since the mailing of the letters was usually handed over to me, and I knew for sure that my husband's irritation would subside in a day and that he would be sorry for having expressed himself so strongly, I didn't mail the letters he gave me immediately. And when, the next day, he would express regret for having been so sharp, it would always turn out that this letter had "accidentally" not yet been posted, and then Fyodor Mikhailovich would write in a calmer vein. In my archives are preserved more than a dozen such heated letters, which might have given rise to quarrels between my husband and people he did not really wish to quarrel with; but he had not been able to restrain himself in his vexation or annoyance and had therefore given vent to his opinion without sparing his correspondent's self-esteem. Fyodor Mikhailovich was always grateful to me for this "accidental" failure to mail his letters.

And how many personal negotiations he was forced to participate in! There was a secretary, Viktor Feofilovich Putsykovich, at the office; but most writers wanted to speak with the editor personally, and sometimes major misunderstandings arose. Fyodor Mikhailovich, always sincere in word and act, would express his opinion straight out, and how many enemies he earned himself thereby in the world of journalism!

In addition to material troubles he endured many moral sufferings in the course of his editorial work, for persons not in sympathy with *The Citizen*'s orientation or who disliked Prince Meshchersky would transfer their dislike and sometimes their hatred to Dostoevsky. He acquired a host of enemies in the literary world, or rather enemies of the editor of so conservative an organ as *The Citizen*. Strange as it may seem, in later years, both before and after my husband's death, there were many people who could not forgive him for having edited that journal, and echoes of their dislike still appear in print even today.[6]

During the early period of his new activity he made a blunder: namely, he printed a direct quotation from the Emperor's address to the deputies in an article written by Prince Meshchersky called "Kirghiz Deputies in St. Petersburg".[7] Under the conditions of censorship at that time, speeches made by members of the Imperial household and particularly those of the Emperor could be printed only by permission of a minister of the Imperial court. My husband was unaware of this point of law.

He was brought to trial without a jury. The trial took place on June 11, 1873, in the St. Petersburg district court, the members of which were E. M. Borkh, V. N. Krestyanov, K. A. Bilbasov, and Prosecutor G. Zeger. Fyodor Mikhailovich appeared personally at the court proceedings, pleaded guilty, of course, and was sentenced to a fine of twenty-five rubles and forty-eight hours of arrest in the guardhouse.[8] He was very much disturbed by the uncertainty as to when he would have to serve out his sentence, mostly because it would interfere with his coming to us in Russa. In connection with his arrest he made the acquaintance of the then president of the St. Petersburg district court, Anatoly Fyodorovich Koni, who did everything possible so that my husband's sentence could be served at the most convenient time for him. From then on the friendliest relationship developed between him and Anatoly Fyodorovich, and it continued up to his death.

In order to live somewhat nearer to the offices of *The Citizen* we had to change our apartment and settle on Ligovka Street at the corner of Gusev Lane, in the house of Slivchansky. Our choice of apartment was a very unfortunate one. The rooms were small and badly arranged, but since we moved in midwinter we had to adjust to many inconveniences. One of these was the unstable character of our landlord, a very peculiar old man with various eccentricities which caused both Fyodor Mikhailovich and myself much irritation. My husband mentions these in a letter to me of August 19.

In the spring of 1873 I took the children with me to Staraya Russa on the advice of the doctors, to consolidate last year's salt-bath treatment, which had already proved very beneficial to them. This time we stayed not with Father Rumyantsev, whose house was already let, but in the house of an elderly colonel, Alexander Karlovich Gribbe, who had served in the military colonies as far back as Arakcheyev's time.

The separation from his family was painful to Fyodor Mikhailovich. He missed us and came to Russa several times in the course of the summer. But he had to take on all the financial concerns of the journal in Prince Meshchersky's absence, and consequently to spend the hot months in the capital and endure all the unpleasant aspects of a Petersburg summer.

All these circumstances had such a crushing effect on his nerves and general health that by the autumn of 1873 he began to grow weary of his editorship and to dream of sitting down once more to his beloved and purely creative writing.

In 1873, Fyodor Mikhailovich became a member of the Society of Friends of Spiritual Enlightenment and also of the St. Petersburg Slavonic Benevolent Society,[9] and used to attend meetings and sessions of these groups. Our circle of friendships broadened, and my husband's friends and acquaintances began coming to see us more often. In addition to Nikolai Strakhov, who took Sunday dinner with us regularly for several years, and Apollon Maikov, who visited us often, Vladimir Sergeyevich Solovyov—then still a very young man who had just completed his education—began coming to visit us that winter.[10]

At the beginning he wrote Fyodor Mikhailovich a letter and later came to us at my husband's invitation. He made an enchanting impression on us, and the more often my husband saw and spoke with him the fonder of him he grew and the more impressed he became with his mind and his sound erudition. Once, my husband told Solovyov the reason he was so attached to him.

"You remind me very much of a certain man," he said, "one Shidlovsky, who had a tremendous influence on me in my youth. You are so like him in both looks and personality that I sometimes feel his soul has transmigrated to you."

"And has he been dead long?" asked Solovyov.

"No, only about four years."

"Then you think I went about without a soul for twenty years before he died?" asked Vladimir Sergeyevich, and burst into loud laughter. In general, he could be very gay and had an infectious laugh. But sometimes curious things happened to him because of his absentmindedness. For instance, he assumed that because Fyodor Mikhailovich was over fifty I, his wife, must be about the same age. And once, when we were discussing Pisemsky's novel *People of the Forties*, Solovyov said, addressing both of us, "Yes, it must seem to you people of the forties that . . ."

At these words Fyodor Mikhailovich laughed and said to me

teasingly, "Do you hear that, Anya, Vladimir Sergeyevich includes you too among the people of the forties!"

"And he doesn't err in the least," I answered. "For I really do belong to the forties, having been born in 1846."

Solovyov was very much embarrassed by his mistake. That was perhaps the first time he looked at me and realized the difference in age between my husband and myself.

Fyodor Mikhailovich said of Solovyov's face that it reminded him of one of his favorite paintings by Annibale Carracci, *Head of the Young Christ.*

Fyodor Mikhailovich's friendship with Yulya Denisovna Zasetskaya, daughter of the partisan guerrilla Denis Davydov, dates from the year 1873. She had just founded what was then the first night shelter in Petersburg, at the second company of the Izmailovsky Regiment.

Through the editorial secretary at *The Citizen* she invited Fyodor Mikhailovich to come on an appointed day to inspect her shelter for the homeless. She was a Redstockist, and my husband attended Lord Redstock's spiritual talks several times at her invitation, as well as those of other well-known practitioners of that teaching.

Fyodor Mikhailovich had a high regard for Yulya Zasetskaya's intelligence and uncommon goodness, and visited her and corresponded with her often.[11] She came to see us as well, and I got along very well with her as a dear and good woman who, when my husband died, showed much fellow-feeling for me in my grief.

In 1873 we went often to visit the Kashpiryovs. Vasily Vladimirovich, head of the family, published the journal *Dawn,* and his wife, Sofya Sergeyevna, was editor and publisher of the children's magazine *Family Evenings.* We liked both of them very much, and Fyodor Mikhailovich loved visiting them. That year they organized an interesting evening attended by many men of letters, at which the well-known writer A. F. Pisemsky read from his not yet published novel *The Burghers.* Pisemsky's appearance did not make a good impression. He seemed fat and clumsy to me, but he read superlatively and brilliantly portrayed the different character types in his novel.

That year Fyodor Mikhailovich renewed his old friendship

with the Stackenschneider family, whose center was Elena Andreyevna, daughter of the eminent architect. She was a highly intelligent woman with an excellent literary education who used to collect a group of writers and artists at her home on Sundays. She was always very kind to Fyodor Mikhailovich and to me, and we became very friendly. I rarely went out in society in those years, however, for the children were small and it was dangerous to leave them with a nurse.

Fyodor Mikhailovich was always very regretful of the fact that circumstances forced me to be housebound, and in the winter of 1873 he insisted that I take advantage of the opportunity to subscribe to the Italian opera for the season, where such celebrities as Patti, Volpini, Calzolari, Scalchi, Everardi and others shone. My seat was in the gallery, directly opposite an enormous chandelier. I saw only what was going on at the right-hand side of the stage—sometimes nothing but legs—and I would ask my neighbor, "But who's that in the bright yellow jackboots?" or, "Who's that in the pink shoes?" The uncomfortable seat, however, did not keep me from reveling in the enchanting voices of the artists. I particularly recall the opera *Dinorah,* in which Patti sang like a nightingale. I did not worry about the children because Fyodor Mikhailovich did not leave the house on those evenings, and at every whimper or rustle of a child he would go immediately to see whether something was amiss.

CHAPTER SEVEN

The Years 1874 and 1875

The first months of 1874 were not auspicious ones for us. Fyodor Mikhailovich, who had to leave the house in every kind of weather in connection with *The Citizen*'s affairs, and to sit for hours in an overheated proofreading room before each issue went to press, began to catch frequent colds. His slight cough became acute and a shortness of breath appeared; and Professor Koshlakov prescribed the compressed air treatment. He recommended Dr. Simonov's clinic on Gagarinskaya Street, where Fyodor Mikhailovich would sit under the bell for two hours at a time, three times a week. The treatment was very beneficial to him although it consumed an inordinate amount of time and broke up his whole day. He had to get up early, hurry to his appointment, wait for the arrival of late patients scheduled to sit under the bell with him, and so forth. All this had a bad effect on his frame of mind.

He was also troubled by the fact that, because of his editorial duties and ill health, he had not yet been able to serve the forty-eight-hour prison term to which he had been sentenced the previous year for the article printed in *The Citizen*. Finally, he arranged things with A. F. Koni, and the date of arrest was set for the second half of March. On the morning of March 21 we were visited by a police officer whom Fyodor Mikhailovich was already expecting, and they went first to the district court, while I was to go to the police station two hours later to learn exactly where my husband had been put.

As it turned out he was put in the guardhouse on Sennaya Square (now a municipal laboratory). I took a small suitcase there right away with his overnight necessities. Times were simple then, and I was admitted to see him immediately. I found him in an amiable mood. He asked whether the children missed him, and wanted me to give them some goodies for him and tell them he had gone to Moscow for toys.

In the evening after putting the children to bed, I couldn't hold out any longer and went again to visit my husband. But because of the lateness of the hour they did not let me in, and all I could do was transmit a letter and some fresh rolls to him through the guard. I felt so badly at not being able to speak with him and reassure him about the children that I stood under the guardroom window (the last one on the Spassky Lane side), and caught sight of him sitting at the table reading a book. I stood there for a few minutes and then rapped softly; he got up right away and looked through the window. When he saw me he smiled gaily and began nodding to me. At that moment a sentry approached and I had to go away.

I went to see Apollon Maikov, who lived close by on Sadovaya Street, and asked him to visit Fyodor Mikhailovich the next day. He was good enough to inform Vsevolod Solovyov about the arrest, and he too paid a visit to my husband.[1] On that second day I was there twice (in the evening at the window again—this time he was waiting for me). And at about twelve o'clock of the third day the children and I joyfully greeted their papa, just returned "from Moscow." He had stopped in at a shop on the way home and bought them some toys. He was in a blithe mood after his imprisonment and said he had passed a very pleasant two days. His cellmate, an artisan of some kind, slept for hours on end during the day, and so Fyodor Mikhailovich was able to reread Victor Hugo's *Les Misérables* (a work he had a high regard for) without any interference.

"Wasn't it a good thing they put me in jail!" he said gaily. "Otherwise how would I have found the time to refresh my old, wonderful impressions of that great book?"

At the beginning of 1874 Fyodor Mikhailovich decided once and for all to resign his editorship of *The Citizen.* The last issue under his signature came out on [April 15].[2] He was drawn once more to purely creative work. New ideas and characters had sprung up in his imagination and he felt the need to embody them in a new work.[3] He was concerned, of course, about the question of where to publish it in the event that the *Russian Messenger* already had its material collected for the following year. And, as a matter of fact, he always found it onerous to have to offer his work. But then something happened that resolved this troublesome matter happily.

One April morning at about twelve the maid handed me a visiting card on which the name "Nikolai Alexeyevich Nekrasov" was printed. Knowing that Fyodor Mikhailovich was already dressed and would appear shortly, I had the visitor shown into the drawing room and gave the card to my husband. Within a few minutes Fyodor Mikhailovich, apologizing for the delay, invited the guest into his study.

I was terrifically curious about the arrival of Nekrasov, the former friend of my husband's youth and later his literary enemy. I recalled that Fyodor Mikhailovich had been upbraided in the pages of [Nekrasov's] *Contemporary* as early as the sixties, when [the Dostoevsky brothers] were publishing *Time* and *The Epoch*, and that hostile attacks by the critics Mikhailovsky, Skabichevsky, Eliseyev and others had appeared more than once in the journal[4] in recent years as well.

I knew also that Fyodor Mikhailovich had not yet met Nekrasov face to face since our return from abroad, so that this visit must have a certain importance. My curiosity was so great that I could not hold myself in check and stood behind the door leading into the dining room from the study. To my great joy I overheard Nekrasov inviting my husband to contribute to *National Notes*, asking him to give it a novel for the next year, and offering payment of two hundred and fifty rubles per sixteen-page signature (whereas Fyodor Mikhailovich had been receiving one hundred and fifty up to then).

Seeing how modestly we lived, Nekrasov probably assumed that Fyodor Mikhailovich would be extremely happy to have such an increase in his honorarium and would say yes immediately. But Fyodor Mikhailovich thanked him for his offer and said, "I cannot give you an affirmative answer, Nikolai Alexeyevich, for two reasons. In the first place I have to be in touch with the *Russian Messenger* and find out whether they need my book. If they have enough material for next year, I'm free and can promise you the novel. I've been contributing to the *Russian Messenger* for a long time now. Katkov has always been very good about meeting my requests, and it would be tactless of me to leave them without offering my work to them first. That can probably be cleared up in a week or two. I think I should warn you, Nikolai Alexeyevich, that I always take an advance for my work—an advance of two or three thousand."

To this Nekrasov indicated full consent.

"But the second question," Fyodor Mikhailovich continued, "is how my wife will react to your offer. She is at home, and I'll ask her right now."

And my husband went to look for me. At this point something amusing happened. When Fyodor Mikhailovich came to my room I told him impatiently, "What is there to ask about? Say yes, Fedya, say yes right away."

"Say yes to what?" my husband asked in amazement.

"Oh, my Lord! To Nekrasov's offer, of course."

"And how do you know about Nekrasov's offer?"

"Because I overheard the whole conversation—I was standing at the door."

"So you were eavesdropping? Aren't you ashamed of yourself, Anechka?"

"Not in the least! After all, you don't have any secrets from me and you would certainly have told me all about it anyway. Then what's so important about my listening in? It's not other people's business, after all, but our common business."

Fyodor Mikhailovich could only drop his hands in dismay at this logic of mine.

He returned to the study and said, "I've talked it over with my wife, and she is very pleased that my novel will be published in *National Notes*."

Nekrasov was evidently a bit put out that my consent was required in this matter and said, "Now I would never have imagined that you were under your wife's heel."

"What is there to be surprised at?" Fyodor Mikhailovich retorted. "She and I live together very harmoniously, I confide all my affairs in her and have faith in her intelligence and business sense. How then could I not ask her advice in a matter so important to us both?"

"Oh, well then, I understand, of course . . ." said Nekrasov, and changed the subject. He stayed another twenty minutes or so and then left after saying goodbye very warmly to my husband and asking him to let him know the moment an answer was received from the *Russian Messenger.* In order to clear up the question of the novel as quickly as possible, Fyodor Mikhailovich decided to go to Moscow himself instead of writing to the *Russian Messenger,* and left at the end of April. When Katkov heard about Nekrasov's offer he agreed to pay the same price; but when Fyodor Mikhailovich requested an advance of two thousand rubles Katkov said that a large sum had just been spent to acquire a certain novel, *Anna Karenina,* and that the office was short of funds. Thus, the matter of the novel was decided in Nekrasov's favor.

After spending the month of May with me and the children in Staraya Russa, Fyodor Mikhailovich went to Petersburg on June 4 so as to proceed to Bad Ems for treatment, on the advice of Professor Koshlakov.[5] In Petersburg Prince Meshchersky and some relative of his tried to convince my husband to go to Soden instead of to Ems. The same advice was given by his regular physician, Dr. Y. B. von Bretzel. This insistent recommendation confused him so much that he decided to consult Professor Fröhrich, the eminent Berlin physician.

He went to see the professor as soon as he arrived in Berlin. The latter kept him for two minutes and merely touched his chest with his stethoscope, then gave him the address of a Dr. Gutentag and recommended consulting him in Ems. Fyodor Mikhailovich, accustomed to the thorough examinations carried out by Russian doctors, was very dissatisfied with the superficiality of the German celebrity.

He arrived in Berlin on June 9, and since all the banking houses were closed he went to the Royal Museum to have a look at the paintings of [Wilhelm] Kaulbach, of which so much had been said and written. He did not care for this artist's work, finding it "no more than cold allegory."[6] The other paintings in the museum, however, especially the old masters, made an excellent impression on him and he expressed regret that we had not seen these art treasures together on our first visit to Berlin.

While in Berlin Fyodor Mikhailovich had to go shopping for a black cashmere shawl like the one he had bought for me in Dresden, at the request of the landlady of our summer house. He carried out this mission successfully and bought an excellent shawl at a comparatively reasonable price. I must say apropos of this that my husband understood quality, and everything he bought was irreproachable.

On the way out of Berlin he was enraptured with the charming scenes of nature. He wrote to me [on June 13], "Everything seductive, tender and fantastic you can imagine in a landscape, the most charming in the world: hills, mountains, castles, cities like Marburg and Limburg with its fascinating towers, in an astonishing conjunction of mountains and valleys—I have never seen anything like it; and so we drove all the way to Ems, on a hot morning glowing with sunlight." He rapturously described the beauty of Ems as well, although later, because of his homesickness and loneliness, it had a depressing effect on him.

He stopped at a hotel and then went on the day of his arrival to see Dr. Ort, to whom he had a letter from Dr. von Bretzel. Ort examined him very thoroughly and found that he had a temporary catarrh but added that his condition was fairly serious, because the more it developed the more difficulty he would have breathing normally. He prescribed the drinking of the waters and promised a full recovery after four weeks of taking the cure.

That same day Fyodor Mikhailovich succeeded, after long searching, in locating two rooms on the second floor of Haus Blücher No. 7, at a rental of twelve thalers a week. In addition, the landlady agreed to a price of one-and-a-half thalers a day for breakfast, dinner, tea, and a light supper.

Fyodor Mikhailovich wrote me on June 16, "I've been reading nothing but Pushkin and getting drunk on [him]; every day I find something new." In the same letter he says, "Yesterday evening while taking my walk I met Kaiser Wilhelm for the first time: a tall old man with an imposing air. Here, all rise (including the women), remove their hats and bow; while he bows to no one, merely waves his hand sometimes. Our Tsar, on the other hand, bows to everyone here, and the Germans set great store by that. I have been told that both the Germans and the Russians (particularly our high society ladies) do everything they can to meet the Tsar on the walk somehow and curtsey before him."

By the time a week or so had gone by Fyodor Mikhailovich was already feeling homesick for the family, from which up to now he had been separated only for short intervals, besides which there had always been an opportunity to come to us if the necessity arose. His homesickness was aggravated also because my letters were not being dispatched on time and were taking a long time to arrive. Knowing that he would worry, I myself used to take my letters to the post office to mail, and each time I would ask the postmaster to send them off immediately. I would bring along Fyodor Mikhailovich's letters to me with their complaints about the sluggishness of the Staraya Russa post office, I would implore him not to hold up our correspondence, but it was all for nothing. My letters would remain in Russa for two or three days, and it was not until the spring of 1875 that we found out why this delay was occurring.

After three weeks at Haus Blücher, where the landlady was overcharging him and was planning to transfer him to the top story, Fyodor Mikhailovich moved over to the Hotel Ville d'Alger No 4–5. He lived very comfortably in those quarters, since the ceilings were higher and there was a balcony which remained open till late evening.

Fyodor Mikhailovich had several Russian acquaintances in Ems whom he liked. Thus, he saw [M. E.] Kublitsky, A. A. Stackenschneider, a Mr. X, and Princess Shalikova, whom he used to meet at Katkov's house. This very nice and kind old lady, with her gay, direct manner, helped him greatly to bear his loneliness. I was very grateful to her for that.

My husband's melancholy was intensified also because he was deprived of the pleasure of taking his accustomed long walks twice a day. It was out of the question to stroll in the small garden of the *Kursaal* park, in the crowd and the crush, and the condition of his health did not permit climbing the mountain. He was also worried about the way we would have to live during the coming winter. The rather substantial advance received from Nekrasov was already spent, part of it on the payment of pressing debts, part on Fyodor Mikhailovich's trip abroad. To request another before delivering at least a part of the novel was unthinkable.

All these circumstances taken together affected him. His nerves went to pieces (possibly due also to the drinking of the waters), and among the other guests he had the reputation of a "testy" Russian who lectured everybody on how to behave. My letters and my stories about the children, their pranks and sayings, were a great comfort to him. "Your anecdotes about the children, my darling Anya," he wrote on July 9, "breathe new life into me, just as though I were with you." In the same letter he mentions a defect in our children's upbringing: "They don't have *their own* friends, that is, girlfriends and boyfriends, other little children like themselves." It was true that among our friends there were few with children of the same age as our own, and only in summer did they find friends in Father Rumyantsev's family.

Anticipating Fyodor Mikhailovich's trip abroad the previous spring, we had assumed that after completing his course of treatment he would stay somewhere for a while for a *Nachkur,* and that if there was sufficient money he would have a short stay in Paris as well. So I had the idea of sending him fifty rubles to buy me some black silk fabric in Paris for a going-out dress which I needed for certain occasions. I amazed my husband by sending this money; under the influence of a seizure, he even reprimanded me, not having correctly understood or rather clarified my words.

Nevertheless, the thought of carrying out my wish did not leave him; and while he was traveling through Berlin he went to many shops and brought back some marvelous silk cloth for me. Although he declared his purchase at the customs they paid no attention to his declaration, but zealously went through all his books and notebooks, expecting to find something forbidden.

Fyodor Mikhailovich did not have enough money to make the trip to Paris, but he was not able to deny himself his deep desire to visit once more the grave of our first daughter, Sonya, whose memory he still cherished in his heart. He went to Geneva and visited the children's cemetery of Plain Palais twice; and from Sonya's grave he brought me a few sprigs of cypress, which in the course of six years had grown thick over our little girl's monument.

After spending two or three days in Petersburg, Fyodor Mikhailovich returned to Russa about August 10.

In his letters to me from Ems in the summer of 1874, Fyodor Mikhailovich returned several times to the oppressive thought of the difficult times ahead for us in the near future.[7] In truth, our situation was such as to give us—for whom things had never been easy in a financial sense—serious pause.

I have already mentioned that Nekrasov had come to us in April to ask Fyodor Mikhailovich to place his future novel [*A Raw Youth*] with *National Notes* for 1875. My husband was very pleased at the renewal of friendly relations with Nekrasov, whose talent he regarded highly; both of us were pleased also because Nekrasov had offered an honorarium a hundred rubles higher than my husband was receiving from the *Russian Messenger*.

But for Fyodor Mikhailovich there was also a difficult side to this matter. *National Notes* was an organ of the opposing camp, and he had waged an intense struggle against it quite recently,[8] when he was editing *Time* and *The Epoch*. Several of my husband's literary enemies were members of its staff: Mikhailovsky, Skabichevsky, Eliseyev, and, to a degree, Pleshcheyev, and they might demand that my husband make changes in the novel in the direction of their own political tendency. And Fyodor Mikhailovich could not under any circumstances compromise his basic convictions. Whereas *National Notes* in its turn might not want to print my husband's contrary opinions, and then at the first serious difference Fyodor Mikhailovich would undoubtedly ask that his novel be returned, no matter how sad the consequences might be for us. Troubled by the same thoughts, he wrote me on December 20, 1874, "Now Nekrasov can make things hard for me if something contrary to their tendency turns up . . . but I will not yield a single line of my own convictions, even if we have to go begging alms this year."

What would we do in the event of a disagreement with *National Notes?* That thought worried us both very much. I am not even speaking of the advance, which would have to be returned immediately although it was already partially spent, so that paying it back right away would present a very great hardship. But there was another thought as well—how would we live until such time as Fyodor Mikhailovich could place the novel? For the *Russian Messenger* was the only journal of that period for which my husband, because of his views, was able to work.[9]

In trying to devise different alternatives in the event of the anticipated difficulties, I felt that we should reduce our family living expenses as much as possible. No matter how modestly we lived, we spent no less than three thousand rubles a year on top of the debt payments and interest which which we were plagued, since our ever-modest living quarters alone cost seven or eight hundred rubles a year, and a full thousand including firewood. And then it came into my mind to remain in Russa through the winter, the more particularly because we had firmly resolved to return to Russa the following spring for the beneficial effects of the bathing on our children. So that we would be moving to the capital for no more than eight or nine months, of which a month-and-a-half or two would go for the search for an apartment and settling into it, and the spring would be spent in preparing for departure again. All that time would be lost for work, and Fyodor Mikhailovich was extremely anxious to complete the novel as soon as possible, so as to embark on the fulfillment of his cherished dream: the publication of his own independent organ, *Diary of a Writer.*

Even without taking into consideration the low cost of an apartment in Staraya Russa, food and groceries were three times cheaper than in Petersburg; and other expenses unavoidable in Petersburg life would be curtailed as well. And apart from material considerations, I personally found very tempting the chance of living throughout a whole winter that peaceful, serene, and pleasant family existence we had in summer, which we used to recall in winter with such a happy feeling.

In Petersburg in winter Fyodor Mikhailovich hardly belonged to his family. He had many social obligations, had to attend meetings of the Slavonic Benevolent Society,[10] of which he had been a member since 1872; and we had to invite people to our house often. All this took him away from me and the children, with whom he could spend less time; and the company of our children was the highest happiness for my husband. If we stayed in Staraya Russa we would be freed at one stroke of much that was interfering with our happy family life.

After deciding to spend the winter in Staraya Russa I set about hunting for an apartment. It was impossible for many reasons to spend the winter at the Gribbe villa. But finding a larger apartment was not difficult. Villas renting for three or four hundred rubles in season were empty in winter and could be rented for fifteen or twenty rubles a month. Still, I could not make the final decision without Fyodor Mikhailovich. In passing through Petersburg he might locate a suitable apartment, and in that case there was no point in considering wintering over in Russa.

Fyodor Mikhailovich returned to Russa at the end of July. He spent two or three days in Petersburg but did not find an apartment, and as a matter of fact didn't even try to look for one because he was very homesick for us and hurried home. Several days later we started discussing the question of winter quarters and when we should leave Russa. At that point I suggested, "Well, and what if we were to stay in Russa over the winter?"

This proposal met with a heated protest from him. The reason for his refusal was unexpected, but very flattering to me. He began by saying I would find it boring in Russa, living the solitary life we lived in summer.

"Even in winters past," he said, "you never went anywhere and never had any pleasure, but this winter, God willing, my work will go well and there will be some more money. You'll have some pretty dresses made up, you'll go out in society—I am firmly decided on that. Why, you'll waste away in Russa!"

I began trying to convince him that the forthcoming winter was for work, that it was necessary to continue and complete *A Raw Youth,* and that I could not even think of pretty dresses and social diversions for that reason.

"And I don't need them in the least—for me, the nicest and most precious thing is the peaceful, quiet family life we lead here, where we're not bothered by all kinds of unexpected happenings."

I added that I feared only that he might find life boring in Russa without suitable companionship. But this problem could be alleviated by his making a trip to Petersburg two or three times in the course of the winter, to see the friends and acquaintances he found dear and interesting. Trips of that sort for himself alone wouldn't cost a great deal, but would enable him to renew impressions and keep in touch with his literary and artistic interests.

I held up all the advantages, financial and otherwise, of a winter in Russa, for my husband to see. And he himself was tempted by the picture of tranquil family life I drew for him, where he could give himself wholly to his work. He doubted, however, that we would succeed in finding a warm and spacious apartment. Then I suggested that we go that very day, during our walk, to have a look at General Leontyev's villa, which had become available a few days ago and which was always rented for the winter as well.

Our inspection of the house decided the matter conclusively. Fyodor Mikhailovich took a great fancy to the apartment, which was on the lower floor of the Leontyev villa, on lively Ilinskaya Street. It was a large two-story house* renting (that is, both floors) for eight hundred rubles a season. The apartment we chose consisted of six rooms in addition to the kitchen. The main thing that pleased my husband was the fact that his rooms (a bedroom and a study) were separated from our part by a large room with four windows. Thus, the children's noise and running about would not reach him and keep him from working and sleeping; and the children, too, would not be constrained (something my husband was always concerned about) and could shout and make as much noise as they liked.

We came to an agreement at once with the woman in charge of the house and took the apartment until the following May 15 at a rental of fifteen rubles per month. So as not to lose time for work, we decided to move right away and get ourselves settled for winter living.

*It is still standing there today, just as it was. (A.G.D.)

That winter of 1874–75 in Staraya Russa is one of my most beautiful memories. The children were quite well and we didn't have to call the doctor once throughout that entire winter, something which was never true in Petersburg. Fyodor Mikhailovich also felt well. The results of the "cure" at Ems had proved favorable: his cough had lessened, his breathing was much deeper. Thanks to our tranquil and orderly mode of life and the absence of all those unforeseen and unpleasant occurrences so frequent in Petersburg, my husband's nerves grew stronger and his epileptic seizures milder and rarer. And as a consequence he was seldom angry and irritated, and was almost always goodhumored, loquacious and gay. The disease which was to lead him to his grave within six years had not yet developed, he did not suffer from shortness of breath, and therefore he permitted himself to run about and play with the children.

I, my children, and our friends in Staraya Russa vividly remember the way Fyodor Mikhailovich used to play with the children in the evenings, to the sounds of the small organ he himself had bought them (and which his grandchildren play now)—and the way he used to dance the quadrille, the waltz and the mazurka with me and the children. He loved the mazurka particularly and, to do him justice, he danced it with dash and fervor, like a "real Pole," and was very pleased when I once said as much to him.

Our everyday life in Staraya Russa was scheduled by the hour, and this schedule was strictly adhered to. Since my husband worked at night he would get up no earlier than eleven in the morning. When he came out for his coffee he would call the children, and they would run to him joyfully and tell him everything that had happened during the morning and everything they had seen on their morning walk. And Fyodor Mikhailovich was happy looking at them, and carried on the most animated conversations with them. Neither before nor since have I seen a man with such a capacity to enter the world of children and make them so interested in talking to him. In those hours he became a child himself.

After midday he would call me to his study and dictate what he had written during the night. Working with him was always a joy for me, and I privately took great pride in helping him and in being the first of his readers to hear the author's work from his own lips. Usually he dictated his novel directly from the manuscript. But if he was dissatisfied with his work or had doubts about it, he would read the entire chapter to me in one sitting, before beginning to dictate. That way a stronger impression was made than through ordinary dictation.

I should like to say a few words on the subject of our dictations. Fyodor Mikhailovich always worked at night when there was complete quiet in the house and there was nothing to break into the flow of his thoughts. But he would dictate during the day from two to three, and these hours I recollect as some of the happiest in my life. It was my good fortune to hear a new work from the lips of the writer himself, whom I so loved, read with those nuances he gave to his characters' speeches. After finishing his dictation he always turned to me and said, "Well, what do you say, Anechka?"

"I say it's fine," I would reply. But my "fine" meant to Fyodor Mikhailovich that perhaps the just-dictated scene, though successful from his point of view, had not produced any particular effect on me. And my husband placed great importance on my spontaneous reactions. Somehow it always happened that those pages of the novel which had a moving or shattering effect on me had the same effect on most of his readers as well—a fact my husband became convinced of in conversations with readers and through the critics' judgments.

I wanted to be sincere and would not express praise or admiration when I did not feel it. He deeply valued my sincerity. Nor did I conceal my reactions. I remember how I laughed at his reading of the conversations of Madame Khokhlakova or the general in *The Idiot,* and how I teased my husband for the prosecutor's speech in *The Brothers Karamazov.*

"What a pity you're not a prosecutor! With that speech of yours you'd whisk the most innocent man off to Siberia."

"So you think the prosecutor's speech went off well?" Fyodor Mikhailovich asked.

"Fantastically well," I confirmed. "But just the same, I'm sorry you never took up a judicial career. You'd be a general by now and I'd be Madame General, and not the wife of a retired second lieutentant."

And when Fyodor Mikhailovich dictated the speech of

Fetyukovich [counsel for the defense] and addressed his eternal question to me I said, I recall, "And now, my darling, I'll ask you —why didn't you become a lawyer? For you'd whitewash the most hardened criminal whiter than snow. It's the truth— you've missed your vocation! And you have brought Fetyukovich off brilliantly!"

But there were times when I had to weep. I remember that when my husband dictated to me the scene of Alyosha's return with the boys after Ilyusha's funeral, I was so moved that I wrote with one hand and wiped my tears with the other. Fyodor Mikhailovich saw how excited I was, came over to me, and kissed me on the head without saying a word.

In general, Fyodor Mikhailovich idealized me and attributed to me a deeper understanding of his work than I actually had. He was convinced that I understood the philosophical import of his novels. I remember that once, after taking his dictation of a chapter from *The Brothers Karamazov* (it was the chapter called "The Grand Inquisitor") I answered his invariable question, "You know, to be frank, I didn't understand very much of what you were dictating. I think that to understand it, one should have had some training in philosophy different from the education I had."

"Just a minute now," said my husband. "I'll explain it more clearly."

And he expressed the gist of the idea in simpler language. "Well, is it clear now?"

"It's not clear even now. If you told me to repeat it I wouldn't be able to do it."

"No—you did understand it, I can tell that from the questions you asked. And if you can't put it into words, that's only from lack of training, lack of form."

Apropos of this, I would like to say that the longer my life, with its sometimes melancholy complications, went on, the more the framework of my husband's books expanded for me, and the more deeply did I begin to understand them.

Of our life in Staraya Russa, I call to mind that Fyodor Mikhailovich read me a newly written chapter from *A Raw Youth* in which a young girl hangs herself (it was Part 1, Chapter 9; it produced a tremendous impression on Nekrasov, as my husband informed me in his letter of February 9, 1875). After finishing his reading he took one look at me and cried out, "Anya, what's wrong with you, my darling, you look so white—are you tired? Don't you feel well?"

"It's because you've frightened me!" I answered.

"My Lord, does it produce such a painful reaction as that? How sorry I am! How sorry I am!"

To return to the winter of 1874. After finishing his dictation and lunching with me, Fyodor Mikhailovich read *The Wanderings of the Monk Parfeny* that winter, or wrote letters; and at half-past three, no matter what the weather, he would go out alone for a walk along Russa's quiet, deserted streets. Almost always he would drop in to the Plotnikovs' shop (it is described in *The Brothers Karamazov* as the store where Mitya used to buy delicacies on the way to Mokroye) and buy things just delivered from Petersburg (appetizers or sweets), though always in small quantity. They knew and respected him in the shop and, undisturbed by the fact that he bought things in half-pound quantities or less, would hurry to show him any new item that had come in.

At five we would sit down to dine with the children, and then my husband was always in an excellent mood. The first order of the day was to treat our son's nurse, the old woman Prokhorovna,* to a liqueur-glass of vodka.

"Nanny—a drop of vodka!" Fyodor Mikhailovich would call her. She would drink it down with bread and salt.

Dinner was always gay, the children would chatter on without stopping, and we never talked about anything serious or beyond the children's understanding at the table. After dinner and coffee my husband stayed with them for another half-hour or more, telling them fairy tales or reading Krylov's fables to them.

*Fyodor Mikhailovich valued Prokhorovna very much because of her ardent love for our little boy. He often mentioned her in his letters to me, and put her into *The Brothers Karamazov* as the old woman who said prayers for the repose of the soul of her still-living son, from whom she was receiving no news. Fyodor Mikhailovich dissuaded Prokhorovna from doing this and predicted that a letter from him would arrive soon, which did actually happen. (A.G.D.)

At seven Fyodor Mikhailovich and I would set out together on our evening walk and would invariably stop in to the post office on the way back, where by that time they had managed to sort out the Petersburg mail. In those days the railroad went only as far as Novgorod. From there the mail was transported eighty versts by horse (across the lake it was forty versts); so that if we waited for the mailman we did not receive our newspapers until the following day, whereas if we came for the mail ourselves we had our papers on the day they were published. Fyodor Mikhailovich's correspondence was an extensive one, and therefore we sometimes hurried home full of curiosity to start reading our letters and papers.

At nine o'clock we put the children to bed and Fyodor Mikhailovich would unfailingly go to them to "bless them for approaching sleep" and recite with them the Lord's Prayer, the Hail Mary, and his own favorite prayer, "All my hope in Thee I do repose, O Mother of God; shelter me beneath Thy veil."

Toward ten, quiet would descend on the house, since all the household, by provincial custom, went to sleep early. Fyodor Mikhailovich would go into his study to read the newspaper and I, fatigued with the day's commotion and the children's clamor, was glad to sit quietly for a bit in my own room. I would settle down to my game of patience, of which I knew a dozen different variations. I remember with tenderness how many times each evening my husband used to come to my room to tell me what he had read in the latest papers or simply to chat for a bit, and he would always help me finish out my game. He maintained that it didn't come out right for me because I let the best chances slip; and to my surprise he always found the right cards, which had escaped my notice. The games were tricky, and I was seldom able to complete them without his help.

Apropos of cards: it was not customary to play cards in the circles (mostly literary) in which Fyodor Mikhailovich moved. During all our fourteen years of living together my husband played preference only once, at my relatives', and he played superlatively despite the fact that he hadn't held a card in his hands for over ten years, and even won a few rubles from his partners, which embarrassed him very much.

At the stroke of eleven he would appear at the door of my

sitting room, which meant it was time for me to go to bed. I would beg him to let me have one more little game, he would agree, and we would lay out the cards together. I would go to my room, the whole house would be asleep, and only my husband kept vigil over his work until three or four A.M.

The first half of the winter in Russa, from September to March, went very well, and I cannot call to mind any other period when Fyodor Mikhailovich and I enjoyed such undisturbed tranquillity. True, our life was monotonous. One day was so like the next that they all fused in my memory, and I cannot remember any real events during that period. I do recall one tragicomic episode at the very beginning of winter which disturbed our peace for a few days.

I had heard that the merchants in the shopping arcades had received a stock of raw sheepskin jackets for adults and children from the Nizhny Novgorod fair, and I happened to mention this to my husband. He was very interested, mentioned that he himself used to wear a raw sheepskin jacket at one time, and wanted to buy one just like it for our Fedya.

We set off for a shop where we were shown a dozen or so jackets, each nicer than the other. We picked out several and asked that they be delivered to our house to be tried on. Fyodor Mikhailovich was very much taken with one of them, light yellow with elegant embroidery across the chest and along the front edges, and it suited our son's figure perfectly. Dressed in his high coachman's cap and sheepskin jacket belted with a red sash, our plump, rosy little fellow was really handsome. We ordered a smart little coat for our daughter as well, and Fyodor Mikhailovich used to inspect the children and feast his eyes on them every day before their walk.

But our admiration did not last very long. One ill-starred day, I noticed enormous grease spots on the front of the pale yellow jacket, and the grease was lying on the leather in layers. We couldn't understand it, as there was no way the child could have spotted himself with grease during his walk.

But the truth soon came out. Our old cook's purblind husband used to sit in her kitchen every day from morning on. He would dirty his hands while eating lunch and, not finding a towel within reach, would wipe his greasy fingers on the little jacket hanging in the kitchen to dry. We tried to remove the grease from the leather by various means, but the stains became more distinct after each new cleaning, and the pretty jacket was quite spoiled. I was very much put out by the damage to an article there was no way of replacing, and I was quite annoyed with the cook who had failed to look after her kitchen. In my anger I almost dismissed her together with her clumsy husband; but Fyodor Mikhailovich interceded for them and brought me back to my senses. And of course that minor vexation was soon forgotten.

In view of the fact that both of our publications—*The Possessed* and *The Idiot*—were having a great success, we decided to republish *Notes from the House of the Dead* as well while wintering in Russa, since it had gone out of print long before and was often requested by booksellers. The proofs were sent to us in Russa, but for its publication day I had to make a trip to Petersburg to sell a certain number of copies (which I succeeded in doing), distribute the books to be sold on consignment, settle accounts with the printer, and so forth. And besides, I wanted to see my family and friends and put in a supply of toys and sweetmeats for the Christmas party we wanted to give, not only for ourselves but also for the children of Father Rumyantsev, so kindly disposed toward our family.

I left on December 17 and returned on the twenty-third. While returning across frozen Lake Ilmen I had a great fright. Several of the troikas which set out together lost their way on the lake, a blizzard sprang up and we were in danger of spending the night in the raging gale. Luckily the coachman dropped the reins and the wise animals, after straying in different directions for a while, finally brought us back to the beaten path.

In Staraya Russa in those days there were frequent fires, both winter and summer, which sometimes burned down entire streets. They would start mostly at night in some bakehouse or bathhouse. Remembering Orenburg, which had burnt to the ground not very long before, Fyodor Mikhailovich was very perturbed if a fire started and the bells began ringing in the church belfry (or, if it spread, in all the belfries in the vicinity).

What worried him particularly was that he knew how flustered I—normally so cheerful and plucky—would become at any unexpected occurrence and how absurdly I would behave. For this reason we came to an agreement once and for all during our stay in Russa—to wake each other up the moment one of us heard the tocsin sound.

Usually it was Fyodor Mikhailovich who would hear the alarm, shake me quietly by the shoulder and say, "Wake up, Anechka, don't be afraid—there's a fire somewhere. Please don't get excited, and I'll go find out where it is!"

I would get up right away, put stockings and shoes on the sleeping children, and get their outer clothing ready, so that they wouldn't take cold in the event that we had to carry them outside. Then I would take out the big sheets, and inside one of them I would put together as carefully as possible all my husband's clothes, his notebooks and manuscripts. Into the others I would put all the contents of the cupboard and the chest of drawers—my clothing and the children's things.

After doing that I would calm down, knowing that the most important things were safe. At first I used to carry all the bundles into the front hall closer to the exit, but after the time Fyodor Mikhailovich returned from a reconnaissance trip, stumbled in the dark against the bundles, and almost fell, I began leaving them in the rooms.

More than once he made fun of me, saying, "The fire is three versts away and she's already getting ready to rescue our property." But when he saw that he couldn't talk me out of it and that this gathering up of our possessions made me feel calmer, he let me "pack up," demanding, however, that all his things be put back in place immediately after the imaginary danger was past.

I remember that when we moved back to the Gribbe villa from the Leontyev house in the spring of 1875, the watchman told me as he was taking leave of us, "I'm sorriest of all that the master is going away."

"Why is that?" I asked, since I knew my husband had no contact with him.

"It's like this, Madame—the moment there's a fire in the night and they start ringing the church bells, there's the master,

Johnny-on-the-spot. He knocks at the gatehouse—that means there's a fire somewhere! So even the police inspector says about me that 'there's no one in the whole city who does his job better than General Leontyev's watchman—no sooner do they start ringing than he's already at the gates.' And now what am I going to do? So why shouldn't I feel sorry the master is going away?"

Coming home to the new house, I told my husband about the porter's praise. He laughed and said, "So now you see that I do have some virtues whose existence I didn't even suspect myself."

At the beginning of February Fyodor Mikhailovich had to go to Petersburg for two weeks. The main purpose of the trip was to see Nekrasov and agree on publication dates for the future installments of the novel. He also had to consult Professor Koshlakov, since he was planning to go to Ems again to consolidate his successful treatment of the previous year.

The day after his arrival in the capital something annoying happened which caused him some anxiety; he was summoned to the district police station. Since he was not able to make it at nine o'clock, the time set, he went later in the day, did not find anyone there, and had to return again in the evening. It turned out that the reason for the summons was the fact that his passport was a temporary one and he was required to furnish a permanent passport, which he did not possess. He attempted to prove to the police officer's assistant that he had been living with a temporary passport since 1859[11] and was receiving foreign passports on this basis; and that no one had ever required any other kind of passport from him. I quote from his letter of February 7.

The police officer's assistant also started arguing. "We're not giving you a passport, and that's all there is to it. We have to observe the laws." "But what am I supposed to do?" "Give us your permanent passport." "But where in the world am I supposed to get one now?" "That's not our business." And so on and so forth in that vein. But these people have a bee in their bonnet—it's all for the purpose of showing off in front of a writer. So I said to them finally, "There are twenty thousand people in Petersburg without passports, and you're holding a prominent man like a vagrant." "We are aware of that, sir, only too well aware that you are known throughout Russia, but we have our laws. But why disturb yourself? Tomorrow or the day after, we'll issue you a certificate instead of your passport—so won't that be all the same to you?" "Oh, damn it, then why didn't you tell me that in the first place instead of arguing with me?"

It all ended with their holding my husband's passport up to the time of his departure [for Germany] and then returning it to him without replacing it with a new one, but first causing him some needless agitation.

In his letters of February 6 and 9, my husband described with heartfelt satisfaction his friendly meeting with Nekrasov and said that the latter had paid him a visit especially to express his *rapture* on reading the end of Part 1 of *A Raw Youth*.

"I sat up all night reading, that was how carried away I was, and at my age and state of health I'm not supposed to indulge myself in that kind of thing . . . And what freshness you have, my dear fellow . . ." He liked the last scene with Liza best of all. "Such freshness no longer exists in any other writer in our time. Leo Tolstoy's last novel only repeats what he's said before, only he said it better the first time." He finds the suicide scene and the narrative "the height of perfection." And just imagine, he likes the first two chapters also. "Weakest of all," he says, "is your Chapter 8. There are many purely external events." And do you know what? When I myself was reading the proofs, the part I liked least was that very same Chapter 8, and I cut a good deal out of it.

After returning to Russa my husband told me a lot about his talks with Nekrasov, and I realized how precious this renewal of warm relations with the friend of his youth was to him. He had a less favorable reaction to his encounters at that time with several members of his literary circle.[12] In general, his two weeks in the capital were marked by a good deal of fuss and fatigue, and he was glad as could be when he was back with his family at last and found us all happy and well.

Fyodor Mikhailovich's frame of mind was always merry and good-humored while we were living in Staraya Russa, as is shown by his joke on me. Once toward the spring of 1875 he came out of his bedroom in the morning scowling. I was worried and asked him how he was feeling.

"Quite well," he answered, "but something annoying happened—I found a mouse in my bed. I woke up and felt something running along my leg, threw off the blanket, and saw the mouse. It was so repulsive!" he said with a grimace of disgust. "You had better look through the bed."

"Yes, I certainly will," I answered.

He went into the dining room for his coffee while I called the maid and the cook, and all together we set about inspecting the bed. We took off the blanket, sheets and pillows, and changed the bed linens. Finding nothing at all, we began moving the tables and bookcases away from the walls to look for the mouse hole.

Hearing the commotion we raised, Fyodor Mikhailovich at first called me, but since I didn't respond he sent one of the children to come fetch me. I answered that I would come as soon as I finished straightening up his room. Then he told the maid, insistently now, to call me to the dining room. I came at once.

"Well then, did you find the mouse?" he asked me disgustedly, as before.

"How can we find it, it's run away! But the strangest thing is that we couldn't find any hole in the bedroom—it must have run in from the front hall."

"April fool, Anechka, April fool!" he said, and a sweet, merry smile came over his kind face. It turned out that he had remembered that April 1 is the day when people play tricks on each other, and he wanted to have a joke on me. And I went and believed him, forgetting the date completely. Naturally there was a lot of laughter, we started playing "April fool" tricks on one another, and our "kiddies," as my husband used to call them, took an active part.

Our life went along in its usual order, and the work on the novel was going rather well. This was extremely important for us, since Fyodor Mikhailovich had gone to consult Professor Koshlakov during a trip to Petersburg, and the latter was insistently recommending—in view of the beneficial results of last year's water cure—that he consolidate the treatment by going back to Ems again in the spring.

In April of 1875 we had to go through the steps of obtaining a foreign passport. In Petersburg this hadn't presented any difficulties; but living in Russa, my husband had to get his passport through the governor of Novgorod. I went to see the Russa district police officer to find out what kind of petition must be sent to Novgorod, how much it would cost and so forth. At that time the police officer was a Colonel Gotsky, a rather frivolous person, as people said, who liked to drive about visiting the neighboring landowners.

When he was given my calling card Colonel Gotsky invited me into his office, seated me in an easy chair, and asked the nature of my business with him. After rummaging around in his desk drawer he handed me a rather large blue-bound file. I opened it and saw, to my extreme surprise, that the contents consisted of "The Case of Retired Lt. Fyodor Mikhailovich Dostoevsky, under Secret Surveillance and Residing Temporarily in Staraya Russa." I leafed through a few pages and began to laugh.

"What is this? Then we're under your enlightened surveillance and you probably know everything that goes on in our household? That's something I hadn't expected!"

"Yes, I do know everything that happens in your family," said the police officer with an air of importance. "And I can tell you that up to the present I am quite satisfied with your husband."

"May I convey your praise to my husband?" I asked mockingly.

"Yes, please let him know that he is behaving splendidly and that I hope he will not give me any trouble in the future either."

When I reached home I told Fyodor Mikhailovich what the police officer had said, laughing at the idea that a man like my husband could be turned over to the surveillance of a rather stupid policeman. But Fyodor Mikhailovich took the news hard.

"Look at all the evil-intentioned people they let slip through their fingers," he said, "but they suspect me and keep watch over me, a man devoted with all his heart and mind to Tsar and fatherland. That is wounding!"

Thanks to the police officer's garrulousness, a circumstance had come to light which had been causing us extreme annoyance, but whose source we had never been able to discover: namely, why it was that the letters I had mailed to Ems from Russa the previous year were never posted to Fyodor Mikhailovich on the day I brought them to the post office, but for some reason were always held up a day or two by the postmaster. It was the same story with letters from Ems to Russa. And the fact that my husband was not receiving my letters on time not only caused him severe anxiety but also brought on epileptic seizures, as is evident, for instance, in a letter he wrote me on July 16, 1874.

Now it was all clear. Our letters were being censored, and their mailing depended on the permission of a police inspector who frequently went off somewhere in the district for two or three days at a time.

This censorship by one office or another of the correspondence between my husband and myself (and perhaps of all his correspondence) continued through later years also and caused us a good deal of heartache, but there was no way of eliminating this annoyance. Fyodor Mikhailovich himself never raised the question of release from police surveillance, the more particularly because competent persons assured him that, since he had been permitted to edit and publish his journal *Diary of a Writer,* there was no doubt that the secret surveillance of his activity had been removed. In actual fact, however, it went on up to the year 1880 when, during the Pushkin memorial celebrations, Fyodor Mikhailovich had occasion to speak about it to a highly placed personage by whose order the secret surveillance was finally discontinued.[13]

At the end of May he had to go to Petersburg once more for a few days, and from there to Europe. This time he left for Ems with great reluctance, and it cost me a good deal of effort to persuade him not to let the summer pass without taking the cure. His disinclination came from the fact that he was leaving me not entirely well (I was in an "interesting condition"), so that on top of his missing the family as usual, he was feeling great anxiety on my account.

An episode occurred toward the end of my husband's course of treatment which seemed to bode disaster. On July 23 I received a letter from Petersburg informing me that a story about Fyodor Mikhailovich's serious illness had appeared in the *St. Petersburg Gazette.* Putting no credence in the letter, I ran to the reading room in Mineralnye Vody, searched through the previous day's newspapers, and found the following item in the news column of the *Gazette,* No. 159: "We have learned that our prominent writer, F. M. Dostoevsky, is gravely ill."

The effect of this news on me can be imagined. It flashed through my mind that Fyodor Mikhailovich had probably suffered a double epileptic seizure, which always affected him very severely. But it might also have been a nervous stroke or some other horrible thing. In complete desperation I went to the post office to send my husband a telegram, and when I came home I began preparing to leave while waiting for the answer, having decided to leave the children in the care of Father Rumyantsev and his wife. Our landlords tried to persuade me not to make the trip to my husband, but I could not admit even the thought that my dear husband was gravely ill and might die, and that I would not be with him.

Fortunately, I received a reassuring reply by six o'clock. I am appalled to think what might have happened if I had travelled in my "condition" and in the anxious state I was in because of my husband and my children. Truly, the Lord saved us from calamity!

And so I never even succeeded in learning exactly who gave the newspapers this baseless story, which caused my husband and myself some tormenting hours.

But on top of his great anxiety about the children and me, Fyodor Mikhailovich was torn by the feeling that his work was not moving along and that he would not be able to deliver the next installment of *A Raw Youth* on time. He wrote me on June 13: "I am tormented worst of all by the breakdown in my work. Up to now I have been sitting here agonizing and doubting myself, and have no strength to begin. No, that is not the way to produce works of art—on order, under compulsion—but with time and freedom at one's disposal. But it seems that I shall finally sit down soon to my real work, though I'm not sure what will come out of it. In this state of anguish, I am capable of ruining the idea itself."

He was very concerned also about the matter of locating winter quarters for us. Although our life was very good in Russa it would have been difficult to stay there for a second winter, particularly since Fyodor Mikhailovich was planning to start publishing his journal *Diary of a Writer*—which he had been contemplating for so long—at the beginning of the following year of 1876.

The question was whether he should hunt for an apartment while passing through Petersburg, or whether it would be better to bring the entire family to the capital and look for living quarters while we stayed at a hotel. Both solutions had their inconvenient aspects, and I inclined to the idea of coming to Petersburg myself upon my husband's return from Ems, and looking for an apartment together with him. He protested strongly against the latter idea because of my physical condition at that time. It was decided that he would remain in Petersburg for two or three days, and that he would come back to Russa if he wasn't lucky enough to find suitable quarters within that time.

Fyodor Mikhailovich returned to Petersburg from Ems on July 6 and stayed in the city for two or three days. But since it was difficult to locate comfortable quarters in so short a time, he stopped searching after looking at a few apartments and continued on to Russa—he was by now so pulled toward home and family. After turning things over in our minds we decided to remain in Russa until the arrival of the expected addition to the family, particularly since our elderly landlords, who loved our children very much, dissuaded us from taking them away in midsummer.

It was with special pleasure that Fyodor Mikhailovich agreed to stay on, because this gave him the opportunity to work undisturbed on *A Raw Youth* before and after my forthcoming confinement without having to forgo my collaboration. It was true that intensive work was in store for us, so that when he returned to Petersburg he would have the right to ask Nekrasov for some money. And money was very necessary to us for the start of our life in Petersburg.

Everything went well. Fyodor Mikhailovich felt much better, the children were growing bigger and stronger, and as for me, my invariable prenatal terrors of dying disappeared almost completely now that my husband was back with us. In this peaceful mode of life a month went by; and on August 10 God gave us a son whom we named Alexey. (The name of "St. Alexey, the man of God" was particularly revered by my husband and so we gave it to the newborn infant even though we did not have this name in our family.) Both of us were happy and thrilled as could be at our Alyosha's arrival in the world (and an almost painless one at that). Therefore I regained my strength rather quickly and could help my husband out with my stenography again.

The fine weather lasted all through August. In September the so-called "Indian summer" arrived, divinely warm and peaceful. Fearing a change in the weather, however, we decided to leave on about the fifteenth of the month. The road ahead was a difficult one since the steamships, because of the shallowness of the River Polista, did not go as far as the city but stopped at Lake Ilmen opposite the village of Ustriki, eighteen versts away.

We left our house in a long file one warm, beautiful morning: in the first carriage, Fyodor Mikhailovich with the two children; in the second, myself with the newborn baby and his nurse; in the third, our cook rode atop a mountain of trunks, bags and bundles. We drove gaily to the tinkle of the carriage bells, and Fyodor Mikhailovich stopped the horses often to make sure I was all right and to boast about what a good time he and the children were having.

We reached Ustriki about two and a half hours later; but there we were confronted with an unexpected situation. The steamship had arrived the day before and taken on a large load of passengers. The captain had decided that today there would be few and was therefore not returning until the next day. We had to wait over for twenty-four hours—there was no alternative.

Two or three housewives ran outside and invited us to stay with them overnight. We selected the cleanest house and moved the whole family into it. I immediately asked the lady of the house how much money she wanted for the night's lodging. She answered goodhumoredly, "Don't worry about it, my lady, we won't ask for too much, and you'll be good to us."

Our room was of medium size with a very wide bed across which we could put the children. I decided to sleep on some benches we drew together and Fyodor Mikhailovich on an old divan whose style reminded him of his childhood. We were promised that the maids would be put up in the hayloft.

Since we were traveling in gentry fashion with our own food supplies, our cook immediately started preparing dinner for us while we went for a walk. Spreading out our rugs, we sat down comfortably on the hill in sight of the lake. We even took the newborn baby with us and he slept in the open air. The day went most pleasantly. Fyodor Mikhailovich was very gay, played with the children, and even raced around with them. And I was happy that we had succeeded in completing a part of our long trip so well. We had our dinner, and since it soon grew dark we all went early to bed.

In the morning at about eight we were told that the smoke of the steamer had been sighted in the distance, and that it would reach Ustriki in an hour or an hour and a half. We started to pack and get the children dressed for the trip, and I went to settle our bill. Our hostess had disappeared somewhere and so her son appeared in her stead to receive payment—a man who liked his vodka, judging by his puffed-up face.

The bill, badly scrawled, was for the amount of fourteen rubles and some kopecks. Of that two rubles had been charged for a chicken, two for milk, and ten for the night's lodging. I was incensed and began disputing the bill, but the landlady's son would not give in and threatened to keep our suitcases if we didn't pay in full. Naturally we had to pay up, but I couldn't restrain myself and called him a "robber."

Meanwhile the steamer was approaching and stopped about half a verst away from shore, so that we had to get to it by dinghy. But when we went down to the shore itself, it turned out that the dinghies were ten paces from the shoreline. The peasants had taken off their footwear and were wading out to the dinghies. We, however were carried out to them on the backs of stalwart women. One can imagine the fear my husband and I felt for the children. He was carried over first and he then received the children, squealing and screaming in terror. I was

The house in Vevey where Dostoevsky lived in 1868.

Anna Dostoevsky in 1871.

Dostoevsky in 1872, from a portrait in oils by Vasily Perov.

Dostoevsky in 1876.

Anna Dostoevsky in 1878.

Dostoevsky in 1880, photographed by M. M. Panov.

Anna Dostoevsky with her son Fyodor and her daughter Lyubov (1880's).

Dostoevsky's house in Staraya Russa in 1880.

Vladimir Solovyov.

The house in Petersburg in which Dostoevsky died.

The study in which Dostoevsky died.

Anna Dostoevsky in 1912.

taken last, and then the newborn baby. Sitting in the rowboat, I pictured with horror how we would manage the climb up the ladder to the steamer with such tiny children. But happily all went well. The captain sent a sailor to meet us, who carried all the children. Our baggage had come by that time, brought by the landlady's son on another dinghy.

The day was ravishing! Lake Ilmen was the color of turquoise and reminded us of the Swiss lakes. There wasn't the slightest pitching, and we sat out on deck throughout all four hours of the trip. We reached Novgorod at about three. Fyodor Mikhailovich and I took the children directly to the railroad station, while our luggage was to be brought by the carters together with the baggage belonging to the other passengers. It arrived within the hour and I, having no confidence in the servants, went to check it myself. We had two large leather suitcases, a black one and a yellow, plus several traveling bags; when I saw that everything was in order I felt calmer.

The day went rather swiftly. At about seven a guard came up to me and said we had better get our tickets ahead of time and check our luggage before the crowds started arriving. I agreed and bought the tickets, and when I returned I pointed out to the guard the two suitcases and two large traveling bags which were to be checked. Suddenly, to my astonishment, the guard, pointing to the black suitcase, said to me, "Madame, that is not your suitcase. Another passenger gave it to me to hold some time ago."

"What do you mean, not mine? That is impossible!" I exclaimed, and rushed to inspect the suitcase. Alas, although it was exactly the same size and shape as ours (and probably also bought in the Shopping Arcade for around ten rubles), it belonged to someone else, without a doubt, and there were even some half-worn-off initials on its upper lid.

"My Lord, where is our suitcase, then? Go look for it!" I said to the porter, but he answered that there was no other black suitcase there.

I became completely desperate. The lost suitcase contained articles belonging exclusively to Fyodor Mikhailovich: his overcoat, his underwear and, most important of all, his manuscript for *A Raw Youth*, which he was to take to *National Notes* the next day and receive on account of his honorarium the money we needed so badly. Not only was the work of the past two months lost, therefore; it was impossible even to reconstruct the manuscript, because the lost suitcase contained Fyodor Mikhailovich's notebooks, without which he was completely helpless, so that he would have to work out the plan of the novel all over again.

All at once my imagination was confronted with the full dimensions of the disaster. Beside myself with misery, I ran into the main waiting room, where Fyodor Mikhailovich was sitting with the children. When he caught sight of my distraught expression he took fright that something might have happened to the baby, who was in the ladies' room with his nurse. Hardly able to find words, I told him what had occurred.

He was terribly shocked. He actually turned white and said softly, "Yes, that is a great loss. What in the world will we do now?"

I suddenly remembered something. "You know what—it must be that good-for-nothing landlady's son who didn't bring the suitcase to the steamer, to get even with me for calling him a robber."

"You may be right," Fyodor Mikhailovich agreed, "but you know we can't leave things like this. We have to try to find the suitcase. It can't really have disappeared. This is what we'll do. You go on to Petersburg with the children—it's out of the question to stay here in a hotel with the children and the maid—there isn't enough money for that. And I'll stay here and go to see Lerche tomorrow" (he was the governor of Novgorod, whom Fyodor Mikhailovich knew personally). "I'll ask him to assign me a policeman, and I'll take the steamer back to Ustriki the same day. If the landlord is holding the suitcase, he'll certainly give it up when he realizes his house might be searched. But you—you calm down, for goodness' sake! Do you know what you look like? Take care of yourself for the baby's sake! Go wash your face with cold water and come back right away."

I left him, feeling utterly desperate. I blamed myself for the trouble that had befallen us, for the fact that I had failed to watch out for our most precious possession, for the fact that my carelessness had cost my husband two months of labor. And yet,

I thought to myself, I did look, and I was sure it was our suitcase! Why did there have to be such a coincidence, why did an identical suitcase have to turn up right then and there?

I stood in the baggage room leaning against a counter, while the tears kept rolling down my cheeks. Suddenly a thought flashed through my mind. What if the suitcase had been left behind at the steamship dock? In that case it would certainly have been put away. What about inquiring there?

I turned to the station guard and asked whether he could go to the dock for me to find out whether the suitcase was there and bring it back. And if they wouldn't give it to him, to tell them that its owner would come to fetch it the next day. But the guard answered that he couldn't leave because he was on duty.

Then, without thinking twice, I decided to go back to the dock myself. I left the station, found two cabbies outside, and exclaimed, "I'll give a ruble and a half to whoever will take me to the steamship dock, there and back!"

One of them said he wasn't free but the other, a lad of about nineteen, agreed to take me. I jumped into the droshky and we started off. It was about eight in the evening, and quite dark. While we were driving through the city with its street lights and pedestrians I wasn't afraid. But after we crossed the Volkhov Bridge and made a turn to the right past some long warehouses, my heart sank. There in the darkness, deep in the recess of the warehouses, I thought I saw people hiding, and a couple of tramps even started running after us.

My cabby took fright and urged the horse on so hard it broke into a gallop. We reached the docks in about twenty minutes. I jumped out of the droshky and ran along the ramp to the steamship office. It was dark inside: the guard was obviously asleep. I started banging with all my might, first on one wall, then the other, and finally the window, shouting at the top of my lungs, "Guard, open up—open up right away!"

After a few minutes, when I was already losing hope and on the point of returning to the cabby, some kind of old man's cough suddenly sounded, followed by a voice: "Who is that knocking? What do you want?"

"Open up, grandpa, this minute!" I shouted, having decided

by the voice that I was talking to an old man. "A big black suitcase was left here, and I've come to get it!"

"It's here," answered the voice.

"Then bring it out right now!"

"Come here," said the old man, and opened up a wooden partition at the side wall (the kind used for checking one's baggage). And he threw my black suitcase on to the dock. My jubilation can be imagined.

"Grandpa, take the suitcase to the cabby, I'll give you a tip," I begged. But either he didn't hear me or was afraid of the evening dampness, for he moved back the partition and the office grew dead still as before.

I tried to move the suitcase, which was a heavy one, about four poods.[14] I ran up for my young cabby, but he refused to leave his coach box. "You can see for yourself what kind of a place this is. If I get down, they'll steal my rig!"

There was nothing else to do. I ran back, grabbed the suitcase by its handle and dragged it, stopping at every step. And to make matters worse, the ramp was a long one. But I managed to lug it to the cab. The cabby jumped out and put the suitcase between the seat and the coach box, while I sat down right on top of the suitcase, resolving not to give it up if we should be attacked by the hoodlums.

The coachman began to whip his horse on; we dashed quickly past some figures who were calling out to us and reached Market Square in about fifteen minutes. There we were safe. My driver perked up and started telling me what a fright he had taken.

"I felt like going away, but I was afraid to leave you there. Then these two roughnecks came up to me and started asking questions, and I told them that it was a peasant I brought—and when they heard you and someone else shouting, they took off."

I begged the fellow to drive faster, for only now did I realize how much time had elapsed since I left the station, and that Fyodor Mikhailovich might have discovered my absence. As it turned out, he had gone to the ladies' room when I did not come back to him and, not finding me there, had left the children with Alyosha's nurse and gone to look for me. He questioned the guards as to whether anyone had seen me. On of them told him that the lady had rented a cab to go to the other side of the city.

Fyodor Mikhailovich was distraught, not knowing where I could have gone at such a late hour, and went out on the porch to watch for me. Sighting him from a distance, I yelled, "Fyodor Mikhailovich, it's me, and I have the suitcase!"

It's a good thing the station entrance was not very well lighted, since the sight of me—a lady sitting, not on the droshky seat, but on top of a suitcase—was not, I think, very picturesque. When I told him all my adventures, he was appalled and said I was crazy.

"My God, my God!" he cried out. "Only think what danger you put yourself into! After all, when those rogues who followed you saw that the cabby was driving a woman, they might have attacked you, robbed you, maimed you, killed you! Just think what would have happened to us, to me and the children. Truly the Lord saved you for the sake of our angel-children! Oh, Anya, Anya! Your rashness will lead you to no good!"

This impetuosity of mine, or "quickness on the trigger," as they call it—my propensity for making a decision in one second without thinking over the consequences—was called my "vice" by Fyodor Mikhailovich, who mentions it somewhere in his letters as well. Little by little, he calmed down. We left that very evening and reached Petersburg in fine fettle.

I cite the episode as an example of the difficulties and unpleasantnesses of making even so relatively short a journey as the one to Staraya Russa during those far-off days.

CHAPTER EIGHT

The Years 1876 and 1877

On May 18, 1876, something happened that I remember with a feeling almost of horror. That year Sofya Smirnova's new novel, *Strength of Character,* was published in *National Notes.* Fyodor Mikhailovich was friendly with Sofya Smirnova and had a high regard for her literary talent. He was therefore interested in her newest work and asked me to get him a copy of the journal as each installment appeared. I always chose the days when he was relaxing from his work on *Diary of a Writer* to bring him the latest *National Notes.* But since the new periodical issues were normally loaned for two or three days only, I would always rush him to finish the installment, so that I could return the magazine to the library on time and not have to pay a fine.

So it was with the April issue. Fyodor Mikhailovich read the installment and told me how well our dear Sofya (whom I too regarded highly) had succeeded in her portrayal of one of the masculine characters in the novel. That same evening my husband left for a meeting, while I put the children to bed and then settled down to read *Strength of Character.* Among other things, the novel contained an anonymous letter sent to the hero by some worthless scoundrel:

> Most gracious sir, most noble Pyotr Ivanovich![1]
>
> Being entirely unknown to you, but participating in your feelings, I am emboldened to address these lines to you. Your nobility of charac-

ter is very well known to me, and my heart is outraged at the thought that despite your nobleness, a certain person close to you is deceiving you so basely. Having been permitted by you to go away, perhaps more than a thousand versts, she, like some rejoicing dove, has spread wide her wings and soared up to the skies, and does not wish to return to her marital home. You have let her go, to your own and her ruination, into the talons of a man before whom she trembles. But he has bewitched her with his flattering exterior, he has ravished her heart, and no gaze is dearer to her than his gaze. Even her own little children seem tedious to her if he does not caress her with his words. If you want to know who he is, this villain of yours, I will not name his name. But you yourself should look to see who it is who visits your house most often; and beware of dark men. If you see a dark man who is fond of crossing your threshhold, take his measure carefully. This dark man crossed your path long ago, but you never guessed. It is your nobleness alone which impels me to reveal this secret to you. And if perchance you do not believe me, then have a look at the locket hanging around your wife's neck and see whose face she carries next to her heart in that locket.

A well-wisher forever unknown to you.

I should mention that of late I had been in the most placid of moods. My husband had not had an epileptic seizure for a long time, the children were quite recovered from their illness, our debts were being paid off little by little, and the success of *Diary of a Writer* was reaching a crescendo. All this lent encouragement to the high spirits so much a part of my nature. And now under that influence a prankish thought flashed through my mind as I was reading the anonymous letter: to copy this letter over (changing or crossing out two or three lines, changing the name and patronymic) and send it to my husband.

I assumed that since he himself had read the letter in Smirnova's novel only the day before, he would guess right away that it was a joke, and he and I would have a good laugh together. There was also the flicker of another thought: that my husband might take the letter seriously. And in that case I was curious about how he would react to an anonymous letter—would he show it to me or throw it into the wastebasket?

As was my habit, no sooner said than done. At first I was going to copy the letter in my own handwriting, but since, after all,

I used to transcribe my shorthand notes for *Diary of a Writer* for my husband every day, my handwriting was *too* familiar to him. The prank had to be camouflaged a bit, and so I set to copying the letter in another handwriting, more rounded than mine. But this turned out to be quite difficult, and I spoiled several sheets of writing paper before the letter was written in a uniform hand. The next morning I threw it into the mailbox, and it was delivered to us at midday in the same post with other correspondence.

Fyodor Mikhailovich was delayed somewhere that day and returned home at exactly five o'clock. Not wishing to keep the children waiting for dinner, he changed and went straight to the dining room without looking through his mail. Dinner was noisy and gay. Fyodor Mikhailovich was in a good mood and talked and laughed a lot as he responded to the children's questions. After dinner he took a glass of tea to his study as usual, while I went to the nursery. Not till ten or fifteen minutes later did I go to find out what effect my anonymous letter had produced on him.

I entered the room, sat down at my usual place near the desk and deliberately brought up a subject which required an answer from him. But he remained morosely silent and kept walking around the room with steps as heavy as if his feet had weights on them. I realized that he was upset and immediately felt sorry for him. In order to break the silence I said, "Why are you so gloomy, Fedya?"

He stared at me furiously, circled the room once or twice more and then stopped almost directly opposite me.

"Do you wear a locket?" he asked in a choked voice.

"Yes, I do."

"Show it to me!"

"What for? You've already seen it many times."

"Let—me—see—that lock-et!" he bawled at the top of his voice.

I understood that my joke had gone too far, and in order to appease him I began unfastening the collar of my dress. But I had no time to take off the locket myself. Fyodor Mikhailovich could not contain the rage that swept over him. He advanced on me fast and ripped at the chain with all his strength. It was a delicate one that he himself had bought me in Venice. It tore in a second and the locket was left in my husband's hands.

He moved quickly around to the other side of the desk, bent over and started opening it up. He couldn't find the spring and worked over it for a long time. I saw how his hands were trembling and how the locket almost slipped out of them on to the table. I felt terribly sorry for him and terribly angry with myself.

I started to speak in a friendly way and offered to open the locket for him, but he refused my help with an angry movement of his head. At last he found the spring and opened it. On one side of it he saw a portrait of our Lyubochka and on the other—himself. He was quite dumbfounded, continued to scrutinize the portrait, and kept silent.

"Well, what did you find? Fedya, my foolish one, how could you believe an anonymous letter?"

He turned swiftly to me.

"And how do you know about an anonymous letter?"

"What do you mean, how? Because I sent it to you myself!"

"What do you mean, you sent it yourself—what are you saying? A likely story!"

"But I'll prove it to you right now!"

I ran to another desk where that issue of *National Notes* was lying, leafed through it and found a few sheets of writing paper on which I had practiced changing my handwriting the day before.

Fyodor Mikhailovich was so astonished that he made a helpless gesture. "And you yourself composed this letter?"

"There was no 'composing' about it—I simply copied it out of Sofya Ivanovna's novel. My goodness, you read it yesterday yourself. I thought you'd guess at once."

"But how could I remember it! Anonymous letters are all alike. The one thing I can't understand is, why did you send it to me?"

"All I wanted to do was have a little joke," I explained.

"What kind of joke is that? Why, I've been in torment this last half hour!"

"But who could know you'd be such an Othello and go climbing the wall without stopping to think it over?"

"In cases like this, people don't stop to think! It's obvious you've never felt real love and real jealousy."

"Now, now . . . I'm feeling real love right this minute. And if I don't know what 'real jealousy' is, it's your own fault. Why aren't you unfaithful to me?" I teased him, trying to break up his mood. "Please—be unfaithful to me. And even then, I'd be nicer than you. I wouldn't lay a hand on you, but *her* . . . I'd scratch her eyes out, the villainess!"

"You keep on joking, Anechka," Fyodor Mikhailovich said in a guilty voice, "but just think what a terrible thing might have happened! I might have strangled you in my rage! Now we can really say that God saved us and took pity on our children. And just think—even if I hadn't discovered my own portrait, a grain of doubt of your faithfulness would have lodged inside me, and I would have tormented myself with it all my life. I beg of you, don't ever joke about such things—I can't answer for myself when I'm in a fury!"

All the while we were talking, I felt a kind of awkwardness in moving my neck. I passed my handkerchief over the place and saw a streak of blood on it. Evidently the chain had scratched my skin when it was torn off with such force.

When my husband saw the blood on the handkerchief he grew quite overwrought. "My God, what have I done! My darling, Anechka, forgive me! I've wounded you! Does it hurt—tell me, does it hurt very much?"

I began reassuring him that there was no "wound" but only a little scratch which would be healed by tomorrow. Fyodor Mikhailovich was really very anxious, but mostly ashamed of his outburst. All that evening passed in apologies, regrets and the most loving tenderness. And I myself was infinitely happy that my absurd prank had ended so well. I was truly sorry for making my husband suffer and promised myself that I would never again joke with him in that vein, having learned from experience what a frenzied, almost irresponsible state my dear husband was capable of reaching in those moments of jealous suspicion.

Both the locket and the anonymous letter of May 18, 1876, are still in my possession.

In the summer of 1876 Professor Nikolai Petrovich Wagner of the University of St. Petersburg was living in Staraya Russa with his family. He came to us with a letter from Y. P. Polonsky and made a favorable impression on my husband. They began seeing one another quite often, and Fyodor Mikhailovich took a great interest in his new friend as a person fanatically dedicated to spiritualism.[2]

Once I met Wagner in the park and he said, "Well now, Fyodor Mikhailovich really surprised me yesterday!"

"How is that?" I was curious to know.

"I was out walking in the evening and was about to drop in to your place when I met your husband right at your crossroads. I said, 'Are you going out for a walk, Fyodor Mikhailovich?'

" 'No, not for a walk, I'm on business.'

" 'Then may I come along with you?'

" 'Come if you want,' he answered, not very graciously.

"He looked concerned about something, and it was obvious he didn't feel like engaging in any conversation. We reached the first cross street. There we met a woman and Fyodor Mikhailovich asked her, 'Auntie, you haven't by any chance seen a brown cow?'

" 'No, dear sir, I have not,' says she.

"The question about the brown cow seemed strange to me, and I attributed it to a folk belief according to which you can predict the next day's weather by the first cow returning from the fields. I thought Fyodor Mikhailovich was asking about the cow in order to find out about tomorrow's weather. But after we walked another block and he repeated the very same question to a boy we met there, I couldn't keep from asking him, 'Now what is it you need a brown cow for, Fyodor Mikhailovich?'

" 'How is that—"need"? I'm searching for her.'

" 'You're searching for her?'

" 'Yes indeed, I'm searching for our cow. She didn't come home from the fields. The whole household is out looking for her, including me.'

"It was only then that I realized why Fyodor Mikhailovich was looking so absent-minded and was peering so closely into the ditches on both sides of the street."

"But what's so surprising about that?" I asked Wagner.

"Just that it seems queer . . . a great man of literature, whose mind and imagination are always engaged with ideas of a higher order . . . and here he is wandering along the street looking for some brown cow."

"It's obvious you aren't aware, esteemed Nikolai Petrovich," said I, "that Fyodor Mikhailovich is not only a talented writer but also a very affectionate family man. Everything that goes on in the household is very important to him. For if the cow hadn't come home yesterday, our children, the youngest in particular, would have been without any milk or would have had it from a strange cow, and perhaps an unhealthy one. And that's why Fyodor Mikhailovich went out searching for her!"

I should mention that we didn't have a cow of our own. But when we came to Russa for the summer the neighboring peasants used to vie with one other to let us have their cows for the whole season. This was because they hoped to get back a sleek, well-fed cow the next fall, and not one emaciated from its winter fodder. We would pay the peasants ten or fifteen rubles a summer, but in the event the cow died or was injured in some way we were obligated to pay ninety rubles. Every summer it happened three or four times that the cow failed to come home from the fields together with the rest of the herd, and then the entire household (except for the infant Alyosha and his nurse) would go looking for her down different streets. Fyodor Mikhailovich, who held our family joys and sorrows close to his heart, used to help us in this as well, and several times he himself drove our cow home and let her through the gate. I was always very touched by my husband's heartfelt concern for his family.

That winter Fyodor Mikhailovich's circle of social acquaintances broadened a great deal. He was very cordially received everywhere, since he was sought after not only for his intellect and talent, but also for his kind heart, responsive to every human grief.

But I decided not to go out socially that winter. I used to exhaust myself so in the course of the day with work on *Diary of a Writer,* with housekeeping duties and looking after the children, that all I wanted to do by evening was rest and spend a little time with some interesting book; and in social situations I would doubtless have gone about with a vacant look.

I didn't in the least regret not going out, however, and this is why: we had a custom that began when we first came back to Russia and continued until my husband died. Fyodor Mikhailovich, always distressed by the fact that I did not go out in society and might perhaps find things tedious at home, wanted to compensate me a bit by telling me all about the things he had seen, heard, or talked about with this person or that. And his tales were so enthralling and were told so expressively that they completely replaced social life for me.

I remember that I always waited very impatiently for him to come home from a visit. He would usually return by one or half-past one (by that time some freshly brewed tea was ready for him); would change into his wide summer coat, which served him as a dressing gown, drink a glass of hot tea, and start telling me about the encounters of the evening. He knew I was interested in details and therefore didn't spare them but told me all about his conversations, while I would ask, "And what did she say to you then? And what did you tell him to that?"

After coming home from a visit Fyodor Mikhailovich would not sit down to work, but since he was accustomed to going to bed late we used to sit up for these conversations, sometimes until five o'clock in the morning, when he would send me off to bed forcibly, declaring that I would get a headache and that he would tell me the rest tomorrow.

Sometimes he would boast to me that he had taken the upper hand in some literary or political dispute. At other times he would tell me about some social blunder he had made, how he had failed to notice or recognize someone, and the misunderstanding that developed out of it, and he would ask my opinion or advice on how to make amends for his oversight.

There were times when he complained openly about some people's unfairness to him, about the way they tried to insult or wound his self-esteem. Frankly, the men of his profession, even intelligent and talented ones, often behaved mercilessly toward him and tried to show him through their petty digs and insults how unimportant his talent was in their eyes. For instance, there were writers who wouldn't even mention his latest work when they spoke with him—as though not wishing to upset him with unfavorable opinions—although they knew, of course, that what he was waiting for from them was not praise nor compliments, but their sincere reaction as to whether he had succeeded in carrying through his basic idea in the novel.

Or, to Fyodor Mikhailovich's direct question whether his "friend" had read the last chapter of the novel (this was already a month after its appearance in the magazine), the "friend" answered that "the young people seized on it, they pass it from hand to hand and like it a lot"—although the speaker knew perfectly well that what Fyodor Mikhailovich valued was not the opinion of inexperienced youth but the speaker's personal opinion, and that he would be pained by the fact that his "friend" was so uninterested in his work that he hadn't found time to read it for a whole month.

I remember, for example, how a certain literary man who met Fyodor Mikhailovich on some social occasion announced that he had at long last managed to read *The Idiot* (published five years earlier), and that he liked the novel but had discovered an error in it.

"What error?" Fyodor Mikhailovich was curious to know, assuming that it was in the fundamental idea or in the psychology of the characters.

"This summer I was living in Pavlovsk," answered the man, "and while I was out walking with my daughters we looked for that opulent villa in the style of a Swiss chalet where your heroine, Aglaya Epanchina, lived. And by your leave, no such villa exists in Pavlovsk."

As though Fyodor Mikhailovich had the obligation to depict an existing rather than an imaginary villa in his novel!

Another writer (this happened later) stated that he had read the prosecutor's speech in *The Brothers Karamazov* twice, with great interest—the second time with a stopwatch.

"Why with a stopwatch?" my husband asked in surprise.

"You say in the novel that the speech went on for . . . minutes. So I wanted to verify that. And it turned out that it wasn't . . . minutes, but only . . .*minutes.

Fyodor Mikhailovich had at first assumed that it was the prosecutor's speech itself which this writer found so gripping

*Gaps in the manuscript.

that he decided to read it over a second time, as happens when we are struck by something. But the reason turned out to be quite a different one, and so petty that it could have been brought up only for the purpose of insulting or wounding Fyodor Mikhailovich. And instances of that kind of attitude on the part of his literary contemporaries were not rare.

All these things, of course, were no more than petty pinpricks to his self-esteem, unworthy of these talented and intelligent people, but nonetheless they affected my sick husband's sensitive nerves painfully. I was often indignant with these unkind people and—may I be forgiven if I am mistaken—inclined to attribute these hurtful tricks to professional jealousy, which Fyodor Mikhailovich himself, to give him his due, did not have at all. He always gave credit to the talented work of other writers, despite any difference in views between him and the person about whom he was speaking or writing.

I was always interested when Fyodor Mikhailovich, in response to my questions, used to describe the ladies' dresses he had seen during his visit. He would tell me to be sure and have made up for myself some dress he had taken a fancy to.

"You know, Anya," he would say, "she was wearing a charming dress. The style was of the simplest: raised and gathered on the right side, let down to the floor in back, but it didn't drag. I can't seem to remember what it was like on the left side, I think it was also raised. Have one like that made up for yourself, you'll see how nice it will be."

I would promise to do it, although from my husband's description it would have been rather difficult to form a picture of the style.

He sometimes got colors wrong, too, and couldn't distinguish shades very well. He would occasionally mention shades which had long ago gone out of use, the color *masaka*, for example. He assured me that *masaka* would be flattering to my skin and asked me to have a dress made up in it. I wanted to please him and asked around the shops for fabric in *masaka* color. The salespeople weren't familiar with the term, but afterward I found out from a certain old lady that it was a shade of deep purple, and that *masaka*-colored velvet was formerly used in Moscow to upholster coffins. It is possible that deep purple is becoming to certain people, perhaps even to me, but I never succeeded in having a dress made up in it to fulfill my husband's wish.

I would like to say apropos of this that he was always extremely pleased when he saw me in a pretty dress or hat. It was his dream to see me smartly dressed,[3] and that gave him more pleasure than it did me. Our financial affairs were always in such a state that it was impossible to think about fancy clothes. But for all that, how pleased and happy my dear husband was when he had occasion—sometimes even against my wishes—to buy or bring me some pretty thing from abroad! Every time he made a trip to Ems he would try to save up money so as to bring me a gift. Once it was an elegant carved ivory fan of fine workmanship; another time, magnificent opera glasses in sky-blue enamel; the third, a set of amber jewelry—brooch, earrings and bracelet. He would take a long time selecting, examining and pricing these things, and was very pleased if I liked his gifts.

Knowing how pleasant it was for him to give me presents, I always displayed great joy when I received them, though there were times when in my heart I felt upset because he used to buy elegant rather than useful things. I remember, for instance, how badly I felt once when after receiving some money from Katkov he bought me a dozen chemises from the best shop in Moscow, at twelve rubles apiece. Naturally I accepted the gift with apparent rapture, but in my heart I regretted the money, since I already had enough underthings and a great deal I really needed might have been bought with the money he had spent.

This purchase of the luxurious chemises was preceded by a comical incident which gave me much amusement. Once my husband came into my room after one in the morning and woke me up with a loud question.

"Anya, are these your undershirts?"

"What undershirts, they must be mine" (not understanding him in my half-asleep state).

"But how can you wear such coarse underclothing?" he said angrily.

"Of course I can, I don't understand what your're talking about, darling, please let me sleep!"

The next morning the reason for my husband's coming into

my room in such indignation was unriddled. The maid told me that she and the cook had first been frightened and then surprised by "the master." That evening she had washed out her two undershirts and hung them on a clothesline outside the window to dry. A wind came up in the night and the frozen undershirts began banging against the glass. Fyodor Mikhailovich, who was at work in his study, heard the tapping and, fearing the noise would awaken the children, went into the kitchen, got up on a stool, opened up the *fortochka,*[4] and carefully pulled the things inside. Then he painstakingly hung them both on a line above the stove. It was then that he took a good look at this underwear (which was of course made of a coarse gray canvas), was appalled, and went to wake me up.

The next morning I explained the whole thing to my husband and he had a good laugh at his mistake. When I asked him why he hadn't awakened the maid, he answered, "It would have been such a pity to wake them up—after all, they work hard all day, let them have their rest!"

That was always my husband's attitude toward servants, from whom he never demanded any special service for himself.

But Fyodor Mikhailovich was particularly pleased when, two years before his death, he was able to make me a present of diamond earrings, with a single stone in each. They cost about two hundred rubles and my husband consulted P. F. Panteleyev, a connoisseur of precious stones, on the purchase.

I remember wearing his gift for the first time at a literary evening at which he gave a reading. While other writers were reading my husband and I were sitting together along a wall decorated with mirrors. I suddenly noticed that he was looking to the side and smiling at somebody. Then he turned to me and whispered blissfully, "They sparkle, they have a gorgeous sparkle!"

It turned out that the play of the stones was brilliant under the multiple lights, and my husband was as happy as a child.

Of our life in 1876 I recall a certain minor misunderstanding which deeply upset my husband, who had suffered an epileptic seizure two or three days earlier. A young man, Alexander Fyodorovich Otto (Onegin), who lived in Paris and who later compiled a valuable collection of Pushkiniana, paid a visit to Fyodor Mikhailovich. He said he was there by commission of his friend Turgenev to see Fyodor Mikhailovich and obtain from him the money owing to Turgenev.

My husband was surprised at this and asked, hadn't Turgenev received from Pavel Annenkov the fifty thalers given him to transmit to Turgenev the previous July when Fyodor Mikhailovich met him on the train on his way to Russia? Mr. Otto confirmed that the money from Annenkov had been received, but said that Turgenev recalled sending Fyodor Mikhailovich in Wiesbaden not fifty thalers but one hundred, and therefore he considered that Fyodor Mikhailovich still owed him fifty thalers.

My husband, assuming the error was his, was extremely agitated and called me in immediately.

"Tell me, Anya, how much money did I owe Turgenev?" he asked, introducing the visitor to me.

"Fifty thalers."

"Is that right? Are you sure? Could you be mistaken?"

"I remember it perfectly. Why, Turgenev's letter stated exactly how much money he was sending you."

"Show me the letter—where do you have it?" my husband demanded.

The letter, of course, was not at hand, but I promised to locate it, and we asked the young man to drop in again in a couple of days.

Fyodor Mikhailovich was very much disturbed by the possibility that I might have made an error, and fretted so over it that I decided to sit up all night if necessary until I found that letter. His anxiety infected me, and I began to wonder whether some misunderstanding had occurred. Unfortunately my husband's correspondence for the past few years was in complete chaos, and I had to go through at least three or four hundred letters until, at last, I came upon the one from Turgenev. After reading it and realizing for himself that we had not made any mistake, my husband calmed down.

When Mr. Otto came two days later, we showed him Turgenev's letter. He was very embarrassed and asked us to loan him the letter so that he could send it on to Turgenev, promising to return it to us.

About three weeks later Otto came again, bringing a letter with him—not the one we had given him, but a letter Fyodor Mikhailovich himself had written from Wiesbaden, asking Turgenev for a loan of fifty thalers.[5] Thus, the misunderstanding was cleared up to our complete satisfaction. It was only Mr. Otto who bore the brunt of it. In a letter of many years later (December 19, 1888), reminding me who he was, he wrote:

> My brief acquaintance with Fyodor Mikhailovich was based on a misunderstanding unpleasant for him, in which I played an unwitting role. I am the man who came to see you long, long ago, when you were still living in Peski, at a financially difficult time exacerbated by Fyodor Mikhailovich's state of health. I was there at the commission of my friend I. S. Turgenev to receive some money which Fyodor Mikhailovich owed him. I experienced some painful moments then; for you yourself trustingly explained the general situation to me and afterwards Fyodor Mikhailovich, perturbed and fuming, demonstrated to me that Turgenev's demand was more than unjust.
>
> With the unfortunate abruptness characteristic of my nature, I then wrote a biting letter to Turgenev. The matter was cleared up when Turgenev admitted his error, but I almost lost his friendship, as always happens to the third party when he gets involved in the quarrels of the first two![6]

At the beginning of 1877 an event occurred thanks to which I had occasion to make the acquaintance of the St. Petersburg Department of Criminal Investigation: my new fur cloak was stolen.

I should mention that after my return to Russia [in 1871], I went on wearing my gray lamb half-length coat in winter, the same one I used to wear in Dresden. Fyodor Mikhailovich was appalled when he saw me dressed so lightly, and predicted a severe chill with all its consequences. Of course the coat was not adequate for the Russian December and January frosts, and during the cold weather I had to put a thick plaid on top of it, which presented a rather unattractive picture. But during the first years after our return we had to think first of all of paying off the debts which were causing us so much anxiety, and therefore the question of a warm fur coat, which was raised every fall, simply could not be favorably resolved.

Finally, at the end of 1876, it became possible to fulfill our long-standing desire, and I remember how interested Fyodor Mikhailovich was in this small domestic matter. Since he knew how grudging I was when it came to clothes for myself, he made up his mind to take things into his own hands. He took me to Zezerin's fur shop (now Mertens, where he always used to store his fur coat for the summer) and asked the salesman in charge to do his very best to select a fox skin for the coat and a collar of marten.

The salesman, who was an admirer of my husband's work, threw down a whole mountain of fox skins. Pointing out their merits or faults, he finally selected a flawless fur for the agreed-on price of one hundred rubles. The marten collar, which cost almost the same price, was first-rate. They also had samples of black silk satin which Fyodor Mikhailovich examined for weave, color and durability. When the topic of style came up (the ladies' cloak called "rotunda"[7] had only just come into vogue), Fyodor Mikhailovich asked to see this novelty, and immediately set up a protest against the "absurd" fashion. And when the shop assistant jokingly informed him that the rotunda had been invented by a tailor who wanted to be rid of his wife, my husband said, "But I don't in the least want to be rid of my wife. So please make it up in the old-fashioned style—a cloak with sleeves!"

Seeing that the order for the coat was a matter of such interest to my husband, I didn't insist on having a rotunda. When the finished coat was delivered two weeks later and I put it on, he said, pleased as Punch, "Well, now, I've got myself a real prosperous Madame Merchant! Now I won't be afraid of your catching cold in it."

And then the fur coat, completed after so much fluster and so many years of waiting, was stolen!

It happened in broad daylight in the space of ten minutes. I had just come back from somewhere. When I was told that Fyodor Mikhailovich was already up and asking for me I hurried to his study, leaving the coat on a hook in the front hall, though normally I took it into my own room. After speaking with my husband for a bit I returned to the hall, but the coat was no longer on its hook.

A commotion was raised. Both of the maids, who were in the

kitchen, maintained that they had not seen anyone. We looked at the door and at the front staircase. It was unlocked. Obviously the girl had forgotten to lock the door when she helped me off with my coat, and the thief had availed himself of this negligence.

Fyodor Mikhailovich was extremely upset by the disappearance of the coat, particularly because two whole months of cold weather still lay before us. And I felt quite desperate, "stormed and raged," roundly scolded the servants, and was angry with myself as well for leaving the coat in the hall. We called in the head janitor, who notified the police of our loss. That evening a police official came to question the servants, and he advised me to go to the Criminal Investigation Department myself and request a very thorough search.

I went to Ofitserskaya Street the next morning. In view of my literary surname I was received at once by one of the high officials. (While my husband was alive, my name always produced a certain impression in official institutions: "He's a writer, perhaps he'll put it in the newspapers!")

They listened to me attentively, and the official asked whom I suspected. I answered that I was quite sure of my servants, both of whom I had brought from Staraya Russa. They had been with us for three years and I had never seen them doing anything wrong. Nor did I suspect anyone else.

"Tell me, who are your frequent visitors?" asked the official.

"Our friends, and then too messengers come from the shops for books and magazines.[8] But they always come in through the kitchen, and none of them came yesterday."

"But don't you have beggars, that is, people who come for alms?"

"That happens sometimes—quite a few of them, actually. I should tell you that my husband is a very kind person and never has the strength to refuse help to anyone—in accordance with his means, of course. There were times when my husband didn't have any small change, and if people came asking alms near our house entrance, he would bring them into our apartment and give them money there. After that these visitors began coming on their own, and when they learned my husband's name from the nameplate on the door, they started asking for Fyodor Mikhailovich. Of course it was I who came out. They would tell me their troubles and I would hand over thirty or forty kopecks. We aren't very rich people, but we're always able to give that kind of help."

"There you have it! One of those beggars robbed you."

"I don't think so. Allow me to stand up for my paupers!" I said. "Even though they're tiresome and take up a lot of my time, still I can't believe they would be thieves—they look too unhappy and hurt."

"Well now, we'll just have a look," said the official. "Ivanov, bring the album here."

His assistant brought in a thick book and put it on the table in front of me.

"Would you be good enough to take a look?" he said. "Perhaps a familiar face will turn up."

I started looking curiously through the album, and there on the third page I saw a face I knew very well indeed.

"My Lord!" I exclaimed. "I know that man very well. He comes to us often. And this one has been there, too, and also this one," I repeated as I turned over the pages. And under each photograph of my "acquaintances" was the caption "Entry hall thief"; and under one of them—also one I knew very well—was written "Housebreaker caught in possession of firearms."

I was hard hit. People who were often inside our house and whom I usually spoke with alone, had turned out to be thieves, even murderers who might not only rob but also kill Fyodor Mikhailovich or me. Our family might be exposed to terrible danger. A cold chill ran along my spine and a dreadful thought came into my head—all these people would continue coming to our house, and we had no security at all against mortal danger in future! Even if we refused them money from now on, our refusal might make them angry and bring the danger upon ourselves.

For several minutes I sat there feeling as depressed as could be. "What a pity," I said, "that my husband can't see the photographs of these people we both recognize—he may not even believe they're thieves."

"But wouldn't you like to pick out the pictures of the people you recognize? We have duplicates. You'll find them useful to you in another way, too. If one of these people turns up at your door, tell him you've been to the Criminal Investigation Department and they gave you their pictures. Believe me, they'll pass the word around and you'll be rid of them for a whole year."

Rarely have I been so pleased with a gift as with the gift of that remarkable collection, which I still have. As the obliging official said goodbye, he promised to send me an experienced agent who might even very possibly locate the stolen goods, particularly since it was now known in exactly which depraved circles the thief must be hunted.

Fyodor Mikhailovich was no less struck than I when he saw the photographs with their descriptive captions. There were certain faces which he recognized perfectly because he often encountered them during his evening walk near the gates of Prince Oldenburg Hospital, where they used to beg money from passersby to bury their nephews or their children who had allegedly died in the children's hospital. They frequently addressed their importunities to Fyodor Mikhailovich—and he never refused them even though he knew that they were begging under false pretenses.

The collection of photographs I had been given was of real help. I should note that during the first month after the theft no one troubled us with any solicitations. Then one of the most persistent of the beggars turned up. In the course of two years of visits by him my small contributions had helped bury not only his sick mother, but several aunts as well. Now he was here again with a plea for money to buy medicine for a sick aunt.

For my own protection I called out Lukerya, a tall girl, from the kitchen and asked her for thirty kopecks, which she put on the table. Then I addressed myself sternly to the "entry hall thief."

"Listen here—take these thirty kopecks and kindly don't come back here any more. My coat was stolen not long ago. I went to the Criminal Investigation Department about it and they gave me pictures of entry hall thieves and told me to inform the police if any of them came here begging. And your picture was there too, for some reason or other. Would you like to take a look?"

"No, why should you trouble yourself?" said my visitor, and vanished in a trice. He even left the proferred money on the table. Evidently he told his pals about the pictures, since none of them came to see us for a very long time after that. And Fyodor Mikhailovich also stopped bringing people in from the street. If he had nothing to give them he would ask the beggar to wait at the entrance and send some money out with the maid.

The agent the Criminal Investigation Department had promised us came the next day. He made me tell him in the minutest detail what had happened, questioning me about the most unnecessary things, with a mysterious expression on his face. I put a question to him, incidentally: were stolen articles often recovered? And I received the following reply: "That, madame, depends mostly on whether the victim wants to have his article back or not."

"I would assume that everyone wants to have it back."

"Let us assume that everyone does, but some care more about it than others. Let me give you an example. Prince G. was robbed of five thousand rubles' worth of valuables. He said to me straight, 'If you find them, you can keep 10 percent for yourself.' Well, and so the things were recovered. Every agent likes to know his intensive efforts will be rewarded."

And the detective brought up two or three more examples. I excused myself for a few minutes to go talk with my husband, and told him it was obvious that I had to promise [the detective] 10 percent and give him at least five rubles on account. Fyodor Mikhailovich only shook his head and said that nothing would come of these investigations. I returned to the detective, promised him 10 percent, and gave him a five-ruble note, after which he promised to take special measures of some kind right away.

A few days later the detective came to us again and said he was on the trail of the coat thief but couldn't tell me his name because of fear of premature publicity. Again he began questioning me about unnecessary details and took up an hour of my time. Assuming that he would go away sooner if I gave him a bribe, I handed over five rubles and told him I was always very busy, and would he please not come back again until he had something material to tell me regarding the case.

About a week and a half had passed when Lukerya ran into the dining room where my husband and I were sitting and exclaimed, "Good news, Madame! Your fur coat has been found! The detective told us—he's coming right away."

We were all very glad, of course. The detective informed us that the thief had pawned my stolen coat at the Loan Society on the Moika, that he had been caught with the pawn ticket, and that the Loan Society must give back the coat without charge if I could produce proof that it belonged to me. He said I must make an immediate statement of my rights, and suggested that I go with him to the Society right then and there to retrieve my coat.

Fyodor Mikhailovich was very displeased with the agent's suggestion. He wanted to accompany him himself but the detective demurred, saying that my husband, as a man, might not be able to give an accurate description of the lost coat. I wanted to have it back so badly that I talked my husband into allowing me to go with the detective, and I covered my face with a thick veil in case we met anyone I knew. And so there I was, on that bright sunny day, driving through all of central Petersburg accompanied by an agent of the Criminal Investigation Department, and laughing to myself at the idea that all the Petersburg thieves strolling along Nevsky Prospect would be wondering what unknown burglaress was being taken in by the only too well-known detective.

We came to the Moika and I wanted to pay the cabby, but the detective said I would need him to take me home again after getting my coat back. So I told him to wait. We entered the office and were taken into a separate room, and a lady's fox-fur coat was brought out to us within a few minutes. From the very first look at it I saw that it was not my coat and said so to the detective.

"But please look it over carefully. Perhaps you'll recognize it. Look at the sleeves—ladies can tell better by the sleeves."

Then he was called away for a moment, and I saw the [Loan] Society's tag stitched to the edge of the coat. I bent down to read it and saw to my indignation that the coat had been pawned in November of 1876—in other words, four months before my coat was stolen. It was obvious that the detective was perfectly aware of this fact, but assumed either that I wouldn't recognize my own coat or was prepared to take someone else's, since my own had not been recovered.

When the detective returned, I pointed out the tag to him and, in the presence of the director of the Society, I loudly expressed my indignation at this patent deception. He was very much taken aback and moved away at once to look at something in the windows. When I left the Society I told the cabby that I wouldn't be using him, and asked how much I owed him for the trip from Grechesky Prospect and for his time. And how vexed I was when the cabby said I owed him seven rubles, for he had been driving the "gentleman" about since morning! The latter, who came out of the door just then, said, "The lady will pay for everything."

Thus, Fyodor Mikhailovich's prediction was correct, and nothing came of my search for the cloak. To the value of the stolen article itself we had to add another seventeen rubles wasted on the detective. My husband felt there was no point in making a complaint against the detective to the obliging official who had recommended him to us. He would sent a second agent and the same long-drawn-out proceedings would have started all over again. The best we could do was to reconcile ourselves to the loss and promise ourselves never again henceforth in similar circumstances to look to that estimable institution, the Department of Criminal Investigation, for help.

At the beginning of 1877 we had some news which distressed us very much. A. K. Gribbe, the owner of the country house in Staraya Russa where we had spent the past four summers, was dead.[9] In addition to our genuine sorrow at the passing of this kindly old man, who had always showed such warmth to our family, we were disquieted by the question of who would inherit the house and whether the future owner would want us as his summer tenants.

This was an important matter to us. In our five years in Staraya Russa we had grown very fond of the place and highly prized the benefits of the mineral waters and the mud baths for our children; and we wanted to go on taking advantage of them in future. But apart from the town itself we also loved the

Gribbe villa, and it seemed to us that it would be hard to find anything else nearly as good. Colonel Gribbe's villa was not a town house but more like a country manor, with a large, shady garden, a kitchen garden, barns, a root-cellar and so forth. Fyodor Mikhailovich particularly appreciated its excellent Russian bathhouse in the garden, which he, who didn't use bathtubs, enjoyed often.

The Gribbe house stood (and still stands) at the edge of town near Kolomets, on the shore of the Pererytitsa River, lined with elm trees planted back in the days of Arakcheyev. But there were broad streets along the other two sides of the house (alongside the garden), and only one side of our plot touched on the neighbors' garden. Fyodor Mikhailovich, who had a fear of the fires which sometimes burned our wooden towns such as Orenburg to the ground, greatly appreciated the isolation of our villa. He was also fond of our shady garden and the big cobbled courtyard where, on rainy days, when the whole town was drowning in mud and it was impossible to walk the unpaved streets, he used to take the walks so essential to his health. But what particularly pleased us both were the rather small but comfortably laid out rooms of the house, with their heavy old mahogany furniture and the decoration and atmosphere in which we felt so warm and cozy. And besides, the fact that our darling Alyosha had been born in that house made us consider it, somehow, our own.

For a time we felt uneasy at the possibility of losing this favorite spot of ours, but the matter was soon cleared up. The heiress to the Gribbe villa left town, decided to sell the house, and was asking a thousand rubles for it (including the furniture and even ten sazhens[10] of firewood) which seemed a high price to the inhabitants of Russa.

At that time we had no money of our own, but I wanted so badly not to lose the villa that I asked my brother Ivan to buy the house in his own name, with the idea of reselling it to us when we had some money. My brother fulfilled my wish and purchased the house, and I bought it from him in my own name later, after Fyodor Mikhailovich's death.

Thanks to this purchase we had, in my husband's words, "built our nest," where we went joyously in early spring and which we were so reluctant to leave in late autumn. Fyodor Mikhailovich considered our Staraya Russa villa his place of physical and emotional peace and, I recall, always put off reading his favorite books until coming to Russa, where his sought-for solitude was seldom disrupted by idle visitors.

In mid-April Fyodor Mikhailovich had to go to the State Bank on business. Fearing that he might have difficulty locating the right department, I volunteered to go with him. As we were driving along Nevsky Prospect we noticed crowds of people around the news vendors. We stopped our cabby, I squeezed my way through the crowd and bought the announcement which had just come out. It was the "Imperial Manifesto on the Entry of Russian Troops into Turkish Territory issued in Kishinev on April 12, 1877."

The manifesto had been expected for a long while, but now the declaration of war was an accomplished fact. After reading the manifesto Fyodor Mikhailovich ordered the cabby to take us to Kazan Cathedral. There was a large crowd inside and a continuous prayer service was being held before the Ikon of the Virgin of Kazan. Fyodor Mikhailovich instantly disappeared in the crowd. Knowing that at certain solemn moments he liked to pray silently without onlookers, I did not follow him, and not until a half hour later did I seek him out in a corner of the cathedral, so absorbed in his rapt and prayerful mood that he did not recognize me for the first moment.

Our trip to the bank was out of the question, so shaken was Fyodor Mikhailovich by the event and its grave consequences for his beloved motherland. My husband put the manifesto away among his important papers, and it is preserved in his archives.[11]

During the year of 1877 we continued publishing *Diary of a Writer.* Although its moral and material success was growing, the burdens of putting out a monthly journal were growing along with it, namely, mailing out the issues, keeping records of subscribers' accounts, correspondence with readers, and so forth and so on. Since I had no assistant in all this except for a messenger boy, I would become overexhausted, and this had repercussions on my health, which had been robust up to that time. In the course of the past two years I had lost a good deal of weight and developed a cough.

My good husband, who was always concerned for my health, began to insist on a complete rest for me during the summer; but since such a rest was impossible to get in Staraya Russa, where the household management in my hands, he decided to accept my brother's invitation to spend the whole summer in the country with him. At the beginning of May we took the family to my brother's estate, Maly Prikol, near Miropolye, in the province of Kursk.

I vividly remember our long-drawn-out journey with stops in Moscow and at the main railroad stations, where our train had to stand for hours because of the movements of the troops being sent off to war. At every stop Fyodor Mikhailovich would go to the buffet to buy large quantities of rolls, honey cakes, cigarettes and matches, and take them into the cars where he would give them out to the soldiers and have long talks with some of them.

Recalling that long journey, I must say that I never ceased to be surprised that Fyodor Mikhailovich, at times so easily irritated in the course of everyday living, was an uncommonly patient and easy companion on the road. He was agreeable to everything, never made any demands or claims but, on the contrary, tried just as hard as he could to lighten the nurses' and my care of the small children, who tired so quickly while traveling and would start getting cranky. I was positively astounded by my husband's ability to soothe a child. The moment one of the three began acting up, Fyodor Mikhailovich would appear from his corner (he sat in the same car, but at a distance from us), take the naughty child to his own seat, and quiet him down in a twinkling. He had a special ability to talk with children, to enter into their world, win their trust (and this even with strange children he met by accident) and get the child so interested that he would become gay and obedient at once. I account for this in his unflagging love for little children, which told him how to behave in a given situation.

At the end of June Fyodor Mikhailovich had to leave the country for Petersburg to edit and put out the double summer issue of *Diary of a Writer* for May and June. At the same time the two older children and I, who were setting out on a pilgrimage to Kiev, went with him as far as Korenevo station. In bringing up his children Fyodor Mikhailovich put great weight on the vivid, pure impressions experienced in early childhood. Knowing that I had been dreaming for a long time of visiting Kiev to venerate its holy places, my husband suggested that I take advantage of his absence to go there, which we accomplished very smoothly.

In recent years Fyodor Mikhailovich had often expressed regret at not being able to visit Darovoye, the estate belonging to his late mother where he had spent his summers as a child. Since he was feeling quite well that summer, I persuaded him to stop in Moscow and make the trip to Darovoye on his way back to Miropolye from Petersburg. He did just that and stayed with his sister Vera (who had inherited the estate) for two days.

His family told me later that during his stay my husband revisited all the different places in the park and the outskirts dear to him in memory, and even walked to the grove he had loved as a child, Chermashnya, about two versts away from the estate—a name he later gave the grove in *The Brothers Karamazov.* He also went to visit the huts of the peasants he had known as a boy, many of whom he still remembered. The old men and women and those of his own age as well, remembering him from childhood, were very happy to see him, invited him into their cottages, and regaled him with tea.

The trip to Darovoye gave rise to many reminiscences which my husband recounted to us with great liveliness after his return home. He promised the children to take them to Darovoye without fail and show them all his favorite spots in the park. In fulfillment of this wish of my husband's to show his children the places where he had spent his childhood, I took them to Darovoye in 1884[12] and, with his family pointing things out, went everywhere my husband had walked for the last time.

The summer of 1877 passed gaily and happily for our family, and we regretted only that we could not stay in the country through September as well. But we had to put out the double summer issue of *Diary of a Writer* for July–August, and so we returned to Petersburg toward the end of August.

Our normal life, full of petty troubles, began. People familiar and unfamiliar started visiting Fyodor Mikhailovich daily. That fall the writer Vsevolod Solovyov, a great admirer of my husband's work, came to see us quite often. On one such occasion he told my husband that he had met an interesting woman, a Mrs. Field, who first described his past life to him with great accuracy and then foretold certain events which, to his amazement, had already come to pass.

When Solovyov set off for home my husband went with him, since he used to take a long walk every evening. On the way he asked Solovyov how far away Mrs. Field lived, and on learning that she was nearby suggested that they drop in to see her right then and there. Solovyov agreed and they went to visit the fortuneteller.

Mrs. Field of course had no idea who her unknown guest was, but what she foretold to Fyodor Mikhailovich came true exactly. She prophesied for him such great fame as he could never even have imagined, awaiting him in the near future; and this prophecy came to pass at the Pushkin memorial festivities. And, to our deep grief, her sad prediction that my husband would soon be overtaken by a family sorrow also came to pass with the death of our darling Alyosha. This melancholy prediction of hers he told me about only after our loss.

As the year's end drew close, Fyodor Mikhailovich began to ponder the question of whether to continue publishing *Diary of a Writer* during the following year. As far as the journal's financial success was concerned he was quite pleased, and he was pleased at society's sincere and trusting attitude toward him as expressed in letters and in many visits from strangers. The demands of his art prevailed, however, and he decided to discontinue the *Diary* for a period of two or three years and set to work on a new novel. What literary projects excited and gripped him may be judged by a notebook discovered after his death, in which he made the following entry in December of 1877:

Memento—for the rest of my life

1. To write the Russian *Candide*
2. To write a book about Jesus Christ
3. To write my memoirs

4. To write an epic of the *sorokovina.*[13]
(All this in addition to my last novel and proposed publication of the *Diary,* that is, a minimum of ten years' work, and I am now fifty-six.)

In November of 1877 Fyodor Mikhailovich was in a very depressed frame of mind. Nikolai Nekrasov, who had been suffering for a long time with a painful disease,[14] was dying. For my husband, Nekrasov was associated with memories of his own young manhood and the beginnings of his literary career. It was Nekrasov, after all, who was one of the first to recognize Fyodor Mikhailovich's talent and who contributed to his success in the intellectual circles of that day.

It is true that in later years their political views kept them apart, and during the sixties a fierce polemical struggle was waged between the journal [of the Dostoevsky brothers] *Time,* and [Nekrasov's] journal *The Contemporary.* Fyodor Mikhailovich bore no grudge, however, and when Nekrasov suggested that he place his novel [*A Raw Youth*] in *National Notes,* he agreed. His friendly feelings toward the old friend of his youth were revived, and Nekrasov responded to them with genuine warmth.

When Fyodor Mikhailovich learned that Nekrasov was gravely ill, he began dropping in to his house often to inquire about his health. Sometimes he would ask them not to disturb the patient on his account, but merely to convey his warm greetings. Sometimes he found Nekrasov alert, and then the poet would read Fyodor Mikhailovich his latest poems. Pointing to one of them, "The Unhappy Ones" (called "The Mole"), he said, "I wrote that one about you!" My husband was terribly touched by this.

In general, Fyodor Mikhailovich's last meetings with Nekrasov had a profound impact on him, and so, when he heard on December 27 that Nekrasov was dead, he was grieved to the depths of his soul. He spent the whole night reading aloud the verses of the late poet, deeply moved by many of them, which he called "the real pearls of Russian poetry." Seeing his extreme excitation and fearing a seizure, I sat in his study with him until morning; and from the stories he told me I learned several episodes from the days of their young manhood which I hadn't known until then.[15]

Fyodor Mikhailovich attended the offices for the dead and decided to be present at the bearing out of the body and the burial. Early on the morning of December 30 we went to Krayevsky's house on Liteynaya Street, where Nekrasov had lived, and found there a crowd of young people with their arms full of laurel wreaths. My husband accompanied the coffin as far as Italyanskaya Street, but since walking bareheaded in the intense cold was dangerous for him I persuaded him to go home and return to Novodevichy Convent two hours later for the funeral rites. This we did and were at the convent by noon.

After standing in the overheated church for a half hour Fyodor Mikhailovich decided to go out into the fresh air. Orest Miller came with us, and we went together to look for Nekrasov's future grave. The hush of the cemetery had a subduing effect on Fyodor Mikhailovich and he said to me, "When I die, Anya, bury me here or wherever you want, but mind, don't bury me in the writers' section of Volkov Cemetery. I don't want to lie among my enemies—I suffered enough from them while I was alive!"

It was very painful for me to listen to him giving instructions for his own funeral. I started talking him out of it, reassuring him that he was quite well and that there was no reason for him to think about dying. In an effort to dispel his sad mood, I began weaving a fantasy about his future funeral while beseeching him to go on living as long as possible.

"All right then, if Volkov doesn't appeal to you I'll bury you in the Nevsky Lavra next to your beloved Zhukovsky. But please don't die just yet! I'll call in the Nevsky choir and the mass will be served by the bishop, maybe by two bishops. And you know what, I'll arrange things so that not only this huge crowd of young people will follow your coffin, but all Petersburg —sixty thousand people—eighty thousand. And there will be three times more wreaths. See what a brilliant funeral I'm promising you? But only on one condition—that you live many,

many years more, many, many years! Or else I'll be too miserable!"

I spoke my hyperbolic promises deliberately, thinking they might distract Fyodor Mikhailovich from the thoughts weighing him down at that moment, and my effort succeeded. He smiled and said, "All right, all right, I'll try to live a while longer!"

Orest Miller made some remark about my rich vein of fantasy, and the conversation passed to another subject.

At Nekrasov's grave, after several speeches by his colleagues on *National Notes,* the surrounding throng of young people demanded a word from Dostoevsky. Fyodor Mikhailovich, deeply moved, made a short speech in a breaking voice in which he paid high tribute to the genius of the departed poet and commented on the great loss to Russian literature with his death. In the opinion of many, these were the most heartfelt words spoken over Nekrasov's open grave.

This talk, much amplified, was printed in the December, 1877, issue of *Diary of a Writer.* It contained the following chapters: 1. Nekrasov's death. What was said at his grave. II. Pushkin, Lermontov and Nekrasov. III. The Poet and the Citizen: Some general comments on Nekrasov as a human being. IV. A witness for Nekrasov. In the opinion of many writers this article was the best defense of Nekrasov as a man written by any of the critics of that day.[16]

[I should add that] when Fyodor Mikhailovich died three years later and his magnificent funeral ceremony took place, of such impressiveness as the capital had not seen up to that time, Orest Miller reminded me during a visit shortly afterward that I had predicted almost literally everything that happened. Just as I had foretold, Fyodor Mikhailovich found his place of eternal rest in the Alexander Nevsky Lavra, side by side with the grave of the poet Zhukovsky, a location available only by chance. Two bishops officiated and the superb Nevsky choir sang at the funeral rites. Behind the cortege walked sixty to eighty thousand people bearing great masses of wreaths, as I had foretold.

I myself remembered the fantastic promises I had made at Novodevichy Cemetery but was not in the least surprised by the accuracy of my prophesy. I knew I sometimes had the capacity to express a surmise (quite accidentally, as if it had slipped out involuntarily in conversation) which [later] came true almost to the letter.

This capacity usually appeared in me at times when my nerves were strained to the utmost, and that was exactly their condition when we said goodbye to Nekrasov and I saw with disquiet how painfully my husband was affected by the death of his old friend and contemporary. I have read somewhere that the gift of a kind of "foretelling" is inherent in Northern women, that is, in Norwegians and Swedes. Perhaps this capacity—which has given me many painful moments in certain cases—can be accounted for as an inheritance from my Swedish mother.

CHAPTER NINE

The Years 1878 and 1879

During Lent of 1878, Vladimir Solovyov gave a series of lectures in philosophy for the Society of Friends of Spiritual Enlightenment in the lecture hall of Solyanoy Gorodok.[1] These lectures drew a full hall of listeners, among whom were many of our mutual friends. Since things were going well at home, I too went with Fyodor Mikhailovich to hear the lectures.

As we were coming home from one of them my husband asked me, "Did you notice how strangely Strakhov behaved to us today? He didn't come over to us the way he always does, and when we met during intermission he barely said hello and then started talking to someone else right away. Is he angry about something—what do you think?"

"Yes, I had the feeling he was avoiding us," I answered. "Although when I said to him as we were leaving, 'Don't forget Sunday,' he answered, 'I'll be there.' "

I felt a little uneasy that I might somehow, in my impetuosity, have hurt the feelings of our regular Sunday visitor. My husband really treasured his talks with Strakhov and would often remind me before one of our dinners to get a bottle of good wine or prepare our guest's favorite fish.

Strakhov came to dinner the next Sunday, and I resolved to clear up the matter and ask him straight out whether he was angry at us.

"Whatever put that into your head, Anna Grigoryevna?" Strakhov asked.

"Because both Fyodor Mikhailovich and I had the feeling you were avoiding us at Solovyov's last lecture."

"Oh, that was a special case," he laughed. "It wasn't only you, but all our friends I was avoiding. Count Leo Tolstoy came to the lecture with me. He asked me not to introduce him to anyone, and that was why I stayed away from all of you."

"What? Tolstoy was with you?" Fyodor Mikhailovich exclaimed in rueful surprise. "How sorry I am that I didn't see him! Naturally I wouldn't have foisted my acquaintance on him, if the man didn't want it. But why didn't you whisper to me who was with you? I would have taken a look at him, at least!"

"But you know him from his portraits, after all!" laughed Strakhov.

"What are portraits—can they show what a man is? It's another thing entirely to see him face to face. Sometimes one look is enough to imprint a person on your mind for the rest of your life. I'll never forgive you, Nikolai Nikolayevich, for not pointing him out to me!"[2]

And in later years Fyodor Mikhailovich more than once expressed his regret at never having met Tolstoy in person.

On May 16, 1878, our family was struck down by a terrible tragedy. Our younger son Alyosha died. There was nothing to give any intimation of the calamity that befell us. The little boy was always healthy and gay. On the morning of the day he died, he was still prattling away in his not always intelligible speech, and was laughing hard with his old nurse Prokhorovna, who was paying us a visit before our departure for Staraya Russa. Suddenly the little one's face began twitching in a slight spasm. The nurse took it for the kind of cramp children sometimes get when teething, for his molars were beginning to come through just at that time.

I was terrified and immediately called our regular children's doctor, G. A. Choshin, who lived nearby and came at once. Evidently he did not consider the illness very serious. He wrote out a prescription and assured us that the spasms would soon pass. But since they continued I awakened Fyodor Mikhailovich, who was very much upset.

We decided to consult a specialist in nervous diseases and I went to Professor Uspensky. He was receiving patients, and there were twenty or more people sitting in his waiting room. He saw me right away and said he would come to us the moment his patients were gone. He wrote a prescription for some sedative, and told me to take a container of oxygen and give it to the child from time to time to help him breathe.

When I reached home I found my poor little boy in the same state. He was unconscious, and every so often his small body would convulse in spasm. But it was clear that he was not in pain, for he did not groan or cry out.

We did not stir a step from our little sufferer and waited anxiously for the doctor to come. He appeared, finally, at about two, examined the patient, and said to me, "Don't cry, don't worry, it will be over soon."

Fyodor Mikhailovich went to see the doctor out, came back dead white, and got down on his knees next to the couch where we had put our baby to make it easier for the doctor to examine him. I too got down on my knees beside my husband and tried to ask him exactly what it was the doctor had said (I learned afterwards that he told Fyodor Mikhailovich the death agony had already begun). But with a sign he forbade me to speak.

About an hour went by and we noticed that the convulsions were diminishing perceptibly. Lulled by what the doctor had said to me, I was even happy, for I assumed that the spasms were turning into a quiet sleep, a portent of recovery, perhaps. And what was my desolation when suddenly the baby's breathing stopped . . . and he was dead!

Fyodor Mikhailovich kissed him, made the sign of the cross over him three times, and broke into a paroxysm of sobbing. I sobbed too, and so did our children, who so loved our darling Lyosha.

My husband was crushed by this death. He had loved Lyosha somehow in a very special way, with an almost morbid love, as if sensing that he would not have him for long. What racked him particularly was the fact that the child had died of epilepsy—a disease inherited from him.[3] To outward appearance, he was calm and bore with courage the blow that fell on us; but I very much feared that this suppression of his deep grief might react fatally upon his already shaky health.

In an effort to comfort him a little and divert him from his black thoughts I begged Vladimir Solovyov, who used to visit us in those days of our mourning, to persuade Fyodor Mikhailovich to accompany him to Optina Pustyn, the hermitage where Solovyov was planning to go that summer. A pilgrimage to Optina had been a long-time dream of Fyodor Mikhailovich's, but very difficult to realize. Solovyov agreed to help me and began talking my husband into making the trip to Optina with him. I added my own entreaties to his, and it was decided then and there that Fyodor Mikhailovich would go to Moscow in mid-June (he had been planning to go there anyway to offer his future novel [*The Brothers Karamazov*] to Katkov), and use the occasion to make the trip to Optina with Solovyov.

I would not have dared to let Fyodor Mikhailovich make such a distant and wearisome (in those times) journey by himself. But I felt that Solovyov, even though he was a man "not of this world," would be able to look after Fyodor Mikhailovich if he should have an epileptic seizure.

As for me, the death of our darling little boy was shattering. I so lost my bearings, mourned and cried so much that I was unrecognizable. My customary cheerfulness vanished together with my normal flow of energy, which gave way to apathy. I grew impassive to everything: the management of the household, our business affairs, and even my own children; and I gave myself over utterly to my memories of the last three years. Fyodor Mikhailovich recorded many of my doubts, thoughts and even words in the chapter of *Brothers Karamazov* called "Women of Faith," in which a woman who has lost her child unburdens her grief to Father Zossima.

My condition caused Fyodor Mikhailovich much suffering. He kept urging and beseeching me to submit to God's will, to accept with humility the affliction visited upon us, to take pity on him and the children, to whom I had become, in his words, "indifferent." His entreaties and exhortations had an effect on me, and I succeeded in mastering myself so as not to distress my unhappy husband even more with my unrestrained grief.

Immediately after Alyosha's funeral (we buried him in the Great Okhta Cemetery) we went to Staraya Russa, and by June 20 Fyodor Mikhailovich was already in Moscow. There he succeeded in coming to a very quick agreement with the editor of the *Russian Messenger* on the publication of [*The Brothers Karamazov*] during the next year, 1879. After winding up this matter he made his trip to Optina Pustyn. The story of his journey, or rather of his "wanderings," with Vladimir Solovyov was described in his letter to me of June 29, 1878.

My husband returned from Optina seemingly at peace and much calmer, and told me a great deal about the customs of the hermitage where he had passed two days. He met with the renowned elder, Father Ambrosius, three times: once in the presence of others and twice alone. These talks had a profound and lasting effect on him. When he told the elder about the loss we had suffered and about my too violent grief, the latter asked whether I was a believer. And when Fyodor Mikhailovich said that I was, the elder asked him to convey his blessing to me as well as those words which later, in [*The Brothers Karamazov*], Father Zossima spoke to the grief-stricken mother: . . . .*[4] It was clear from my husband's stories about him what a profound seer and interpreter of the human heart this universally respected elder was.

When we returned to Petersburg that autumn, we could not bring ourselves to go on living in that apartment, filled with memories of our dead child, and we moved to No. 5 Kuznechny Lane, where my husband was fated to die two and a half years later.

Our apartment, which was on the second floor, consisted of six rooms in addition to a huge storeroom for books, a front hall, and a kitchen; and seven windows looked out on Kuznechny Lane. A marble plaque is now affixed to the room which was my husband's study. The front entrance (now walled up) was located underneath our drawing room, which was next door to the study.

No matter how my husband and I strove to submit to God's will and not grieve, we could not forget our darling Lyosha. All that autumn and the following winter were darkened by desolate memories. Our loss had the effect on my husband (who had always been passionately attached to his children) of making

*A gap in the manuscript.

him love them even more intensely and fear for them even more.

Outwardly, our life went on as always. Fyodor Mikhailovich worked very hard on the plan for his new book. (Working out the plan for a novel was always the most important and most difficult aspect of his literary work. The plans of several of his novels—*The Possessed*, for instance—were sometimes rewritten many times.) The work went so well that by December of 1878 not only was the plan complete, but about 160 pages of the novel were written as well, and these were published in the *Russian Messenger* for January, 1879.

On December 14, 1878, Fyodor Mikhailovich took part in a literary and musical evening, a benefit for the Bestuzhev Higher Courses for Women, held in the Nobility Assembly Hall. He read Nellie's story from his novel *The Insulted and Injured*. All his listeners were struck by his great simplicity and sincerity, as though it were not the author reading, but an adolescent girl telling about her own wretched life. There was a special art in producing an indelible impression on his listeners by reading so simply. The women students responded to him with fervor, and I remember how very pleasant it was for him to be in the center of that group of enthusiastic young people who felt so warmly toward him. On subsequent occasions he took particular pleasure in their requests to read at student benefits.[5]

When a notice appeared in the next-to-last issue of *Diary of a Writer* [for 1877] that Fyodor Mikhailovich was discontinuing its publication for reasons of health,[6] he began receiving sympathetic letters from subscribers and readers. Some commiserated on his illness and wished him recovery; others expressed regret at the discontinuance of a journal which reacted with such sensitivity to all the issues with which society was then concerned. Some said that if Fyodor Mikhailovich felt overburdened by publishing the journal every month, they wished he would issue his *Diary* irregularly whenever his health and strength permitted, so that it might be possible, even if only from time to time, to have his honest interpretation of the outstanding events of contemporary life.

Over a hundred letters in that vein came in at the beginning of the year, and these letters had a very good effect on my husband. They demonstrated to him that there were people who shared his views and that society valued his objective voice and trusted him. In this connection I have preserved a published letter from Fyodor Mikhailovich to his friend S. D. Yanovsky, which I quote here:

You would simply not believe the degree to which I have enjoyed the acceptance of the Russian people during these two years of publishing. Letters of approval and even some with expressions of sincere affection have come to me in the hundreds. Since October, when I announced that I was suspending publication, they have been arriving daily from all over Russia, from all classes of society (the most heterogeneous) with expressions of regret and entreaties not to abandon the cause. Only modesty prevents me from telling you how much fellow-feeling all express.

And if you could only know how much I myself have learned from these two years of publication, from these hundreds of letters from the Russian people! And the chief thing I've learned is that these are authentic Russians, not people with the distorted outlook of the Petersburg intelligentsia, but with the genuine and right outlook of the Russian man, of whom there have proved to be incomparably more here in our country than I supposed two years ago. So many more that I could not have imagined this result even in my most fervid wishes and fantasies.

Believe it—there is much here in Russia which is not nearly so dismal as we used to think. But mainly there is much testimony to the craving for a new, right life, to profound faith in the imminent change in the mentality of our intelligentsia, who lag behind the people and have not the slightest understanding of the people.

You are angry with Krayevsky, but he is not alone. They all denied the people, laughed and continue to laugh at its awakening and the bright, sacred manifestation of its will, and at the form in which it presented its demands. And therefore these gentlemen will simply disappear; they are too outdated and too played out. Those who don't understand the people must now inevitably join the stockbrokers and the Yids,[7] and there you have the finale to the representatives of our "progressive" thinking. But something new is coming. In the army, our young men and our women (nurses) demonstrated something other than what was expected by all. Let us wait.

(And Krayevsky, after all, is at the service of certain persons and on top of that, in my opinion, has been trying to show off his originality ever since the Serbian war. Having once taken a stand, he could no longer let it go. However there is very little sense here in any of the Moscow papers, except for the *Moscow Gazette* and its lead articles, so highly regarded abroad. The other papers simply exploit the moment.[8]

In all the hundreds of letters I have received during these two years, what I was most highly praised for was my sincerity and honesty of thinking. In other words, that is just what we are missing most, that is just what people are craving, and that is just what they don't have. We have few citizens among the representatives of our intelligentsia.[9]

On February 6, 1878, Fyodor Mikhailovich received the following document from the Permanent Secretary of the Academy of Sciences: "The Imperial Academy of Sciences, wishing to express its high esteem for your literary work, has elected you, respected sir, a corresponding member in the Division of Russian Language and Literature."

His election had taken place at a solemn session of the Academy on December 29, 1877. He was extremely pleased by this recognition even though it was somewhat tardy (in the thirty-third year of his career) in comparision with that of his literary contemporaries.[10]

I recall that at the beginning of 1878 Fyodor Mikhailovich used to attend dinners in different restaurants, organized every month by the Society of Authors—at Borelle's, at the Maloyaroslavets, and so on. The invitations were sent over the signature of the distinguished chemist D. I. Mendeleyev. These dinners were attended exclusively by writers of the most diverse camps, and Fyodor Mikhailovich used to meet there with his sworn literary enemies. He attended three or four of these dinners that winter, returned home each time very much aroused, and described with great gusto his unexpected encounters and the people he had met.

Something else happened at the beginning of 1878 which had a very good effect on him. He was visited by Dmitry Sergeyevich Arsenyev, tutor to the Grand Dukes Sergey and Paul [the sons of Tsar Alexander II]. Arsenyev expressed the desire to acquaint his pupils with the eminent author, whose work was of interest to them. He added that he came in the name of the Tsar, who desired Fyodor Mikhailovich's conversations with the young Grand Dukes to exert a beneficial influence on them.

At that time Fyodor Mikhailovich was deeply engrossed in working out his plan for *The Brothers Karamazov* and it was difficult for him to tear himself away from it, but the wish of the Tsar-Liberator was of course law for him. He found it pleasant to know that it was in his power to carry out even a small desire of a personage he had always revered for his great achievement of emancipating the serfs, for realizing a dream dear to him in his youth, for which he himself had suffered so bitterly in his own day.

On March 15 Fyodor Mikhailovich received the following letter from Arsenev.

> Much time has elapsed since you and I met. After my conversation with you I was surer than ever that it would be best to arrange things so that your acquaintance with the Grand Dukes would not appear to be contrived by parental advice or tutorial decree, but should result from their own wish. And now much time has been spent on inculcating this idea through (apparently) random conversations. During Carnival and the first week of Lent and Communion, however, I feared that experiences of a different order might weaken the impact of their first meeting with you, and that is why I have waited until now to ask you to fulfill your promise.[11]

Fyodor Mikhailovich was highly impressed by his meeting with the Grand Dukes. He found them possessed of kind hearts and superior intelligence, capable in discussion not only of defending their own sometimes still immature opinions, but also of respecting the contrary opinions of their fellow discussants. Evidently Fyodor Mikhailovich made a good impression on them as well, and the invitations began to be repeated. Not finding my husband at home on one occasion, Arsenyev left the following letter for him (April 23, 1878).

> . . . If it is not inconvenient for you to come at 5½ you will be doing me a great favor, since I would like to speak with you *alone* before the Grand Dukes come. I would like to ask you to touch upon the role they might play in the light of the present situation of society, of the useful-

ness they must manifest, and I should very much like to discuss with you the question of how to approach this matter most naturally.

Fyodor Mikhailovich's relations with the Grand Dukes continued up to his death. Their Highnesses, who were abroad in 1881, sent me a telegram expressing deep sympathy on the occasion of my loss.

When he was visiting the Grand Dukes Fyodor Mikhailovich had occasion to make the acquaintance of Grand Duke Konstantin Konstantinovich. The latter was then a kind and sincere young man who struck my husband with his passionate love for everything beautiful in his native literature. Fyodor Mikhailovich felt the presence of a genuine poetic gift in the young Grand Duke and regretted his choice of a naval career after the example of his father, since in my husband's opinion the literary calling was the right one for him; this prediction was brilliantly realized in later years.[12]

Despite the difference in their ages, my husband and the young Grand Duke developed a truly friendly relationship. He often invited Fyodor Mikhailovich to his home for a personal talk or called a select company together and asked him to choose something from his new book to read aloud. Thus, Fyodor Mikhailovich had occasion to read two or three times at the Grand Duke's in the presence of her Highness, the Crown Princess Maria Fyodorovna, of Maria Maximilianovna of Baden and other members of the Imperial family.

I still have several extremely friendly letters from the Grand Duke to my husband, and when he died his Highness sent me a letter of condolence in addition to a telegram. Among the masses of sympathy letters I received in 1881, I was particularly touched by his Highness' letter. Knowing his affectionate feelings toward my husband, I was convinced that he mourned his passing sincerely and with all his heart.

I cannot deny myself the pleasure of quoting this letter of a fine man who, alas, passed away at so early an age!

The Frigate *Duke of Edinburgh*,
February 14, 1881

Deeply respected Anna Grigoryevna!

You have suffered a heavy, irreplaceable loss, and not you alone, but all Russia sadly mourns with you the loss of a great man who gave his whole life to his country. The merciful God who gave you a heavy cross to bear has granted at the same time a rare consolation: your deep grief is shared and lamented by all your fellow countrymen, by all, whether or not they knew Fyodor Mikhailovich personally.

Our far-distant naval cruise prevented me from learning of our nation's sorrow, and not until yesterday was I thunderstruck by the grievous news. Although I have not as yet had occasion to make your acquaintance I cannot now, in these sad moments, refuse myself in my overwhelming desire to express to you my deepest, most sincere and heartfelt sympathy in your grief. As a Russian and a friend who truly and genuinely loved your unforgettable husband, I cannot keep from telling you of my fellow feeling for your heart's wound, of everything I feel now which words cannot convey. Forgive the liberty with which I address you during these high, painful moments when nothing mortal can give you consolation, and believe the candor of my feelings.

Wholly devoted to you,
KONSTANTIN

When the Grand Duke attended the funeral rites for Emperor Alexander II he expressed the desire to meet with me through Countess A. E. Komarovskaya. At the Countess' invitation I paid a visit to her home and passed several hours in conversation with the Grand Duke. With a feeling of sincere gratitude I remember what he said about my beloved husband and his strong, beneficial influence upon him. The Grand Duke wished to see my children, of whom their father had spoken with such delight.

Since he was about to leave on a cruise, the Grand Duke invited me and the children on Thursday of Passion Week; the children painted Easter eggs there and received gifts from him. Later in Holy Week the Grand Duke visited me and presented the two children and myself with a portrait of himself in naval uniform, with a very friendly inscription.

When a school named for Fyodor Mikhailovich was founded subsequently in Staraya Russa, Grand Duke Konstantin Konstantinovich wanted to be among the people helping the school get on its feet and pledged an annual contribution of fifty rubles, which the school accepted with deep gratitude.

One day in the early spring of 1878 the whole family was sitting quietly at dinner. Fyodor Mikhailovich, refreshed after a long walk, was in an excellent mood and was having a lively conversation with the children. Suddenly the bell rang loudly and the girl ran to open the door. Through the half-open door into the front hall we heard a woman's rather shrill voice say, "Is he still alive?"

The girl didn't understand the question and didn't say anything.

"I'm asking you, is Fyodor Mikhailovich still alive?"

"The master is alive, ma'am," the girl answered in confusion.

I wanted to go and find out what this was all about but was forestalled by Fyodor Mikhailovich, who was sitting closer to the door and who quickly jumped up and almost ran out into the hall.

A middle-aged woman rose from her chair to meet him, held out her hands and exclaimed, "Are you alive, Fyodor Mikhailovich? How happy I am that you are still alive!"

"Madame, what is the matter with you?" exclaimed the astonished Fyodor Mikhailovich in his turn. "I am alive and plan to go on living for a long while!"

"But there are rumors going about Kharkov," the woman said excitedly, "that your wife has left you, that you fell seriously ill because of her unfaithfulness, and that you are lying helpless. And so I came immediately to look after you. I'm here directly from the train."

Hearing these exclamations, I too went out into the hall and found Fyodor Mikhailovich in a state of high indignation. "Listen to this, Anya," he said, "some scoundrels have been spreading the lie that you ran away from me—how do you like that? How do you like that, I say!"

"Now calm yourself, my dear, don't upset yourself," I said. "It's some kind of misunderstanding. Please go in, you'll catch a chill here in the hall."

And I began quietly drawing him back toward the dining room. He heeded me and went in, but we could still hear his indignant exclamations coming from the dining room for a long time afterward.

As for me, however, I had a talk with the strange woman, who turned out to be a schoolteacher, a very kind person but probably not very bright. She was doubtless fascinated by the idea of taking care of a famous writer who had been deserted by his good-for-nothing wife, and probably also by the idea of seeing him off into the next world and then priding herself all the rest of her life that he had died in her arms.

I was genuinely sorry for the poor woman, who was obviously quite upset. Excusing myself for a moment, I went to the dining room and told my husband I would like to give her some dinner.

Fyodor Mikhailovich made a gesture of resignation and whispered, "All right, call her in, but just let me get out of here first!" He sprang up from his seat and went off to his study.

I returned to the stranger and invited her to rest awhile and have dinner with us, but she, evidently chagrined by the reception she had received from my husband, refused, asking only that the maid take out to the cabby her large wicker basket, which the janitor had brought in after her. I didn't insist, but inquired where she was staying and what her name was.

When I returned to my husband I found him intensely irritated. "No, really—can you imagine it?" he said, pacing around the room in his excitement. "What a scurvy thing they've invented here—you've left me! What a shabby lie! Which one of my enemies contrived that one?"

The idea that anyone was capable of slandering me was what struck my husband the hardest in this incident. When I saw that this relatively minor affair was causing him so much upset, I suggested that he write to his old friend Professor N. N. Beketov in Kharkov and find out exactly what kinds of rumors were being circulated about us there.[13]

He took my advice and wrote Beketov that very evening, after which he felt somewhat calmer. And the next day he asked me to go and see our strange visitor, but I did not find her; she had gone back home that morning.

The first two months of the new year of 1879 were peaceful ones for us. Fyodor Mikhailovich was working intensively on his novel, and the work was going well. At the beginning of March he had occasion to take part in several literary evenings. On

March 9, for example, he read at a benefit for the Literary Fund in the Nobility Assembly Hall. Our foremost writers took part in that evening: Turgenev, Saltykov, Potekhin and others. Fyodor Mikhailovich chose to read the chapter "A Tale in Secret" from *The Brothers Karamazov.* He read superlatively and evoked a thunderous ovation. The success of the evening was so great that it was decided to repeat it on March 16 with almost the same participants (except for Saltykov). During that reading a bouquet of flowers was presented to Fyodor Mikhailovich on behalf of the students at the Higher Courses for Women. There was a flattering inscription on its ribbon, embroidered in the Russian style.[14]

About the twentieth of March my husband had an unpleasant experience which might have had lamentable consequences. While he was taking his usual pre-dinner walk a drunken man came up behind him on Nikolayevskaya Street and struck him on the back of the head with such force that he fell against the pavement and bruised and bloodied his face. A crowd collected in a moment, and a policeman appeared and led the drunkard away to the police station. My husband was asked to go there as well.

At the station Fyodor Mikhailovich asked the police officer in charge to release the offender, because he "forgave" him. This the latter promised to do; but an item about "the assault" appeared in the papers the following day, and, in view of the victim's literary reputation, a police report of the event was handed over to a Mr. Trofimov, Justice of the Peace for the Thirteenth District, for further consideration.

About three weeks later Fyodor Mikhailovich was summoned to court. During the questioning the defendent, a peasant, one Fyodor Andreyev, explained that he was "plenty drunk and barely touched the 'gentleman' who, however, fell off his feet from it."[15] Fyodor Mikhailovich told the court that he forgave the offender, and asked that he not be punished. The justice of the peace assented to his request but decided nonetheless that the peasant Andreyev should be sentenced to a fine of sixteen rubles or a sentence of four days in jail for "disturbing the peace" and for disorderly conduct on the street. My husband waited for his offender at the entrance to the building and gave him the sixteen rubles to pay his fine.

During the Easter holidays a literary reading for the benefit of the Froebel Society[16] took place at Solyanoy Gorodok on April 3. Fyodor Mikhailovich read "The Little Boy at Christ's Christmas Tree." Since it was a children's festivity he wanted to take his own children along, so they could hear him reading from the platform and see the love shown him by the audience. His reception was enthusiastic this time also, and a group of young listeners brought him a bouquet of flowers. He stayed to the end of the festive occasion walking about the halls with his children, watching the games, and enjoying the children's delight at sights they had never seen before.

Also during Easter, Fyodor Mikhailovich read in the building of the Alexandrovsky Gymnasium for Girls at a benefit for the Bestuzhev Higher Courses for Women. He selected a scene from *Crime and Punishment* and produced an extraordinary effect with his reading. The students not only applauded him with fervor but surrounded him during the intermissions and asked his opinion on various questions they were interested in. And when he was getting ready to leave at the end of the evening, they followed him down the stairs in a huge crowd of two hundred people or more up to the very entrance doors, where they tried to help him put on his coat.

I had been standing next to my husband, but the thrusting crowd pushed me aside and I remained far behind, sure that he would not leave without me. And indeed, after putting on his coat he looked about him and, not seeing me, said plaintively, "Wherever is my wife? She was with me. Please find her!" And he turned to his throng of feminine admirers, who started shouting my name in concert. Luckily they did not have to call me for long, and I went over to my husband right away.

Spring arrived. As was our custom, we began preparing hurriedly to leave for Staraya Russa, especially since Professor Koshlakov had stringently prescribed a trip to Ems to take the waters, and my husband wanted to stay with the family at our country house for a while and work undisturbed, if possible.

Unfortunately that spring was rainy and cold, and my husband not only did not improve in health at the villa but even lost weight, which upset us all very much. Summer, however, began very pleasantly. Anna Jaclard-Korvin, of whom we were both very fond, came to Russa with her family for the season. Almost every day after his walk my husband would go to have a talk with this fine, intelligent woman, who had been so important in his life.

During the second half of July Fyodor Mikhailovich left for abroad and was in Ems by the twenty-fourth. He stayed in his old quarters at the Ville d'Alger and went to see his physician, Dr. Ort. Although it was already three years since his last visit, the doctor recognized him and even reassured him with the promise that "the Kränchen waters will give you new life."

"He found," my husband wrote on July 25, "that some part of my lung has become displaced and shifted its position, just as my heart has shifted its former position and is now in another place. All this is a consequence of the emphysema, although" (as he added in consolation) "my heart is quite sound and all these shifts of position don't mean very much and aren't particularly dangerous. Naturally, as a doctor he is obliged to say reassuring things, but if the emphysema has already produced such an effect at its very inception, what will happen later? However, I place high hopes on the waters."

Dr. Ort's explanations confused and worried me terribly, since after seeing my husband well and strong during these last years, I had not realized that his disease had made such ominous progress. But since I knew what great benefit he always derived from drinking the Kränchen waters, I lulled myself with the thought that they would bring about an improvement in his health this time too.

I was counting heavily on the possibility that he would meet some people he liked and that these contacts would distract him, so that he wouldn't feel as homesick as he always felt when separated from his family. But to my genuine regret my hopes were not realized. During his entire five-week stay in Ems he did not meet a single familiar face, and he complained bitterly of utter loneliness.

"To make my frustration complete," he wrote me on the tenth of August, there is nothing in the reading room but the *Moscow Gazette,* which arrives very late, and the vile *Voice,* which only enrages me. My sole distraction is to look at the children, of whom there are a good many here, and to talk to them. Even there nasty things happen. Today I met a little boy going to school in a crowd of other children. He was perhaps five years old, walking along covering his eyes with the palm of his hands and crying. I asked what was the matter with him and learned from German passersby that for a whole month he's been suffering from an inflammation of the eyes (terribly painful)—but his father, a cobbler, *doesn't want* to take him to the doctor, so as not to have to spend a few pfennigs on medicine. This disturbed me horribly, and in general my nerves are going to pieces and I'm feeling very low. No, Anya, tedium is not "nothing." When things are tedious even work can be a torment. Better penal servitude—as a matter of fact, penal servitude was better than this![17]

His letters to me were very despondent. On August 13 he wrote:

The news of poor Emilya Fyodorovna saddened me greatly. True, things were coming to the point where she couldn't have gone on much longer, with her illness. But with her death it's as though every last reminder of my brother remaining on this earth for me is gone. Only Fedya is left, Fyodor Mikhailovich, whom I rocked in my arms. My brother's other children grew up unconnected with me, somehow. Please write Fedya of my deepest regret, because I don't know where to reach him. . . .

Just imagine what a dream I had on the fifth (I wrote down the date). I see my brother lying on the bed, an artery in his neck is cut, and he is bleeding. And I think, appalled, I'd better run to the doctor—but I'm stopped by the thought that he'll bleed to death before the doctor can get there. A strange dream, and the main thing is that it was on August 5, the day before she died.

I don't think I need feel any guilt toward her. I helped her out whenever it was possible, and stopped giving her regular help only after she had closer providers, a son and a son-in-law. And in the year my brother died I not only spent my entire ten thousand rubles on his business affairs but also sacrificed without regrets or reservations my health and my literary reputation, which fell into disrepute with the failure of the journal. I worked like an ox. Even my late brother could not have reproached me from the other world.

At the end of the letter he added: "Tomorrow there will be exactly two weeks left of my *silence* here, since this is not only solitude but silence. I have quite forgotten how to speak, I even talk to myself, like a lunatic."

On August 16 he wrote: "I have become hypochondriac through solitariness and I keep picturing bad and hopeless things. My longing is so great that it cannot be described. I've even forgotten how to speak. I'm amazed at myself if I say a word aloud, even accidentally. It's more than three weeks since I've heard the sound of my own voice."

I too suffered over my husband's painful emotional state, particularly because I knew that on top of it all he was worried about some money I had promised to send him. I couldn't send it, however, because there had been a misunderstanding with the editor of the *Russian Messenger.* He had sent me a money order in care of the office of Aschenbach and Kolli in Petersburg. Since I had given Fyodor Mikhailovich my word that I wouldn't leave the children even for a day, I couldn't go to get the money. I had to return the money order and ask that the money be sent to me in Staraya Russa, in cash. I sent it to my husband as soon as I received it.

Reflecting on what would happen to his family if he died or had to slacken the pace of his literary work, Fyodor Mikhailovich often dwelt on the idea of buying a small estate after his debts were paid off, and living partly on the income from it. In a letter from Ems on August 13, 1879, he wrote me:

> I keep thinking, my darling, of death (my thoughts here are serious ones) and of what I would be leaving for you and the children. Everybody assumes that we have money, while we have nothing. Right now the Karamazovs are sitting on my neck. It must be finished well, polished like a piece of jewelry. And it's a difficult and risky thing and will consume much of my strength. And it's also a fateful thing. It will have to establish my name securely, or else there will be no hope at all.
>
> I'll finish it, and toward the end of next year I'll announce a subscription for *Diary of a Writer* and buy an estate with the subscription monies. And somehow I'll manage to go on living and publishing until the next subscription by selling books. Strenuous measures are neces-

sary, or else there will never be anything for us.

But enough of that—you and I will have time to discuss it and argue about it, since you don't care for the country, while I am completely convinced that, 1) real estate is capital which will triple by the time the children are grown, and 2) a man who owns land possesses also a share of political power in the State. It is the children's future and the determination of what they will become: solid and independent citizens, as good as anyone else, or nullities.[18]

In the letter of August 16 I find: "I keep dreaming here about building our future and buying an estate. It's almost driving me crazy—would you believe it? I tremble for our children and their fate."

In principle, I was in complete agreement with my husband on this question, but I felt that under our present circumstances the idea of securing our children's future with an estate might be unfeasible. The first and most important question was, who would be in charge of it if we should manage to acquire one? Even though Fyodor Mikhailovich knew something about farming, he would hardly be able to take an active part, preoccupied as he was with his literary work. And I understood nothing at all about agriculture, and it would in all probability be several years before I could master it or adjust myself to this completely unfamiliar occupation. We would have to entrust the estate management to a steward, but from the experience of many landowners we knew I foresaw the consequences of putting an outside manager in charge.

But Fyodor Mikhailovich dwelt so persistently on this reassuring idea of his that I was genuinely sorry to oppose him. I asked only that he wait until at last our portion of the inheritance from my husband's aunt, A. F. Kumanina, was allotted to us, so that we could begin to set up our farm little by little on land which was already ours. Fyodor Mikhailovich agreed and decided to leave his payment for *The Brothers Karamazov* with the *Russian Messenger*, so as to have it in reserve when it was needed for setting up our estate.

This inheritance from Fyodor Mikhailovich's aunt had been left as far back as the beginning of the seventies. It consisted of an estate of six thousand desyatinas a hundred versts from Ryazan, near the settlement of Spas-Klepiki. One-third of the estate, or approximately two thousand desyatinas, had been allotted to the four Dostoevsky brothers, who in turn were to pay the sisters their share in money. Of this land, five hundred desyatinas[19] represented Fyodor Mikhailovich's share.

Since Madame Kumanina, as it turned out, had many heirs, coming to an agreement with them proved extremely difficult. There were no purchasers who would buy the estate as a whole, and meanwhile we, like the other heirs, were being required to lay out money to pay taxes. Our lawyer was also demanding money for his trips to the estate, for documents, court costs, and so on. So that this inheritance was giving us nothing but trouble and expense.

Finally the heirs came to a decision: to take the land in kind. But since it was of diverse character, ranging from ancient forest to sheer swamp, my husband and I decided to accept a considerably smaller acreage provided that the land was of good quality. In order to pick out such a plot, however, we had to make a trip to inspect the estate. Every spring, the question arose of a meeting of all the heirs at the estate, so that each might choose and survey a certain number of desyatinas as his portion. But it always turned out that one or the other of the co-heirs was not able to come, and the matter would be put off to the following year.

Finally, in the summer of 1879, the heirs decided to meet in Moscow in order to come to some definitive agreement, and if that worked out, all were to proceed to Ryazan and from there to the estate, and there they would settle the matter on the spot, once and for all. Fyodor Mikhailovich was taking the cure in Ems at that time and was not expected to return for another month. It would have been a pity to let slip the chance to put an end to this affair, so burdensome to us. On the other hand, I was in a quandary. Should I let my husband know about the proposed trip to the estate—particularly since it might not even take place? Knowing how passionately he loved his children and worried about their health, I was afraid to upset him with the prospect of a prolonged journey and thereby cause some setback in his treatment.

Luckily, I had received my husband's prior consent to take

the children to the monastery of Saint Nil of Stoloben, a hundred versts away from Staraya Russa, and since the journey would take a week, I decided to go first to Moscow for two or three days. But when I reached there I found that the chief heirs were already on their way to the estate. I decided to utilize the occasion, and went with the children to look over the land and pick out what would best suit my husband's desires. Our trip, which took about ten days, went very well, and I succeeded in selecting as my husband's share two hundred desyatinas of timberland in the so-called Pekhorka plus a hundred desyatinas of arable land.

Fyodor Mikhailovich was pleased with my choice, but his letter from Ems scolded me roundly for my "secretiveness." For my part, I always found it hard to conceal anything from him, but there were times when this was unavoidable, just precisely so as not to disturb him and not to bring on an epileptic seizure through these upsets (if they could be averted), since their consequences were so distressing to my husband, particularly if an attack occurred while he was far away from us.

We returned home from Russa at the beginning of September, and our normal routine began again. By two in the afternoon several visitors would be assembled at our house, some of them friends and some strangers. They would go in to Fyodor Mikhailovich in turn and sometimes sit there with him for an hour. Knowing how exhausting these prolonged conversations were for my husband, I would sometimes send the maid to ask him to come to my room for a minute, and there I would give him a glass of freshly brewed tea. He would gulp it down fast, ask about the children, and hurry back to his visitor. Sometimes, when a session was dragged out for too long, I had to have him called out to the dining room to receive some delegation or other which had come to ask him to read at a literary benefit for some institution, or to see one of his friends who could not wait his turn in line with the strangers.

That winter the public's acceptance of Fyodor Mikhailovich (thanks to the success of *The Brothers Karamazov*) increased even more, and he began receiving honorary invitations and tickets to balls, literary evenings, and concerts. He had to compose gracious refusals and thank-you letters; and sometimes, not wishing to offend the people who had invited him, he would send me in his stead. After spending a boring couple of hours there, I would find the patroness of the festivity and express to her, in my husband's name, my thanks for her graciousness and his apologies for not coming himself because of urgent work. All this complicated our lives and brought us little pleasure.

In December of 1879 Fyodor Mikhailovich had occasion to take part in several literary readings. Thus, on December 16 he read at a benefit for the Society for Assistance to Needy Students of the Larin Gymnasium. He read "The Little Boy at Christ's Christmas Tree." The reading took place during the day, at one o'clock. One of the participants was the famous actor and storyteller I. F. Gorbunov, and I recall that everyone backstage was particularly lively because he was there. After reading their selections the writers did not go out into the hall but remained in the readers' waiting room. Gorbunov was at the top of his form, had many new and witty things to tell, and even drew someone's portrait on a playbill.

On December 30 there was another "literary morning," at which Fyodor Mikhailovich gave a masterful reading of "The Grand Inquisitor" from *The Brothers Karamazov.* His reading had an extraordinary success, and the audience called the author back for repeated curtain calls.[20]

Fyodor Mikhailovich had frequent occasion to read at benefits for different philanthropic societies, such as the Literary Fund and so on, during the years 1879 and 1880. In view of his fragile health I always went with him to these literary evenings and, as a matter of fact, I myself wanted very much to listen to his truly masterful reading, to be present at those tumultuous ovations he was constantly being given by admiring Petersburg audiences.

On these evenings I always took along the book my husband was to read from, his cough medicine (the pastilles from Ems), an extra handkerchief in case he misplaced his, a plaid to wrap around his throat when he went out into the cold air, and so forth. Seeing me always loaded down, Fyodor Mikhailovich used to call me his "faithful armor-bearer." These evenings, for the most part, took place in the hall of the Municipal Credit Society opposite the Alexandrinsky Theater, or at the Nobility Assembly Hall near Politseysky Bridge.

Unfortunately, these sorties of mine into society were often darkened by Fyodor Mikhailovich's jealous outbursts—utterly unexpected and entirely groundless—which sometimes put me into an absurd position. I shall cite one such instance.

On one of those evenings Fyodor Mikhailovich and I arrived a little late and the other participants had already assembled.

When we came in they all greeted Fyodor Mikhailovich very cordially and the men kissed my hand. This social custom of hand-kissing apparently had an unpleasant effect on my husband. He drily said hello to all of them and moved away. I realized at once what was wrong. After exchanging a few phrases with those present I sat down next to my husband with the object of dissipating his bad mood. But I failed. He did not reply to two or three of my questions and then, glaring furiously at me, said, "Go to him!"

"Who is 'him'?" I asked in surprise.

"You don't un-der-stand?"

"No, I do not. To whom am I supposed to go?" I laughed.

"To the one who kissed your hand so *passionately* just now!"

Since every man in the room had kissed my hand out of politeness, I could not of course know who the guilty party was in the alleged crime.

He carried on this entire conversation in an undertone, but still those sitting nearby could hear perfectly. I became very embarrassed and said, fearing a domestic scene, "All right, Fyodor Mikhailovich, I see you're out of sorts and don't want to talk to me. So I had better go into the hall and find my seat. Goodbye!"

And I left. Not five minutes later, P. A. Gaideburov came up to me and said that Fyodor Mikhailovich was asking for me. Assuming that he was having difficulty in locating the excerpt in the book he was to read from, I went immediately to the readers' room. My husband met me antagonistically.

"You couldn't restrain yourself? You came to have another look at him?"

"Oh yes, of course," I laughed, "and also at you. Do you need anything?"

"I do not need anything."

"But didn't you call for me?"

"Nothing of the sort! Don't go imagining things!"

"Well then, if you didn't call for me, goodbye, I'm leaving."

In another ten minutes or so one of the organizers came up to me and said that Fyodor Mikhailovich wanted to know where I was sitting, and therefore he assumed my husband wanted to see me. I said I had just been in the readers' room and didn't wish to prevent Fyodor Mikhailovich from concentrating all his attention on his forthcoming reading. So I didn't go that time.

But at the first intermission an usher approached me again with an insistent summons from my husband. I hurried into the readers' room, went up to my dear husband, and saw his embarrassed, guilty face. He bent down to me and said in a barely audible voice, "Forgive me, Anechka, and give me your hand for luck: I'm going on stage now to read!"

I was terribly glad he had calmed down, but I still couldn't understand which one of the men present (all of them to a man were of an advanced age) had come under suspicion of a sudden passion for me. But then his contemptuous remark, "Take a look at the Frog over there, how he plays up to people" made me realize that the object of Fyodor Mikhailovich's jealous suspicions turned out on this occasion to be the old man D. V. Grigorovich,[21] whose mother was a Frenchwoman.

When we came home that evening I scolded my husband roundly for his completely baseless jealousy. As usual he begged my forgiveness, admitted that he was at fault, swore it would never happen again, and suffered sincerely in his repentance; but he maintained that he hadn't been able to master his sudden outburst and had been feeling miserable and seething with jealousy for a whole hour.

Scenes of this sort recurred at almost every literary evening. Fyodor Mikhailovich would invariably send an usher or some friend to find out where I was sitting and whom I was talking to. He would often go over to the half-open door of the readers' room and look for me from afar in the seat I had mentioned. (Usually, the participants' relatives were given seats along the right-hand wall, a few steps from the first row.)

After appearing on the platform and bowing to the applauding audience, he would not start reading but would instead peer closely at all the women sitting along the right-hand wall. To help him find me faster, I would either wipe my brow with a white handkerchief or half rise from my seat. Only after convincing himself that I was in the hall would he begin his reading.

Naturally my friends, as well as the managers, noticed all this peeping and questioning on my husband's part, and they would chaff both of us a bit, which I sometimes found infuriating. I was fed up with it all, and once, as we were on our way to a literary evening, I told Fyodor Mikhailovich, "You know, my dear, if you keep peering at me and searching for me in the audience today too, I give you my word that I'll simply get up from my seat and walk past the stage and out of the hall."

"And I'll jump off the stage and run after you to find out what happened to you and where you went."

He said this in the most serious voice, and I believe that he was quite capable of making just such a scandalous scene if I had left suddenly.

Fyodor Mikhailovich's epileptic seizures were seriously damaging his memory, chiefly his memory for names and faces; and he earned a good many enemies by his failure to recognize people. Even when they told him their names, he was completely unable to figure out just who it was he was speaking to without detailed questioning. People who either didn't know or had forgotten about his disease were offended, regarded him as an arrogant person and felt that his forgetfulness was deliberately calculated to give offense.

I recall an episode when we met the writer F. M. Berg on the staircase, on our way to visit the Maikovs. He had once worked on *Time,* but my husband had already succeeded in forgetting who he was. Berg greeted Fyodor Mikhailovich very cordially and, seeing that he didn't recognize him, asked, "Fyodor Mikhailovich, you don't know who I am?"

"Excuse me, but I don't."

"I am Berg."

"Berg?" Fyodor Mikhailovich looked at him questioningly (later he told me that his mental association on hearing the name "Berg" was: "a typical German, the Rostovs' son-in-law in *War and Peace*").

"The poet Berg," he explained. "Do you really not recognize me?"

"The poet Berg?" repeated my husband. "It's a pleasure, a real pleasure!"

But Berg, who had been forced to explain himself so laboriously, was deeply convinced that Fyodor Mikhailovich had deliberately failed to recognize him and remembered this slight for the rest of his life. And how many enemies, particularly literary ones, Fyodor Mikhailovich acquired through his lapses of memory!

This forgetfulness and non-recognition of people he met socially sometimes put me too into an absurd position, and I would have to make excuses for him. In this connection I remember a comical episode.

Three or four times a year during the holidays my husband and I used to visit with my cousin Mikhail Snitkin, who loved to gather his family around him. We would almost always see there my godmother, Alexandra Pavlovna [Neupokoyeva], whom I never visited after my marriage because her husband's political views were so different from Fyodor Mikhailovich's. She was very much hurt that my husband greeted her courteously but never sat down to chat with her. She spoke of this to mutual relatives, and they in turn told me.

At our very next visit to the Snitkins, therefore, I begged my husband to talk to Alexandra Pavlovna and behave toward her as graciously as possible.

"All right, all right," he promised. "Just point out which of the ladies is your godmother and I'll find an interesting topic of conversation. You'll be satisfied with me!"

When we arrived at the house I pointed out to Fyodor Mikhailovich a woman sitting on the couch. He peered closely, first at her, then at me, then at her again, and said hello to her very politely, but never came near her again for the balance of the evening.

After we returned home I rebuked him for not being willing to carry out such a small request of mine.

"But just tell me, Anya, please," he answered in embarrassment, "which one of you was godmother to the other? Were you hers or was she yours? I was looking at the both of you—there is very little difference between the two of you! I was in doubt about it and so, in order not to make a mistake, I decided it was better not to go near her."

The point was that the difference in age between me and my godmother was comparatively small: sixteen years. But since I always dressed very modestly, almost always in something dark, while she loved dressing up and used to wear beautiful head-dresses, she looked considerably younger than her years. And it was that youthfulness of hers which confused my husband.

But the most curious thing of all was what happened a year later, once more at Christmas time. Knowing that I would be certain to meet my godmother at the Snitkins, I addressed the very same request to Fyodor Mikhailovich, earnestly explaining to him the degree of our relationship. To all appearances, he listened to me with close attention (although he was obviously thinking about something else). He promised me that this time he would speak with her, but again he failed to keep his word. His confusion of the previous year returned, and he couldn't decide the question of "which one of us was godmother to the other," and felt awkward about asking me in the presence of other people.

His inability to remember the most ordinary, familiar names and surnames placed him in a very uncomfortable position at times. I remember that he once came to our Consulate in Dresden to attest to my signature on some document (I was unable to go myself because of illness). Seeing through the window that he was hurrying home, I went to meet him. He came in, all excited, and asked me crossly, "Anya, what's your name? What's your last name?"

"Dostoevskaya," I answered in confusion, surprised at such a strange question.

"I know it's Dostoevskaya, but what's your maiden name? They asked me your maiden name at the Consulate and I forgot what it was, and now I have to go back there again. The clerks no doubt were laughing at me for forgetting my own wife's name. Please write it down for me on your calling card, or else I'll forget it again on the way!"

Such incidents were not infrequent in Fyodor Mikhailovich's life and, unfortunately, they gained him many enemies.

CHAPTER TEN

The Last Year

The start of the year 1880 was marked by the opening of our new business: "F. M. DOSTOEVSKY, BOOKSELLER (TO THE PROVINCES ONLY)." Although our financial affairs were improving with each passing year and most of the debts which had been lying heavy on Fyodor Mikhailovich ever since the sixties were settled, still our material position was shaky. Life was growing more complicated and expensive, and we could never manage to put anything aside for a rainy day. This made us very anxious, particularly because Fyodor Mikhailovich himself was aware that it was becoming more and more difficult for him to work.

His emphysema had indeed made inroads, and one might well fear that his worsening health could put a stop to his literary activity. It was for just such a sad contingency that we wanted to have a certain sum of money in reserve, or some kind of auxiliary occupation that would bring it in. But even today a woman's sphere of activity is quite limited, and in those times it was far worse.

For a long while I thought about the question of what kind of work to undertake that might serve us, even if only as a small measure of support. After long reflection and questioning of experienced people, I decided to start a book service for out-of-towners, particularly since the several works I had already published had given me some familiarity with the book trade.

The enterprise I was embarking on had two advantages. First and foremost for me, it did not force me to leave the house, and

I could continue to look after my husband's health, my children's upbringing, and my own housekeeping and other affairs just as I had done before. The second advantage consisted in the fact that almost no capital had to be expended to open a book business. It wasn't necessary to rent premises and lay in a stock; one might limit oneself at the beginning to the purchase of books ordered and paid for in advance. The only expense was the payment of the "trade license" and the employment of an errand boy to go out and buy the books, pack them for shipping, and take them to the post office. This amounted to 250 or 300 rubles a year, and we could well risk such an amount.

Of course we would have to put advertisements in the newspapers to insure the success of the business. To start with, however, I was putting my hopes on the hectographed announcements I had sent to the former subscribers to *Diary of a Writer*, and for the following year I planned to send out many thousands of copies of a big announcement, sharing the costs with the woman who was the publisher of *Family Evenings.*[1] (This announcement was mailed at the beginning of 1880, but already too late to have any effect on sales.)

Naturally, our business undertaking could count on success only on condition that the business was the property of F. M. Dostoevsky. In taking out a sales license at the Regional Board of Trade, therefore, Fyodor Mikhailovich had to become a merchant—a circumstance his journalistic enemies lost no opportunity to scoff at. This jeering did not injure my husband's self-esteem in the least, for once he looked into the matter he approved of my idea and believed in the success of our enterprise just as I did.

My hopes for success were based chiefly on the assumption that the subscribers to *Diary of a Writer* for 1876 and 1877, accustomed to its reliable editorial management, would also have confidence in a service operated by the same publisher which would obtain for them the books they needed. These hopes proved justified, and before two or three months were out a group of persons (perhaps thirty) was formed from former *Diary* subscribers who ordered books every month through our service. I recall a bishop from Poltava, for instance, who gave us monthly orders for many expensive books for his personal library and for gifts, through a member of his staff, a Prince Eletsky. I remember also an engineer from Minsk who used to order books for large sums of money, and not only in his own field.

In addition to this nucleus of regular customers there were also quite a few single individuals who made use of our new book service. There were, of course, irritating clients as well, such as subscribers to some newspaper or other through whom the business received a net profit of twenty-five kopecks. But even more exasperating were those buyers who made us search for some book that turned out to be long out of print; and after prolonged and conscientious searching we would have to return their money to them.

The book service did not take too much of my personal time. All I had to do was to keep the accounts, enter the orders and write out the bills. And the boy who was recommended to me had worked in a bookstore previously, although he was only fifteen years old. Pyotr managed the buying and shipping of the books extremely well.[2]

Fyodor Mikhailovich was very interested in the progress of our undertaking. I would compile a little report of income and expenses for him at the end of each month. Our profit usually ranged between eighty and ninety rubles a month at the beginning and end of the year (because of magazine and newspaper subscriptions), and between forty and fifty rubles during the summer months. All in all, our first year in business yielded a clear profit of eight hundred and eleven rubles after deducting all expenses, and we considered such a result a good augury for the future.

Our business might have been put on a larger scale from the very start, of course. There were orders from educational institutions and Zemstvo[3] storehouses asking that books be sent them on credit. But since we would need to lay out large sums of money to acquire these books, we had to decline such orders despite their potential profits.

A book service for out-of-town residents is a very profitable enterprise provided that it is competently and accurately conducted. I have seen similar small services transformed into substantial book firms before my very eyes within three decades—

the Bashmakov brothers, Panafidin, Klyukin—and I firmly believe that if I had gone on with my own activity I would today have a shop on a par with the *New Times* bookstore. I did not, however, continue in the book business because I undertook the publication of my husband's complete works, which demanded all my energy and time.

When I announced my intention of discontinuing the book service after Fyodor Mikhailovich's death, many persons asked me to transfer my enterprise to them. Some even wished to buy the firm and offered approximately fifteen hundred rubles for it. But to this I did not consent. To carry on an enterprise bearing the name of F. M. Dostoevsky was something only I myself could do, since I held myself responsible for the firm's integrity. How that matter would be viewed by someone purchasing the firm or receiving it gratis was an unknown quantity, and might have subjected Fyodor Mikhailovich's name, so precious to me, to censure or mockery in the event the firm's management proved incompetent or dishonest.

The book trade of F. M. Dostoevsky, therefore, ceased to exist at the beginning of March, 1881. I think back on my short-lived enterprise with a pleasant feeling, however, chiefly because of the good relationships established between the business and its clients. Some of these people innocently assumed that F. M. Dostoevsky was actually handling the book sales himself, and would address their orders to him personally. Others, writing to the business, would ask to have their delight with *The Brothers Karamazov* or other works of his conveyed to him. Still others requested that the bill sent to them should contain some information on the state of health of "the great writer." Some of these artless and enthusiastic letters touched him deeply, and he would ask me to convey respects and greetings in his name. My husband, who had so often encountered ill-will from his literary and other friends and critics, deeply appreciated these simple and sometimes naïve expressions of delight in his talent—the respect and devotion of people who felt a deep affinity for his art although they were total strangers to him.

Generally speaking, the year 1880 began auspiciously for us. Fyodor Mikhailovich's health seemed much stronger after his trip to Ems of the previous year, and his epileptic attacks were a good deal less frequent. Our children were quite well. *The Brothers Karamazov* was an undoubted success and Fyodor Mikhailovich, always so severe with himself, was highly pleased with certain chapters.[4] The business enterprise conceived by us, our book service, was a reality, our own books were selling nicely, and all in all our affairs were going not too badly.

All these circumstances taken together had a good effect on him, and his general mood was elated and blithe. At the beginning of the year he was very much interested in Vladimir Solovyov's forthcoming defense of his doctoral dissertation, and wanted to be present without fail for that solemn occasion. I also went along, mostly so as to guard him against catching a chill in the crowd.

The debate was a brilliant one and Solovyov successfully parried the attacks of his formidable opponents. Fyodor Mikhailovich stayed until the audience had dispersed, so as to have the opportunity to shake the hand of the hero of the hour. Solovyov was obviously pleased to see that Fyodor Mikhailovich, despite his frail health, had wanted to be there at the university among his friends on such a memorable day in his life.[5]

Despite his intensive work on *The Brothers Karamazov* Fyodor Mikhailovich had frequent occasion that year to read at literary benefits for different organizations. His masterly reading always attracted an audience, and if he was feeling well he never declined such invitations, no matter he busy he was at the time. I remember that he made the following appearances at the beginning of the year.

On February 2, at the request of P. I. Weinberg, he gave a reading at the Kolomna Gymnasium for Girls. On March 20 he read in the auditorium of the Municipal Duma at a benefit for the children's section of the St. Petersburg Refuge of Charity. For his reading he chose "Father Zossima's Talk with the Women" [an excerpt from *The Brothers Karamazov*].

I cannot keep from describing something amusing that happened to me that evening. The auditorium of the Municipal Duma[6] was full to overflowing with a well-dressed crowd in which men predominated. As I looked about at the audience I was struck by one particular fact: that the faces of almost all the men seemed strangely familiar. I told Fyodor Mikhailovich about this, and he marveled at such a peculiar phenomenon.

But the matter was cleared up during intermission, when all the participants and their wives were invited into the next room. There bowls of champagne, fruits and sweets were set out on large tables, and the sponsors of the evening, I. I. Glazunov, Mayor of Petersburg, and his wife extended their cordial hospitality to the singers and writers. Madame Glazunova was a patroness of the [children's] section of the St. Petersburg Refuge of Charity, and all the merchants and salesmen of the Gostiny Dvor had, of course, responded to her invitation to attend this literary evening for the benefit of her institution. And since only a few days before I had been round to all the shops there, looking for fabrics and pretty patterns for the children's summer clothing, the salesmen's faces had stayed in my mind and now seemed familiar. I was very pleased that a phenomenon I had been on the point of taking for the effect of some mysterious disease was cleared up so simply.

The next day, March 21, Fyodor Mikhailovich also participated in a benefit reading, this time for the Pedagogical Courses, at the Nobility Assembly Hall. He chose an excerpt from *Crime and Punishment,* "Raskolnikov's Dream of the Exhausted Horse." His reading had an overwhelming effect. With my own eyes I saw the spectators white with emotion, some of them even in tears. Nor could I hold back my own tears. His last reading that spring was "Raskolnikov's Conversation with Marmeladov," given in the Nobility Assembly Hall on March 28, for the benefit of the Society for Aid to Needy Students of St. Petersburg University.

The audiences at these literary readings received Fyodor Mikhailovich with uncommon warmth. His appearance on stage would call forth thunderous applause which continued for several minutes. He would get up from his reader's desk, bow, and thank the audience, but they would not let him begin to read; and later they repeatedly interrupted the reading itself with deafening applause. It was the same story when he was finished, and he would have to come out three or four times for curtain calls.

Naturally, the public's rhapsodic response to his talent could not fail to give him pleasure, and he felt a sense of moral satisfaction. Before a reading he was always afraid that his weak voice would not be audible beyond the first few rows, and he would be upset by this thought. But his nervous excitement on these occasions was so great that his normally thin voice resounded with great clarity, and every word carried to all the furthest corners of the large hall.[7]

To give him his due, Fyodor Mikhailovich was a first-rate reader. Whether he was reading his own or someone else's work, he conveyed all the nuances and highlights of each with a special vividness and skill. And he read simply, moreover, without resorting to oratorical devices of any kind. His reading produced a shattering effect (particularly Nelly's story from *The Insulted and Injured* or Alyosha Karamazov's story about Ilyusha), and I saw tears in the eyes of the spectators. I too used to weep even though I knew those excerpts by heart. He would preface each reading with a brief explanation for the benefit of those who had either not read the work or had forgotten it.

In substantiation of the foregoing I would like to quote S. A. Vengerov on the impression Fyodor Mikhailovich's reading produced on him.

It was my great happiness to hear him read at one of the evenings organized by the Literary Fund in 1879. . . . Dostoevsky had no equal as a reader. The word "reader" applies to him only in the sense that no other term exists for a man who appears on stage in a black frock coat and reads his own work.

On the same evening I heard Dostoevsky, there were also readings by Turgenev, Saltykov-Shchedrin, Grigorovich, Polonsky, and Alexey Potekhin. Except for Saltykov, who read badly, and Polonsky, who read in an affectedly pompous manner, all read very well. But it was just precisely "reading" that they did; whereas Dostoevsky prophesied, in the full sense of the word. In a thin but penetratingly distinct voice, gripping his listeners with inexpressible excitement, he read one of the electrifying chapters from *The Brothers Karamazov,* "The Confession of a Passionate Heart," Mitya Karamazov's account of how Katerina Ivanovna comes to him for money to save her father. And never since have I felt such deathly stillness in an auditorium, such total absorption of the spiritual life of a crowd of a thousand people in the mood of one man. While the others were reading the listeners did not lose their sense of their own ego; they reacted to what they heard in one way or another, but each in his own way. Even Turgenev's superb joint reading with Savina did not make them forget themselves and did not bear them aloft.

But when Dostoevsky read, the listener—just like the reader of his novels of nightmarish genius—lost his "I" completely and fell utterly under the hypnotic power of this emaciated, unprepossessing, elderly man, with his piercing gaze fixed somewhere away on the distance and burning with mystic fire: that very fire, perhaps, which once blazed in the eyes of the Archpriest Avvakum.[8]

Besides taking part in literary evenings, Fyodor Mikhailovich often visited friends during the winter of 1879–80. On Saturdays he used to go to see Ivan Petrovich Kornilov, (a respected former trustee of the Vilna Educational District), where he met many scholars and men in high official positions.

He used to attend the soirees given by Elena Andreyevna Stackenschneider (daughter of the noted architect), whose "Tuesdays" were the gathering place of many distinguished writers who sometimes read from their work. She used to organize home theatricals as well. I recall, for instance, that my husband and I attended a performance of *Don Juan* there during the winter of 1880; the performers were S. V. Averkieva (Doña Anna), who displayed much talent in the performance of her part, the poet K. K. Sluchevsky, and Nikolai Strakhov. The latter's role suited him so well that Fyodor Mikhailovich applauded him and was very animated that evening. At the Stackenschneider house that winter Fyodor Mikhailovich met Lydia Ivanovna Veselitskaya, who later gained prominence as the authoress V. Mikulich. I should take note here of his sensitivity and foresight. After two or three talks with this young girl, he divined in her (notwithstanding her youth and understandable embarrassment) an uncommon young woman who held the promise of something higher: aspirations toward an ideal and, in all probability, a literary flair. In this he was not mistaken; and the author of *Mimochka* left a noticeable imprint on Russian literature.

Fyodor Mikhailovich deeply respected and loved Elena Stackenschneider for her unwavering goodness and the equanimity with which she bore her constant illnesses. She never uttered a word of complaint but, on the contrary, cheered other people up with her cordiality. In the Stackenschneider family Elena's brother Adrian Andreyevich, a man of great intellect and a sincere admirer of Fyodor Mikhailovich's work, was particularly likable. My husband used to consult him, as a brilliant jurist, in all those instances which concerned the judicial process. Thanks to his knowledge every detail of Mitya's trial in *The Brothers Karamazov* was so accurate that the most malicious critic (and there were not a few of those) could not discover any omission or error.

Fyodor Mikhailovich loved to visit with K. P. Pobedonostsev; he derived keen intellectual enjoyment from conversations with him as with an uncommonly subtle, profoundly understanding mind, albeit one of a sceptical bent.

But more and more often during the years 1879 and 1880, he used to visit Countess Sofya Andreyevna Tolstaya, widow of the poet A. K. Tolstoy. She was a woman of great intellect, highly educated and well read. Talking with her was extremely pleasant for my husband, who never ceased to be amazed at her ability to understand and respond to the many subtleties of philosophic thinking so rarely accessible to any woman. But in addition to her outstanding mind, Countess Tolstaya possessed a tender and responsive heart; and the joy she was able to give my husband on one occasion was something I remembered in gratitude all through my life.

In speaking once with the countess about the Dresden Art Museum, Fyodor Mikhailovich said that he considered the Sistine Madonna the greatest work of painting, adding that he had unfortunately never managed to bring home a good, large-sized photograph of the Madonna from abroad, and that it was impossible to obtain one here.

Whenever he went to Ems he invariably tried to buy a good reproduction of this painting, but had never yet succeeded in carrying out his intention. I too used to look for a large reproduction of the Madonna in the Petersburg print shops, also with no success.

About three weeks after this conversation, Vladimir Solovyov arrived one morning while Fyodor Mikhailovich was still asleep, carrying a huge cardboard package containing a magnificent photograph of the Sistine Madonna in its actual size but without the figures surrounding the Madonna. Vladimir Sergeyevich, who was a great friend of Countess Tolstaya's, told me that she had written to her friends in Dresden, that they had sent this photograph to her, and that she asked Fyodor Mikhailovich to accept the picture from her "in fond remembrance."

This was in mid-October of 1879, and the idea came to me of having it framed right away and so give Fyodor Mikhailovich joy on the occasion of his birthday on October 30. I told Solovyov my idea and he approved, particularly since the photograph might be damaged if left unframed. I asked him to convey my heartfelt thanks to the countess for her kind thought and to forewarn her at the same time that Fyodor Mikhailovich would not see her gift until his birthday.

So it was. On the day before the thirtieth a beautiful dark carved oak frame, with the photograph mounted in it, was delivered by the framer, and a nail for it was hammered into the wall directly over the divan (Fyodor Mikhailovich's bed), where all the special qualities of this masterpiece showed to the best advantage.

The next morning, on the day of our family celebration, the picture was hung in place after Fyodor Mikhailovich went to the dining room for his tea. Following lively congratulations and talk, we went into the study with the children. And what was Fyodor Mikhailovich's astonishment and delight when his eyes beheld his much-beloved Madonna!

"Wherever did you find it, Anya?" he asked, assuming it was I who had bought it. But when I explained that it was a gift from Countess Tolstaya, he was touched to the depths by her heartfelt kindness and went that very day to thank her. How many times during the last year of his life I found him standing before that great picture in such deep contemplation that he did not hear me come in; and I, not wishing to disrupt his prayerful mood, would quietly leave the room. My gratitude to Countess Tolstaya is understandable, for her gift made it possible for my husband to experience some deeply felt and ecstatic moments before the image of the Madonna. This photograph is now our family relic, my son's cherished possession.

Fyodor Mikhailovich was fond of visiting with Countess Tolstaya also because of the very lovely family around her: her niece, Sofya Petrovna Khitrovo, an extremely warmhearted young woman, and her three children—two boys and a darling little girl. The children of this family were the same age as our own children. We brought them together and they became friends, which gave Fyodor Mikhailovich much joy.

At Countess Tolstaya's home Fyodor Mikhailovich met many ladies of fashionable society: Countess A. A. Tolstaya (a relative of Count Leo Tolstoy), E. Z. Naryshkina, Countess A. E. Komarovskaya, Yulya F. Abaza, Princess Volkonskaya, E. F. Vanlyarskaya, the singer Lavrovskaya (Princess Tseretelli), and others. Some of them were great admirers of his talent, and Fyodor Mikhailovich, who in male society was so often exasperated by literary and political arguments, greatly enjoyed their feminine talk, always delicate and restrained.

Among the people he loved to talk with and often visited during the last years of his life I should mention Countess Elizaveta Nikolayevna Geiden, president of the St. George Society. Fyodor Mikhailovich respected her deeply for her tireless philanthropic activity and ever-elevated thoughts. He was fond of visiting Yulya Denisovna Zasetskaya (daughter of the partisan fighter Denis Davydov) and often had friendly arguments with her on the question of her religious beliefs. Occasionally he used to visit with Anna Pavlovna Filosofova, whom he valued highly for her energetic labors. He used to say that she had "an intelligent heart."

I should mention in passing that Fyodor Mikhailovich had many genuine friends who were women, and they willingly confided their secrets and doubts to him and asked his friendly advice, which he never refused to give. On the contrary, he entered into the interests of women with heartfelt kindness and would express his opinions honestly, at times even taking the risk of hurting his confidante's feelings. But the women who gave him their confidence realized intuitively that it was a rare thing to find a man who understood a woman's heart and her sufferings as deeply as Fyodor Mikhailovich understood and divined them.

In March of 1880, rumors started circulating in literary circles that the monument in Moscow in honor of Pushkin was finished and was to be unveiled that spring, and that the unveiling was to be observed with a special ceremonial. The forthcoming event caused a great stir among our intellectuals, and many of them prepared to attend the festivities.

A Pushkin Memorial Committee was organized in Moscow, and the Moscow University Society of Friends of Russian Letters resolved to observe the unveiling with public meetings. S. Yuryev, president of the society, sent out invitations to the foremost men of letters to attend the solemnities.

Such an invitation was received by Fyodor Mikhailovich. The letter invited him, among others, to give a speech dedicated to Pushkin's memory at the solemn session, if he so desired. Fyodor Mikhailovich was very much agitated by rumors circulating in the capital about these speeches, which were to be given by representatives of the two parties of that period, the Westerners and the Slavophiles. He declared that he would certainly make the trip to Moscow if illness did not prevent it, and that he would set forth in his Pushkin speech all the things that had been lying on his mind and heart for so many years. And he expressed the wish that I accompany him. I was, of course, terribly happy to go to Moscow, not only to witness such a rare ceremony but also to be near him during those hectic days (as I realized in advance).

To my great grief and Fyodor Mikhailovich's sincere regret, our journey together could not take place. When we began to calculate how much the trip might cost, we came to the conclusion that we could not manage it. After the death of our son Alyosha, Fyodor Mikhailovich, who had always felt passionately toward his children, grew even more over-anxious for their life and health, and it was out of the question for both of us to go away and leave them in the care of a nurse. We would have to take the children along with us.

But since the journey and the stay in Moscow could not be for less than a week, a stop at a good hotel with the children, in addition to the fare to Moscow and back, could not come to less than three hundred rubles extra. For a ceremony of that nature, moreover, I would have to appear in a light-colored gown—if not luxurious, then at least respectable—and that would add to the expense of the trip.

As ill luck would have it, our accounts with the *Russian Messenger* were somewhat confused, and it would have been awkward to ask the editor for funds. In a word, after long reflection and hesitation my husband and I decided that I would have to forego the tempting idea of going to Moscow for the festivities. I must say that in later years I regarded my inability to be present at the rare triumph vouchsafed to my dear husband on the occasion of the Pushkin memorial festivities as the greatest deprivation of my life.

So as to be able to think through his Pushkin speech and write it down in peace and leisure, Fyodor Mikhailovich wanted to go to Staraya Russa earlier, and at the very beginning of May we were already at our country house with the whole family. In April, friends had begun mentioning to Fyodor Mikhailovich an article by P. V. Annenkov entitled "A Remarkable Decade" which had appeared in *Messenger of Europe* and in which the author discussed Dostoevsky. Fyodor Mikhailovich was very curious about this article and asked me to borrow the April issue of the journal from the library. I managed to get it from friends just before our departure for Russa, and we took it with us.

After reading the article my husband was incensed. Annenkov's reminiscences alleged that Dostoevsky had such a high opinion of his own literary talent that he demanded that his first novel, *Poor Folk,* should be printed in a special manner—namely, "with a border around the edges." Fyodor Mikhailovich was outraged by this slander and wrote a letter to Suvorin immediately, asking him to put an announcement in *New Times* in his name to the effect that *nothing resembling P. V. Annenkov's story in "Messenger of Europe" about a "border" had ever happened or could possibly have happened.*

Many of Fyodor Mikhailovich's colleagues (Apollon Maikov, for example) who had an excellent recollection of that period were also angered by Annenkov's article. Suvorin wrote two excellent paragraphs (on May 2 and 16, 1880) on the subject of "the border," based on Fyodor Mikhailovich's letter and the testimony of contemporaries, and published them in *New Times.* In answer to my husband's refutation, Annenkov stated in . . .* that an error had occurred and that Fyodor Mikhailovich's demand for "a border" was in connection with a different work of his entitled "Plismylkov's Story" (which Fyodor Mikhailovich never wrote). My husband was so infuriated by Annenkov's slander that he resolved not to recognize him if he met him at the Pushkin memorial festivities, and if Annenkov should approach him he would refuse to shake hands.[9]

The unveiling of the monument was set for May 25, but Fyodor Mikhailovich decided to go [to Moscow] several days ahead of time to arrange without haste to obtain the tickets required for attendance at all the solemn sessions. As vice-president of the Slavic Philanthropic Society, moreover, he was the society's representative at the festivities and had to order wreaths to be placed on the monument.

He left on May 22, and the children and I went to the station to see him off. I remember with real emotion how my dear husband said to me at parting, "So you couldn't manage it after all, my poor little Anechka! What a pity, how sad! I dreamed so hard that you'd be with me!"

Upset by our imminent separation, but mostly terribly anxious for his health and frame of mind, I answered, "Well, it wasn't fated—but then you have to make up for it by writing to me every day without fail—tell me every single detail so that I can know everything that's happening to you. Otherwise I'll worry every moment. Do you promise to write?"

"I promise, I promise," Fyodor Mikhailovich said. "I'll write you every day."

And as a man true to his word he carried out his promise and wrote me not only once but sometimes even twice a day, so much did he want to relieve my mind of anxiety about him, and also to share all his impressions with me, as was his habit.

At the time we said goodbye both of us assumed that his absence would last no longer than a week: two days on the journey to Moscow and back, and five days for the festivities he had to attend. And he gave me his word not to stay in Moscow one extra day. But as things turned out, it was not a week but twenty-two days later than he came home, and I can state that

*A gap in the manuscript.

the three weeks of his absence were a time of tormenting worry and anxiety for me.

I should mention that at the end of the previous year, after Fyodor Mikhailovich's return from Ems, he had visited my cousin, Dr. Mikhail Snitkin, and asked him to examine his chest and tell him whether his treatment in Ems had produced some good results. Although my relative was a pediatrician he was also an expert in diseases of the chest, and Fyodor Mikhailovich trusted him as a physician and loved him as a kind and intelligent man.

He reassured Fyodor Mikhailovich, of course (as any doctor would have done) and promised that the winter would go very well for him and that he need have no fears for his health, but should merely take certain precautions.

But to me, in response to my persistent questioning, the doctor had to admit that the disease had made ominous inroads, and that in Fyodor Mikhailovich's present state of health his emphysema might be a threat to his life. He explained that the small blood vessels in the lungs had become so delicate and fragile that there was always a possibility of rupturing them from any physical strain; and therefore he advised him not to make sharp movements or carry or lift heavy objects, and in general he advised that he be shielded from any kind of excitement, pleasant or unpleasant.

True, the doctor tried to reassure me with the statement that these arterial ruptures are not always fatal. Sometimes a so-called "plug" is formed, a clot which prevents great loss of blood. My terror can be imagined, as well as the oversolicitousness with which I began watching over my husband's health. So as not to let him go alone to visit families where he might have unpleasant encounters or conversations, I began complaining that I was bored at home, and expressed the desire to go out in society. Fyodor Mikhailovich, who had always regretted that I went out so little, was pleased with my decision. During the winter of 1879 and all through 1880 I often went with him to visit friends or to attend literary evenings. I ordered an elegant black silk going-out dress for myself and acquired two colored headdresses which my husband assured me were very becoming.

At parties and gatherings I sometimes had to resort to ruses in order to guard Fyodor Mikhailovich from unpleasant meetings and conversations. Thus, for example, I would ask my hostess to seat him at the table further away from such-and-such a man or woman; or I would call him over to me with some plausible pretext if I saw that he was becoming excited and involved in some heated argument. In a word, I was always on the alert, and consequently my excursions into society afforded me small pleasure.

And now, when I was in such terrible fear for my husband's health, we had to be parted not for a week, as I had anticipated, but for twenty-two days. My Lord, how I suffered during that time, especially when I saw from his letters that his return was being pushed further and further away, while the upsets and excitements so dangerous to him were mounting.

I imagined that these excitements must culminate in a seizure, if not in a double seizure, particularly because it was already a long time since his last epileptic attack, so that one might anticipate the imminent onset of one. The darkest imaginings came into my head. I pictured him having a seizure; I imagined that before fully regaining consciousness he would wander through the hotel looking for me* and that there he would be taken for a lunatic, defamed throughout Moscow as a madman; that there would be no one to guard his peace and quiet after the seizure; that he might be exacerbated, pushed to the point of some irresponsible action. All these thoughts tormented me without surcease, and more than once I decided to make the trip to Moscow and stay there without showing myself to anyone but only watching over Fyodor Mikhailovich.

But since I knew that he would be in a state of anxiety for the children, left in the care of a nurse, I could not bring myself to go through with the trip. I asked my friends in Moscow to

*He would always come to me before fully recovering from an attack, for during those moments he experienced a kind of mystic dread and was soothed by the presence of someone close to him. (A.G.D.)

telegraph me at once in the event that Fyodor Mikhailovich had an attack, so that I could leave by the first train. Day followed day and the unveiling of the monument kept being put off; situations unpleasant to Fyodor Mikhailovich (judging by his letters) kept piling up,[10] and together with them my emotional sufferings mounted as well. Even now, after so long an interval, I cannot think back over that time without a feeling of pain.

To that period belongs an episode which would not be worth writing down if Fyodor Mikhailovich had not brought it up in a letter, written immediately after his return from the meeting at which the Moscow public responded so ardently to his Pushkin speech. I refer to the purchase of the colt.

Our elder son Fedya had passionately loved horses from infancy. During our summers in Staraya Russa, Fyodor Mikhailovich and I were always afraid he might be injured by a horse. When he was two or three years old he would sometimes tear away from his elderly nurse, run up to a strange horse, and throw his arms around its leg. Luckily they were country horses, used to having children around them, and so everything turned out all right.

As the child grew, he began begging us to give him a real live horse. Fyodor Mikhailovich promised to buy him one, but somehow never managed to do so. In May of 1880 I bought a colt, quite accidentally, and repented my act bitterly afterwards. This is how it happened.

Early one morning the children and I were going to the town market. While we were walking along the shores of our River Pererytitsa a cart dashed past us, driven by a rather tipsy peasant. Behind the cart a young foal was running, a very beautiful one, now overtaking the horse, now running behind it. We were very much taken with the animal and my son said that it was exactly the kind of little colt he wanted.

As we approached the square a quarter of an hour later, we saw several peasants crowding around the horse and colt and arguing about something. We came up to them and found out that the drunken peasant was selling the colt "for its hide" and asking four rubles for him. There were already buyers; but because of my son's begging and my own feeling of pity that the colt would be killed, I offered six rubles, and the animal was mine.

Knowing nothing about horses or about farming, I began asking the peasants (while the colt's former owner went "to strengthen himself") whether my foal could survive without his mother. Opinions were divided. Some maintained he could not, while others advised us exactly what to feed him and said that if he were properly looked after he would grow up into quite a passable horse.

There was no point in further hesitation, however, and we went home behind the cart, with the foal running alongside. That same day I wrote Fyodor Mikhailovich about our acquisition; and as luck would have it, my letter arrived on the very day he gave his memorable Pushkin speech, when all those present at the meeting responded to him with such ardor. As he read over my letter Fyodor Mikhailovich, still under the influence of his elation, added the words, "I kiss the foal"[11]—so intensely did he feel the need to pour out on everything and everyone the feelings of tenderness and joy which filled his being.

Our first few days with the colt went well. He drank five pots of milk a day, was gay, and ran about after the children like a puppy. But then things took a turn for the worse. Fyodor Mikhailovich, who knew about horses, thought the colt had a "dejected" look and sent for a veterinarian. He gave us his advice, but probably too late, since three weeks later the colt was no more. The children were in despair, and I could not forgive myself for having bought the colt. Of course he would have died in any case even if someone else had owned him, but then I would not have felt responsible for his death, as I felt now.

At last the happy day arrived when my sufferings came to an end. Fyodor Mikhailovich returned to Staraya Russa on June 13, as content and elated as I had not seen him for a very long time. Not only had he not had an epileptic seizure in Moscow, but, owing to the nervous stimulation, he felt very cheerful during his entire stay. There was no end to his anecdotes or to my questions about the events in Moscow, and he told me many interesting things I never heard in anyone else's description of the Pushkin festivities. He had some special capacity to notice everything and retain it all for a short while.

He told me, among other things, how he returned from the second evening session (the one which concluded the entire Pushkin celebration) terribly exhausted but also terribly happy over his ecstatic reception by the Moscow public as they bade him farewell. In utter exhaustion he lay down to rest, and then late at night he went to the Pushkin monument once again. The night was warm, but there was almost no one on the street. Arriving at Strastnaya Square,[12] he lifted with difficulty an enormous laurel wreath which had been presented to him at the morning session after his speech, laid it at the foot of the monument to his "great teacher," and bowed down to the ground before it.

His genuine happiness at the thought that at long last Russia understood and valued the high import of Pushkin's genius and had erected a monument to him in Moscow, "the heart of Russia"; his joyous awareness of the fact that he himself, a fervent admirer of the great national poet since early youth, had been able through his speech to offer the tribute of his veneration; and, finally, his intoxication with the enthralled response of the public to his own personal talent—all these things fused to create for him, in his own words, "moments of the highest possible happiness." In describing to me what he felt then he had an inspired look, as though he were reliving those unforgettable moments anew.

He told me also that the best photographer in Moscow, the artist Panov, had come to see him the next morning and persuaded him to let him do a photographic study of him. Since my husband was in a hurry to leave Moscow, he and Panov went to the studio right away so as not to lose any time. Fyodor Mikhailovich's reactions to the events of the previous day, so memorable for him, are vividly caught in the artist's photograph, and I consider this portrait by Panov the most successful of the many portraits of my husband, always varied because of his changeability of mood. In this photograph I recognized the expression I had seen many times on my husband's face when he was experiencing moments of deep joy and happiness.[13]

But ten more days went by, and Fyodor Mikhailovich's mood underwent a sharp change. It was the newspaper articles he read every day in the reading room of the local spa which were responsible for this. A veritable avalanche of accusations, refutations, slanders, and even abuse was heaped on his head by the newspapers and magazines. Those very men of letters who had listened with such enthusiasm to his Pushkin speech and been so thunderstruck by it that they stormily applauded the speaker and went up to shake him by the hand —suddenly recovered themselves, as it were, awoke from their trance, and began to excoriate the speech and demean its author. As one reads contemporary reviews of Fyodor Mikhailovich's Pushkin speech, one grows indignant at the unceremonious effrontery with which their writers treated him, forgetting that in their articles they were debasing a man of enormous talent who had worked for thirty-five years at his chosen calling and earned the respect and love of many tens of thousands of Russian readers.

I must say that these unworthy attacks upset and wounded Fyodor Mikhailovich deeply. He was so perturbed by them that the double epileptic attack I had foreseen lost no time in happening, and it clouded his mind for the next two weeks. In a letter to Orest Miller of August 26, 1880, Fyodor Mikhailovich wrote: "As for my speech in Moscow, you see what a beating I took from our press, almost to a man, as though I had committed some burglary, swindle or bank fraud. Even Yukhantsev didn't have as much swill flung at him as I have."[14]

Yes, Fyodor Mikhailovich had to endure much pain, too much pain from his literary confreres! He did not consider himself defeated, however, and since he had no way of replying to all the attacks he decided to address his rejoinder to a person who might be considered an opponent worthy of him in literary dispute: namely, to A. D. Gradovsky, a Petersburg University professor, for his article "Dreams and Reality." Fyodor Mikhailovich published his reply in the single issue of *Diary of a Writer* for 1880 together with his Pushkin speech (originally published in the *Moscow Gazette*), which was in ever-increasing demand from the public.

In order to put out that issue I had to make a three-day trip to Petersburg. The *Diary,* with its article "Pushkin" and the reply to Gradovsky, had a colossal success. Six thousand copies were sold in those few days, so that I had to order a second edition of the issue, this time in larger quantity, and that one, too, was sold out by autumn.

After composing the reply to his critics, Fyodor Mikhailovich felt somewhat calmer and settled down to the completion of *The Brothers Karamazov.* All of Part Four of the novel had still to be written—about 320 pages—and it had to be finished before October, since we planned to issue the novel in book form. For convenience in working we remained in Staraya Russa till the end of September. There was nothing to regret in that, however, for the autumn was a beautiful one.

The literary readings were revived that autumn. V. P. Gayevsky, president of the Literary Fund, who had attended the Pushkin festivities and heard Fyodor Mikhailovich read Pushkin's poem "The Prophet" at an evening reading, persuaded him to read it again at a benefit for the fund on October 19, the anniversary of the founding of the Lyceum.[15] He read Scene Two, the scene in the cellar, from *The Covetous Knight,* followed by the poem "Once on a Warm Spring Day," and when the audience began calling for an encore he read "The Prophet," which evoked an electrifying response. The very walls of the Credit Society seemed to be shaking with the tumultuous applause. He bowed and walked off stage, but was recalled over and over again, and this went on for ten minutes or more.

In view of the tremendous success of this reading Gayevsky decided to repeat it a week later, on October 26, with the same program and the same performers. Since it was the talk of the town, the evening attracted a huge mass of people who not only took up all the seats but stood in the aisles in a dense throng. When Fyodor Mikhailovich came out on stage the audience started applauding him and for a long time would not let him begin reading. Then they applauded after each stanza and refused to let him leave the rostrum. Their enthusiasm reached its peak when he read Pushkin's "The Prophet."

On November 21 there was another reading for the Literary Fund at the Nobility Assembly Hall. During the first half he read Nekrasov's poem, "When from the Murk of Sin," and in the second part excerpts from Part One of Gogol's *Dead Souls.* On November 30 there was a benefit evening for the Society for Aid to Needy Students of Petersburg University, at which he read "Ilyusha's Funeral" [from *The Brothers Karamazov*]. Although his voice was very quiet his reading was so consummate, so moving, that I saw faces all about me sorrowing and in tears, and not only women's faces. The students presented him with a laurel wreath and accompanied him in a huge crowd up to the very entrance gates; so that he could see with his own eyes how the young people loved and respected him. This knowledge was very precious to him.

A reading for the benefit of St. Petersburg University students followed on December 14, and finally, on December 22, he read at a benefit for the Shelter of Saint Xenia at the home of Countess Mengden. At the latter reading, during intermission, he was invited into the interior rooms by express wish of Empress Maria Fyodorovna, who thanked him for his part in the reading and had a long talk with him.[16]

Fyodor Mikhailovich willingly took part in these literary readings, and the tumultuous ovations which accompanied his reading were precious and pleasant to him, but unfortunately they caused him great excitement and consumed much of his strength, of which he had so little.

During his last winter he was particularly loved by our always responsive young people. Honorary tickets for concerts and balls organized by higher educational institutions were sent to him constantly. He was always surrounded at these concerts. Young people followed him in throngs, kept putting questions to him to which he had to respond almost in speeches. Sometimes they would engaged in heated arguments with him and listen to his rejoinders with interest. This lively contact with young people who loved and valued his genius was extremely pleasurable for him, and he would come home after such talks physically exhausted but pleasantly aroused, and would recount to me all the details of these conversations, so interesting to him. (I was always present at these evenings, but used to stand aside, though never far away.)

At the beginning of December, 1880, *The Brothers Karamazov* came out in a separate edition of three thousand copies. This edition had an immediate and enormous success, and within a few days the public had bought up half the printing. Naturally Fyodor Mikhailovich found great satisfaction in this proof of the interest aroused by his new novel. This was, I may say, the last joyous event in his life, so rich in every kind of misfortune.

CHAPTER ELEVEN

The Death of Dostoevsky

Fyodor Mikhailovich was by nature a man who loved work to an extraordinary degree. I believe that even if he had been rich, with no need to concern himself with the means of subsistence, even then he would not have remained idle but would constantly have found themes for unremitting literary work.

By the beginning of 1881 we had settled all the debts which had plagued us for so long and even had some funds in reserve with the *Russian Messenger* (about five thousand rubles in payment for work done). There did not seem to be any pressing need to set to work immediately, but Fyodor Mikhailovich did not want to take a rest. He decided to start publishing *Diary of a Writer* again, since a number of disquieting thoughts on Russia's political situation had been accumulating in him during the past few troubled years, and he could express these freely only in his own journal. Moreover, the sensational success of the single issue of the *Diary* published in 1880 gave us the hope that renewed publication would find a large circle of readers, and Fyodor Mikhailovich set much store by the dissemination of his cherished beliefs.

He proposed to put out *Diary of a Writer* for two more years and then to fulfill his dream of writing a sequel to *The Brothers Karamazov* in which almost all the former characters would reappear after an interval of twenty years, almost in our own day, after accomplishing and experiencing much in their lives. The plan he had in mind for this future novel of his, judging by his remarks and notes on the subject, was extraordinarily interesting, and it is truly a pity that this novel was not fated to come into being.[1]

The subscription list for *Diary of a Writer* went well, and by the third week in January we had about . . .* subscribers. Fyodor Mikhailovich always preserved the good habit of regarding subscription monies as not belonging to him personally until such time as he satisfied his subscribers. Therefore he opened an account in his name at the State Bank, in which I deposited the subscription fees as they were received. Thanks to this circumstance, I was able to refund their money to the subscribers immediately [after his death].

During the first half of January Fyodor Mikhailovich felt extremely well. He visited his friends and even agreed to participate in the home theatricals which were to take place at Countess Tolstaya's at the beginning of the next month. It was proposed to put on two or three scenes from *The Death of Ivan the Terrible*, [the first play of] A. K. Tolstoy's trilogy, and Fyodor Mikhailovich volunteered to play the role of the eremite monk.

It was three months since he had suffered an epileptic seizure, and his cheerful, lively air gave us all the hope that the winter would go well. He had been working since mid-January on the January issue of the *Diary*, in which he wanted to express his thoughts and feelings on the subject of the Zemsky Sobor. This theme was such that it might be stopped by the censor,[2] an eventuality which caused Fyodor Mikhailovich a good deal of concern. Nikolai Savvich Abaza, who had just been appointed chairman of the Censorship Committee, learned of my husband's anxiety through Countess Tolstaya, and asked her to tell him not to worry, since he himself would censor the article. It was finished by January 25 and handed over to the printers to be set up in type, so that all that remained was to read the final proofs, deliver the article to the censor, and print it, so as to have the issue out on the last day of the month.

January 25 was a Sunday and we had many guests. Professor Orest Miller dropped in and asked my husband to read at a

*A gap in the manuscript.

literary benefit for students on January 29, the anniversary of Pushkin's death. Uncertain as to the fate of his article on the Zemsky Sobor[2] and whether he might not have to substitute another article for it, he declined at first to take part in the evening, but finally agreed. He was quite well and happy, as all our guests observed, and there was nothing at all to betoken what was to happen in a few hours.

On the morning of January 26 he got up as usual at one in the afternoon. When I went into his study he told me that there had been a minor episode during the night. His penholder had fallen on the floor and rolled under the bookcase (and he set great store by this penholder, which he used not only to write with but also for rolling cigarettes). In order to get at it he had to move the bookcase aside. Evidently it was heavy and he had to expend some effort, which caused an artery in his lung to break open suddenly, and he started to spit blood. But since there was only a very small amount of blood he hadn't considered it very important and hadn't even wanted to disturb me during the night.

I was horribly alarmed. Without saying anything to Fyodor Mikhailovich I sent our messenger boy Pyotr to Dr. Y. V. von Bretzel, my husband's regular doctor, to ask him to come at once. Unfortunately he had already left on his visiting rounds and could not come to us until after five o'clock.

Fyodor Mikhailovich was quite calm, talked and joked with the children, and settled down to read *New Times*. At about three a visitor arrived, a very nice man whom my husband liked, but with one fault: a great fondness for argument. They started discussing an article in the forthcoming issue of the *Diary*. The visitor began trying to argue some point; Fyodor Mikhailovich, who was feeling somewhat anxious about his hemorrhage of the previous night, disagreed with him—and a hot discussion blazed up between them.

My attempts to restrain the discussants were in vain, although I told our guest twice that Fyodor Mikhailovich was not entirely well and that it was bad for him to talk so much and so loudly. Finally the visitor left at about five and we started getting ready for dinner, when Fyodor Mikhailovich abruptly sat down on the couch and was silent for a minute. Suddenly, to my horror, I saw that his chin was red with blood, running down his beard in a thin stream.[3]

I cried out, and the children and servants came running. But Fyodor Mikhailovich was not frightened. On the contrary, he tried to soothe me and the weeping children. He took them over to the desk and showed them the new issue of *Dragonfly,* with a cartoon about two fishermen tangled up in their own nets and fallen into the water.[4] He even read the accompanying verse to the children, and with such verve that they quieted down. About an hour passed peacefully in this way, and the doctor—whom I had sent for a second time—arrived.

When the doctor started examining and tapping the patient's chest the hemorrhage recurred, this time with such violence that Fyodor Mikhailovich lost consciousness. When he was brought round, the first words he addressed to me were "Anya, please tell the priest to come right away, I want to confess and take communion."

Although the doctor started assuring him that there was no particular danger, I carried out the patient's wish in order to calm him down. We lived near St. Vladimir's and the priest, Father Megorsky, was at our house within a half hour. Fyodor Mikhailovich greeted him serenely and benignly, and was a long time at confession and communion. After the priest had gone and the children and I went into his study to congratulate him on receiving the Sacrament, he blessed us, asked the children to live in peace, to love one another, to love and keep me. He sent them away and then thanked me for the happiness I had given him, and asked me to forgive him if he had ever caused me pain. I stood there neither dead nor alive, without the strength to say anything in reply.

The doctor came in and put him down on the couch, forbade him to speak or make the slightest movement, and immediately advised us to send for two other doctors: his friend A. A. Pfeiffer and Professor D. I. Koshlakov, whom my husband sometimes consulted.

Koshlakov, who understood from Dr. von Bretzel's note that the patient's condition was grave, came at once. This time he was not disturbed with an examination, and Koshlakov decided that since the hemorrhaging was comparatively slight (about two glassfuls, from three hemorrhages) a "plug" might form and then the patient would be on the road to recovery. Dr. von Bretzel stayed up all night at Fyodor Mikhailovich's bedside, while he apparently slept peacefully. I also fell asleep, but only toward morning.

The whole of that day of January 27 passed quietly. The hemorrhage did not recur. Fyodor Mikhailovich seemed calmer and more cheerful, had the children called, and even spoke to them a bit, in whispers. At midday he started worrying about *Diary of a Writer.* The make-up man from Suvorin's printing house arrived, bringing the final proofs, and it turned out that there were seven lines too many, which had to be cut to make the material fit the two signatures. Fyodor Mikhailovich was troubled over this, but I suggested deleting several lines on the previous pages and he agreed to this. Although I kept the make-up man for a half hour, the matter was straightened out after two corrections which I read to Fyodor Mikhailovich. On learning from the make-up man that the issue had been sent to [the censor] N. S. Abaza in galleys and had been passed by him, my husband calmed down considerably.

Meanwhile the news of Dostoevsky's grave illness had spread all over town, and the doorbell kept ringing from two in the afternoon until late at night, and had to be tied up. People—friends and strangers—came to inquire about his health, letters with good wishes were delivered, telegrams kept arriving.

Nobody was allowed in to see the patient, and I only came out to friends for a few minutes to tell them how he was doing. He was enormously pleased by the general attention and sympathy, asked me about it in a whisper, and even dictated to me a few words of response to one kind letter.

Professor Koshlakov arrived, found the patient's condition considerably improved, and gave him hope that he would be out of bed in a week and completely recovered within two weeks. He ordered him to sleep as much as possible; therefore our whole household went to bed quite early. Since I had spent the previous night sitting up in an armchair and had slept badly, I had a mattress made up for myself on the floor next to Fyodor Mikhailovich's couch, so that it would be easier for him to call me. Exhausted by my sleepless night and anxious day, I fell asleep quickly, got up a few times in the night, and saw by the light of the night lamp that my dear patient was peacefully asleep. I awoke at about seven and saw my husband looking at me.

"Well, how do you feel, my darling?" I asked, bending over him.

"You know, Anya," he answered in a half whisper, "I've been awake for about three hours and I'm thinking all the time; and it's only just now that I realized clearly that I'm going to die today."

"My darling, why should you think such a thing?" I said in terrible uneasiness. "Why, you're better today. The bleeding is stopped, it's obvious the "plug" is formed, just as Koshlakov said it would. For God's sake, don't torture yourself with doubts—you're going to go on living, I tell you!"

"No. I know I have to die today. Light a candle, Anya, and give me the Gospel."

This Gospel had been presented to Fyodor Mikhailovich by the Decembrists' wives, P. E. Annenkova, her daughter Olga Ivanovna, N. D. Muravyova-Apostol,[5] and N. D. Fonvizina, in Tobolsk, on his way to serve his term at hard labor. They had entreated the prison warden to let them see the newly arrived political prisoners, spent an hour with them, and "blessed us on our new journey, made the sign of the Cross over us, and gave each one a Gospel—the only book allowed in the prison."[6]

Fyodor Mikhailovich did not part with that holy book during all his four years at hard labor. After that it always lay on his writing desk within sight, and often, when he was looking for an answer or in doubt about something, he would open up this Gospel at random and read what was on the left-hand page. And now, he wanted to verify his doubts by the Gospel. He opened the holy book himself and asked me to read to him.

The Gospel opened at Matthew, chapter 3, verse 14: "But John held him back, saying, I need to be baptized by You, and do You come to me? But Jesus said to him in answer, Do not hold me back,* for thus it is fitting for us to fulfill a great truth."

*In editions of the Gospel printed in the 1820's this phrase reads "Do not hold me back." In more recent editions it has been replaced by the phrase, "Let it be now." The passage as set forth in later editions reads, "But John held him

"Do you hear? 'Do not hold me back.' That means I'm going to die," my husband said, and closed the book.

I could not hold back my tears. Fyodor Mikhailovich began comforting me, said fond and loving words to me, thanked me for the happy life he had lived with me. He entrusted the children to my care, said that he believed in me and hoped I would always love and protect them. Then he told me something very few husbands can say to their wives after fourteen years of married life: "Remember this, Anya, I always loved you passionately and was never unfaithful to you even in my thoughts."

These earnest words moved me to the depths but also disquieted me terribly, for I feared his emotion might do him harm. I beseeched him not to think of dying, not to give pain to all of us with his doubts, begged him to rest, to sleep. He obeyed me and stopped talking, but it was clear

---

back, saying, I need to be baptized by You, and do You come to me? But Jesus said to him in answer, Let it be now, for thus it is fitting for us to fulfill every truth."

The words of the Gospel revealed to Fyodor Mikhailovich on the day he died had a profound significance and meaning in our life. It is possible that my husband might even have recovered for a time, but his recovery would have been of short duration. He would undoubtedly have been deeply shocked by the news of the villainous deed of March 1 [the assassination of Alexander II by members of the revolutionary People's Will party], for he idolized the Tsar as liberator of the serfs. His barely healed artery would have burst again, and he would have died. His death even at that troubled time would of course have produced a great reaction but not such a colossal one as it evoked when it actually occurred. All of society would have been too deeply plunged into reflection on the crime and the complications which might have followed at this tragic time in the life of the State. In January, 1881, when everything appeared peaceful, the death of my husband was a public event. He was mourned by people of the most diverse political views and the most disparate social circles. The extraordinary solemnity of the funeral procession and burial of Fyodor Mikhailovich attracted a host of readers and admirers from among people hitherto indifferent to Russian literature. In this way, my husband's lofty ideas were disseminated much more widely and evaluated in a fitting manner, worthy of his gifts. It is also possible that after the death of our magnanimous Tsar-Liberator our family might not have been vouchsafed the royal benevolence by which my husband's long-cherished dream was fulfilled: that our children should receive an education and might later become useful subjects of Tsar and Fatherland. (A.G.D.)

from his softened face that the thought of death had not left him and that the passage to another world was not frightening to him.

At about nine in the morning he fell quietly asleep without letting go of my hand. I sat without stirring, fearing to disturb his sleep with some movement of mine. But at eleven he woke up abruptly and raised himself from his pillow, and the hemorrhage began again. I felt utterly desperate, although I tried with all my might to keep a cheerful expression on my face and kept reassuring him that there was very little blood and that another "plug" would probably form just as it had done the day before yesterday. In answer to my words of solace he only shook his head sadly, as if fully convinced that his prediction of death would come to pass that very day.

At midday the relatives, friends, and strangers again started coming; letters and telegrams were delivered again. Fyodor Mikhailovich's stepson Paul Isayev, whom I had informed of my husband's illness the day before by letter, arrived. He wanted to go right in to see him, but the doctor would not allow it. So he stood peeking into the room through the crack of the door. Fyodor Mikhailovich noticed this peeking, became agitated, and said, "Anya, don't let him in here, he'll get me all upset!"

Paul meanwhile was very wrought up and informed everybody who came to ask about Fyodor Mikhailovich's condition—friends and strangers—that his "father" did not have any will and that a notary must be brought to the house so that he might personally dispose of his possessions.

When Professor Koshlakov, who had come to see the patient, heard from Fyodor Mikhailovich's stepson that he intended to bring in a notary, he opposed it. He stated that we must keep watch over the patient's strength with all the means at our command, that a business transaction of that sort requiring instructions and explanations could only confirm his thoughts of imminent death, that the least excitement might prove fatal to the sick man.

Actually, there was no need for any will. Fyodor Mikhailovich had assigned the literary rights to his works to me back in 1873. Aside from the five thousand rubles being held for him by the *Russian Messenger* Fyodor Mikhailovich had nothing at all, and we were the heirs to this small sum, that is, the children and myself.

I did not stir a step away from my husband for a moment all through that day. He held my hand in his and kept whispering, "My poor darling, my dearest . . . what am I leaving you with . . . my poor girl, how hard it will be for you to live!"

I reassured him and tried to comfort him with the hope of recovery, although it was clear that he himself had no hope and was in anguish at the thought that he was leaving his family almost without means. For those four or five thousand being held at the office of the *Russian Messenger* were our only resources.

Several times he whispered, "Call the children." I called them, my husband offered his lips to them, they kissed him and left immediately at the doctor's command; and Fyodor Mikhailovich followed them with his sad eyes. When the children came at his summons about two hours before the end, he asked that his Gospel be given to his son Fedya.

In the course of that day a great number of people called on us, but I did not go out to speak to them. Apollon Maikov came and talked for a little with Fyodor Mikhailovich, who responded in whispers to his greeting.

At about seven a great mass of people assembled in our drawing room and dining room and waited for Koshlakov, who visited us about that time. Suddenly, without any apparent cause, Fyodor Mikhailovich shuddered and raised himself slightly on the couch, and a thin stream of blood again reddened his face. We began giving him pieces of ice, but the bleeding would not stop.

At about this time Maikov came again with his wife, and kind Anna Ivanovna decided to go fetch Dr. N. P. Cherepnin. Fyodor Mikhailovich was unconscious. The children and I got down on our knees at the head of his bed and wept, choking back our noisy sobs with all our might, for the doctor had warned us that hearing is the last sense to leave a human being, and that any disruption of his peace and quiet might slow down his final agony and prolong the dying man's suffering. I held my husband's hand in mine and felt his pulse beat growing weaker and weaker. At 8:38 that evening Fyodor Mikhailovich passed into eternity.[7] Dr. Cherepnin arrived then but could catch only his last heartbeats.[8]

When the end came, my children and I gave full vent to our despair. We wept, sobbed, said incoherent things, kissed the face and hands of our dear departed, not yet grown cold. All this I remember only as a blur. I was clearly aware of one thing only: that from that moment on, my personal life filled with immeasurable happiness was finished, and that I was orphaned in my heart forever. For me, who loved my husband so passionately, so utterly, who gloried in the love, friendship and respect of this man so rare for his nobility of spirit, the loss was irretrievable. In those dreadful moments of parting I thought I could not survive my husband's passing, that my heart would burst any minute, so hard did it beat in my breast, or that I would simply go out of my mind right then and there.

Nearly everyone, of course, has experienced the loss of near and dear ones in his life, and everyone knows and understands the deep grief of parting with them. But in most cases people live through this heartache in the bosom of their own family and among their intimates, and give vent to their feelings as they can and wish, without being constrained and without holding back. So great a happiness did not fall to my lot. My dear husband died in the presence of a multitude, some of them deeply attached to him but others entirely indifferent both to him and to the inconsolable sorrow of our orphaned family.

As if to increase my pain, among those present was the writer B. M. Markevich, who never came to see us but who was there now at the request of Countess Tolstaya to inquire about the doctor's opinion as to Fyodor Mikhailovich's condition. Knowing Markevich, I was sure he would not abstain from describing my husband's last moments, and I felt deeply sorry that my beloved could not die in peace, alone with those devoted to him heart and soul.

My fears proved well grounded. I learned with pain the next day that Markevich had sent an "artistic" description of the sad event to the *Moscow Gazette.* In two or three days I read the article itself, and there was much in it that I did not recognize. I did not recognize even myself in the words attributed to me, so little did they correspond either to my character or to my frame of mind in those agonizing moments.[9]

But God in His mercy sent me consolation as well. That grievous evening, at about ten o'clock, my own brother Ivan arrived. He had been in Moscow from the country on business and was already on the point of leaving for home when he took it into his head, without knowing why himself, to come to Petersburg and pay us a visit. True, he had read in some newspaper that Fyodor Mikhailovich was ill, but did not ascribe any great importance to this news, assuming that he had suffered a double epileptic attack, as happened on occasion.

His train arrived late. He took a room at a hotel and then decided to come to us that evening. As he was approaching our entrance he saw with surprise that all the windows of our apartment were brightly lit and that two or three suspicious-looking people in long coats were standing by the door.

One of these individuals ran up the stairs after my brother and began whispering to him, "Sir, please be kind and see to it that I get the order . . ."

"What are you talking about, what order?" asked my bewildered brother.

"We're the coffin-makers from so-and-so, it's about the coffin."

"But who died here?" my brother asked mechanically.

"It's some writer or other, I can't remember the name—the porter was saying . . ."

My brother's heart sank, as he told us later. He rushed upstairs and ran into the unlocked vestibule, where some people were crowding around. He threw off his greatcoat and hurried into the study, where, still resting on the couch, Fyodor Mikhailovich's body was slowly stiffening.

I was on my knees beside the couch. When I saw my brother come in I rushed to him in sobs. We threw our arms around each other and I asked, "Who told you, Vanya, that Fyodor Mikhailovich was gone?" (forgetting completely that my brother didn't even live in Petersburg and was now supposed to be in Moscow, and could not have known and come to us so fast). Apparently, I was so overcome both by grief and by the suddenness of his passing (for only the day before, Professor Koshlakov had given me firm hope of his recovery) that I had lost the capacity to reason clearly.

I felt that my brother's arrival at that moment of agony was God's veritable grace toward me. It was not only that the presence of my beloved brother and true friend gave me a measure of consolation, but also that a close and devoted person was near, whose advice I could ask and whom I could entrust with all the minor but complicated details of the burial. Thanks to my brother I was relieved of practical matters and spared much unpleasantness and pain during those sad days.

That whole evening of January 28 (like the next four days from January 29 to February 1) I remember as a kind of nightmare oppressing my soul. Much of what happened I can picture vividly, much slipped out of my memory entirely, and some things I know from what others told me. I remember, for instance, that A. S. Suvorin came to us about midnight of that evening, distressed by the death of my husband, whom he deeply respected and loved. Suvorin described his visit in *New Times.*

Toward 1:00 A.M. all the necessary preparations were finished, and our dear departed was lying on a raised catafalque in the middle of his study. Near his head was a stand with an ikon and a lighted lamp. His expression was peaceful and he seemed not dead but asleep, and smiling in his sleep at some "great truth" he now knew.

All the outsiders went away toward midnight. I put my children to bed. They were terribly distressed by the death of their papa and had been crying all evening. The three of us—my mother, my brother, and I—could be near the body of our dear one without interference. With deep gratitude to fate I recall that last night, when my dear husband still belonged wholly to his family and I could give way to my grief without witnesses, without constraint or reserve, cry my fill, pray fervently for the rest of his soul, and ask his forgiveness for all those petty hurts that happen inevitably in the course of everyday living and which I might have inflicted on him, my dearly beloved husband.

My brother and I stood or sat by the coffin until four in the morning, when my brother forcibly sent me off to bed, insisting that I needed all my strength for the inevitable upsets of the coming day.

On January 29, at about eleven o'clock, a very imposing gentleman came to me on behalf of the then Minister of Internal Affairs, Count Loris-Melikov. After expressing sympathy in the name of the Count on the occasion of my loss, this official said he was empowered to give me a sum of money to pay for my deceased husband's funeral expenses. I do not know how much money was involved, but I did not want to take it. I was aware, of course, that it was the custom in all the ministries to extend aid to an orphaned family for the burial of one of its deceased members, and that no one ever took offense at such assistance. And still I felt almost offended when this help was offered to me. I asked the official to thank Count Loris-Melikov very much for the assistance proffered but said I could not accept it, since I considered it my moral obligation to bury my husband with the money he had earned.

Besides that, the official stated in the count's name that my children would be accepted in any educational institution in which I desired to place them, at the expense of the State. I asked him to convey my sincere gratitude to the count for his kind offer, but in my heart I decided right then and there that my children must be educated not at the expense of the State but by the labor of their father and later the labor of their mother.

To my great joy, I succeeded in fulfilling the obligation I had undertaken, and my children were educated subsequently on the proceeds received from the publication of their father's complete works. I am deeply convinced that when I refused to accept money for the funeral and for the education of his children, I did what my cherished husband would have done himself.

From eleven o'clock on, people known and unknown, who had learned of Fyodor Mikhailovich's death from the newspapers, arrived to pray at his coffin. There was such a multitude of them that soon all five dwelling rooms were packed with a dense crowd, and when the office for the dead was recited the children and I had a hard time pushing through the crowd to stand near the coffin.

I had asked Fyodor Mikhailovich's confessor, Father . . .,* to perform the requiem masses. On the first day the choir was from the Church of St. Vladimir. On the last two days, at their own wish and with the consent of the church warden, the full choir of St. Isaac's Cathedral, directed by E. V. Bogdanovich, came to perform the main offices for the dead, announcements of which appeared in the newspapers, at one in the afternoon and eight in the evening.

But on top of those requiem masses designated by me, two or three delegations from various institutions arrived each day together with the priests of their churches and the members of their choirs, asking permission to serve a requiem mass at the coffin of the late author. I recall a delegation from the Naval Academy, whose archpriest celebrated a splendid mass assisted by an excellent naval choir.

I shall not enumerate here the names of those who attended the services at my husband's coffin. All the foremost representatives of our literature, in sympathy with Fyodor Mikhailovich and valuing his talent, were there. Also among those present were men who had been downright antagonistic to him but who, after learning of his death, understood the enormity of the loss to Russian literature and wished to pay tribute to the memory of one of the noblest of their number. One of those evening masses was attended by the young Grand Duke Dmitry Konstantinovich and his tutor, a gesture which touched all those present.

On the day of January 29 many people asked where Fyodor Mikhailovich was to be buried. Recalling that at Nekrasov's funeral my husband had taken a liking to the cemetery at Novodevichy Convent, I decided to have him buried there. I asked my brother-in-law, P. G. Svatkovsky, to make arrangements for the grave and my daughter Lilya to choose the location. It was mostly to give her the opportunity to drive through the city and breathe some fresh air that I sent her to Novodevichy with my brother-in-law.

My poor unfortunate little ones! Throughout the entire three

*A gap in the manuscript.

days before the funeral, they stayed indoors in rooms crammed with outsiders. They attended every requiem mass, and my daughter Lilya distributed flowers from the wreaths lying on her father's breast as keepsakes for his admirers.

While my daughter and brother-in-law were on their way to Novodevichy we had a visit from Vissarion Vissarionovich Komarov, editor of the *St. Petersburg Gazette.* He said he was there on behalf of the Alexander Nevsky Lavra[10] to offer any location desired in its cemeteries as my husband's last resting place.

"The Lavra requests that a place be accepted without charge," said Komarov, "and will consider it an honor for the ashes of the writer Dostoevsky, who zealously defended the Orthodox faith, to rest inside its walls."

This proposal of the Alexander Nevsky Monastery was such an honor that it would have been a real pity to decline it. But it was possible that my brother-in-law had already purchased a plot at Novodevichy Convent. I did not know what decision to make nor how to answer Komarov. Fortunately, my brother-in-law returned just then and said that the Mother Superior at the convent had raised some difficulties about the plot my daughter had selected, and therefore the purchase of the grave site was postponed until tomorrow.

I was very pleased, and since the monastery was allowing us to choose a grave site in any of its cemeteries, I asked Mr. Komarov to select a plot in Tikhvin Cemetery close to the graves of Karamzin and Zhukovsky, whose work Fyodor Mikhailovich had so loved. By fortunate coincidence, there was a site available next to the monument of the poet Zhukovsky, and this was the location chosen for my cherished husband's everlasting rest.

On January 30, during the afternoon service, Chamberlain Abaza arrived and gave me a letter from the Minister of Finance in which my children and I were granted an annual pension of two thousand rubles by the Emperor "in gratitude for my late husband's services to Russian literature." After reading the letter and thanking Mr. Abaza warmly for his kind news I hurried into my husband's study right away, to give him joy with the good news that the children and I would be secure from that day forward. Not until I entered the room where his body was lying did I remember that he was no longer in the world, and burst into bitter tears.

I should add that this inexplicable forgetfulness went on for at least a month or two after my husband died. Either I would hurry home so as not to keep him waiting for dinner, or I would buy sweets for him, or, hearing some news or other, I would think to myself that I must tell him about it right away. The next moment, of course, I would remember that he was dead, and I would feel an inexpressible pain.

I must say that I recall with a certain horror the two and a half days while the body of my dear husband was lying in our house. Most agonizing of all was the fact that our apartment was not free of strangers for a single hour. A solid stream of people kept coming in the front door, another passed through all our rooms from the back and stopped in the study, where at times the air grew so thick, there was so little oxygen left, that the ikon-lamp and the tall tapers surrounding the catafalque would go out.

There were strangers in our house not only during the day but even through the night. Some wished to spend the night by Dostoevsky's coffin, others wanted to recite psalms for his soul and did this for hours on end. I remember that on the last night before the bearing out of his body, Count Adjutant Nikolai Fyodorovich Geiden, a great admirer of Fyodor Mikhailovich's work, recited psalms at the coffin.

All this, of course, bore witness to the genuine sorrow felt by Fyodor Mikhailovich's admirers and their deep respect for his memory, and I could only feel and express my sincere thanks to these people so devoted to my husband. Still, along with the most sincere gratitude, I felt deep in my heart a certain resentment that the outside world had deprived me of my husband, that although he was surrounded by people who loved him, I myself—the one being closest in the world to him—could not be alone with him, could not kiss his dear face and hands again and again and lay my head on his breast, as I did the first night after he died.

The presence of strangers forced me to hold back every show of feeling, out of fear that some idle reporter would write a preposterous description of my grief the next day. The only refuge where I could yield freely to my despair was the little room where my mother stayed. When things were more than I could stand I would run to her room, lock the door, throw myself on her bed, and try to comprehend somehow what had happened.

But even behind locked doors I was not to have peace. Someone would knock and tell me that a delegation had arrived from such-and-such an institution, and that they would like to express their sympathy to me personally. I would come out to see them and the representative of the delegation, who had prepared an eloquent speech in advance, would start speaking about my late husband's importance for Russian literature, would expound the noble ideas he advocated, and would tell me "what a great loss Russia had suffered" in his passing. I would hear them out in silence, thank them heartily, shake their hands, and go back to my mother. And then, a little while later, there would be another delegation which simply had to see me and personally express its sympathy. And I would go out and listen to their speeches about the importance of my husband and "what Russia has lost in him."

After three days of listening to the many speeches of condolence, I finally became desperate and said to myself, "My God, how they torture me! What is it to me, 'what Russia has lost'? What do I care about Russia now? Can't you understand what *I've* lost? I've lost the best person in the world, the joy and pride and happiness of my life, my sun, my god! Take pity on me, take pity on me as a person, and don't tell me at this time about Russia's loss!"

When, out of the members of those many delegations, one person showed some pity for me as well as for "Russia," I was so touched that I seized this stranger's hand and kissed it.

I am quite convinced that during those days my thoughts were disordered and abnormal, a situation to which, among other things, the fact that I was leading the most unhygienic life contributed. For five days between January 26 and 31 I did not leave those stifling rooms and took no food but tea and rolls. My kind friends would take the children out for walks and to their own homes for dinner, since it was out of the question for the cook to prepare anything in view of the crowds going through the apartment via the back door, and everyone ate cold food.

On the last day, January 30, I started getting attacks of hysteria. During one such seizure something happened that might have caused my death. After one of the requiem masses I felt a nervous lump in my throat, and asked a friend to bring me some valerian drops. The people standing near me in the drawing room hastily started calling the servant and saying, "Get the valerian right away, where's the valerian?" Since "Valerian" is also a person's name, a funny thought came into my overwrought mind: a widow is weeping and everybody is calling some "Valerian" to come and comfort her. This absurd image sent me into a frenzy of laughing and exclaiming, "Valerian, Valerian!" just as they were all doing. And I went into real hysterics.

As ill luck would have it, the maid couldn't find the valerian drops and was dispatched to the apothecary for them and told to buy spirits of ammonia at the same time, in case I fainted and had to be brought round. In about ten minutes both medicines were brought in, while I went on laughing and struggling in the arms of the women around me. One of them, the good Sofya Viktorovna Averkieva, a person of decisive character, poured thirty or more drops of some liquid into a wineglass and forced me to drink it in spite of my resistance.

I felt a terrible burning in my tongue, grabbed a handkerchief, and spit up everything I had drunk into it. It seems that in her haste Sofya Viktorovna had mixed up the phials and given me thirty or more drops of spirits of ammonia instead of valerian.

That night all the skin peeled off my mouth and tongue and kept peeling for almost a week after that. Later, I was told that if I had swallowed the liquid I would have received the same burn in my esophagus and stomach, leading to possible illness, if not death.

I have forgotten to mention that among our many visitors on the day after Fyodor Mikhailovich's death was the celebrated painter I. N. Kramskoy. On his own initiative he wanted to do a full-sized portrait of the deceased, and he produced a brilliant work of art. In that portrait Fyodor Mikhailovich seems not dead but only asleep, with a hint of a smile on his illumined face, as if he had already learned the mystery, unfathomed by us, of life beyond the grave.[11] Several artists and photographers besides Kramskoy also painted or photographed portraits of my husband for the illustrated periodicals. We had a visit from the sculptor Leopold Bernstamm, prominent now but quite unknown at that time, who made a mask of my husband from which he was later able to do a bust bearing a striking resemblance.

The bearing out of Fyodor Mikhailovich's body from our apartment to the Alexander Nevsky Monastery took place on Saturday, January 31. I will not attempt to describe the funeral procession; that has been done by many others. And indeed I did not see the entire procession, or saw it only in illustrations, since I walked directly behind the coffin and could see only what was nearest to me. According to the accounts of spectators, it was a majestic spectacle: a long file of wreaths borne aloft on poles; large choirs of young people intoning funeral chants; the coffin raised high above the throng; and a vast mass of humanity, several tens of thousands, following the cortege. All this had a powerful impact.

The chief merit of this mournful homage to Fyodor Mikhailovich's remains consisted in the fact that it was quite spontaneous. Since then elaborate funerals have become customary, and it is not difficult to arrange them. In those days, however, solemn funeral processions (except for Nekrasov's, which was relatively modest) did not yet exist, and indeed the time (about two days) would not have sufficed to prepare and organize one.

On the day before the bearing out of the body my brother, wishing to please me, said that eight different institutions were intending to bring wreaths to Fyodor Mikhailovich's grave; but by the next morning there were already seventy-four wreaths or possibly even more. Later it came out that all the institutions and associations, each on its own initiative, had ordered their own wreaths and picked a delegation. In a word, all parties of the most diverse orientations united in common sorrow at Dostoevsky's passing and the genuine wish to honor his memory in the greatest possible solemnity.

The funeral procession left the house at eleven and did not reach Alexander Nevsky Monastery until after two. I walked side by side with my son and daughter, and my bitter thoughts would not leave me. How was I to bring up my children without their father, without Fyodor Mikhailovich, who had loved them with such a passion? So heavy a responsibility to my husband's memory lay on me henceforth—would I be able to carry out my obligations with dignity? As I walked behind his coffin, I swore an oath to myself to live for our children; I vowed to dedicate all the remainder of my life, insofar as it lay within my power, to the glory of my beloved husband's memory and the dissemination of his noble ideals. Now, as I face the approaching close of my life, I can say truthfully that all the things I promised myself, in those painful hours when I walked behind my husband's mortal remains, I have fulfilled to the degree that my capacity and strength allowed.

On that same evening of January 30, a memorial service of solemn vespers was celebrated in the Church of the Holy Spirit of Alexander Nevsky Monastery, where the coffin of Fyodor Mikhailovich was placed. I attended the service with my children. The church was filled with worshippers. Especially numerous were the young people, students from various institutions of higher learning and from the Ecclesiastical Academy as well as young women students. Most of them stayed in church all through the night and took turns reciting psalms over Dostoevsky's coffin.

Later I was told an interesting fact—that when the porter came to clean out the church, there wasn't a single cigarette butt. This amazed the monks, since normally during long services there is always someone in church who will have a furtive smoke and throw the butt away. But in this instance none of those present could bring himself to smoke, out of respect for Fyodor Mikhailovich's memory.

The funeral service took place in the Church of the Holy Spirit attached to the monastery. The church had a majestic air.

The coffin, on its catafalque raised high in the center of the church, was covered with great numbers of wreaths. The remaining wreaths, with their broad ribbons on which inscriptions printed in gold and silver were visible, stood along the walls of the church on tall poles, and lent the temple a special beauty.

On the day of the funeral rites my brother took my son and my mother to the monastery. As for my daughter and me, we were promised a ride there by Yulya Zasetskaya, daughter of the partisan fighter Denis Davydov and an ardent enthusiast for my husband's work. We left at ten. While we were still several yards away from the monastery, Madame Zasetskays's carriage drew up alongside a cab in which a colonel was sitting. He bowed, and Zasetskaya waved to him.

An enormous crowd several thousand strong was standing in the square, and it was impossible to drive up to the gates. We were forced to stop in the middle of the square. My daughter and I got out and walked toward the gates, while Zasetskaya stayed in the carriage to wait for the colonel, saying that he would accompany her into the cathedral.

With difficulty we pushed our way through the throng, but then we were stopped and asked for our tickets. In all the fuss and misery, naturally, it had never entered my head to bring any tickets along, since I assumed we would be admitted even without them. I replied, "I am the widow of the deceased and this is his daughter."

"There are plenty of Dostoevsky's widows here who have gone inside already, and some of them are with children, too," was the retort.

"But you can see that I am in deep mourning."

"Oh, they were wearing veils, too. Kindly show me your visiting card."

Naturally I had no visiting card with me either. I tried insisting, begged them to call one of the funeral officials, mentioned the names of Grigorovich, Rykachev, Averkiev, but was told, "How are we supposed to find them—do you think we can find them so fast in a crowd of thousands of people?"

I felt desperate. Not to mention the opinion people who did not know me might receive if they did not see me at my husband's funeral rites, I myself had an agonizing need to say goodbye to him for the last time, to pray and cry for a while at his coffin. I did not know what to do, for I assumed Zasetkaya had already managed to get in and could not rescue me.

Luckily this did not happen. Zasetskaya's companion authoritatively vouched for my identity, we were admitted, and my little girl and I made our way to the church at a run. Fortunately the services had only just started.

The funeral liturgy was celebrated by the Archpriest and very Reverend Nestor, Bishop of Vyborg, assisted by archimandrites and priestly monks. I. L. Yanyshev, rector of the Ecclesiastical Academy, and Archimandrite Simeon, acting vicar of the Lavra, who had known my husband personally, performed the funeral rites. An augmented choir of the Lavra plus the choir of St. Isaac's Cathedral sang very movingly. Before the requiem, the very Reverend Father Yanyshev gave a beautiful eulogy in which he vividly set forth all Fyodor Mikhailovich's merits as a writer and as a Christian.

After the funeral service the coffin of Fyodor Mikhailovich was lifted and borne out of the church by his admirers, among whom the young philosopher Vladimir Solovyov was conspicuous for his anguished face. All of Tikhvin Cemetery was clogged with people. They clambered on to the monuments, climbed the trees and clung to the fences, while the processional slowly moved ahead, passing under the arched wreaths of the various delegations on both sides.

After the coffin was lowered, speeches were made over the open grave. First to speak was A. K. Palm, a former member of the Petrashevsky Circle. He was followed by Orest Miller, Professor K. N. Bestuzhev-Ryumin, Vladimir Solovyov, P. A. Gaideburov, and many others. Many poems dedicated to Fyodor Mikhailovich's memory were also recited over the open grave. Visitors covered the coffin with wreaths massed almost to the top of the crypt. The rest of the wreaths were ripped into shreds, and those present took leaves and flowers away with them as keepsakes. Not until nearly four o'clock was the grave closed, and I and the children, weak with tears and hunger, went home. But the vast throngs did not disperse for a long time afterward.

CHAPTER TWELVE

After Dostoevsky's Death

Only once in my life did I have the happiness of seeing and speaking with Count Leo Tolstoy, and since our conversation was concerned entirely with my husband, I think it appropriate to include it in these reminiscences.[1]

It was in 1885 that I first met Countess Sofya Andreyevna Tolstaya during one of her trips to Petersburg. Unknown to me until then, she came to ask my advice in connection with book publishing. She explained that the works of her famous husband had previously been published by the Moscow bookseller Salayev, who paid a relatively modest sum for the publication rights (I believe it was twenty-five thousand rubles). When she learned from friends that I was successfully publishing the works of my husband, she decided to make the attempt to publish Count Leo Tolstoy's work herself, and wanted to find out from me whether book publishing presented very many complications and problems.

The countess made a very favorable impression on me. It was with genuine pleasure that I confided to her all the "secrets" of my publishing work, gave her samples of subscription books and announcements I had distributed, cautioned her against certain mistakes I had made, and so forth. Since there were many details, I had occasion to visit her at the home of her sister, Tatyana Andreyevna Kuzminskaya, and she came to see me two or three times to clear up the things that seemed puzzling to her.

To my great joy, my advice on publishing proved valuable to Countess Sofya Andreyevna. Her publication went marvelously well and brought in a large profit. She went on publishing the works of Leo Tolstoy herself, with enormous success, for over twenty years. Our frequent meetings and talks made it possible for us to come to know one another, and we became good friends. I was convinced that she was the veritable guardian angel of her husband's genius. She used to visit me when she was in Petersburg. I too would invariably go to see her whenever I was in Moscow, and later I made it possible for her and her family to watch from the windows of the F. M. Dostoevsky Memorial Museum as the body of the late Emperor Alexander III was borne into the Cathedral of the Archangel.

I used to come to Moscow mostly in spring to visit my Museum, or in fall on my way home from the Crimea. But no matter when I visited Sofya Andreyevna, I never found Count Leo Tolstoy at home: either he had left in early spring for Yasnaya Polyana or was spending the autumn there. One evening in winter, however, while paying the countess a visit, I learned that Tolstoy was in Moscow but was not well and not receiving anyone. After speaking with me for a bit Sofya Andreyevna went to her husband's room, while I stayed behind to chat with her family. She returned about ten minutes later and said that Tolstoy, on being told that I was there, wanted to see me very much and asked that I come to him. She warned me that he had had a liver attack that day and was feeling very weak, and therefore she asked me to keep my conversation with him brief.

The countess and I went through some passageways from house to house (the kind you find only in Moscow), and while I was on my way to him I didn't even feel very pleased at the idea. Despite all my desire to meet this great literary genius whose poetic works had always enthralled me, I was overwhelmed by a feeling of awe, and I was afraid of making an unpleasant impression on him, which was something I did not in the least want to do.

We entered a large but low-ceilinged room where Count Lev Nikolayevich was sitting on a couch, dressed in the gray peasant blouse familiar to everyone from photographs. My fright vanished in a second at the cordial exclamation he greeted me with: "How astonishing that our writers' wives look so much like their husbands!"

"Do you really think I look like Fyodor Mikhailovich?" I asked happily.

"Extraordinarily like! It was just precisely someone like you that I've been picturing as Dostoevsky's wife!"

Actually, there was no resemblance whatever between my husband and myself. But nothing Tolstoy might have said could have given me greater pleasure than that downright untruth that I looked like my cherished husband. Somehow, he instantly became close and dear to me. He seated me in an armchair next to him and, pointing to his chest, which was covered with some kind of little bags (filled with hot ashes or oats), he complained of his ill health. We were silent for a moment.

"I've been dreaming for a long time of meeting you, dear Lev Nikolayevich," I said, "to thank you with all my heart for the wonderful letter you sent Strakhov when my husband died. Strakhov gave that letter to me, and I preserve it as something precious."

"I wrote what I genuinely felt," said Lev Nikolayevich. "I still regret that I never met your husband."

"And how *he* regretted it! And there was an opportunity to meet, you know. It was when you attended Vladimir Solovyov's lecture at Solyanoy Gorodok. I recall that Fyodor Mikhailovich even reproached Strakhov for not telling him you were there. 'I might at least have had had a look at him,' my husband said at that time, 'even if there was no opportunity to speak with one another.' "

"Really? And your husband was at that lecture, too? Then why in the world didn't Strakhov let me know?[2] How sorry I am! To me Dostoevsky was a precious person[3]—perhaps the only person I might have asked about many things, and who might have given me answers about many things."

Sofya Andreyevna came in. Mindful of her warning, I rose to go, but Tolstoy kept me, saying, "No, no, stay a while longer. Tell me, what kind of person was your husband, how does he remain in your heart, in your memory?"

I was deeply touched by the heartfelt way he spoke of Fyodor Mikhailovich.

"My dear husband," I said excitedly, "was an ideal person! All the loftiest moral and spiritual qualities that can grace a human being appeared in him in the highest degree. He was kind, generous, compassionate, just, unmercenary, tactful, sympathetic—as no one else! And his directness, his incorruptible honesty, which gained him so many enemies!

"Was there ever a person who left my husband without receiving advice, comfort, help in one form or another? It's true that when he was feeling ill after an attack or when he was deep in work he was harsh—but that harshness would change to kindliness in a moment if he saw that a person needed his help. And how much real gentleness he would show then, to make up for his sharpness or brusqueness.

"You know, Lev Nikolayevich, a person's character is never so vividly expressed as in his everyday life with his own family. And here I dare say that after living with him for fourteen years I could only be astonished and touched when I saw his actions. And even though I was fully aware at times of how impractical some of them were, and even harmful to us personally, I had to admit that in certain cases my husband behaved just exactly as a man must behave if he prizes nobility and justice!"

"I have always thought of him like that!" said Count Lev Nikolayevich, thoughtfully and with real emotion. "I have always imagined Dostoevsky as a man of deep Christian feeling."[4]

Sofya Andreyevna entered the room again. I rose, warmly pressed the proffered hand of my favorite author, and left under the spell of such charm as I have rarely experienced. Yes, that man knew how to conquer hearts!

As I returned home along Moscow's deserted streets, reliving the deep impressions I had just experienced, I made a promise to myself, and kept it—that I would *never* again see Count Leo Tolstoy—and this despite the fact that the good countess invited me many times, even to stay with them at Yasnaya Polyana. I feared that at our next meeting I might find him ill, out of sorts or unresponsive, and I would see a different person in him. And then the enchantment I had felt and which was so precious to me would vanish forever. Why then should I rob myself of those treasures of the spirit, sent us so rarely by fate along our life's journey?

I have had a good deal of grief in my long lifetime from the "reminiscers"—that is, from people who knew or who allegedly knew my late husband personally, and who wrote reminiscences of him. Whenever I used to see that this or that person's memoirs, in one journal or another, contained a discussion of my husband, my heart would contract with a dreary premonition and I would think to myself, "Here we go again with some kind of exaggeration, invention, or gossip."

And I was seldom mistaken. Nor was I mistaken in the fact that even conscientious memoirists did not always apprehend Fyodor Mikhailovich's real nature and behavior nor accurately appraise his moral character. (I refer here, of course, to personal reminiscences only and not to literary analyses. Some of those, on the contrary, came close to Fyodor Mikhailovich's conception and evaluation of his own work.)

I was always struck by the general tone of these reminiscences of my husband, which were almost stereotyped. As if by common consent, all the memoirists would depict Fyodor Mikhailovich (judging, probably, by his books) as a gloomy man, difficult in company, impatient of other people's opinions, constantly arguing, and always with the design of wounding his interlocutor—and on top of that, puffed up with pride and filled with "delusions of grandeur." Only a few persons, such as V. Mikulich,[5] the Moscow relatives of Fyodor Mikhailovich, and a gentleman who remembered him during a summer's stay at a dacha near Moscow, Mr. N. N. von Vocht,[6] could receive and express an entirely different impression of him, one which corresponded to reality.

How many times was I compelled both to hear and to read that Fyodor Mikhailovich would enter a drawing room with an air of gloom, shake hands wordlessly, not vouchsafing a verbal greeting to anyone, would seat himself in an armchair and maintain a sullen silence—thereby showering a stream of cold water on the other guests, so animated and merry until his arrival! After maintaining this "majestic" silence for a full half hour or sometimes even longer, or perhaps replying to questions and greetings now and again with a word or two, Fyodor Mikhailovich would at long last bring himself to "condescend" to ordinary mortals, and would begin to converse. But even then it would not usually be with the company in general, but only with a selected one of their number, someone he knew to be an obsequious or deferential admirer. With this person he would carry on a conversation in an undertone, merely tossing out to the other guests some belittling or denigrating *mot* now and then. This would be seized immediately, commented upon by the other members of the company. Then, embellished with various ornamentations, it would make its way into literary circles as a fresh example of Fyodor Mikhailovich's intolerance or his inflated opinion of himself.

As a matter of fact, Fyodor Mikhailovich's social behavior had a very simple explanation. Ever since his return from abroad, or rather since 1872, he had been suffering from a catarrh of the respiratory passages: emphysema. This disease, despite his trips to Ems [to take the cure], grew worse with each passing year. His lungs progressively lost their capacity to take in the necessary air. Sometimes, even when he was sitting in his own home, he struggled so hard for breath, fell into such a frenzied spell of coughing, that it seemed his chest could not withstand the strain, and that a catastrophe would occur. And that, indeed, was what did happen: Fyodor Mikhailovich died of a lung hemorrhage.

And so one can imagine what my poor husband had to endure after driving in the frost or even worse, in the damp, when he made his way up to someone located on the third floor (such as the Credit Society or the Nobility Assembly halls) or sometimes (for instance to the Polonskys, whom he loved to visit) on the fifth floor. He would climb the stairs, stopping at every step to catch his breath, and would say to me at times, "Don't hurry—let me rest, I can't breathe. I feel as if I'm breathing through a wool kerchief folded over double."

Naturally I did not hurry. Our ascent to the third or fourth floor would take twenty or twenty-five minutes; and still Fyodor Mikhailovich would arrive exhausted, drained, almost suffocating. We were lucky if the porter did not ring upstairs to announce the arrival of a new guest, so that we could take our time going up. But since visitors usually arrive at about the same time, we would often be overtaken on the staircase by acquaintances, who would inform our hosts that Fyodor Mikhailovich would be right along. He, however, might not appear for another half hour, having sat down to rest at the landings. And so persons hostile to him would think or say, "Well, then—since he forces people to wait so long for him to appear, doesn't he regard himself as 'an Olympian deity'?"

The expectant hosts, and sometimes Fyodor Mikhailovich's devotees as well, would shower him with greetings, help him remove his greatcoat, his hat, his scarf (and it is so hard for a person with a chest disease to endure rapid and superfluous movements); and Fyodor Mikhailovich would enter the drawing room utterly drained of strength and incapable of articulating a word, trying only to catch his breath a little and come back to normal. That was the true cause of his gloomy appearance on those occasions when he went out in society.

Most of the people who knew him were aware that it was not only epilepsy that he suffered from. But since he disliked complaining about his health and always tried to keep up outward appearances, never refusing to participate in benefit readings for charitable societies nor to make business or social visits, most of his acquaintances ascribed no importance to his chest disease up to the very end. And therefore, through normal human frailty, they were capable of attributing his gloom and taciturnity to qualities entirely untypical of my husband's noble and elevated character.

When we visited private homes (Countess Tolstaya, the Stackenschneiders, the Polonskys, the Gaideburovs, and so forth) Fyodor Mikhailovich sought relaxation from his work, the chance to chat with someone, to unburden himself. That was why he liked to converse quietly with people congenial to him (it wasn't at all out of pride or "Olympian" arrogance). And sometimes, particularly after a seizure, he would even show distaste at meeting new people. I can bear witness to the fact that, contrary to gossip, he particularly disliked holding forth in company, starting arguments, or making spiteful or mocking remarks to anyone.

I recall how unpleasantly and painfully I was struck by the remarks of a Mr. I. I. Yanzhul,[7] in which he mentioned meeting Fyodor Mikhailovich at a Gaideburov Sunday gathering. Mr. Yanzhul described a whole scene which supposedly outraged all those present, during which Fyodor Mikhailovich is alleged to have made some remarks about science and scientists. This description left the impression (and not on me alone) that my husband envied people with a higher university education than his own (since he, after all, was only a Military Engineering School graduate) and that he wished to insult and wound any and every man of science whenever an opportunity presented itself.

Fyodor Mikhailovich deeply valued true learning, and he had warm friends of long standing among wise and gifted scholars and professors, with whom he always found it pleasant and interesting to meet and talk. Such, for example, were the Orientalist V. V. Grigoryev, V. I. Lamansky, N. P. Wagner, A. F. Koni and A. M. Butlerov. On the other hand, he regarded as nonentities those mediocre scholars of his acquaintance whose academic or publicistic activity left no beneficial trace; and I believe he was entitled to do so.

Knowing my husband's habit of conversing with one person at a time (as many memoirists, for example Mikulich, Vsevolod Solovyov and de Boland attest) it seemed strange to me that Mr. Yanzhul was able to overhear my husband's quiet conversation with his hostess (my husband had a muffled, unresonant voice) and to understand that his remark was pointed directly at him with the aim of giving offense. Unfortunately, Mr. Yanzhul's reminiscences appeared at a time when no witnesses to this scene were still alive, so that their accuracy could not be verified. No less strange to me was a second meeting of this "reminiscer" with my husband [at the theater]. Not to mention the fact that Fyodor Mikhailovich went to the theater only too rarely and always with me (and I do not recall the meeting) my husband would hardly have recognized Professor Yanzhul unaided, since he had no memory at all for faces (and particularly faces he had seen only once).

Some reminiscences of a student at the St. Petersburg Ecclesiastical Academy were published in the *Historical Messenger* for March, 1901, in which every word was a fabrication. [This individual] described an encounter with Dostoevsky at the Cathedral of the Alexander Nevsky Monastery on Good Friday, when the Shroud of Christ is borne out. I can vouch for the fact that my husband and I always went together to all the major religious services during Holy Week and Easter Week (I was afraid he might have a seizure because of the crush and the stuffiness), and that we used to be either in the right side-chapel of the Znamenskaya Church or, in the last three years, at St. Vladimir's. It would never have entered my husband's head to make the trip to the Nevsky Monastery (about five versts from our apartment) on a day in spring when the frost-bearing floes of ice from the Neva or from Lake Ladoga were floating down the river, for he took very careful precautions against catching cold during his last years.

The bust of Pushkin seen by this "reminiscer" in the corner of my husband's study during his visit did not exist, since we did not own any busts of any sort.

And finally, this memoirist could not have printed a last kiss on the body of Fyodor Mikhailovich in the Church of the Holy Spirit, since the coffin was not opened for this purpose, even for members of the family. The coffin cover was lifted only for the rite of "committing to the earth." In a word, I would suggest that all these things appeared to the memoirist in his sleep, and that he mistook his dream for reality and published it in his reminiscences.

Still, I am most grateful for him for the fact that he did not attribute to my husband such bad habits as a recent "reminiscer," N. N. Firsov, did in an article in the *Historical Messenger* for June, 1914, entitled "Reminiscences of a Man of the Sixties." The author of this article saw Fyodor Mikhailovich during a stay in Staraya Russa, where my husband allegedly made a daily appearance at the outdoor musicales. There, in a state of deep contemplation, he would walk around and around the military band while *dragging his feet,* evidently composing his works under the spell of the music, since immediately on reaching home he is supposed to have dictated several pages of his novel (once again walking around the room).

What is all the more curious is that when [this person] *first* met Dostoevsky at the home of the poet Pleshcheyev in Moscow in 1858 or 1859, Fyodor Mikhailovich—who must have been thirty-seven or thirty-eight years old at the time—was also *drag-*

ging his feet (an allusion to the fetters) while pacing back and forth about the room all the while.

Every word of this is an invention. Fyodor Mikhailovich loved walking and used to go on long walks, but he never dragged his feet. He walked with measured steps—a habit remaining from his period of military service. The author of the article fails to notice the incongruity of his description. Only people with leg ailments drag their feet, and people as ill as that prefer to sit, and not to be constantly walking about.

Fyodor Mikhailovich never attended the outdoor musical performances at Staraya Russa. He used to go either to the reading room to look at the newspapers or to the park at Mineralnye Vody, always away from the public. There was no military brass band in Russa, but only a small string orchestra of ten or twelve members, whose performances could hardly be called inspiring. It would indeed have been ridiculous to go strolling around and around an orchestra in full view of the assembled audience; and my husband never put himself into a ludicrous position. I ask myself: to what end did this memoirist find it necessary to invent such a fable and drag the name of Dostoevsky into it?

And only now, as the end of my life draws close, am I compelled to defend my beloved husband's radiant memory against the contemptible slander of a man whom my husband, I, and all our family regarded for decades as our true friend. I refer to Nikolai Strakhov's letter to Count Leo Tolstoy of November 28, 1883, which was published in *Contemporary World*, October, 1913.[8]

In November of that year, when I returned to Petersburg after the summer and met with friends and acquaintances, I was rather surprised that almost all of them asked me whether I had read Strakhov's letter to Tolstoy. When I asked where this letter was published, they answered that they had read it in some newspaper but couldn't remember exactly where.

I didn't ascribe any special importance to such forgetfulness and didn't take any particular interest in the news. What, after all, could Strakhov write but good (I thought) about my husband, who had always spoken of him as an outstanding writer, commended his work, and suggested ideas and themes for it? Not until later did I realize that none of my "forgetful" friends or acquaintances wanted to wound me mortally, as our false friend did with his letter.

It was not until the summer of 1914 that I read that wretched letter for myself when I was sorting out the profusion of newspaper and magazine clippings sent me by an agency to augment the collection of the F. M. Dostoevsky Memorial Museum in Moscow. It reads as follows.

I shall write you a short letter, my inestimable Lev Nikolayevich, although my subject is of the richest. But I am not feeling well, and it would take a very long time to develop this theme in full.

You have probably already received my *Biography of Dostoevsky.*[9] Please give it your attention and indulgence; let me know what you think of it. And it is in this connection that I would like to make a confession to you.

All during the writing of it I was in conflict. I was struggling against my own rising revulsion, trying to suppress that ugly feeling in myself. Help me find a way out of it. I cannot consider Dostoevsky either a good or a happy man (actually, the two coincide). He was malicious, envious, dissolute; and he lived his whole life in a state of agitation which made him pitiful and would have made him ridiculous if he had not also been so malicious and so intelligent. For his part, he considered himself, like Rousseau, the best and the happiest of men.

Because of the *Biography* I recall these character traits vividly. Once in Switzerland in my presence he ordered a waiter about so roughly that the man took offense and declared, "I too am a human being, after all!" I remember how struck I was then by the fact that this remark was addressed to a man who preaches *humanity,* and that it was an expression of free Switzerland's concept of *the rights of man.*

Such scenes were continual with him, because he could not restrain his spite. There were many times when I did not reply to his remarks, which he made just like a woman, unexpectedly and by innuendo. But once or twice I had occasion to say some very wounding things to him, although in the matter of insults, it goes without saying, he had the upper hand over ordinary people. And what made it worst of all was the fact that he wallowed in it, that he never completely repented of all his nasty actions. He was drawn to nasty acts and he bragged about them.

Viskovatov once began telling me how [Dostoevsky] had boasted of having . . . a little girl in the bath house, delivered over to him by her governess. Bear in mind here that with all his animal lust he had no taste, no feeling for feminine beauty and charm. This is evident in his novels. The characters most resembling him are the hero of *Notes from Underground,* Svidrigailov in *Crime and Punishment,* and Stavrogin in *The Possessed.* There was one scene with Stavrogin (the rape of a child, and so forth) that Katkov refused to publish[10] but which Dostoevsky read to many people here.

And yet, with such a nature, he was very much inclined toward sweet sentimentality, toward lofty humanitarian fantasies, and these fantasies are his tendency, his literary muse and course. In essence, however, all his novels are *self-justification,* they argue that every variety of loathsomeness can live side by side with nobility in the same human being.

How it pains me that I cannot throw off these thoughts, that I cannot find a way of coming to terms with them! Is it that I am malicious? Is it that I envy him? Do I wish him ill? Not in the least—I am simply ready to shed tears that this memory which *might have been* radiant only oppresses me!

I call to mind your remarks that people who know us too well naturally do not love us. But the reverse is also true. In a close relationship you can discern in a man a trait of character for which you are ready to forgive him everything later. *An impulse of true goodness, a spark of real warmth of heart,* even a single moment of genuine repentance—can make up for everything; and if I could recall anything of that sort in Dostoevsky I would forgive him and rejoice in him. But nothing but building himself up as a wonderful human being, nothing but cerebral and literary humanitarianism—my God, how revolting that is!

He was a truly unhappy and wicked person who imagined himself happy and a hero, and tenderly loved himself alone. Since I am aware that I myself am capable of arousing antipathy and have learned to understand and forgive this feeling in others, I thought I would find a way out of my feelings toward Dostoevsky, too. But I cannot, I cannot find any way out!

Here you have a small commentary on my *Biography.* I could have written down and narrated this side of Dostoevsky [in the book] as well —there are many episodes which I recall much more vividly than those I did describe; and the account would have been much closer to the truth. But let this truth perish, let us flaunt only the façade of life, as we do everywhere and in everything!

. . . I sent you two more books (copies) which I myself like very much and which you were interested in, as I noticed when visiting you. Pressensé is a charming book of first-rate scholarship, and Joly of course is the best translation of Marcus Aurelius, delighting me with its mastery.[11]

I quote from Tolstoy's reply to Strakhov.[12]

I too have read Pressensé's book, but all the scholarship is wasted because of a difficulty. There are magnificent pure-bred horses; a racer can bring a price of a thousand rubles. But suddenly you detect some kink and the price for that beauty, that magnificent animal, drops to a farthing. The longer I live, the more I value people without a kink. You say you've come to accept Turgenev; while I've grown very fond of him—and, amusingly enough, just because he doesn't have a kink, and he takes you where you need to go. Whereas the other one is a racehorse, but you'll get nowhere on him, and you're even lucky if he doesn't land you in the ditch. Both Pressensé and Dostoevsky, both of them have a kink. And in one case all the scholarship, in the other his intellect and his heart, go for nothing. For Turgenev will outlive Dostoevsky—and not because he is the greater artist, but because he didn't have a kink.

Strakhov replied as follows on December 12, 1883.

If that is so, then do please write about Turgenev, inestimable Lev Nikolayevich. How I thirst to read something with a background as profound as yours! For what we others write is some kind of self-pampering or comedy, which we play out for others.

In my *Memoirs* [of Dostoevsky] I stressed the literary aspect of the matter; I wanted to write a page in "the history of literature." But I could not completely overcome my indifference. With regard to Dostoevsky as a man, I strove to set forth his virtues only; but I did not attribute to him merits he did not possess. My account of literary matters probably had little interest for you. But may I speak frankly? Even your evaluation of Dostoevsky, though it clarified a good deal for me, was nonetheless too easy on him. How can a person experience an organic change when nothing can penetrate his soul beyond a certain point? I say "nothing," in the literal sense of the word: that is the way I visualize his soul. Oh, luckless and pitiful beings that we are! And the only salvation is to renounce one's own soul.

Strakhov's letter outraged me to the depths of my soul. A man who visited our family for decades, who was treated by my husband with such heartfelt warmth, turned out to be a liar who made bold to utter such despicable slanders against him! I was wounded for myself, for my trustfulness, for the fact that both my husband and I had been so deceived by this unworthy individual.

I was astounded by Strakhov's remark in his letter that "all during the writing of [the *Biography*] . . . I was struggling against my own rising revulsion." But then why—if he felt a revulsion against the work he had undertaken to do, and evidently felt no respect for the person he had agreed to write about—why did Strakhov not refuse to go on with the work, as any self-respecting person would have done in his place? Was it because he did not wish to put me, the publisher, into an embarrassing position in seeking another biographer? But Orest Miller had also undertaken to write the biography, and there were other writers available as well—Averkiev, Sluchevsky—who wrote it for the later editions.

Strakhov says in his letter that Dostoevsky was *malicious,* and as proof of this cites a rather silly episode with a waiter whom he is alleged to have "roughly ordered about." My husband, due to his illness, was very irascible at times, and it is possible that he shouted at a waiter who was slow in bringing some food he had ordered (how else would the "ordering about" of a waiter be demonstrated?), but this signified not malice but only impatience. And how implausible is the servant's reply, "I too am a human being, after all!" In Switzerland the plain folk are so rude that a waiter answering an offensive remark would not confine himself to pathetic words, but could and would dare to answer back with barefaced insolence, placing perfect reliance on his own impunity.

I cannot comprehend how Strakhov could lift his hand to write that Fyodor Mikhailovich was "malicious" and "tenderly loved himself alone." For Strakhov was witness to the dreadful position both of the Dostoevsky brothers were put into when *Time* was banned—and this was caused by Strakhov's own clumsily written article, "The Fatal Question."[13] If Strakhov had not expressed himself so ambiguously in this article, the journal would have continued to exist and prosper even after the death of Mikhail Dostoevsky, and all its obligations would not have fallen on my husband's shoulders. He would not have been compelled to spend the rest of his life paying off the journal's indebtedness, for which he accepted responsibility. I can state in truth that Strakhov was my husband's evil genius, not only in his lifetime, but, as it now turns out, even after his death.

Strakhov was also witness to the fact that Fyodor Mikhailovich gave help over a long period to the family of his dead brother Mikhail, his sick brother Nikolai, and his stepson Paul Isayev. A man with a "malicious" heart, who loved himself alone, would not have undertaken financial burdens difficult to fulfill, nor to concern himself with the fate of his relatives. And for Strakhov, who was familiar with the smallest details of Fyodor Mikhailovich's life, to say of him that he was "malicious" and "tenderly loved himself alone" is utterly without conscience.

For my own part I, who lived with my husband for fourteen years, consider it my duty to bear witness that Fyodor Mikhailovich was a man of infinite kindness. He demonstrated this not only in relation to the people who were close to him, but to all whose misfortune, failure or trouble he had occasion to learn of. One didn't have to ask him, he himself would volunteer to help out. Possessed of influential friends—K. P. Pobedonostsev, T. I. Filippov, I. A. Vyshnegradsky—my husband used their influence to help other people out of trouble.

How many aged men and women he found a place for in old-age homes, how many children he got accepted into asylums, how many jobless he found work for! And other people's manuscripts—how many of them he had to read and revise, how many frank confessions he listened to, how much counsel he gave in the most intimate matters. He begrudged neither his time nor his strength if he could do any service for his neighbor.

He helped out with money, too, and if he didn't have any would put his signature to notes and sometimes had to pay dearly for that. Fyodor Mikhailovich's kindness was sometimes at cross-purposes with the interests of our family, and I was sometimes vexed by his unlimited kindness, but still I had to admire him when I saw what happiness he derived from the opportunity to do some good deed.

Strakhov writes that Dostoevsky was *envious.* But whom then did he envy? Everyone interested in Russian literature knows that Fyodor Mikhailovich worshiped Pushkin's genius all his life, and that the best article celebrating the great poet was the speech given by Fyodor Mikhailovich in Moscow at the unveiling of the Pushkin monument.

It is difficult to concede envy for the talent of Count Leo Tolstoy in Fyodor Mikhailovich, if we bear in mind what my husband wrote about him in his articles in *Diary of a Writer.* Take for example the *Diary* for January, 1877, when, in discussing the hero of [Tolstoy's] *Childhood and Youth,* Fyodor Mikhailovich stated that it was "a highly important psychological study of a child's inner world, astoundingly written." In the February issue, my husband calls Tolstoy "an artist of rare stature." In the *Diary* for July–August he sees in *Anna Karenina* "a fact of special import which could be our answer to Europe, which we could hold up to Europe." Further in the same article he says, "It is limned with poetic genuis in the novel's great scene, the scene of the heroine's mortal illness." At the end of the article he says, "People like the author of *Anna Karenina* are society's teachers—our teachers—and we are merely their pupils."

As for the famous novelist Goncharov, Fyodor Mikhailovich not only valued his "great intellect" but had a high regard for his talent, was genuinely fond of him, and called him his favorite author.[14]

My husband's attitude to Turgenev in his youth was deeply admiring. In a letter to his brother of November 16, 1845, he wrote of Turgenev, "But, brother, what a man he is! I too have practically fallen in love with him. A poet, a talent, an aristocrat, handsome, rich, intelligent, cultivated, twenty-five years old—if nature denied him anything, I don't know what it was. And finally, an unswervingly direct character, a splendid character wrought in a good school."

In later years Fyodor Mikhailovich's views diverged from Turgenev's, but in a letter of March 28, 1877, Turgenev wrote, "I resolved to write this letter to you despite the misunderstandings which have arisen between us and which caused a break in our personal relations. You have no doubt, I feel sure, that these misunderstandings could have no possible influence on my evaluation of your first-rate talent and of the high place you occupy by right in our literature."[15] At the Pushkin memorial festivities in Moscow in 1880, Fyodor Mikhailovich referred to Pushkin's Tatyana in these terms: "A positive type of Russian woman of such beauty is almost unique in our imaginative literature—except, perhaps, for the image of Liza in Turgenev's *A Nest of Gentlefolk.*"

Shall I mention Fyodor Mikhailovich's feelings toward the poet Nekrasov, who remained precious to him from the memories of his youth, and whom he called "the great poet who created the great Vlas"? Fyodor Mikhailovich's article at the time of Nekrasov's death, in which he said, "He stands right after Pushkin and Lermontov in the hierarchy of poets, that is, those who brought something new to Russian literature," has been acknowledged by men of letters to be the best article written on the occasion of the poet's passing.

These were my husband's attitudes toward the talent and the work of our distinguished writers, and Strakhov's statement that Dostoevsky was "envious" is cruelly unjust.

But an even more glaring injustice is Strakhov's statement that my husband was "dissolute," that he "was drawn to nasty acts and he bragged about them." As proof of this, Strakhov cites a scene from *The Possessed* which "Katkov refused to publish, but Dostoevsky read to many people here."

For artistry of characterization of one of the novel's chief characters, Nikolai Stavrogin, Fyodor Mikhailovich had to impute to him some odious crime. It is true that Katkov did not want to publish this chapter of the novel and asked its author to change it. Fyodor Mikhailovich was chagrined by the rejection and, to test the correctness of Katkov's reaction, read this chapter to his friends Pobedonostsev, Maikov, Strakhov and others. But this was not to show off, as Strakhov explains it, but to seek their opinion and, as it were, judgment of himself. And when they all found the scene "too real," my husband began to compose a new version of this scene which he considered indispensable for the characterization of Stavrogin.

There were several variants, among which was the scene in the bath house (an actual event, which someone had described to my husband).[16] In this episode a criminal role was played by "a governess." Therefore the persons to whom my husband narrated this variant (Strakhov included) and from whom he sought counsel, expressed the opinion that this might provoke from readers reproaches that Fyodor Mikhailovich was accusing "governesses" of such dishonorable acts, and was thereby putting himself in opposition to the so-called "woman question." In the same way, people used to reproach Dostoevsky at one time for having portrayed the student Raskolnikov as a murderer, alleging that he was thereby accusing our younger generation, our students, of committing such crimes.

And now Strakhov in his spite does not hesitate to ascribe this version of a novel, this foul role of Stavrogin, to Fyodor Mikhailovich himself, forgetting that the perpetration of a profligacy so refined requires large sums of money and is accessible only to the very rich—whereas my husband was in financial straits all his life. Strakhov's reference to Professor P. A. Viskovatov in this connection is even more striking to me, since the professor was never even in our house, and Fyodor Mikhailovich regarded him as a rather lightweight person. The story he tells in his letter to Maikov about meeting a certain Russian in Dresden bears this out.[17]

For my own part, I can testify to the fact that, notwithstanding his sometimes very graphic portrayal of base acts committed by characters in his novels, my husband was completely alien to "dissoluteness" all his life. It is obvious that a great artist's talent makes it unnecessary for him to commit the crimes perpetrated by his characters. Otherwise one would have to admit that Dostoevsky himself did away with somebody, since he succeeded in depicting Raskolnikov's murder of two women with such great artistry!

It is with profound gratitude that I think back on Fyodor Mikhailovich's treatment of me, how he kept me away from the reading of immoral novels and how indignant he was when I, because of my youth, told him an off-color story someone had told me. My husband was always extremely restrained in his speech and did not permit "cynical" expressions. Everyone who remembers him will doubtless agree with this.

When I first read Strakhov's contemptible letter, I resolved to protest. But how to do it? Too much time had elapsed to respond to the letter itself. It appeared in October of 1913, and I did not learn of it until almost a year later. And, in fact, what would a reply printed in the newspapers amount to? It would be lost in the current news, would be forgotten, and how many people would even read it? I began to seek counsel from my friends and acquaintances, certain of whom had known my late husband.

Their opinions differed. Some said that these foul slanders should be treated with the contempt they deserved. They maintained that Dostoevsky's importance in Russian and world literature was so great that these libels could not harm his radiant memory. They pointed out also that the publication of [Strakhov's] letter had not even evoked any response in the current press, so clearly did most writers perceive the nature of the slander and the slanderer.

Others, on the contrary, said that I must protest, bearing in mind the proverb, *"Calomniez, calomniez, il en reste toujours quelque chose!"*[18] They said that the fact that I, who had dedicated my entire life to serving my husband and his memory, was unable to refute this calumny might lead to the conclusion that there was some truth in it. My silence might appear to be a confirmation of the slander.

Many of those who were outraged by Strakhov's letter, however, considered that *my* denial alone was inadequate, and that those friends and people with fond memories of Fyodor Mikhailovich should write a protest against Strakhov's vilification. Several persons undertook to compose a protest and collect signatures for it. Others wished to express their outrage in individual letters. Many of my friends said that, in counterweight to the defamation, one should append articles of reminiscence to the protest, which would appear in the journals at different times and show Fyodor Mikhailovich as a rarely kind and responsive human being. Following the advice of friends, therefore, I append both my protest and my articles to my memoirs.

In my conversations with many people on the subject of this

wretched letter which so darkened my last years, I asked them how they understood it. What was Strakhov's motivation for writing such a letter? Most of them inclined to the opinion that it was *jalousie de métier,* so common in the literary world; that Fyodor Mikhailovich in his honesty and perhaps his sharpness had given offense to Strakhov (who even mentions this himself), and that he thus developed the desire to take revenge, even if on a dead man. He did not dare to express his feelings in print, for he knew he would arouse too many defenders of Dostoevsky's memory against himself, and quarreling with people was not in Strakhov's nature.

One of those who knew him intimately expressed the thought that he hoped through his letter to "blacken, to debase Dostoevsky in Tolstoy's eyes." When I indicated some doubt of that assumption, my interlocutor gave me a rather original analysis of Strakhov:

> Who, in essence, was Strakhov? He was a type of "noble sponger" vanished in our time but quite common in the old days. You remember that he would stay with Tolstoy, with Fet, with Danilevsky for months on end, and in winter he would go to friends on fixed days to dine and carry rumors and gossip from house to house. As a writer and philosopher he was of small interest, but as a guest he was in universal demand, for he could always tell you something new about Tolstoy, since he was considered his friend. He set great store by that friendship, and because he had a high opinion of himself it is possible that he regarded himself as someone Tolstoy relied on.
>
> What then must have been Strakhov's indignation when Tolstoy, on learning that Dostoevsky was dead, called him his "moral support" and expressed genuine sorrow at never having met him?[19] It is possible that Tolstoy admired Dostoevsky's talent often and talked about him, and that Strakhov was jarred by this. And in order to put an end to this admiration, he decided to direct a series of slanders against Dostoevsky in order to darken his bright image in Tolstoy's eyes.
>
> Possibly also Strakhov had the idea of avenging himself on Dostoevsky for some offense inflicted at one time, by blackening him for posterity—since, seeing the degree of public fascination commanded by his friend Tolstoy's genius, he might well assume that his correspondence would be published later and thus the malicious goal would be achieved, even though many, many years afterwards.

Since I do not share my interlocutor's rather special opinion, I shall conclude this painful episode in my life with the words of Strakhov's own letter: ". . . that every variety of loathsomeness can live side by side with nobility in the same human being."

An Afterword to My Reminiscences

Throughout my life it has always seemed a kind of mystery to me that my good husband not only loved and respected me as many husbands love and respect their wives, but almost worshiped me, as though I were some special being created just for him. And this was true not only at the beginning of our marriage but through all the remaining years of it, up to his very death. Whereas in reality I was not distinguished for my good looks, nor did I possess talent nor any special intellectual cultivation, and I had no more than a secondary (gymnasium) education. And yet, despite all that, I earned the profound respect, almost the adoration* of a man so creative and so brilliant.

This enigma was cleared up for me somewhat when I read V. V. Rozanov's note to a letter of Strakhov dated January 5, 1890, in his book *Literary Exiles* (p. 208). Let me quote.

No one, not even a "friend," can make us better. But it is a great happiness in life to meet a person of quite different construction, different bent, completely dissimilar views who, while *always remaining himself* and in no wise echoing us nor currying favor with us (as sometimes happens) and not trying to insinuate his soul (and an insincere soul at that!) into our psyche, into our muddle, into our tangle, would stand as a firm wall, as a check to our follies and our irrationali-

*Those who have read my cherished husband's letters to me will not consider my words boastful. (A.G.D.)

ties, which every human being has. Friendship lies in *contradiction* and not in agreement. Verily, God granted me Strakhov as a teacher and my friendship with him, my feelings for him were ever a kind of firm wall on which I felt I could always lean, or rather rest. And it won't let you fall, and it gives warmth.

In truth, my husband and I were persons of "quite different construction, different bent, completely dissimilar views." But we always remained ourselves, in no way echoing nor currying favor with one another, neither of us trying to meddle with the other's soul, neither I with his psyche nor he with mine. And in this way my good husband and I, both of us, felt ourselves free in spirit.

Fyodor Mikhailovich, who reflected so much and in such solitude on the deepest problems of the human heart, doubtless prized my non-interference in his spiritual and intellectual life. And therefore he would sometimes say to me, "You are the only woman who ever understood me!" (That was what he valued above all.) He looked on me as a rock on which he felt he could lean, or rather rest. "And it won't let you fall, and it gives warmth."

It is this, I believe, which explains the astonishing trust my husband had in me and in all my acts, although nothing I ever did transcended the limits of the ordinary. It was these mutual attitudes which enabled both of us to live all the fourteen years of our married life in the greatest happiness possible for human beings on earth.

ANNA DOSTOEVSKY
1916

Notes

Chapter One: Childhood and Youth

1. A verst is thirty-five hundred feet, or about two-thirds of a mile.
2. The Swedish name for Turku, Finland.
3. Mikelli, Finland.
4. Found in Russian Orthodox churches. A large square of linen fabric painted as if Christ's crucified body had been wrapped in it for the tomb.
5. A desyatina is equal to 2.7 acres.
6. In addition to Anna there was an older sister, Maria (Masha) and a younger brother, Ivan (Vanya).
7. Finnish carriages with their harnesses decorated with bells and ribbons. They made their appearance in St. Petersburg during Carnival week.
8. Secondary school (the Russian word is *gimnaziya*). In Anna Grigoryevna's time, there was a seven-year system for eligible pupils between the ages of ten and seventeen or eighteen.

Chapter Two: My Acquaintance with Dostoevsky and Our Marriage

1. *The Gambler.*
2. In discussing the length of a literary work, Dostoevsky habitually used the printer's term "signature" (a printed sheet folded in multiples of four pages) instead of "pages." The Russian signature of that period normally consisted of sixteen pages, except for the so-called "large format" used in certain periodicals, in which seven signatures were equivalent to ten or eleven normal signatures. Thus, the seven

contemplated "large format" signatures of *The Gambler* equalled approximately one hundred seventy-five pages. For the reader's convenience henceforth, most of Anna Grigoryevna's future references to "signatures" are given directly in terms of pages.

3. The phrase "girl of the sixties" had a very definite meaning for Russians of that period, for whom it was common practice to characterize the *Zeitgeist* of an era by naming its decade. The sixties began auspiciously with the proclamation by Alexander II of the emancipation of the serfs in 1861, followed by a number of other reforms in the military and the judiciary. It was also the period when the so-called "woman question" first came forcibly to public notice and discussion. Zeal to achieve social justice; passionate interest in the natural sciences as the truth which was to make humankind free, accompanied by a disparaging attitude toward religion; an attempt to throw off old stereotypes of clinging dependence; agitation for admission to universities or for the creation of "higher courses for women" which would enable them to pursue independent careers as teachers, doctors, lawyers; aversion to the forms of established authority—these were some of the hallmarks of the "girl of the sixties." To what extent Anna Grigoryevna actually participated in such aspirations is discussed by Helen Muchnic in her introduction to these *Reminiscences.*
4. A huge arcade of shops in St. Petersburg, facing Nevsky Prospect at one end and next to the Municipal Duma building.
5. He was actually forty-five.
6. A letter of the pre-1917 Russian alphabet, inserted after consonants but having no phonetic value of its own.
7. Actually, *Crime and Punishment* was not yet completed. A large part of it had already appeared in installments in the *Russian Messenger,* but the last two sections were dictated to Anna Grigoryevna by Dostoevsky for inclusion in the November and December, 1866, issues, after *The Gambler* was finished.
8. The Petrashevsky circle was a group of young admirers of the French Utopian socialists. Between 1846 and 1849 they met secretly at the home of M. V. Petrashevsky to discuss politics and literature. In the wave of hysteria which swept Russia after the European revolutionary uprisings of 1848, the group was caught and arrested, and twenty-one of their number (including Dostoevsky) were sentenced to death. Although the sentence was later commuted to prison terms of varying lengths at hard labor in Siberia, the condemned prisoners were forced to undergo the experience of being prepared for public execution. They were then informed at the last moment that their lives were being spared through the Tsar's infinite mercy. Dostoevsky's original death sentence was commuted to four years in fetters at hard labor followed by an indefinite term in Siberia as a common soldier.

9. It is questionable whether this statement conveys Dostoevsky's real feelings. In *The Idiot* he gives the following speech to the hero, Prince Myshkin:

> To execute a man for murder is a punishment incomparably greater than the crime itself. To be executed is incomparably more terrible than to be murdered by a highwayman. . . . There is a death sentence, and the whole horrible torture resides in the fact that there is no escape. . . . Who can tell whether human nature is able to endure this without going mad? Why this hideous, unnecessary, useless humiliation? Perhaps there is some man who has been sentenced to death, been exposed to this torture and has then been told, "You can go, you are reprieved. Perhaps such a man could tell us."

10. The original title of *The Gambler* was *Roulettenburg*.
11. Not accurate. *Time* was closed down by government censorship in April, 1863, and was succeeded by *The Epoch*. When Mikhail Dostoevsky died in July, 1864, Fyodor Mikhailovich became *The Epoch*'s publisher until its demise a year later, and in this capacity he assumed personal responsibility for the journal's debts, which amounted to thirty-three thousand rubles.
12. "Milyukov refers to this episode in his reminiscences in the *Historical Messenger* in 1881." (A.G.D.) Actually, Milyukov's memoir first appeared in *Russian Antiquity*. He cites the following dialogue between himself and Dostoevsky:

> "How about doing it this way? Let's get a few of our friends together. You tell them the plot of the novel, we'll keep the different sections in mind, divide it up by chapters and pool our efforts. I'm sure no one will refuse to take part. Afterwards you can look it all over and smooth out the rough spots, or whatever contradictions might show up. If you collaborate, you might be able to finish by the deadline. You can hand the novel over to Stellovsky and escape his clutches. And if you don't feel like giving away your plot like that, we can think up a new plot."
> "No," [Dostoevsky] answered with finality. "I'll never sign my name to somebody else's work."

13. An affectionate diminutive, literally "little dove."
14. I.e., his sister Vera, who was married to a physician, Alexander Ivanov. They had seven children, of whom Dostoevsky's favorite was his deeply beloved niece Sofya Alexandrovna (Sonya or Sonechka). Dostoevsky had a high regard for his niece's intelligence and esthetic judgment, and his letters to her contain many confidences about his creative work and the details of his personal life. He dedicated *The Idiot* to her and named his first-born daughter after her.

15. A very basic Russian dish consisting of hulled grain, usually buckwheat or semolina. Used as a vegetable or as a cereal.
16. "Letter to Baron A. E. Wrangel, included in the *Biography* on p. 288." (A.G.D.) This probably refers to a letter of February 18, 1866, since there is no extant letter of the end of 1866. ". . . You, at least, are happy in your family, but fate has denied me this great and *only* human happiness."
17. There is no evidence that Anna Korvin-Krukovskaya was ever actually engaged to Dostoevsky, nor that he broke the engagement because of ideological considerations, although it is true that she was a political radical. According to her younger sister, Sofya Kovalevskaya, who wrote a book, *Vospominaniya detstva* (Memories of Childhood), Dostoevsky proposed marriage to Anna but was rejected by her. Sofya quotes her sister as telling her:

> He needs an entirely different kind of wife from me. His wife will have to dedicate herself to him utterly, utterly, to give her whole life to him, to think about nothing but him. And I can't do that—I want to live myself! . . . He always seems to be taking possession of me and sucking me up into himself. When I'm with him, I can never be myself.

18. *The Gambler* contains many autobiographical elements. It reflects Dostoevsky's passionate infatuation with roulette and with his mistress, Polina Suslova, during a European trip with her in 1863, with a disastrous stopover at the gambling tables of Baden-Baden. Anna Grigoryevna's "literary" judgment of the novel should be noted: "I was sympathetic to the grandmother who gambled away her fortune, and to Mr. Astley; but my contempt was aroused by Polina." It is interesting that the name of Polina Suslova never appears in these memoirs although Anna Grigoryevna was fully aware of her importance in Dostoevsky's life and, indeed, suffered pangs of violent jealousy which she faithfully recorded in the diary she kept in shorthand during the first year of her marriage.
19. "You and I are in the same boat."
20. She was in mourning for her father.
21. Dostoevsky's childhood was not as happy and serene as Anna Grigoryevna indicates, largely because of his relationship with his father, a man of sullen and explosive temperament who was murdered by his own serfs in 1839, when Dostoevsky was eighteen years old. A letter to his friend Wrangel in this connection is revealing:

> What troubles me for you, my friend, more than anything else, is your relationship with your father. I know, I know extremely well, from personal experience, how unbearable such unpleasant scenes are. . . . Personalities like your father are a peculiar

> mixture of the blackest suspiciousness, morbid sensitivity and generosity. I conclude these things about him even though I don't know him personally, for twice in my life I have known exactly such relationships as yours with your father.

His mother, on the other hand, is depicted by his younger brother Andrey as a woman of rare goodness, sensitivity and tenderness, possessing literary and musical talent. Dostoevsky's memories of his mother are reflected in the passages dealing with the mother of Alyosha Karamazov.

22. The episode referred to does not appear in the manuscript.
23. Not accurate. Jaclard was imprisoned in Chantiers prison in Versailles and fled to Geneva.
24. Suspect as a political radical, Jaclard was ordered by the Minister of Internal Affairs on March 22, 1887, to leave Russia within three days. On April 2 Anna Grigoryevna wrote to Pobedonostsev's wife requesting an extension. Her intercession on Jaclard's behalf roused Pobedonostsev to institute an inquiry into the matter, and she succeeded in gaining a ten-day postponement of the deportation order. (See Glossary, "Pobedonostsev.")
25. Word-play on the title of Dostoevsky's novel *Netochka Nezvanova* and on the adjective *nezvanaya,* "unbidden" or "uninvited."
26. "Letter to me of May 17, 1867." (A.G.D.)
27. "I too have read Mikhailovsky's article on Dostoevsky [A Cruel Talent]. He has accurately noted the underlying quality of [Dostoevsky's] work. He might also have mentioned that there was a similar phenomenon in French literature, namely the notorious Marquis de Sade." (Letter from Turgenev to the writer Saltykov-Shchedrin, Sept. 24, 1882.) Turgenev repeated the statement in a letter to P. V. Annenkov written the following day.
28. The famous jurist A. F. Koni describes such an instance:

> Maikov met with me, still under the spell of the first installment of *Crime and Punishment,* which he had just finished reading in the last issue of the *Russian Messenger.* "Listen to what I shall read to you," he said. "This is something astounding!" And, closing his study door so as not to be disturbed, he read aloud the famous story of Marmeladov in the tavern, and then lent me the magazine for a few days. To this day, after all these years, I am moved when I think back to the first time I read this work. And what I felt then revives in me, not in the least muted nor changed—a feeling of rapturous tenderness.

29. December 29, 1866, and January 2, 1867.

Chapter Three: The First Stage of Married Life

1. I.e., common-law marriage.
2. There is no positive proof that Milyukov was the author of the article.
3. Actually, Paul Isayev was only a few months younger than Anna Grigoryevna, as she herself indicates a few pages later in the text.
4. Actually, he was born in 1846.
5. Dostoevsky left Petersburg for Revel (the Russian name for Tallinn, capital of Estonia) in July, 1842, and again during the summer of 1846 to visit his brother Mikhail.

Chapter Four: Living Abroad

1. "Our first marital quarrel (from my stenographic notebook)." (A.G.D.)
2. "Letter of . . ." (A.G.D.) The letter has not been located, but the incident appears in Anna Grigoryevna's diary.
3. "Fedya has taken me at last to see the Sistine Madonna. No painting has ever produced such an impression on me as this. What beauty, what innocence and grief in that divine face, how much meekness, how much suffering in those eyes! Fedya sees sorrow in the Madonna's smile." (A.G.D., diary entry for April 18, 1867.) The Sistine Madonna is mentioned several times in Dostoevsky's work. Svidrigailov in *Crime and Punishment* says of his young bride-to-be: "But you know, her little face is like Raphael's Madonna. For the Sistine Madonna has a fantastic face, the face of a sorrowing Fool of God."
4. "According to Fedya, this magnificent painting can stand on the same plane with Raphael's *Madonna.* The face of Christ expresses amazing gentleness, majesty, suffering." (A.G.D., diary entry for April 20, 1867.)
5. An error. Anna Grigoryevna means Lorraine's *Acis and Galatea,* which Dostoevsky called "the Golden Age." This painting had the symbolic meaning of a secular Utopia for Dostoevsky, and he develops the theme at length three times in his work: in Stavrogin's confession *(The Possessed),* in Versilov's story of the early days of European civilization *(A Raw Youth),* and in the short story "The Dream of a Ridiculous Man." The paintings of Lorraine titled *Morning* and *Evening* are not in Dresden but in the Hermitage in Leningrad.
6. "Although the music here is good, it's rarely Beethoven or Mozart, but always Wagner (the most boring German *canaille,* notwithstanding all his fame) and every kind of trash." (Letter from Dosto-

evsky to his wife from Ems, Germany, August 7, 1879.)

7. Twenty-seven years later, in 1897, Anna Grigoryevna began the work of transcribing two notebooks of her diary entries of April 14 to August 24, 1867, describing the Dostoevskys' life in Berlin, Dresden and Baden-Baden. This work was published by N. F. Belchikov in Moscow in 1923. A third diary notebook, covering the Geneva residence of the Dostoevskys from September to December, 1867, was partially decoded over a period of several years, starting in the mid-1950's, by a Leningrad stenographer, T. M. Pomeshanskaya. The results were published in *Literaturnoye nasledstvo* (Literary Heritage), Volume 86, in Moscow, in 1973. A fourth diary notebook mentioned by Anna Grigoryevna in her last will and testament has not been discovered.
8. ". . . In our women, one observes more and more sincerity, perseverence, seriousness and honesty, truth-seeking and sacrifice. . . . Woman is more persevering and more patient in work; she is more *serious* than man, aspires to the cause for the sake of the cause and not for appearance's sake. And in that cause, is it not from that direction that we can expect great help?" ("Something About Lies," *Diary of a Writer* for 1873.) Dostoevsky's attitude toward what is today termed "women's liberation" but was then known as "the woman question" is a good deal more complicated than Anna Grigoryevna indicates. On the one hand, he savagely parodies "Nihilist women" in his novels and makes it appear that higher education and careers for women go hand in hand with sexual promiscuity, social coarseness and physical repulsiveness. On the other, he maintained personal relations of close mutual friendship and respect with highly intelligent and educated "liberated" women of liberal or radical views: A. P. Filosofova, Sofya Kovalevskaya, and Anna Korvin-Krukovskaya, among others. He also used his connections with highly placed reactionary figures, such as Pobedonostsev, on more than one occasion to intercede on behalf of radical women in political trouble. (See Beatrice Stillman, "Sofya Kovalevskaya: Growing Up in the Sixties," *Russian Literature Triquarterly,* No. 9, Spring, 1974.)
9. A gap in the manuscript. Actually the story appeared in the *National Zeitung* of June 22, 1867: "At the last general meeting of the Stenographic Institute, a Russian lady was present who has studied the Gabelsberger System and uses this system frequently in St. Petersburg."
10. Anton Berezowski, a Polish émigré, attempted to assassinate Tsar Alexander II at the World's Fair in Paris on May 25, 1867. Almost the entire Paris press, as well as the legal profession (which organized a demonstration under the slogan *"Vive la Pologne!"*) rose to Berezowski's defense, viewing his attempt as an act of justifiable reprisal for Russia's partition of Poland. Berezowski was sentenced

by a Paris jury to life imprisonment at hard labor. Dostoevsky, who was opposed to capital punishment, was nonetheless outraged by the jury's focus on the historical context of Berezowski's act rather than on the act itself, an approach which went counter to Dostoevsky's precept of man's personal responsibility for his deeds. "I am terribly shaken by the event in Paris," he wrote Maikov on July 28. "Those Paris lawyers who screamed 'Vive la Pologne!' are really something. Ugh—what loathsomeness, and mostly, what stupidity and what a bureaucratic mentality! This strengthens me even more in my old feeling that it is an advantage to us, to some extent, that Europe does not know us, or knows us so execrably."

11. Dostoevsky, as a "political criminal," had been stripped of all property rights after the Petrashevsky trial in 1849. On April 7, 1858, Alexander II presented a decree to the State Senate restoring Dostoevsky's former right of hereditary nobility. The right to reside in Petersburg, however, was not granted until almost two years later (December, 1859) when the Emperor gave him permission to live in Petersburg—but under secret police surveillance.
12. Dmitry Karakozov, a Russian revolutionary youth, had made an unsuccessful attempt to assassinate Alexander II in April, 1866, for which he was tried and executed.
13. According to A.G.D.'s diary, he promised to be back in four days, but stayed for eleven.
14. There is a gap in the manuscript at this point. A letter exists in which Dostoevsky told Strakhov that Belinsky "used obscene expressions about Christ" (May 18, 1871). Anna Grigoryevna, however, tends to oversimplify the complex relationship between Belinsky and Dostoevsky. They doubtless did disagree on religious questions, but these differences of opinion were not the underlying cause of their rupture. (See Glossary, "Belinsky.")
15. "*Niva*, 1884. Article by Y. P. Polonsky, 'The Reminiscences of A. Y. Golovacheva-Panayeva.' " (A.G.D.) Dostoevsky's problems with the *Contemporary* circle were both literary and psychological. The trouble began with Belinsky's negative response to Dostoevsky's second novel, *The Double,* in which he complained that it was "fantastic" and that the fantastic belonged "only in lunatic asylums, not in literature. It is the business of doctors and not of poets." This review, which appeared in February, 1846, plunged Dostoevsky into deep depression. The problem was complicated by Dostoevsky's social gaucherie and his increasingly strained personal relations with the members of the coterie. He offered his next story, *Mr. Prokharchin,* not to the *Contemporary* but to a rival publication, Krayevsky's *National Notes.* "I can tell you," he wrote his brother Mikhail in November, 1846, "that I have had the unpleasant experience of a final break with the *Contemporary* in the person of Nekrasov. . . . Now they're saying that I'm infected with

amour propre, have an inflated opinion of myself, and have transferred myself to Krayevsky because Maikov praises me." (See Glossary, "Panayeva," "Nekrasov," "Turgenev.")

16. Probably inaccurate, since Babikov died in 1873. The article apparently never reached him; he wrote to Dostoevsky at the end of December, 1867, complaining that he had been waiting in vain all year for the promised article.
17. It must be assumed that Dostoevsky fulfilled his intention at least partially in an article he wrote about Belinsky and Herzen, "Old-Timers" ("Starye lyudi"), published in *Diary of a Writer* for 1873. Maikov, who had read the original article, was convinced that it was unpublishable. "It conveys the impression," he wrote Dostoevsky, "that its author started out by wanting to tell the whole story; but when he began writing it down he realized that it was impossible. No, this kind of thing is possible only in *posthumous* memoirs."
18. "Letter to Maikov, July 28, 1867." (A.G.D.)
19. This is evidently a reflection of Dostoevsky's reaction. "With the soul of a clerk, without ideas and with the eyes of a boiled fish endowed by God—as if for fun—with brilliant talent." (Letter from Dostoevsky to A. E. Wrangel, November 9, 1856.)
20. There are two fuller "Dostoevsky" versions of the celebrated quarrel between Dostoevsky and Turgenev, to which Anna Grigoryevna devotes a single sentence in these pages. One of these versions is contained in a letter from Dostoevsky to Maikov on August 16, 1867. The other is Anna Grigoryevna's own account, which she confided to her diary. (See Glossary, "Turgenev.")
21. She was pregnant.
22. "This reaction is reflected in his novel *The Idiot.*" (A.G.D.) The painting was Hans Holbein's *The Dead Christ.* Anna Grigoryevna's diary entry for August 12 reads: "In the city museum there, Fyodor Mikhailovich saw Hans Holbein's painting. It struck him with terrific force, and he said to me then, 'A painting like that can make you lose your faith.' "
23. Dostoevsky's first literary work was a translation of Balzac's *Eugenie Grandet;* his last one, the Pushkin speech, compares Balzac's Rastignac with Raskolnikov, the hero of *Crime and Punishment,* in relation to the superman theory, i.e., the inherent right of the superman to transgress the codes of human behavior. Like Balzac, George Sand strongly influenced the young Dostoevsky's developing *Weltanschauung.* He translated her novella *La derniére Aldini* when he was twenty-three years old. At a period when many other Russian writers were condemning her savagely because of the potentially "pernicious" effect on Russian womanhood of her advanced sexual views, Dostoevsky continued to hold her in the highest regard. V. V. Timofeyeva quotes him as saying, "In all the

world, there is only one woman writer worthy of the name—and that is George Sand." His obituary article for her said, "[She] was not a thinker but one of the most clear-sighted prophets . . . of a happier future which mankind will achieve through the attainment of the ideas she optimistically and magnanimously believed in all her life." (*Diary of a Writer,* June, 1876.)

24. Erroneous. The first part of Balzac's *Les parents pauvres* is *La cousine Bétte.* And Victor Hugo's novel *Les misérables* is inadvertently given the title *Les humiliés et les offensés* by Anna Grigoryevna—a translation from Dostoevsky's novel *The Insulted and Injured (Unizhonnye i oskorblyonye).*
25. Dostoevsky's favorite poem was the refrain from N. P. Ogaryov's "Tyurma" (Prison), written in 1857–58, when Dostoevsky himself was still in Siberian exile:

    From the Bible, I foretold the future
    And I thirsted, and I dreamed alone
    That by the will of fate would come to me
    A prophet's life, a prophet's grief, a prophet's death.

26. The first congress of the League for Peace and Freedom was held in Geneva September 9 to 12, 1867.
27. "The Case of the Landowner's Daughter Olga Umetskaya, Accused of Arson, and of Her Parents, Vladimir and Ekaterina Umetsky, Accused of Abuse of Parental Power" (headline in the newspaper *Moscow,* September 23 and 24, 1867). The Umetskys were landowners in the town of Kashir. As the trial continued a picture of barbaric child abuse came to light. The fifteen-year-old daughter Olga tried to retaliate by setting fire to her parents' house on four occasions. In Dostoevsky's first plan for *The Idiot,* Olga Umetskaya was the prototype of the character Mignon. Although the Umetsky case was eliminated from the final version of the book, Dostoevsky utilized certain elements of it in his elaboration of the idea of "the accidental family," with which he was preoccupied at that period.
28. As a result of Alexander II's judicial reforms of 1864, the old class-based courts were replaced by institutions to which all classes of Russian society were subject. In the new courts, as distinct from the pre-reform courts, hearings were open to the public, and there was a jury and an attorney for the defense. Reports of court sessions were printed in the newspapers. Dostoevsky's fascination with the content and procedure of jury trials was reflected in *The Idiot,* in *Diary of a Writer,* and most notably in *The Brothers Karamazov.*
29. "Those were the exact words with which Fyodor Mikhailovich described his first wife's character in a letter to Baron A. E. Wrangel on March 31, 1865." (A.G.D.)
30. There is a gap in the manuscript after the line ". . . do I see the

image of my dead Sonya." The balance of the quotation has been supplied by the Russian editors.

31. Dostoevsky's name appears on a list of persons under police surveillance for 1867: "Secret. To the Chief of the Odessa Police Department. I entrust to your Excellency the mission of carrying out a comprehensive search of the baggage of Retired Lieut. Fyodor Dostoevsky upon his return to Russia from abroad. If anything reprehensible is found, it is to be delivered immediately to the Third Section, to the personal office of his Imperial Highness, having in the latter case first dispatched the said Dostoevsky himself to this Section, under arrest. (Signed) Major-General Mazentsov, Director of the Department of his Majesty's Personnel." (Instructions given to the Third Section No 1292 for Nov. 28, 1867. These were turned over to the chief of the Odessa District Customs Office, which in turn informed the mayor of Odessa "in absolute secrecy.")
32. The book was Paul Grimm's novel *Les mystéres du palais des czars (sous l'Empereur Nicolas I),* published in Wurzburg in 1868. For a while after its publication it was thought that the author was August Theodor Grimm, tutor to the grand dukes, who had left Russia for Germany in 1860. This theory was categorically denied by Maikov in a letter to Dostoevsky of September 17, 1868.
33. December 12, 1868.
34. Actually done in Rome in the first century B.C., mistakenly attributed to the Athenian sculptor Cleomenes.
35. Dostoevsky's interest in Voltaire developed in connection with a novel he was planning at the end of the sixties, *Atheism.* A year before he began *The Brothers Karamazov,* he wrote in his notebook: "*Memento*—for the rest of my life. . . . To write a Russian *Candide. . . .*"
36. *Lyubov* is the Russian word for "love."
37. From Dickens' *David Copperfield.* Dostoevsky again refers to himself as "Mr. Micawber" in a letter to Maikov on March 25, 1870. It is thought that Micawber may have provided the initial impetus for the character of General Ivolgin in Dostoevsky's *The Idiot.*
38. His lifelong preoccupation with problems of religious faith and doubt took the form of a project for an "enormous" new philosophical novel about a Russian who "loses his faith in God . . . runs around here and there and everywhere with the new generation, the atheists, the Slavs and the Europeans, the Russian fanatics and anchorites, the ecclesiastics . . . and finally attains both Christ and the Russian land." This plan, conceived in Florence in the spring of 1869, went through a series of transformations and was given the title *The Life of a Great Sinner.* Dostoevsky regarded it as a confession, a creative summation, and wrote to Strakhov and Maikov in the spring of 1870, "This will be my last novel." It is clear from

his letters and notebooks of this period that he was working on this novel concurrently with *The Possessed;* and gradually *The Possessed* displaced "the great sinner," although elements of his original idea are evident in the figure of Stavrogin.

39. A not quite verbatim quotation from a letter of September 17, 1869.
40. February 26, 1870.
41. "The overall title of the novel is *The Life of a Great Sinner,* but each story will have a separate title. The main question, which runs throughout all the parts, is that very question with which I have consciously and unconsciously tormented myself all through my life—the existence of God. . . ." (Letter to Maikov, March 25, 1870.)
42. "I want to make Tikhon Zadonsky the protagonist of the second story. . . . I shall, perhaps, bring forth a majestic, *positive* holy figure. . . . Who can tell? It may be that it is precisely Tikhon who will turn out to be the Russian *positive* type our literature is seeking. . . ." (Ibid.) (See Glossary, "Tikhon Zadonsky.")
43. Many European and particularly German papers, such as the *Kölnische Zeitung, Frankfurter allgemeine Zeitung* and *Neue preussische Zeitung,* were indeed printing stories to the effect that a widespread network of conspiratorial revolutionary organizations existed in Russia, and that an uprising was imminent. As to the fact that Dostoevsky foresaw that it was precisely in the Moscow Agricultural Academy that the agitations would break out, no corroborative source exists other than Anna Grigoryevna's memoirs.
44. The underlying theme of *The Possessed* was based on an actual event. A student at the Moscow Agricultural Academy and classmate of Ivan Snitkin, one Ivan Ivanov, was murdered. It came out at the trial that he had belonged to a secret society headed by the revolutionary terrorist Sergey Nechayev, who ordered him killed. Nechayev was the prototype for Dostoevsky's Pyotr Verkhovensky in *The Possessed.* (See Glossary, "Nechayev.")
45. "All year I have done nothing but tear up and make changes. I have scribbled over such heaps of paper that I have lost even my system for referring to my own notes. I have changed the entire plan and rewritten the entire first part no less than ten times." (Letter to Strakhov, December 2, 1870.)
46. The dispatch of October 17 (not 19), 1870, informed the various Foreign Offices of Russia's decision to abrogate the second article of the Treaty of Paris of 1856, on the neutralization of the Black Sea. All the great powers agreed to review this provision of the treaty and to grant Russia the right to maintain her naval fleet on the Black Sea, as was later confirmed at the London Conference of 1871.
47. A slip of the pen. The date of the letter is April 4. Dostoevsky replied to it on April 21.

48. Maikov advised Dostoevsky to ask the Literary Fund for four hundred rubles, not one hundred—that is probably an error in the telegram. At the same time, he requested the Fund to extend the sum of five hundred rubles to Dostoevsky to help out with the lawsuit against Stellovsky. The Fund replied that it could extend the money not to help out with the lawsuit, but as "a loan with security." Anna Grigoryevna exaggerates when she speaks of the Literary Fund's biased and hostile attitude toward Dostoevsky. The Fund did not object to giving Dostoevsky the loan he needed; but they did require security, probably because Dostoevsky had been living abroad for over four years, and his contacts with Russian literary circles had almost ceased. It should be noted that when Dostoevsky was brought to trial in 1873 in connection with an article written by Prince Meschersky, it was V. P. Gayevsky, president of the Literary Fund, who served as his defense attorney.
49. The quotation has been supplied by the Russian editors from Dostoevsky's letter to Maikov of April 21, since there is a gap in the manuscript at this point.
50. The quotation is not verbatim.
51. The notebooks were later published and are an invaluable source for study of the creative process in Dostoevsky.
52. "*Biografiya i pis'ma* (Biography and Letters), p. 294." (A.G.D.)

Chapter Five: In Russia Once Again

1. The trip actually took place at the end of July or the beginning of August.
2. Anna Grigoryevna kept a list of all the books in Dostoevsky's library during the last period of his life, in a notebook discovered by L. P. Grossman in the spring of 1917.
3. The record books for the journals *Time* and *The Epoch* were not located among Anna Grigoryevna's archives, but E. M. Dostoevskaya, the daughter of Dostoevsky's brother Mikhail, presented a similar book to the Dostoevsky Museum in the late 1920's. It is now preserved in the Lenin Library.
4. Dostoevsky's letters contain several mentions of the Tarasov house, with which he was threatened on more than one occasion:

> As a matter of fact (and I'm not trying to make a *mot* or speaking for effect) the debtors' prison, from one point of view, would have been quite useful to me—as reality, as raw material, a second *Notes from the House of the Dead*—in a word, four or five thousand rubles' worth of material. But I've only just married, after all, and besides that, could I stand a stifling hot summer in the Tarasov house? That was the unanswerable

question. And if I couldn't write in the Tarasov house because of exacerbated epileptic seizures, then how could I settle my debts? [Letter to A. M. Maikov, August 16, 1867.]

5. Most of the literary critics of Dostoevsky's day were incapable of comprehending the innovative form of his work. The reviewer for *The Cause* praised the "humanitarian feelings" which had inspired Dostoevsky to write *The Brothers Karamazov,* but considered the novel highly unsatisfactory in the artistic sense. The eminent critic V. V. Chukko said of it: "The novel glows in spots with pages of striking talent; but as a whole, in its entirety, it consists of various absurdities and incongruities . . . and finally bores you to tears with its length and repetitiveness." Dostoevsky himself saw the immense scale of his novels and their multiplicity of themes as a "defect," although he realized that he could not write in any other way. As he wrote to Strakhov:

> You have pointed out my chief defect with horrible precision. Yes, I have suffered from it and still suffer from it. I am utterly incapable, have not yet learned, to control my means. I cram a profusion of individual stories and novels into one, so that both proportion and harmony are lacking. . . . But there is something even worse. Carried away by a poetic surge and failing to take account of my means, I undertake to express an artistic concept beyond my powers.

6. This is the first mention of the fact that Dostoevsky suffered from emphysema as well as epilepsy.
7. Anna Grigoryevna is referring here to Maikov and Strakhov.
8. Dostoevsky's younger brother, Nikolai, was educated as a civil engineer and architect. He worked at first in Estonia, then in Petersburg; but he was unemployed because of illness from the 1860's on, and Dostoevsky, who felt a special love and sympathy for him, helped him constantly.
9. Anna Grigoryevna mentions the dinner party for Danilevsky again in an almost identical but slightly fuller version in Chapter Six, in which she says the party took place at the end of the following winter of 1872–73. Danilevsky was no longer in Petersburg at that time, however, as evidenced by a letter from Strakhov of January 14, 1873. Therefore the two accounts of the party have been combined and placed where they chronologically belong, during the winter of 1871–72.
10. Citadel.
11. Long, open carriages with benches running down the middle, back to back.
12. A. A. Roikhel, director of the Staraya Russa Mineral Waters Administration.
13. "Letter to me of May 30, 1872." (A.G.D.)

Chapter Six: The Years 1872 and 1873

1. The liberal as well as the radical press was almost unanimously negative in its reception of *The Possessed,* attacking its political viewpoint while ignoring it as literature. Even the reviewer for the conservative *Russian World,* V. G. Avseyenko, reproached Dostoevsky with prolixity, general absence of artistry, and "grotesqueness." (He later softened his approach in an article for the *Russian Messenger.*) Perhaps the only article which maintained a calm and relatively objective tone was N. K. Mikhailovsky's "Literary and Journalistic Jottings" in the magazine *National Notes* in 1873.
2. Actually, the idea for *Diary of a Writer* was conceived even before that. Dostoevsky mentions it in a letter to Baron Wrangel as early as 1865.
3. The *Citizen* was founded in 1872. Meshchersky applied for official permission to hire Dostoevsky as editor on December 15 of that year. Since Dostoevsky, as a former "political criminal," was under secret police surveillance, Meshchersky had to address his application to the director of the Third Section (i.e., the political police). Dostoevsky's readiness to assume editorship of the journal was a consequence not only of his difficult financial situation, but also of his eagerness to enter the literary and public arena more directly. He was attracted by the opportunity to express his political and social views via the journal. His decision to edit *The Citizen* (probably the most reactionary of all the Petersburg magazines), coming as it did in conjunction with the publication of his novel *The Posessed* (viewed by liberal and radical critics as a libel on contemporary youth and the revolutionary movement as a whole) was interpreted almost unanimously by the Petersburg press as an indication of Dostoevsky's passage to the reactionary camp. In accepting the position of editor of the journal, Dostoevsky had hoped for complete independence and freedom of action. These hopes soon proved illusory. Meshchersky kept Dostoevsky under constant personal supervision and frequently interfered with his decisions; and the attacks of the Petersburg press markedly lowered his standing with the literary journals. It was therefore not only from Meshchersky's "enemies" that he suffered, but from almost every magazine in Petersburg, with the possible exception of *Domestic Chat.* (See Glossary, "Meshchersky.")
4. Anna Grigoryevna is evidently referring here to the critics' mixed reception of *The Idiot* and their deeply hostile response to *The Possessed.* Her opinions naturally reflect those of her husband, who was inclined to number literary critics among his "enemies." To critical articles on his work, which he usually regarded as either tendentious or shallow, he would counterpose the opinions of ordinary readers. "I was always supported not by the critics, but by the

public. Which of my critics knows the ending of *The Idiot?*—a scene of such power that it is unique in literature." (Diary entry in a notebook of 1876.)

5. "Letter to me of July 29, 1873." (A.G.D.)
6. "Jeers, stupid and vulgar, were heaped on the new editor from all sides. The author of *Crime and Punishment* and *Notes from the House of the Dead* was called a madman, a maniac, an apostate, a traitor. The public was even invited to an exhibition at the Academy of Arts to view Perov's portrait of Dostoevsky, as direct evidence that he was a lunatic who belonged in an insane asylum." (Vsevolod Solovyov, "Vospominaniya o Dostoevskom" [Reminiscences of Dostoevsky].)
7. The article appeared on January 29, 1873. The controversial quotation read:

> The senior deputy, Sultan Mahomet . . . began his speech, which he had written in the name of the entire [Kirghiz] nation. His first words, pronounced firmly and correctly, were "Your Imperial Majesty" . . . but when the Tsar broke in with the remark, "But are you speaking Russian?" Mahomet became so confused that all he could do was to mumble a few words in the Kirghiz language from his prepared speech of thanks, and after that he grew positively mute.

8. Anna Grigoryevna is mistaken in her statement that Dostoevsky "pleaded guilty, of course." Dostoevsky appeared in court but did not plead guilty. His defense attorney, V. P. Gayevsky (who was also president of the Literary Fund) argued that the Censorship Committee had no juridical power to institute a case.
9. An error. Anna Grigoryevna means the Petersburg Slavonic Benevolent Committee. The Slavonic Benevolent Society was formed out of the Committee four years later, in 1877, with the objective of providing financial aid for the Balkan Slavs and for Russian volunteers for the Russo-Turkish theaters of war.
10. It is true that Vladimir Solovyov became acquainted with Dostoevsky at the beginning of 1873, but he left for abroad the next year after defending his master's thesis, and did not return to Russia until 1877, when his real intimacy with Dostoevsky developed. Anna Grigoryevna, therefore, is probably referring here to Vladimir's brother Vsevolod, the historical novelist and literary critic, who also met Dostoevsky at that time.
11. None of these letters from Dostoevsky to Yulya Zasetskaya has been located up to the present. They were concerned primarily with religious questions: Zasetskaya had converted from Orthodoxy to Lutheranism, and Dostoevsky was attempting to bring her back into the Russian Orthodox fold.

Chapter Seven: The Years 1874 and 1875

1. "Reminiscences of Vsevolod Solovyov," *Historical Messenger*, 1881. (A.G.D.)
2. In actuality he had been no more than its nominal editor since the end of the previous year. ". . . I compile the issue, read the articles, rewrite them, and write one of my own from time to time. That is my work. As for all the rest of it, I couldn't have any idea about it, even if I wanted to." (Letter to M. P. Pogodin, November 12, 1873.)
3. *A Raw Youth.*
4. Anna Grigoryevna confuses *The Contemporary* here with *National Notes. The Contemporary* ceased publication in 1866.
5. Bad Ems was a fashionable German spa where the *haut monde* of Europe went "to take the waters"—i.e., to drink from the Kränchen and Kesselbrünnen mineral springs, which were supposed to possess remarkable curative powers for a variety of diseases. Dostoevsky was sent to Ems for treatment of his emphysema. He made four trips there, in 1874, 1875, 1876 and 1879.
6. "Letter to me of June 13, 1874." (A.G.D.)
7. "June 24, July 14, and others." (A.G.D.)
8. Anna Grigoryevna means *The Contemporary.* The last issue of *The Epoch* appeared in 1865, and Nekrasov did not become editor of *National Notes* until 1868.
9. It should be noted that *A Raw Youth* was actually published in Nekrasov's Populist-dominated *National Notes* in spite of the sharp divergence between its ideological orientation and Dostoevsky's. Conversely, in spite of the ideological affinity of Dostoevsky and Katkov, publisher of the conservative *Russian Messenger*, their personal relationship was frequently strained, and the publication of *Crime and Punishment, The Possessed,* and *The Brothers Karamazov* was marked by serious conflicts.
10. Should read "the Petersburg Slavonic Benevolent Committee."
11. I.e., since receiving permission to leave Tver and reside in Petersburg. It should be noted that Russia, both before and after the Revolution, has always had a system of internal passports.
12. With Maikov and Strakhov. His publication of *A Raw Youth* in the progressive *National Notes* led to a disagreement with them, as Dostoevsky states in a letter to Anna Grigoryevna of February 12, 1875.
13. Anna Grigoryevna is mistaken on this point. Secret surveillance of Dostoevsky was actually discontinued in the summer of 1875, but Dostoevsky himself was unaware of this fact until the spring of 1880, when he applied for removal of the surveillance through "a highly placed personage," i.e., the publicist A. A. Kireyev, a mem-

ber of Grand Duke Konstantin Nikolayevich's staff. He was then informed that he had been freed from surveillance back in 1875.

14. One pood equals thirty-six pounds.

Chapter Eight: The Years 1876 and 1877

1. The actual salutation is "Esteemed Ivan Pavlych!"
2. Dostoevsky himself was interested in spiritualism for a while and attended a seance, presided over by a medium, in February of 1876. He wrote three heavily ironic articles on the subject of spiritualism in the January, March and April, 1877, issues of *Diary of a Writer* (the last of these twice mentions the name of N. P. Wagner). Wagner and Dostoevsky first met in the summer of 1875 and not 1876, as Anna Grigoryevna states.
3. "Letter to me of July 24, 1876." (A.G.D.)
4. A small hinged windowpane used for ventilation.
5. Not accurate. Dostoevsky asked Turgenev for a loan of a hundred thalers, but Turgenev sent him only fifty. (See Glossary, "Turgenev.")
6. "The letters of both Fyodor Mikhailovich and A. F. Otto are still preserved." (A.G.D.)
7. A long cape without sleeves.
8. I.e., for copies of *Diary of a Writer.*
9. A. K. Gribbe died on January 1, 1876; therefore the purchase of his summer house was consummated in 1876, and not in 1877, as stated.
10. A sazhen is seven feet.
11. As an ardent Panslavist, Dostoevsky viewed Russia's entry into the war against Turkey as the first step in the fulfillment of Russia's historic destiny to unite, first the Slavic peoples and then all of humanity, on the basis of the Christian principles of love and brotherhood. His position was contrary to that of the liberals and radicals, who opposed Russia's participation in the war with Turkey.
12. Three years after Dostoevsky's death.
13. The fortieth day after a death, on which a memorial mass was celebrated.
14. He died in horrible agony after suffering for two years from cancer of the rectum.
15. "The Unhappy Ones" was not among Nekrasov's last poems: it was published in 1856. The confusion probably arose from the fact that Dostoevsky referred to the poem in his description of his last meeting with Nekrasov (in his lengthy obituary in *Diary of a Writer* for December, 1877):

> Nekrasov is dead. The last time I saw him before his death was one month ago. Then he looked so much like a corpse that it was strange to see that he could speak and move his lips.

. . . On the morning of the twenty-eighth I learned that he had passed away the evening before. . . . On returning home, I was unable to work. I took Nekrasov's three volumes and began to read them, starting with the first page. I sat reading all night till six o'clock in the morning, and once more I lived through those thirty years. . . .

Thereupon, as I kept reading—and I read one poem after another—my whole life passed rapidly before me. I recognized those of his poems which I read first in Siberia, when after serving my four years of penal servitude and being discharged from prison, I finally received permission to lay my hands on a book. . . . In a word, I read virtually two-thirds of everything Nekrasov wrote that night, and I understood—literally for the first time—how much Nekrasov had meant in my life as a poet. As a poet, of course. . . .

We met rarely, and only once with a wholly unreserved, warm feeling, at the very outset of our acquaintance, at the time of *Poor Folk* in 1845. But this I have already recorded. . . . After that—very soon, as I recall—we parted. Our mutual intimacy lasted no more than a few months, thanks to misunderstandings, external circumstances, and the meddling of good people. Thereafter . . . even though we frequently disagreed . . . we said strange things when we used to meet from time to time, as though something that had begun in our youth, in 1845, was persisting in our lives; as though this refused to be interrupted and could not be, even though we sometimes did not see one another for years and years. Thus, once (I believe it was in 1863) he handed me a little volume of his poems and pointed to one of them, "The Unhappy Ones," and told me, "When I wrote this, I was thinking about you (i.e., about my life in Siberia). This was written about you."

16. Most of the Nekrasov obituaries which appeared in the Petersburg press concentrated their attention on Nekrasov's alleged "vices" and "sharp business practices" rather than on his writing. Dostoevsky's article contained a literary analysis in which he ranked Nekrasov immediately below Pushkin and Lermontov in the hierarchy of Russian poets, and also attempted a psychological explanation of the contradictions in Nekrasov's personality and behavior.

Chapter Nine: The Years 1878 and 1879

1. An agricultural museum and lecture hall in Petersburg.
2. This lecture at which both Tolstoy and Dostoevsky were in the audience took place on March 10, 1878. For more details, see Chapter Twelve.
3. Dostoevsky's daughter Lyubov, who was six years old when

Alyosha died, states in her memoirs that the doctors explained that the child's death was due to "the malformation of his skull, which had prevented his brain from expanding." She adds that the death occurred so quickly that she and her brother Fedya were in the room when it happened, and that she had a fit of hysterics when she saw her parents sobbing over the small, lifeless body.

4. In her *Notes to the Works of F. M. Dostoevsky,* Anna Grigoryevna quotes Father Zossima's remarks to a grieving mother in *The Brothers Karamazov:*

> "And I shall pray for the peace of your little boy's soul. What was his name?"
> "Alexey, Father."
> "A sweet name. After Alexey, the man of God?"
> "Yes, Father—Alexey the man of God!"
> "What a saint he was! I will pray for him, mother, and I will remember your sorrow in my prayers, and I will pray for your husband's health. But it was a sin for you to leave him. Go to your husband and care for him. Your little one will see from heaven that you have forsaken his father, and will weep over you. . . . For how can he come into your house when you say the house is hateful to you? And to whom can he go if he finds you not together, his father and mother? You dream about him now, and you grieve. But later he will send you gentle dreams. Go to your husband, mother. Go this very day."

The character of Father Zossima is a composite of Father Ambrosius and Tikhon Zadonsky (See entries in Glossary). In the first chapter of Book 7 of *The Brothers Karamazov,* "The Breath of Corruption," Alyosha is traumatized by the fact that the saint's remains decompose and give off a stench. The real Father Ambrosius was in the habit of saying, "During my life I received much glory from people, and therefore there will be a stench from me." Dostoevsky's descriptions of the hermitage and of Zossima's cell were also modeled upon Optina Pustyn.

5. Anna Grigoryevna's estimate of audience reactions to her husband's readings was not exaggerated. S. V. Pavlova, wife of the world-renowned physiologist Ivan Pavlov, wrote of one of Dostoevsky's readings at the Petersburg Pedagogical Courses in 1879:

> Suddenly I heard a loud voice and, looking at the stage, I saw "The Prophet." Dostoevsky's face was transformed. His eyes flashed lightning which seared people's hearts, and his face glowed with an inspired power from on high! . . . I kept saying to myself over and over, "Yes, he has kindled people's hearts to the service of truth and right."

6. The notice appeared in the October, 1877, issue. Publication of the journal was suspended because of Dostoevsky's intensive work on *The Brothers Karamazov.*
7. Readers interested in Dostoevsky's attitudes toward "the Jewish Question" are referred to *Diary of a Writer* for March, 1877. See also Glossary, "Vladimir Soloyvov," on the impossibility of reconciling Dostoevsky's message of universal love with his "prejudices, preconceived ideas, and . . . numerous attacks . . . on the Jews, the Poles, the French, the Germans, the whole of Europe, and the other Christian creeds."
8. Krayevsky was editor of the progressive journal *National Notes* as well as the newspaper *The Voice.* To understand Dostoevsky's contemptuous reference, it must be borne in mind that Krayevsky was strongly opposed to Russian participation in the war against Turkey. His position in this respect, as in almost every other, was diametrically opposed to that of Dostoevsky. Moreover, he wrote a column for the *Voice* in which he used to attack the two journals to which Dostoevsky was a regular contributor: Prince Meshchersky's *Citizen* and Katkov's *Russian Messenger.* Katkov was also editor of the ultra-conservative *Moscow Gazette,* which he proudly characterized as "the organ of a party which may be called Russian, ultra-Russian, exclusively Russian."
9. From a letter to S. D. Yanovsky dated December 17, 1877.
10. Leo and Alexey Tolstoy, Turgenev, Goncharov, Ostrovsky, Maikov, Tyutchev, Khomyakov, and Konstantin Aksakov, all contemporaries of Dostoevsky, were already members of the Academy of Sciences by the time Dostoevsky was elected to membership.
11. The quotation is not completely verbatim.
12. Grand Duke Konstantin Konstantinovich, a nephew to the Tsar, was the son of Konstantin Nikolayevich, Naval Minister during the 1850's. He later achieved some prominence as a poet, signing himself "K.R." (Konstantin Romanov).
13. This letter is lost. Beketov's reply to it is preserved in the Lenin Library. Based on Beketov's remarks about an L. A. Ozhigina, it appears that she was the "female admirer." Ozhigina was a writer who published a novel called *Svoim putyom. Iz zapisok sovremennoy devushki* (Going Your Own Way: Notes of a Modern Girl).
14. Book 3, Chapter 3, "Confession of a Passionate Heart—in Verse." V. V. Timofeyeva writes of that reading:

> For many, including myself, it was something like a revelation of all destinies. . . . Listening to this reading, I seemed to discern two phrases which explained to me everything in Dostoevsky and in each one of us. It seemed to me that the audience didn't understand at first what he was reading and kept whispering to one another, "Maniac! Holy fool! Strange . . ."

But Dostoevsky's voice, full of nervous strain and passionate excitement, rose above the whispering. . . .

So let it be strange! Let it even be "holy foolishness." But let *the great idea* live on!

And that moving, passionate voice shook our hearts to the depths. . . . Not I alone—the entire hall was aroused. I remember the way a young man, a stranger to me who was sitting beside me, nervously shuddered and sighed, how he flushed and paled, shook his head convulsively and clenched his fingers as if trying hard to restrain them from involuntary applause. And how, at last, that applause thundered out. These sudden bursts of applause, breaking into the reading, seemed to wake Dostoevsky up. He shuddered, stood up, and remained standing for a moment, motionless, not taking his eyes off his manuscript. But the applause grew louder and louder, more and more prolonged. Then he roused himself, as if awakening with difficulty from a sweet dream; and after bowing to the audience, he sat down again to read.

15. *The Voice,* No. 102, April 14, 1879. (A.G.D.)
16. The Froebel Society was founded in Russia by adherents of Friedrich Froebel, the distinguished German educational reformer and founder of the kindergarten system. In the course of his work on *The Brothers Karamazov,* Dostoevsky consulted many works on the education of children. One of his notebooks to the novel contains the entry: "On Pestalozzi, on Froebel. Article of Leo Tolstoy on present-day school instruction . . ."
17. "Letter to me of August 10, 1879." (A.G.D.)
18. The word Dostoevsky uses is *stryutskiye,* a Petersburg slang term roughly equivalent to "rabble." He devotes an item in the November, 1877, issue of *Diary of a Writer* to the question, "What Does the Word *Stryutsky* Mean?": "A *stryutsky* is a vain, trashy man, a nullity. . . . I believe that a man who owns money, a house, property of some kind, also one who has even a somewhat steady and fixed job, say that of a factory worker, cannot be called a *stryutsky.*"
19. Over thirteen hundred acres.
20. The audience's wildly enthusiastic response to this reading (a benefit for the Society for Aid to Needy Students of Petersburg University) had an alarming effect on the Trustee of the Petersburg Educational District, M. S. Volkonsky. As Dostoevsky wrote V. P. Gayevsky, president of the Literary Fund: "The Trustee himself was present at the reading. But he told me when it was over that he was forbidding me to read it again because of the impression it produced. So 'Inquisitor' is absolutely impossible to read now, and I'll have to use something else."
21. Grigorovich was then fifty-seven years old, one year younger than Dostoevsky.

Chapter Ten: The Last Year

1. Sofya Sergeyevna Kashpiryova.
2. Pyotr Grigoryevich Kuznetsov, who grew up to become a well-known Leningrad bookseller and wrote a memoir, "Sluzhba u Dostoevskogo" (Working for Dostoevsky).
3. Elective district council in pre-Revolutionary Russia.
4. "As for me, I consider this *Book 3,* enclosed herewith, *not bad at all*—on the contrary, *a success.* (Kindly forgive this little bit of bragging. Remember what the Apostle Paul said—'Since they don't praise me, I'll start praising myself.' " (From Dostoevsky's covering note to N. A. Lyubimov, included with the installment of *The Brothers Karamazov* sent to the *Russian Messenger* on January 30, 1879.)
5. Solovyov defended his doctoral dissertation, "A Critique of Abstract Principles," at the University of Petersburg on April 6, 1880.
6. Town Council.
7. "You think I read with my voice? I read with my nerves!" was Dostoevsky's frequent comment on his own literary readings, according to the testimony of contemporaries.
8. *Speech,* April 25, 1915. (A.G.D.)
9. The first person to describe this episode was I. I. Panayev in *The Contemporary* in 1855. P. V. Annenkov, who wrote about it in the April, 1880, issue of *Messenger of Europe,* was the second. Suvorin printed a denial of Annenkov's allegation in *New Times* (April 4 and May 2, 1880) stating that Dostoevsky's *Poor Folk* had been published in the *Petersburg Miscellany* for 1846 without any "border." In response to the *New Times* denial, an item appeared in the May issue of *Messenger of Europe* (written by its editor and not, as Anna Grigoryevna states, by Annenkov, who was abroad at the time) to the effect that the affair of the "border" had occurred not in connection with *Poor Folk* but with a certain "Plismylkov's Story," intended by Dostoevsky for inclusion in Belinsky's proposed collection *Leviathan.* In actual fact, there was no "Plismylkov's Story." Still troubled by the affair of the "border," Dostoevsky wrote Suvorin again and asked him to print an item on the subject. On May 18 (not May 16, as Anna Grigoryevna states) an announcement appeared in *New Times:* "F. M. Dostoevsky, presently in Staraya Russa, where he is undergoing medical treatment, requests us to announce in his name that no such incident as described by P. V. Annenkov with respect to a 'border' ever occurred or could possibly have occurred."
10. "I am now in a fearful dilemma and state of unrest. On the one hand, the consolidation of my influence not only in Petersburg but also in Moscow, which means a lot to me; and on the other hand —being separated from you, my difficulties with the Karamazovs,

the expenses and so on." (Letter of Dostoevsky to Anna Grigoryevna, May 25–26, 1880.)

11. June 8, 1880.
12. Now Pushkin Square.
13. The photograph is preserved in Pushkin House. The artist I. N. Kramskoy wrote about it:

> During [Dostoevsky's] last years, his face grew even more impressive, more tragic and profound, and it is a great pity that there is no portrait of the last period equal in artistic merit to Perov's. Fortunately and quite accidentally, this deficiency has been overcome by photography. The Moscow photographer Panov has done just such a photographic study. The portrait is not technically brilliant, perhaps—Panov has done technically superior portraits of Dostoevsky—but what is remarkable in it is the expression. . . . Rarely do photographs convey the sum total of what a human face contains, but Panov's photograph is a rare and happy exception. One can surmise that in this instance a high point in Dostoevsky's life, such as the Pushkin festivities in Moscow, came to the photographer's aid. [*I. N. Kramskoy. Ego zhizn, perepiska i khudozhestvenno-kriticheskiye stat'i 1837–1887* (I. N. Kramskoy: His Life, Correspondence and Critical Essays, 1837–1887), St. Petersburg, 1888.]

14. K. N. Yukhantsev, a special assistant in the Ministry of Finance, who was tried in 1879 for the embezzlement of a large sum of money from the Society for Mutual Land Credit.
15. The school from which Pushkin was graduated in 1817.
16. An error. Maria Fyodorovna was not yet Empress. Dostoevsky's daughter Lyubov gives a completely different version of this episode.

> [He] chose to read . . . the chapter in *The Brothers Karamazov* where Father Zossima receives the poor peasant women who have come on pilgrimage. . . . It was his own sorrow which Dostoevsky painted in this chapter. He too could not forget his little Alyosha. . . . The Crown Princess Maria Fyodorovna, the future Empress of Russia, was present at one of these evenings. She too had lost a little son and could not forget it. As she listened to my father's reading, the Crown Princess cried bitterly. When the reading was over, she turned to the ladies who had organized the evening and told them she would like to have a word with my father. The ladies hastened to carry out her wish, but evidently they were not too bright. Knowing Dostoevsky's rather suspicious disposition, they feared he might refuse to obey the Crown Princess' command, and decided to oblige him to do it through a stratagem. They ap-

proached my father and, with mysterious expressions on their faces, said that "a certain very, very interesting personality" would like to have a talk with him about the reading he had given.

"What interesting personality?" Dostoevsky asked, surprised.

"You will see for yourself! She is extremely interesting. . . . Please come with us right away!" the young women answered, taking possession of my father. Laughing, they pushed him into a little boudoir and closed the door behind him.

Dostoevsky was astonished by this mysterious behavior. The little room where he was standing was dimly lit by a shaded lamp; a young woman was seated modestly at a small table. At that period of his life, my father no longer looked at young women. He bowed to the stranger as one bows to a lady one meets in a friend's drawing room; and, since he assumed that the two young pranksters were playing a joke on him, he simply left the room by the opposite door.

Dostoevsky doubtless knew that the Crown Princess had attended the evening, but either thought she had already left or, perhaps, had already forgotten her presence, due to his habitual absentmindedness. He returned to the main drawing room, was immediately surrounded, became involved in an interesting discussion and completely forgot about the "joke."

A quarter of an hour later, the young women who had led him into the little boudoir rushed up to him.

"What did she say to you? What did she say to you?" they asked eagerly.

"Who?" asked my father in amazement.

"Who? The Crown Princess, of course!"

"The Crown Princess? But where is she? I never saw her! [Aimée Dostoevsky, *Fyodor Dostoevsky: A Study* (London: William Heinemann, 1921).]

Chapter Eleven: The Death of Dostoevsky

1. Alyosha was to be the hero of Dostoevsky's next novel about the Karamazovs, according to A. S. Suvorin. Dostoevsky was planning to "take him through the monastery and make him a revolutionary. He would commit a political crime. He would be executed. He was to have searched for the truth and in those searchings would naturally have become a revolutionary." (A. S. Suvorin, *Dnevnik* [Diary].) A. M. Slivitsky, a writer of books for children, says that Dostoevsky was planning a novel, *Children*, in which the main characters were to be the children in the previous novel. There was also a German

scholar, Frau N. Hofmann, who in 1899 published a book on Dostoevsky based partly on personal interviews with Anna Grigoryevna, and who quotes her as giving the following account of the plot for the future novel:

> It was the author's plan for Alyosha, by Father Zossima's last testament, to go out into the world, to take upon himself its suffering and its guilt. He marries Liza and then leaves her for the beautiful sinner Grushenka, who arouses the "Karamazov sensuality" in him. After a stormy period of moral straying, doubt, and negation Alyosha, left alone, returns to the monastery once more. There he surrounds himself with children and dedicates all the rest of his life to them, loves them truly, teaches and guides them.

2. The Zemsky Sobor was an institution of the sixteenth and seventeenth centuries, a kind of popular assembly of representatives of various social groups. This final issue of *Diary of a Writer* can be seen as Dostoevsky's "testament." It is filled with anxiety for Russia's future, and at the same time expresses his Utopian dream of a delegation of "gray homespuns" whose mission it would be to transform the Zemstvo, the institutions of local self-government, in the spirit of democracy, and so save Russia. The article so vividly depicted the disintegration of Russian society as a whole that Dostoevsky evidently became fearful for the fate of the issue, and asked N. S. Abaza, head of the Central Department of Press Affairs, to change the censor. Abaza himself then volunteered to act as censor for the issue.
3. Anna Grigoryevna's account of the circumstances leading to Dostoevsky's last illness cannot be regarded as completely authentic. She fails to mention one very important fact: the family quarrels of that time over the inheritance from Aunt A. F. Kumanina, who had died back in 1871. By special disposition of her landed property, Dostoevsky was to come into his inheritance of a portion of her Ryazan estate in the year 1881, with the condition that he was to pay out a sum of money to his sisters. His sister Vera, however, asked him to turn his entire share in the estate over to them. According to the memoirs of Dostoevsky's daughter Lyubov, there was a stormy discussion at the dinner table between brother and sister, which ended in Vera's bursting into tears and leaving the table. Dostoevsky went to his study, where the throat hemorrhage occurred. Lyubov erroneously dates this quarrel as taking place on January 25 instead of the twenty-sixth.
4. An error. What Dostoevsky showed his children was a reproduction of comic drawings from the series, "Desire is Worse than Compulsion (for the Fisherman)," printed on the back of the subscription announcement for the journal *Splinters.* This sheet, now preserved

in Pushkin House, contains a penciled notation in Anna Grigoryevna's handwriting: "Fyodor Mikhailovich looked at this drawing on the day of his illness, January 26, 1881."

5. Inaccurate. Anna Grigoryevna means Josephine Adamovna Muravyova, widow of the Decembrist A. M. Muravyov, who was living in Tobolsk at that time.
6. "'Old People,' *Diary of a Writer* for 1873." (A.G.D.)
7. "One of those present (I believe it was Markevich) noted the exact minute of his death." (A.G.D.)
8. "He told me many years later that he had preserved the stethoscope as a relic." (A.G.D.)
9. "A Few Words on the Passing of F. M. Dostoevsky," *Moscow Gazette,* February 1, 1881. Anna Grigoryevna's dislike of Markevich was in all probability transmitted directly from Dostoevsky himself. Markevich was a regular contributor to both of Katkov's publications, the *Russian Messenger* and the *Moscow Gazette,* in which capacity he wrote offensively couched *feuilletons* denouncing such writers as Saltykov-Shchedrin and Turgenev. He accused Turgenev of having close ties with "Nihilists and terrorists." He also published several scurrilous articles attacking a deeply respected friend of Dostoevsky's, Madame A. P. Filosofova, a social leader who was close to radical circles.
10. A *lavra* is a monastery of the highest rank and importance.
11. "Informed of F. M. Dostoevsky's death early in the morning of the next day by one of the latter's friends, Kramskoy went immediately to the deceased's apartment, set up his paraphernalia, and drew a portrait in pencil and India ink within a few hours, one of the best things he has ever done. The likeness of this portrait is striking. The attempts of the photographers to take this [same] picture of the deceased in the small room, with poor lighting and of necessity in profile, moreover, failed completely. Kramskoy has requested the widow of the deceased to accept the original of the portrait from him as a small compensation for those hours of delight received by the artist from the work of Dostoevsky." [*Historical Messenger,* No. 3, 1881.]

The portrait is now in Pushkin House.

Chapter Twelve: After Dostoevsky's Death

1. The meeting took place in 1902.
2. In Chapter 9, Anna Grigoryevna quotes Strakhov as saying that Tolstoy himself had asked not to be introduced to anyone. It is possible that Strakhov decided on his own initiative not to introduce Tolstoy and Dostoevsky to one another, out of jealousy and because of his growing dislike of Dostoevsky, although he was still attempt-

ing to maintain an appearance of friendship with him.

3. " 'When [Dostoevsky] died, I felt that he had been a very important and precious person for me.' From Valentin Speransky's reminiscences of Tolstoy, published in *Speech,* No. 307, November 7, 1915." (A.G.D.)
4. "Speransky says the same thing in his article (op. cit.)." (A.G.D.)
5. *"Encounter with a Celebrity."* (A.G.D.)
6. *"Historical Messenger,* December, 1901." (A.G.D.)
7. *"Reminiscences of F. M. Dostoevsky,* by Vsevolod Solovyov." (A.G.D.)
8. It should be noted that neither Strakhov nor Tolstoy was responsible for the publication of the letter. Strakhov died in 1896, Tolstoy in 1910.
9. *Biografiya, pis'ma i zametki iz zapisnoy knizhki* (Biography, Letters and Notebook Entries), Petersburg, 1883. The biography was to comprise the first volume of Dostoevsky's complete collected works, and was written by Strakhov and Orest Miller at Anna Grigoryevna's request.
10. This was the chapter "At Tikhon's" (in English-language editions, "Stravrogin's Confession"). It was supposed to have followed the chapter "Ivan-Tsarevich" and was already set up in type for publication in the *Russian Messenger* when Katkov decided to delete it. The suppressed chapter has a curious history. Dostoevsky himself, although he considered it central to the book's structure, did not include it in his own separate publication of *The Possessed* (possibly out of fear of social repercussions). The first publication of the chapter appeared as a separate edition in the Soviet Union in 1922 as part of the wave of brilliant Dostoevsky scholarship of that period. The thirteen-volume Soviet edition of Dostoevsky's works (1926–30) contained the chapter plus a discussion of it, but it was deleted once again in the ten-volume Soviet edition of 1956–58. The fate of the suppressed chapter in English is equally interesting. Constance Garnett's translation of the novel in its early editions did not include the chapter, but the 1936 Modern Library edition of her translation contains one by Avrahm Yarmolinsky (not where it was to have been placed according to Dostoevsky's intention, but separately, as an appendix). This was not the first translation of the chapter into English; it had been done by S. S. Koteliansky and Virginia Woolf in 1922 as a separate edition published by Hogarth Press. A recent translation of the chapter by F. D. Reeve also exists. But David Magarshack's otherwise excellent translation of the book (*The Devils,* Penguin, Baltimore, 1953) again excludes the chapter; nor does his introduction mention its existence.
11. Edmond Pressensé, nineteenth-century French Protestant theologian. Which of his works Strakhov is referring to here is not known. Tolstoy was familiar with at least two of Pressensé's books, *Historie*

des trois premiers siécles de l'Eglise Chrétienne and *Jésus Christ, son temps, sa vie.* Joly was the translator of Marcus Aurelius' *Alone with Myself* into French.

12. December 5, 1883. Another part of the same letter, which Anna Grigoryevna does not quote, seems more to the point:

> . . . It seems to me that you have been the victim of a wrong, false attitude toward Dostoevsky, of his exaggerated (not by you alone, but by everybody) importance, and of a kind of stereotyped exaggeration: of exalting into prophet and saint a man in the most fervid process of struggle between good and evil. He is moving, fascinating—but to put a man who is all struggle on a pedestal, as an example to humanity—it can't be done."

13. The article in question, on the subject of the Polish uprising of 1863, was written by Strakhov but appeared anonymously over the signature "A Russian" in the April, 1863, issue of *Time.* Although Strakhov treated the uprising from an official patriotic Russian standpoint, his article was misinterpreted by the authorities as glorifying Polish culture at the expense of Russian; and after its appearance the further publication of *Time* was prohibited by Imperial command.
14. Letter to K. D. Alchevskaya, April 9, 1876.
15. This quotation, which Anna Grigoryevna failed to include in her manuscript, has been supplied by the editors on the basis of her reference to the first collected edition of Turgenev's letters and the sense of the quotation.
16. The possibility also exists that the entire episode was invented by Dostoevsky for the purpose of pulling Turgenev's leg. The memoirs of I. I. Yasinsky state very definitely that Dostoevsky once came to see Turgenev in apparent repentance for some putative crime: " 'Akh, Ivan Sergeyevich, I have come to you to fathom the depths of my baseness by the heights of your moral standards!' Turgenev of course was outraged by Dostoevsky's story, and as he left Dostoevsky remarked, 'But you know, Ivan Sergeyevich, I invented the whole thing, purely out of love for you and for your amusement.' " Yasinsky states that Turgenev agreed after Dostoevsky's departure that the whole story was an invention. (I. I. Yasinsky, *Roman moey zhizni* (The Novel of My Life).
17. The allusion is to a letter of August 16, 1867, in which Dostoevsky described an encounter in Germany with a certain Russian who lived abroad permanently, hated Russia, and went home only to receive the income from his estate. On what grounds Anna Grigoryevna states that this individual was P. A. Viskovatov is not known.
18. "Slander, slander, something will stick in any case!"

19. Tolstoy wrote to Strakhov at the beginning of February, 1881, a few days after Dostoevsky's death:

> I never saw this man and had no direct relationship with him; and yet when he died I suddenly understood that he was the very closest, the very dearest person, the person I needed most. . . . Some kind of support fell away from me. I felt lost; and then it became clear how dear he was to me, and I wept, and am still weeping."

Russian Newspapers and Periodicals

The Bell	*Kolokol*
The Cause	*Delo*
Chat	*Beseda*
The Citizen	*Grazhdanin*
The Contemporary	*Sovremennik*
Dawn	*Zarya*
Diary of a Writer	*Dnevnik pisatelya*
Domestic Chat	*Domashnyaya beseda*
Dragonfly	*Strekoza*
The Epoch	*Epokha*
Family Evenings	*Semeynye vechera*
Historical Messenger	*Istorichesky vestnik*
Light	*Svyet*
Messenger of Europe	*Vestnik Evropy*
Moscow	*Moskva*
Moscow Gazette	*Moskovskiye vedomosti*
National Notes	*Otechestvennye zapiski*
New Times	*Novoye vremya*
Petersburg Gazette	*Peterburgskiye vedomosti*
Russian Antiquity	*Russkaya starina*
Russian Messenger	*Russky vestnik*
Russian Thought	*Russkaya mysl*
Russian Wealth	*Russkoye bogatstvo*
Russian Word	*Russkoye slovo*
Russian World	*Russky mir*
Son of the Fatherland	*Syn otechestva*
The Spark	*Iskra*
Speech	*Rech*
Splinters	*Oskolki*
Time	*Vremya*
The Voice	*Golos*

whereas Slavic (by which he meant Russian) civilization was in its period of growth and ascendancy. He predicted a struggle between Europe and the Slavic world which would culminate in Russia's inevitable victory and establish world peace and order. The new Slavic Empire, with Russia at its head, was to locate its capital in Constantinople. Danilevsky's most important book, *Russia and Europe* (1869) acclaimed by Dostoevsky and hailed by Strakhov as "the most complete catechism of Slavophilism," influenced the German philosopher Oswald Spengler.

DAVYDOV, DENIS VASILYEVICH (1784–1839). Poet, leader of a partisan group in the War of 1812 against Napoleon's invading forces. Supposedly the prototype for the character of Denisov in Tolstoy's novel *War and Peace.*

DOBROLYUBOV, NIKOLAI ALEXANDROVICH (1836–1861). Leading radical critic of the mid-nineteenth century: "The merit of literary works is determined by what and how they propagandize." Died of tuberculosis at the age of twenty-five.

DOLGOMOSTYEV, IVAN GRIGORYEVICH (?–1867). Translator, journalist, regular contributor to *Time* and *The Epoch.* A passionately fanatical adherent of the Pochvennik movement. One of the trio (with Maikov and Milyukov) who proposed the writing of a collective novel signed by Dostoevsky to save him from the ruinous contract with the publisher Stellovsky.

DOSTOEVSKAYA, LYUBOV (AIMÉE) FYODOROVNA (1869–1926). Daughter of Fyodor Mikhailovich and Anna Grigoryevna. Sickly and nervous from childhood, she was present in the room when her baby brother Alyosha died of convulsions. At the age of eleven she was called to her dying father's bedside (as was the custom of that time) to say goodbye to him, and had a fit of hysterics when an attempt was made to put her forcibly out of the room during the actual progress of his death. Afterward she described repeated fantasies that he was not dead but nailed into his coffin in a lethargic sleep, from which he would awaken and return to his family. Her relationship with her mother grew increasingly strained and cold as she grew up, and finally a quarrel took place which resulted in their living separately. She wrote two novels, *A Woman Lawyer* and *An Emigrant Girl,* and a collection of short stories, *Sick Girls,* published in Petersburg between 1911 and 1913. These works, of negligible literary merit, are obsessively concerned with the theme of hereditary pathology and degeneracy. She went abroad permanently in 1913 and settled in Germany, where she earned her living

Biographical Glossary

ABAZA, NIKOLAI SAVVICH (1837–1901). Senator, member of the Council of State, director of the Department for Press Affairs, served as censor for the final issue of Dostoevsky's *Diary of a Writer.*

ALEXANDER NEVSKY (1220–1263). Great Prince of Vladimir. His victory over the Swedes in 1240, at the confluence of the Neva and Izhora rivers, brought him the name "Nevsky."

ALEXEY, THE "MAN OF GOD." St. Alexius, son of a fifth-century Roman nobleman; dedicated his life to Christ and was canonized by the church. His *Life* was a mainstay of Old Russian translated literature.

AMBROSIUS, FATHER (1812–1891). Secular name: Alexander Mikhailovich Grenkov. Renowned elder of the cloister at Optina Pustyn.

ANNENKOV, PAVEL VASILYEVICH (1812–1887). Writer, critic, memoirist, close friend of Gogol, Belinsky, Herzen, Turgenev and other major nineteenth-century literary figures. Dostoevsky appears rather peripherally and not very flatteringly in his memoir, *A Remarkable Decade (1838–1848).* The tone of these remarks undoubtedly reflects the prevailing attitudes of the *Contemporary* coterie of that period, with whose members he had a close personal relationship.

ARAKCHEYEV, ALEXEY ANDREYEVICH (1769–1834). Soldier and statesman, favorite of the Emperors Paul I and Alexander I.

ARSENYEV, ADMIRAL DMITRY SERGEYEVICH (1832–1915). Head of the Petersburg Naval Academy and tutor to the sons of Alexander II.

AVERKIEV, DMITRY VASILYEVICH (1836–1905). Dramatist, critic, belletrist. In the early sixties he drew close to the Pochvennik circle, in which Dostoevsky and Strakhov were prominent (the concept of "Pochvennik" had been the coinage of an earlier thinker, Apollon Grigoryev, deriving from the word *pochva* (soil), and advancing the view that literature must be an organic outgrowth of a nation's cultural "soil"). Averkiev became a regular contributor to the Dostoevsky brothers' journals *Time* and *The Epoch.* After Dostoevsky's death, Averkiev for a time carried on with Dostoevsky's idea of a one-man journal, *Diary of a Writer* (in 1885 and 1886), and he published a memorial article on Dostoevsky in it.

AVVAKUM, ARCHPRIEST (c. 1621–1682). Leader of the schismatic sect of Old Believers during the mid-seventeenth century. Opposed the reforms in Russian Orthodox ritual carried out by the Patriarch Nikon; was exiled, imprisoned, burned at the stake. A brilliant, earthy writer in the Russian vernacular, he was the author of the first autobiography in Russian literature.

BEKETOV, NIKOLAI NIKOLAYEVICH (1827–1911). Professor of chemistry at the Universities of Petersburg and Kharkov. Together with his brothers Alexey and Andrey he set up a communal household with Dostoevsky (which they called an "association") shortly after Dostoevsky's rupture with the *Contemporary* circle. This was one of the important friendships in Dostoevsky's life: he said of the Beketov brothers that he "felt reborn, not only psychologically but even physically" in their presence.

BELINSKY, VISSARION GRIGORYEVICH (1811–1848). Foremost Russian philosopher and literary critic of incalculable influence, not only on the opinions and tastes of his own day, but on the development of Soviet literary criticism as well. As a "civic" critic he stressed the primacy of the social, political and moral values of a literary work as opposed to "pure" esthetics. Dostoevsky's relationship to Belinsky was a complex and ambivalent one. It was to Belinsky, the undisputed arbiter of literary merit, that Dostoevsky's first manuscript, the novel *Poor Folk,* was delivered by an ecstatic Nekrasov and Grigorovich, hailing the neophyte writer as "a new Gogol." Belinsky's first meeting with Dostoevsky, in which he lectured to him on the meaning of his own work ("Do you yourself understand . . . what it is you have written? . . . You have touched the very essence of the matter. . . . The truth has been revealed and announced to you as an artist.") was an experience whose emotional impact imprinted itself permanently on Dostoevsky's psyche. As his writing began to throw off Gogol's influence, however, and develop its own peculiar psychological coloration, Belinsky's enthusiasm diminished markedly, and a series of bitingly negative reviews (*The Double, The Landlady,* etc.) plunged Dostoevsky into deep depression and led him to offer his next story, *Mr. Prokharchin,* to a rival journal. After Dostoevsky's break with the Belinsky-Nekrasov coterie, Belinsky again played an ironically decisive role in his fate, for it was Belinsky's celebrated letter denouncing his old literary hero Gogol as a renegade which Dostoevsky read aloud at a Petrashevsky circle meeting and which was one of the reasons for his arrest. After the ideological crisis of the period of imprisonment and exile, and with his increasing closeness to the Slavophile movement in later years, Dostoevsky tried to free himself completely from Belinsky's influence, which by this time he regarded as the incarnation of noxious atheistic socialism. In 1877, however, a new turn appeared with the death of Nekrasov, who had been the original intermediary between Belinsky and Dostoevsky. At that time Dostoevsky said in *Diary of a Writer* that his first meeting with Belinsky had been "the most exquisite moment in all my life. When I thought about it in prison camp in Siberia, I was strengthened in spirit."

BELOV, EVGENY ALEXANDROVICH (1826–1896). Slavophile historian, frequent contributor to *The Citizen.* Like Dostoevsky, he was a Utopian socialist in his youth and went through a similar evolution of views.

BERNSTAMM, LEOPOLD ADOLFOVICH (1859–1939). Sculptor; did busts of Pushkin, Dostoevsky, Saltykov-Shchedrin and Flaubert.

BESTUZHEV-RYUMIN, KONSTANTIN NIKOLAYEVICH (1820–1897). Historian, president of the Slavonic Philanthropic Society.

BURENIN, VIKTOR PETROVICH (1841–1926). Poet, publicist, literary critic. Wrote frequently, sometimes venomously, on Dostoevsky; but said of *The Brothers Karamazov* that "it turns out to be ten times more contemporary than the most contemporary stories, novels, dramas and comedies."

DANILEVSKY, NIKOLAI YAKOVLEVICH (1822–1885). Philosopher, historian, botanist, intransigent opponent of Darwin's theory of evolution. In his youth a Utopian socialist, he was arrested in connection with the Petrashevsky case but was never brought to trial, although he was exiled for a time to Vologda and Samara. A militant Panslavist, he believed that Western civilization had entered a state of decay,

as a writer. She wrote a biography of her father in French which was translated into German and published in Munich as *Dostojewski geschildert von seiner Tochter* (Dostoevsky Portrayed by His Daughter). This work, despite its unreliability in many respects, is of undoubted interest, particularly where she relates the family stories she remembered hearing from her parents. She never married, and died of leukemia in 1926.

DOSTOEVSKY, FYODOR FYODOROVICH (1871–1921). Son of Fyodor Mikhailovich and Anna Grigoryevna; expert in the art of horse-breeding. He earned degrees in law and in the natural sciences from the University of Dorpat (Tartu), Estonia. He owned a large racing stable in Petersburg at one time, and was considered one of the foremost specialists in his field. His financial means were substantial up to the Revolution, but the last months of his life were lived in destitution. His death at fifty was diagnosed as "angina pectoris"; his burial was paid for by the Moscow Historical Museum. Like his sister, Fyodor suffered with nervous problems from childhood. His first marriage ended in divorce after two or three years. He had two sons by his second wife: Fyodor, a gifted youth who died of typhoid fever in 1921 at the age of sixteen, and Andrey (1908–1972), an engineer whose last years were dedicated to the preservation of everything connected with his grandfather's memory.

ELISEYEV, GRIGORY ZAKHAROVICH (1821–1891). Populist writer and journalist, contributor to the *Contemporary,* member of editorial staff of *National Notes,* editor of *The Spark.*

FILIPPOV, TERTY IVANOVICH (1825–1899). Government official, public figure, prominent Slavophile writer. His views on the necessity of Russia's return to her pre-Petrine patriarchal structure strongly influenced the Pochvennik group and left an imprint on the thinking of such writers as Ostrovsky, Pisemsky, Pogodin, and Apollon Grigoryev as well as Dostoevsky. In 1871 Dostoevsky consulted Filippov as a specialist in church history, and a close friendship developed between them from that time forward.

FILOSOFOVA, ANNA PAVLOVNA (1837–1912). A remarkable public figure, social and philanthropic worker, and leader in the women's movement with whom Dostoevsky developed a deep friendship during the late seventies. Despite the fact that her husband was an important Tsarist functionary (he held the post of Chief Military Procurator) Anna Pavlovna found herself close to the ranks of the political opposition, kept illegal literature in her apartment, and wrote her husband:

"I hate our present government . . . this gang of thieves who are destroying Russia." It is believed that she gave shelter to the revolutionary Vera Zasulich after her trial and before she went underground. For a time, her high connections notwithstanding, Anna Pavlovna was in danger of arrest and deportation to Switzerland. Dostoevsky, who prized above all her rare ability to put herself in the other person's position, said of her that she had an "intelligent heart," and she spoke of him as her "beloved moral teacher." Her friendship with Anna Grigoryevna continued unbroken after Dostoevsky's death.

GABELSBERGER, FRANZ (1769–1849). Founder of stenography in Germany and inventor of a system based on the theory that the visible signs conveying a language's sounds must be adapted to the mechanisms of human speech.

GAYEVSKY, VIKTOR PAVLOVICH (1826–1888). Lawyer, literary historian and bibliographer, a founder and long-time president of the Literary Fund.

GONCHAROV, IVAN ALEXANDROVICH (1812–1891). Leading Russian novelist, author of *Oblomov.* Anna Grigoryevna's diary (but not her *Reminiscences*) records several meetings between him and Dostoevsky in the gambling halls of Baden, during which he rather grudgingly advanced Dostoevsky small sums of money.

GRADOVSKY, ALEXANDER DMITRIEVICH (1841–1889). Professor of state law at the University of Petersburg, critic, and writer on public issues. He accused Dostoevsky's Pushkin speech of utilizing the work of Pushkin to elaborate Dostoevsky's own romantic, Slavophile-oriented glorification of the Russian people as the repository of eternal truths. Dostoevsky published a lengthy reply in *Diary of a Writer* for 1880, in which he ridiculed Gradovsky's "Westernism."

GRIGOROVICH, DMITRY VASILYEVICH (1822–1899). Sentimental novelist, author of *The Village* and *Anton, the Poor Wretch.* Close friend and schoolmate of Dostoevsky; a "co-discoverer" (with Nekrasov) of Dostoevsky's writing gifts. Wrote a memoir of Dostoevsky.

GRIGORYEV, VASILY VASILYEVICH (1816–1881). Orientalist, writer on public affairs, professor at the University of Petersburg. Dostoevsky's publicistic articles on Russia's "Eastern mission" show clear traces of Grigoryev's influence. It has also been pointed out that the character in *The Possessed,* Stepan Verkhovensky (whose actual prototype was the liberal historian T. N. Granovsky) owes a good deal to Grigoryev's earlier depiction in an article, "T. N. Granovsky Prior to His Professorship."

HERZEN, ALEXANDER IVANOVICH (1812–1870). Revolutionary thinker, philosopher, novelist, brilliant memoirist, author of *From the Other Shore* and *My Past and Thoughts.* Herzen was arrested for socialist activity as a youth of twenty-two. He exerted great influence on the critical thinking of Belinsky in the early forties, and later on the development of the Russian Populist movement and the Socialist Revolutionary Party. The failure of the European revolutions of 1848 destroyed much of his early optimistic faith in human progress. He lived for years as an exile in England where, with his friend the poet Nikolai Ogaryov, he published a newspaper, *The Bell,* smuggled into Russia and read by Russians of all classes up to and including Alexander II. Dostoevsky's longest meeting with him took place in 1862, when he visited Herzen in London; they produced a mutually excellent impression on one another. Their later encounters were less agreeable: a chance meeting on a steamer in the company of Polina Suslova, who flirted with Herzen's son, and—at the height of Dostoevsky's gambling fever in 1863—a request for a loan, to which Herzen did not respond. The extent of Herzen's influence on Dostoevsky's work is controversial, and much research remains to be done in this area.

KATKOV, MIKHAIL NIKIFOROVICH (1818–1887). Professor of philosophy, leading editor and publisher, founder of the influential conservative literary journal *The Russian Messenger* and the reactionary daily *Moscow Gazette.* Katkov began his career as a liberal and a disciple of Belinsky but developed increasingly reactionary views in response to the rise of Nihilism in Russia and the Polish insurrection of 1863. He exercised enormous influence in the highest government circles.

KONI, ANATOLY FYODOROVICH (1844–1927). Distinguished jurist and writer; presided over the Petersburg court which acquitted the revolutionary Vera Zasulich in 1878. Met Dostoevsky in connection with the latter's arrest for permitting a direct quotation from the Tsar to appear in the pages of *The Citizen.* Became a lifelong friend: arranged for Dostoevsky to attend important court trials, made it possible for him to visit a colony of child "criminals" in 1875. Koni's erudition and counsel were of great help to Dostoevsky in his writing of the trial scenes from *The Brothers Karamazov.* He left several memoirs of Dostoevsky.

KORVIN-KRUKOVSKAYA, ANNA VASILYEVNA (1843–1887). Promising writer who published two stories in Dostoevsky's *The Epoch* in her early twenties. Dostoevsky proposed marriage to her and was rejected. Later she married the militant radical Charles-Victor Jaclard and participated with him in the Paris Commune of 1871.

KOVALEVSKAYA, SOFYA VASILYEVNA (1850–1891). Gifted writer, distinguished mathematician, one of the first woman professors in the world, sister of Anna Korvin-Krukovskaya. Author of *Vospominaniya detstva* (Memories of Childhood), which contains a brilliant chapter on Dostoevsky. (See also note 8, Chapter Four, above.)

KRAYEVSKY, ANDREY ALEXANDROVICH (1810–1889). Petersburg journalist of progressive views, publisher of *National Notes* and the newspaper *The Voice.*

LAMANSKY, EVGENY IVANOVICH (1825–1902). Eminent financier, public figure, director of the State Bank and brother of the Slavist and historian V. I. Lamansky. First met Dostoevsky as a fellow member of the Petrashevsky circle.

LAVROVSKAYA, ELIZAVETA ANDREYEVNA (PRINCESS TSERETELLI) (1845–1919). Extremely popular singer. Tchaikovsky dedicated six romances and a vocal quartet to her. Became friendly with Dostoevsky in the 1870's.

LORIS-MELIKOV, COUNT MIKHAIL TARIELOVICH (1825–1888). Prominent statesman. In 1880, headed the Supreme Administrative Commission for the Maintenance of Public Order and Social Tranquillity. Minister of the Interior under Alexander II; dismissed by Alexander III in 1881 at the instigation of Pobedonostsev.

MAIKOV, APOLLON NIKOLAYEVICH (1821–1897). Poet, translator and critic. Allied himself with the group of Parnassian poets (including Fet and Yakov Polonsky), which advocated art for art's sake and opposed the "civic" critics Belinsky, Chernyshevsky and Dobrolyubov. His poetry stresses nature and classical themes used as vehicles for philosophic discussion. He was Dostoevsky's oldest and closest friend from the days of their youth, when both had ties with the Petrashevsky circle. It was to Maikov that Dostoevsky confided the plan of a few left-wing members (Pleshcheyev, Speshnev, Durov) to secede from the group and form a separate society with a secret printing press. After Dostoevsky's return from exile a decade after his arrest, the friendship was renewed and became even more intimate as Dostoevsky drew closer to the Slavophiles—a process of development Maikov had gone through several years earlier. In their later life there was a short period of coolness between the two when Dostoevsky published *A Raw Youth* in the leading organ of the Populists, *National Notes.* A second angry episode occurred in 1879 when a member of "the younger generation" asked Dostoevsky at a public dinner, "Why is it that you publish your work in the *Russian Messenger?*" and received the reply, "Because they have more money and you're surer of getting paid, and they pay in advance." That day Maikov wrote to him bitterly: "I was expecting you to say . . . that it was out of affinity and respect for Katkov, even out of agreement with his views on many basic issues . . . you evaded, you didn't say that. What is this? Is it so that you publish with Katkov for money?" Despite such ups and downs the deep friendship between Maikov and Dostoevsky continued to the end. Maikov's wife, Anna Ivanovna, was in many respects Anna Grigoryevna's confidante, and both Maikovs were present at Dostoevsky's deathbed.

MENDELEYEV, DMITRY IVANOVICH (1834–1907). Distinguished chemist who developed the "periodic table" on the basis of which he was able to predict the properties of elements as yet unknown. Like the zoologist Wagner and the chemist Butlerov, he shared for a time a fascination with spiritualism and parapsychic phenomena.

MESHCHERSKY, PRINCE VLADIMIR PETROVICH (1839–1914). Arch-conservative publisher, highly influential in Court circles. His weekly *The Citizen,* which Dostoevsky edited for about a year between 1872 and the beginning of 1874, enjoyed official protection and received a heavy annual subsidy from the government. It was at Meschersky's home that Dostoevsky first met Senator K. P. Pobedonostsev. Meshchersky was a violent opponent of reform (for which he was given the nickname of "Prince Deadstop"). As editor of *The Citizen,* Dostoevsky was forced not only to print his employer's frequent and badly written publicistic utterances, but sometimes to correct their grammar as well. For one of them, which directly quoted a remark of the Tsar, Dostoevsky was forced to take responsibility and to spend forty-eight hours in a prison cell (see Chapter Six, note 7). The final rupture between Meshchersky and Dostoevsky was precipitated by an article of Meshchersky's advocating the construction of dormitories for university students, for the purpose of maintaining police surveillance over them. Even Dostoevsky's conservatism was outraged by this; he replied that he had children of his own and that Meschersky's proposal was deeply repugnant to his convictions. So ended what Dostoevsky called "the accursed year."

MIKHAILOVSKY, NIKOLAI KONSTANTINOVICH (1842–1904). Political thinker, sociologist and literary critic; follower of Herzen and Lavrov. Member of the editorial staff of *National Notes* when it was the organ of the Populists; later became an editor of the prestigious Populist monthly *Russian Wealth.* Author of several penetrating critical articles on Tolstoy and Dostoevsky ("A Cruel Talent").

MIKULICH, V. (1857–1936). Real name: Lydia Veselitskaya. Novelist, author of *Mimochka.* She left a memoir of her acquaintance with Dostoevsky, *Vstrecha s znamenitostyu* (Encounter with a Celebrity).

MILLER, OREST FYODOROVICH (1833–1889). Literary historian and critic, professor at Petersburg University, eminent folklorist. Wrote the first biography of Dostoevsky in collaboration with Nikolai Strakhov.

MILYUKOV, ALEXANDER PETROVICH (1817–1897). Teacher and writer. An early follower of Belinsky. Became Dostoevsky's friend in the 1840's as a fellow member of the Petrashevsky circle; the friendship resumed unbroken in the sixties after Dostoevsky's return from exile, when he took up once more his old ties with Maikov and Yanovsky and met Strakhov for the first time. Milyukov left a memoir of Dostoevsky in his book *Literaturnye vstrechi i znakomstva* (Literary Encounters and Acquaintances).

NECHAYEV, SERGEY GENNADIEVICH (1847–1882). Revolutionary conspirator who collaborated with the anarchist Mikhail Bakunin in the writing of *The Catechism of a Revolutionary.* "Day and night [the revolutionary] must have one thought, one aim only: pitiless destruction. He pursues his aim coldly and relentlessly, and must be prepared to perish himself, as well as to destroy with his own hands anyone who stands in his way." Returning to Russia toward the end of 1869, Nechayev proceeded to put his principles into practice by organizing a terrorist secret society, the People's Vengeance (Narodnaya Rasprava), whose actual structure existed largely in his own imagination. It supposedly consisted of a network of cells of five, no cell knowing the identity nor location of the others. One of these cells was in the Agricultural Academy, where Anna Grigoryevna's brother Ivan Snitkin was a student; and it was there that a lurid crime was perpetrated. The student Ivan Ivanovich Ivanov, a cell member, tried to secede from the group. Nechayev falsely accused Ivanov of being a police spy and ordered the others to murder him. He then abandoned his fellow conspirators to Tsarist justice, while he himself fled abroad. (He was extradited several years later and condemned to imprisonment in the Peter and Paul fortress, where he died.) See Chapter Four, pp. 158–159 and notes 43 and 44.

NEKRASOV, NIKOLAI ALEXEYEVICH (1821–1877). Great Russian mid-nineteenth-century poet, leading exponent of realism and of the "civic" tendency in poetry. His life was marked by intense contradictions. A political radical, he was also a brilliantly successful publisher with a reputation for unscrupulousness in his business dealings and for profligacy in his personal life. His journal *The Contemporary,* purchased in 1846, published the work of the youthful Turgenev and Tolstoy as well as the radical critics Belinsky, Chernyshevsky and Dobrolyubov. After 1856 it became the rallying ground of the extreme left and was suppressed by the government in 1866. In 1868, together with the writer Saltykov-Shchedrin, he acquired *National Notes,* which became an outstanding Populist organ. With the writer Grigorovich, Nekrasov was "co-discoverer" of Dostoevsky's first novel, *Poor Folk.* He brought it to the attention of Russia's foremost critic, Belinsky, whose enraptured reception of it made Dostoevsky an instant literary success. Nekrasov's falling-out with Dostoevsky in 1846, and their dramatic reunion toward the end of their lives, are described by Anna Grigoryevna in Chapter Eight (see also notes 14, 15, and 16 to that chapter). There was also a middle period in the relationship during the early sixties when the Dostoevsky brothers' journal *Time* (in its first phase) was attempting to maintain a middle-of-the-road position between Slavophiles and Westerners. It was then that *Time* published Nekrasov's poems "Peasant Children" and "The Death of Prokl."

NIL OF STOLOBEN (NIL STOLBENSKY) (?–1555). Monk, founder of a hermitage on the island of Stoloben in Lake Seliger.

OGARYOV, NIKOLAI PLATONOVICH (1813–1877). Minor poet, writer on public issues, intimate friend of Alexander Herzen and co-editor for many years of his radical newspaper-in-exile *The Bell.*

OLKHIN, PAVEL MATVEYEVICH (1830–?). Physician, translator, one of the first teachers of stenography in Russia, author of the textbook *A Guide to Russian Shorthand Using the Gabelsberger Method.*

OPTINA PUSTYN. Renowned fourteenth-century monastery near the ancient city of Kozelsk, in the district of Kaluga. With certain other cloisters, Optina gave rise to the institution of the monastic elder *(starets)* or keeper of one's conscience. Optina Pustyn's elders attracted the attention of many distinguished Russian writers including Gogol, Tolstoy, Turgenev and Gorky, who made visits there. The character Father Zossima in *The Brothers Karamazov* is a composite based on the Optina Elder Father Ambrosius and Tikhon Zadonsky.

OTTO (ONEGIN), ALEXANDER FYODOROVICH. Owner of a rare collection of Pushkiniana including original manuscripts, and founder of the

Pushkin Museum in Paris. His collection was acquired by the Russian Academy of Sciences in 1909.

PALM, ALEXANDER IVANOVICH (1822–1885). Minor poet and novelist, member of the Petrashevsky circle who stood at the scaffold with Dostoevsky and who, as one of the circle's last survivors, delivered a eulogy at his funeral. Author of the novel *Alexey Slobodin* (under the pseudonym P. Alminsky), in which Petrashevsky, Durov and Dostoevsky are depicted. The book was not permitted in public libraries, and it circulated underground until 1905.

PANAYEVA, AVDOTYA YAKOVLEVNA (GOLOVACHEVA) (1819–1893). Wife of I. I. Panayev and later of A. F. Golovachev. Long-time mistress of the poet Nikolai Nekrasov and hostess at the literary gatherings of the *Contemporary* circle, she wrote a memoir in which such figures as Belinsky, Chernyshevsky, Dobrolyubov, Turgenev and Dostoevsky played a prominent part. Dostoevsky confesses to being "a little in love with her" in letters to his brother Mikhail. Madame Panayeva's memoir gives a vivid psychological portrait of the young, gauche, hypersensitive Dostoevsky, as his social behavior in her drawing room developed from intense shyness to intense self-importance; the teasing to which he was subjected by the more sophisticated members of the group egged on by Turgenev; and his humiliation at the epigram jointly composed by Turgenev and Nekrasov, in which Dostoevsky was described as "a new pimple on literature's nose."

PARFENY THE MONK (?–1868). Secular name: Pyotr Ageyev. Priestly monk consecrated at Mount Athos, abbot of the Guslitsk Monastery of the Transfiguration, author of *Tales of the Wanderings and Travels of Parfeny the Monk in Russia, Moldavia, Turkey and the Holy Land.*

PEROV, VASILY GRIGORYEVICH (1833–1882). Popular painter of the naturalistic school; did portraits of Dostoevsky and Anton and Nicholas Rubinstein.

PLESHCHEYEV, ALEXEY NIKOLAYEVICH (1825–1893). Poet, translator, critic, served on the editorial staff of *National Notes.* In his youth he was host to the "secessionist" radical wing of the Petrashevsky circle.

POBEDONOSTSEV, KONSTANTIN PETROVICH (1827–1907). High government official, ultra-conservative public leader and thinker, one of the most powerful influences on Russian internal policy during the reign of two Tsars. He was tutor to the sons of Tsar Alexander II, a member of the State Council, Chief Procurator of the Holy Synod (the highest church office in Russia) from 1880 to 1905. An intellectual and something of a mystic, he translated Thomas à Kempis' *Imitation of Christ* into Russian. He was a fanatical adherent of the union of autocracy and Orthodoxy, and tenaciously opposed a constitution, trial by jury, and freedom of the press. He first met Dostoevsky through Prince V. P. Meshchersky and maintained a warm friendship with him to the end of his life. Although his views coincided in many respects with Dostoevsky *qua* publicist, his attempts to influence the direction of Dostoevsky's creative work were not so successful. The protean breadth of Dostoevsky's creative genius, so intractable to ideological co-optation, left Pobedonostsev with feelings of uneasiness and mistrust. In *The Brothers Karamazov,* for example, in the section entitled "Pro and Contra," which treats Christianity's explanation of the existence of evil as a necessary prerequisite to man's free will, Pobedonostsev complained that Dostoevsky had made Ivan Karamazov's attack much more powerful and cogent than the Christian answer. He even advised consigning the "rebellious" pages of the novel to the flames: "When a sculptor's statue is a failure . . . all the metal goes back into the furnace. . . . And you, if you had bided your time, might have decided not to publish this work." There is a rich and interesting correspondence between Dostoevsky and Pobedonostsev. For a comparative analysis of their views on public issues, see R. F. Byrnes, "Dostoevsky and Pobedonostsev," in *Essays in Russian and Soviet History,* ed. John S. Curtiss (New York: Columbia University Press, 1963).

POLONSKY, YAKOV PETROVICH (1819–1898). Lyric poet; belonged to the Russian "Parnassian poets." An opponent of the civic school of Russian poetry, he contributed to *Time* and *The Epoch* although his social views were close to the Westerners.

REDSTOCK, LORD GRENVILLE. British Army colonel who came to St. Petersburg in 1874 as a self-appointed religious missionary, preaching that faith in Christ alone is necessary for salvation and that good works are an obstacle to it; that the Church must be abolished as an ecclesiastical institution; that the sacraments are worthless; and that sin can be washed away by holy blood which has already been spilled. Redstock's doctrine was fashionable for a time among the upper classes of Petersburg society. A disciple of his, Vasily Pashkov, established the Society for the Encouragement of Religious and Ethical Reading in Petersburg in 1876. Dostoevsky was predictably antagonistic to Redstock and wrote about him in *Diary of a Writer.*

REPIN, ILYA EFIMOVICH (1844–1930). Prominent Russian painter of the naturalistic school; noted for historical scenes and portraits.

ROZANOV, VASILY VASILYEVICH (1856–1919). Philosopher, writer, critic. Basic to his philosophic thought is the sexual principle as a reflection of the creative and generative spirit of the universe. As a literary critic he first achieved prominence for his remarkable study *F. M. Dostoevsky's Legend of the Grand Inquisitor* (1894). His fascination with Dostoevsky's work and thought was so intense that at the age of twenty-four he married Dostoevsky's former mistress, Polina Suslova (seventeen years older than himself), partly as a link with the man he had never managed to meet. Rozanov and Suslova separated after six years. She refused to grant him a divorce, and he later wrote a bitter memoir in which he compared her to Catherine de Medici.

SAVINA, MARIA GAVRILOVNA (1854–1915). Leading actress of the Alexandrinsky Theater in St. Petersburg.

SEMYONOV, NIKOLAI PETROVICH (1823–?). Government official, brother of the noted explorer and natural scientist Pyotr Semyonov-Tyan-Shansky, with whom Dostoevsky had been friendly since the Petrashevsky days and again in exile in Semipalatinsk.

SHIDLOVSKY, IVAN NIKOLAYEVICH (1816–1872). Romantic poet, sometime monk and debauchee in periodic alternation. Enjoyed an intense friendship with Dostoevsky during the latter's student years at the Military Engineering Institute. He quickly became Dostoevsky's literary mentor and introduced him to Balzac and Shakespeare, Schiller and Hofmann. Dostoevsky attributed great importance to Shidlovsky's influence on his literary development, and begged Vsevolod Solovyov to write about him so that his name might not be lost to posterity.

SIMEON, ARCHIMANDRITE. Superior of the Alexander Nevsky Monastery. His explanation of monastic burial rites served as the basis for Dostoevsky's description of Father Zossima's funeral in *The Brothers Karamazov.*

SKABICHEVSKY, ALEXANDER MIKHAILOVICH (1838–1910). Radical critic and literary historian; regular contributor to *National Notes.*

SLUCHEVSKY, KONSTANTIN KONSTANTINOVICH (1837–1904). Writer and critic. A metaphysical poet, he was attacked by the radical "civic" critics.

SMIRNOVA, SOFYA IVANOVNA (1852–1920). Novelist and playwright who published in *New Times* and *National Notes.* She was the wife of the actor N. F. Sazonov.

SOLOVYOV, VLADIMIR SERGEYEVICH (1853–1900). Leading philosopher, seminal poet, precursor of the Russian Symbolists, he exerted great influence on the poetic development of Alexander Blok and Andrey Bely. Solovyov first met Dostoevsky as a youth of twenty, but went abroad shortly thereafter and returned in 1877, when his friendship with Dostoevsky deepened. He was for a time an admirer of Dostoevsky's Christian Slavophilism, and is commonly regarded as a model for Dostoevsky's Alyosha Karamazov. His public lectures on "God-manhood" in 1877–78 attracted great attention and were attended by huge crowds. Solovyov's university career was cut short within a year after his brilliant defense of his doctoral dissertation, when he made a public speech in 1881 calling on Tsar Alexander III to forgive the assassins of his father, Alexander II. For this he was dismissed from the university and forbidden to make public statements thereafter. Later in his development, Solovyov turned away from Slavophilism and wrote a cogent criticism of Danilevsky and Strakhov. He advocated a universal church based on principles of social justice and individual liberty. Despite his deep affection for Dostoevsky, he clearly saw the contradictory nature of Dostoevsky's thinking. ". . . Dostoevsky announced the formula of a Russian and Christian ideal which was intended to be universal and to bring about unity and peace. But it was not enough to proclaim the ideal. [He] would have had to apply his ideal as a standard by which to regulate all the practical questions of our collective life. . . . Such a labor would demand the renunciation of his many deeply rooted prejudices, preconceived ideas, and primitive nationalist instincts. . . . Thus none among us can accept his entire spiritual heritage. If we acknowledge with Dostoevsky that the true Russian national character, its dignity and value, consists in its capacity to understand and love all alien elements, then we cannot accept the numerous attacks of the selfsame Dostoevsky on the Jews, the Poles, the French, the Germans, on the whole of Europe, and on the other Christian creeds."

SOLOVYOV, VSEVOLOD SERGEYEVICH (1849–1903). Historical novelist, brother of Vladimir Solovyov and son of the distinguished historian Sergey Solovyov. He was deeply influenced by Dostoevsky's work and personality, and left a perceptive memoir describing Dostoevsky's charismatic effect on him as a youth. "He was my teacher and my confessor; he had a very definite influence on me, and I ascribed deep significance to almost every word he uttered." Solovyov was author of the novels *Tsar-Devitsa* and *Exile.*

STACKENSCHNEIDER, ELENA ANDREYEVNA (1836–1897). Sister of the jurist Adrian Stackenschneider; daughter of the architect and builder of the Mariinsky Palace Andrey Stackenschneider, and hostess of a prominent literary salon. Dostoevsky visited her often and maintained a correspondence with her. She wrote an unfinished memoir of him in 1884.

STELLOVSKY, FYODOR TIMOFEYEVICH (?–1875). Publisher of the humorous weekly *Anchor* and a caricature supplement, *The Wasp*. Began publishing the collected works of serious writers at the beginning of the sixties, and put out a four-volume edition of Dostoevsky's works from 1865 to 1867. Notorious for his unscrupulous dealings with writers, he published the works of Pisemsky and Krestovsky under very exploitative terms, and bought the complete works of the composer Mikhail Glinka for the sum of twenty-five rubles.

STRAKHOV, NIKOLAI NIKOLAYEVICH (1828–1896). Philosopher, critic, writer, ingrained Slavophile, defender of everything "organically Russian" against incursions from the West. A disciple of the Panslavist Nikolai Danilevsky, Strakhov was a violent opponent of the Darwinian theory of evolution and sought to refute it over a period of many years. His most important work is the three-volume collection of his critical thought, *The Struggle with the West in Russian Literature*. One of Dostoevsky's oldest and presumably most intimate friends, Strakhov first met him in 1859. He was co-editor of the Dostoevsky brothers' first journal *Time* from its inception in 1861 until its suppression in 1863. At the beginning *Time* sought to maintain a middle position acceptable to the moderates in both the Westerner and Slavophile camps, but under Strakhov's influence the journal quickly took on its distinctive Pochvennik stamp. In Strakhov's practice, this amounted to the wholesale rejection of Western culture and values. The misreading by government authorities of Strakhov's article "The Fatal Question," which led them to close the journal down in 1863, is described by Anna Grigoryevna in Chapter Twelve (see also note 13 to that chapter). In his later years Strakhov became a close friend of Leo Tolstoy. His notorious letter to Tolstoy written after Dostoevsky's death, in which he so shabbily reveals the vengefulness he had striven over decades to cover up, is itself a study in psychopathology worthy of Dostoevsky's pen, had the latter been alive to make creative use of it.

SUSLOVA, APOLLINARIA PROKOFYEVNA (POLINA) (1839–1917/18). Writer *manqué*, revolutionary *manqué* with whom Dostoevsky had an intermittent and very turbulent love affair between 1862 (when she first came to his notice with a manuscript submitted to *Time*) and approximately 1866. The most celebrated of their junkets was a trip together (while his first wife lay dying of consumption) to the casinos of Wiesbaden and Baden-Baden in the summer of 1863, which later became transmuted into Dostoevsky's novel *The Gambler,* the writing of which is so vividly described in the present book. That the relationship was still alive, at least in the form of correspondence, after Dostoevsky's marriage to Anna Grigoryevna, is shown in his half-explanatory, half-apologetic letter to Suslova written on his honeymoon from Dresden in April, 1867: ". . . My novel *The Gambler* was finished on November 28. . . . By the end of the novel I had become aware that my stenographer was sincerely in love with me, although she never said a word of this to me. And I was getting to like her more and more all the time. Since my life had been horribly dreary and depressing ever since my brother's death, I asked her to marry me. She accepted, and here we are, married. . . ." This letter produced a reply from Suslova which Anna Grigoryevna steamed open secretly in her husband's absence. Her jealous fears are described in some of her diary entries of that year, after which Suslova seems to have disappeared completely from Dostoevsky's life. She is usually considered to have been one of the prototypes for the gallery of "infernal" women in his novels.

SUVORIN, ALEXEY SERGEYEVICH (1834–1912). Journalist, editor, playwright, publisher of the prestigious, conservative *New Times.* Maintained a close friendship with Dostoevsky and also with Chekhov (until the Dreyfus case brought about a rupture in their relations). Perhaps best known as the recipient of some of Chekhov's finest letters on literature.

TIKHON ZADONSKY (1724–1783). Secular name: Timofey Savelyevich Kirillov. Born into abject poverty, studied and taught at the seminary in Novgorod, then became rector of the Tver Seminary and Bishop of Voronezh. Retired to the monastery at Zadonsk where, as a revered elder, his life was an exemplar of active love for his fellow man. Wrote prolifically. Dostoevsky was deeply interested in him; his influence is evident not only in the character Father Zossima (in *The Brothers Karamazov*) but also in Father Tikhon *(The Possessed)* and Makar Dolgorukov *(A Raw Youth).*

TOLSTAYA, COUNTESS SOFYA ANDREYEVNA (1844–1892). Wife of the eminent nineteenth-century poet, playwright and novelist A. K. Tolstoy. After her husband's death Madame Tolstaya settled in Petersburg in the late seventies and began receiving his old literary friends in her home. Her salon was frequented by Dostoevsky, Turgenev, Goncharov and Vladimir Solovyov, among others. Dostoevsky dined with her often and attended her "evenings," at several of which he read aloud chapters from *The Brothers Karamazov* before their publication. Lyubov Dostoevskaya's memoirs of her father recall that "he soon developed the habit of going to see Countess Tolstaya during his afternoon walk to talk over the news of the day with her. My mother, who was of a rather jealous disposition, made no objection to these visits, for by this time the countess was past the age of seductiveness."

TRETYAKOV, PAVEL MIKHAILOVICH (1832–1898). Mayor of Moscow and founder of the famed Tretyakov Art Gallery. A great admirer of Dostoevsky throughout his life, he maintained a correspondence with him during the period of the Pushkin memorial festivities.

TURGENEV, IVAN SERGEYEVICH (1818–1883). Great nineteenth-century Russian novelist and playwright; aristocrat by birth, cosmopolite in spirit, liberal in politics, Western in style of life and thought. The history of his relationship with his contemporary Dostoevsky is complex, tortuous, and dramatic (and is given here only in barest outline). The two men first met in 1845 as equals, both of them budding literary talents newly accepted into the influential *Contemporary* circle headed by Belinsky and Nekrasov. Their early friendliness (see Dostoevsky's letter to his brother of that period, quoted by Anna Grigoryevna in Chapter Twelve) soon developed into an animosity exacerbated by Turgenev's patronizing attitude toward his colleague and Dostoevsky's hypersensitivity and social clumsiness. During the next decade their paths diverged completely. Turgenev's career flourished, whereas Dostoevsky's was cut short by his arrest and imprisonment. By the time Dostoevsky was permitted to return to Petersburg and founded the journal *Time* together with his brother Mikhail, Turgenev was already a prominent author whose name could not fail to add luster to the new publication. Dostoevsky asked Turgenev to contribute a story to it, and Turgenev responded with "Phantoms," which Dostoevsky accepted with fulsome thanks, comparing it to a piece of music (the story was eventually published in *Time*'s short-lived successor, *The Epoch*). During the first half of the sixties there was an extensive and friendly correspondence between the two writers, filled with expressions of admiration for one another's work. Turgenev, whose *Fathers and Children* appeared in 1862 and was attacked by critics from both the radical and reactionary camps, wrote to Dostoevsky, "You have grasped so fully and sensitively what I was trying to say through [the character] Bazarov that I am left with nothing more to express but astonishment and pleasure." The next phase of the relationship was marked by that extreme confusion between personal feelings and political ideology which had characterized Dostoevsky's behavior at many critical points in his life. The problem began during the summer of 1865 when Dostoevsky, destitute and desperate at the gambling tables of Wiesbaden with Polina Suslova, wrote a begging letter to Turgenev asking for a loan of a hundred thalers which "I possibly shall not be able to repay for three weeks." Turgenev sent him fifty thalers, half of what he had requested; the debt was to remain humiliatingly unpaid for the next ten years. In 1867, two years after the loan, Dostoevsky and his bride Anna Grigoryevna, honeymooning in Baden-Baden, learned that Turgenev was in town. Honor demanded that Dostoevsky should call upon his compatriot and that neither should bring up the matter of the unpaid debt. What ensued was an "ideological" quarrel which became a notorious episode in Russian literary history. Since all the accounts come from Dostoevsky's side it is impossible to reconstruct both parts of the dialogue accurately, but we know that it quickly became intensely hostile. Dostoevsky attacked Turgenev in his tenderest spot: the critical and popular fiasco of his latest novel *Smoke,* calling it a calumny on the Russian people which deserved burning by the public executioner. He made disparaging comments about Turgenev's long residences abroad and advised him to "buy himself a telescope so as to be able to understand what was happening in Russia." Despite their heated words the two men parted with a show of correctness, and Turgenev even returned the call the next day (at a time when he knew Dostoevsky would not be receiving callers). A lengthy account of the episode was transmitted by Dostoevsky in a letter to his friend Maikov in which he accused Turgenev of being an out-and-out atheist and of considering himself more of a German than a Russian. The story quickly became a favorite subject of Petersburg literary gossip. A copy of the relevant passages in the letter to Maikov was sent anonymously (possibly by Strakhov) to the editor of a historical review. Turgenev learned of this and remained convinced all his life that Dostoevsky himself was the culprit. At this point the story acquires a sinister tinge. Dostoevsky's novel *The Possessed,* which denounces revolutionary terrorism as the inevitable fruit of the liberalism of the previous generation, contains a portrait of a writer named Karmazinov ("Pinko") which is not only a vicious caricature of Turgenev (and a parody of that very story, "Phantoms," which Dostoevsky had accepted so gratefully from Turgenev some years earlier) but hints that Karmazinov-Turgenev was a secret sympathizer with the terrorists. This finally stung Turgenev into a reply. "I hear Dostoevsky has caricatured me. Well, let him have his fun. He came to me five years ago in Baden, not to pay back the money he borrowed from me, but to abuse me for *Smoke*. . . . I listened to this whole harangue in silence, and what do I hear now? That I expressed all sorts of criminal opinions. It would be simple libel, if Dostoevsky weren't insane—of which I don't have the slightest doubt. He was probably hallucinating." At the end of their lives there was a reconciliation of sorts which took place in the hyper-charged emotional atmosphere of the Pushkin memorial festivities. And as writers with a profound understanding and love of Russian literature, they always retained their recognition of one another's genius even at the height of their personal enmity.

VALIKHANOV, CHOKAN CHINGISOVICH (1835–1865). Kazakh educator, folklorist, ethnographer and explorer, whose researches were published by the Russian Geographic Society. He met Dostoevsky during his exile in Omsk in 1854. They became warm friends and maintained a correspondence for some time thereafter.

VASNYETSOV, VIKTOR MIKHAILOVICH (1848–1926). Mediocre painter of historical and epic subjects. Revived and stylized Byzantine religious painting in his murals executed for the Cathedral of St. Vladimir in Kiev.

VISKOVATOV, PAVEL ALEXANDROVICH (1842–1905). Professor of Russian philology and literature at the University of Dorpat.

VLADIMIR SVYATOSLAVICH (978–1015). Grand Duke of Kiev, virtual founder of Kievan Russia. Introduced Christianity as Russia's official faith and was canonized by the Russian Church.

WAGNER, NIKOLAI PETROVICH (1829–1907). Professor of zoology at the Universities of Kazan and Petersburg. Author of *The Fairy Tales of Kot Murlyka.* His fascination with spiritualism and seances was part of an extraordinary vogue in Russian society during the seventies and eighties which affected even such distinguished scientists as the chemists Butlerov and Mendeleyev. As a contributor to the organ of the Russian spiritualists, *Rebus,* Wagner wrote a number of articles on the study of parapsychic phenomena. (See note 2, Chapter Eight.)

WRANGEL, BARON ALEXANDER EGOROVICH (1838–?). Diplomat, archaeologist, jurist. An intimate friend of Dostoevsky's from his Siberian exile in 1854, he carried on an extensive and revealing correspondence with him. Wrote a memoir, *Vospominaniya o F. M. Dostoevskom v Sibiri* (Reminiscences of F. M. Dostoevsky in Siberia).

YANOVSKY, STEPAN DMITRYEVICH (1817–1897). Physician and later government official. A warm friend of Dostoevsky's from the days of his impoverished literary beginnings; the first to treat Dostoevsky's nervous ailments of that time, with some intimation (though no actual diagnosis) of the incipient stages of epilepsy. Yanovsky was also the first of Dostoevsky's intimates to come to see him in Tver at the end of his Siberian exile, before he was given permission to reside in Petersburg. He left a memoir of Dostoevsky.

YANYSHEV, IOANN LEONTYEVICH (1826–1910). Writer and theologian, rector of the Petersburg Ecclesiastical Academy. A long-time friend of Dostoevsky's, he delivered the eulogy at Dostoevsky's funeral.

YURYEV, SERGEY ANDREYEVICH (1821–1888). Literary critic, translator of Shakespeare and of the Spanish dramatists, editor and publisher of the journals *Chat* and *Russian Thought,* president of the Society of Friends of Russian Literature.

ZHUKOVSKY, VASILY ANDREYEVICH (1783–1852). Foremost Russian poet before Pushkin; one of the creators of the vocabulary of Russian Romantic poetry. Translated Scott, Byron, Schiller, Goethe, Bürger, and, notably, Gray's *Elegy* into Russian.

Selected Bibliography

Source Material

Dostoevsky, Fyodor. *Dostoevsky's Notebooks,* edited by Edward Wasiolek. Chicago, University of Chicago Press: *The Notebooks for "Crime and Punishment"* (1967); *The Notebooks for "The Idiot"* (1967); *The Notebooks for "The Possessed"* (1968); *The Notebooks for "A Raw Youth"* (1969); *The Notebooks for "The Brothers Karamazov"* (1971).

———. *The Unpublished Dostoevsky: Diaries and Notebooks 1860–1881* Introduction by Robert Belknap, general editor Carl Proffer. Ann Arbor, Mich.: Ardis, Vol. 1, 1973, Vols. 2 and 3, 1975.

———. *The Diary of a Writer.* Translated and annotated by Boris Brasol. New York: Charles Scribner's Sons, 1949.

———. *The Letters of Dostoevsky to His Wife.* Translated by Elizabeth Hill and Doris Mudie. London, Constable, 1930.

———. *Letters of Dostoevsky to His Family and Friends.* Translated by Ethel Colburn Mayne, introduction by Avrahm Yarmolinsky. New York: McGraw-Hill, 1964.

———. *Letters and Reminiscences.* Edited by S. S. Koteliansky and J. Middleton Murry. New York: Alfred A. Knopf, 1923.

———. *The Gambler, with The Diary of Polina Suslova.* Edited by Edward Wasiolek, translated by Victor Terras. Chicago: University of Chicago Press, 1972.

Dostoevskaya, Anna. *The Diary of Dostoevsky's Wife.* Translated from the German by Madge Pemberton. New York: Macmillan, 1928. (Record kept during the first year of the Dostoevskys' marriage.)

———. *Dostoevsky Portrayed by His Wife.* Translated from the Russian and edited by S. S. Koteliansky. London: George Routledge, 1926. (Excerpts from the Diary and the Reminiscences.)

Dostoevsky, Aimée (Lyubov Dostoevskaya, the writer's daughter). *Fyodor Dostoevsky:* A Study. London: William Heinemann, 1921.

Biographies and Criticism

Berdyaev, Nicholas. *Dostoevsky.* New York: Meridian Books, 1960.

Carr, E. H. *Dostoevsky.* London: Allen and Unwin, 1931.

Grossman, Leonid. *Dostoevsky.* Translated by Helen Mackler. Indianapolis: Bobbs-Merrill, 1975.

Magarshack, David. *Dostoevsky.* New York: Harcourt, Brace and World, 1963.

Mochulsky, K. *Dostoevsky: His Life and Work.* Translated and with an introduction by Michael Minihan. Princeton: Princeton University Press, 1967.

Muchnic, Helen. *Dostoevsky's English Reputation.* New York: Octagon Books, 1969.

Simmons, Ernest J. *Dostoevsky: The Making of a Novelist.* New York: Alfred A. Knopf, 1940.

Slonim, Mark. *Three Loves of Dostoevsky.* London: Redman, 1957.

Steiner, George. *Tolstoy or Dostoevsky: An Essay in the Old Criticism.* New York: Dutton, 1971.

Wellek, René, editor. *Dostoevsky: Critical Essays.* Englewood Cliffs, N.J.: Prentice-Hall, 1962.

Yarmolinsky, Avrahm. *Dostoevsky: His Life and Art.* New York: Criterion Books, 1957.

Index